VILLAGE HYMNS

FOR

SOCIAL WORSHIP

SELECTED AND ORIGINAL

DESIGNED AS

A SUPPLEMENT

TO THE

PSALMS AND HYMNS

OF

DR. WATTS

By Asahel Nettleton

"And the ransomed of the Lord shall return, and come to Zion with songs and everlasting joy upon their heads." Isaiah xxxv. 10.

International Outreach, Inc.
P. O. Box 1286, Ames, Iowa 50014

International Outreach, Inc.
P. O. Box 1286, Ames, Iowa 50014
(515) 233-2932

© 1997 by International Outreach, Inc.

ISBN 0-9641803-8-3

District of Connecticut, SS.
BE IT REMEMBERED, That on the fifteenth day of March, in the forty-eighth year of the Independence of the United States of America, CALVIN CHAPIN, of the said district, hath deposited in this office the title of a book, the right whereof he claims as proprietor, in the words following, to wit:
"Village Hymns for Social Worship. Selected and original. Designed as a Supplement to Dr. Watts' Psalms and Hymns. By Asahel Nettleton. 'And the ransomed of the Lord shall return, and come to Zion with songs and everlasting joy upon their heads.'—Isaiah."
In conformity to the act of the Congress of the United States, entitled, "An act for the encouragement of learning, by securing the copies of maps, charts, and books, to the authors and proprietors of such copies, during the times therein mentioned."
CHARLES A. INGERSOLL, *Clerk of the District of Connecticut.*
A true copy of record, examined and sealed by me,
CHARLES A. INGERSOLL,
Clerk of the District of Cannecticut.

Preface to the Original Edition

With great satisfaction and pleasure have I often heard the friends of the Redeemer express their unqualified attachment to the sacred poetry of Dr. Watts. Most cordially do I unite with them in the hope, that no Selection of hymns which has ever yet appeared may be suffered to take the place of his inimitable productions.

Deficiencies, however, he unquestionably has. Numerous have been the attempts to supply them; but, hitherto, the judicious have been constrained to regret, that these attempts have succeeded only in part. Whether the book here published will add something to that supply, is submitted to the decision of the religious community.

The compiler does not overlook the valuable labors of those who have preceded him in this department; while he concurs in the opinion, very generally adopted by his brethren in the ministry, that the various benevolent operations, and especially the prevalence of revivals, which are so characteristic of the present day, demand a New Selection of Hymns.

In the year 1820, the General Association of Connecticut appointed a committee to devise rneasures for the prosperity of religion within their limits. I well remember, that at a meeting of this committee, the first item proposed was a New Selection of Hymns. Four years have nearly elapsed, and nothing has been done pursuant to their appointment.

When, in the providence of God, I had the happiness of spending a short season, as a labourer for Christ, within the limits of the Albany Presbytery, the call for such a work in that region; and, as I learned from the most respectable sources, very extensively in the West and South, was not less imperious and pressing, than in districts where I had been more particularly conversant. In personal experience, and discoveries of this description, originated the resolution to undertake the work. The compilation here presented is the result. The task has occupied my attention much of the time for nearly two years. Especially has it cheered and comforted me, during the long continued retirement which a severe sickness subjected me.

The book, whatever may be its defects, is now most affectionately presented "To Zion's friends and mine."

I anticipated difficulties, but am fully persuaded, that whoever undertakes a work of this kind will have to encounter many unforeseen embarrassments in the execution.

I had hoped to find, in the style of genuine poetry, a greater number of hymns adapted to the various exigencies of a revival. Laborious research has, however, led me to conclude, that not many such compositions are in existence.

This volume contains a number of original hymns, which I esteem a valuable accession.—To their authors, whose signatures are prefixed, or at their own request omitted, I tender my sincere thanks.

I have obtained permission to insert a few of the originals from the Hartford Selection. These, though already familiar to many, will yet be consulted with feelings of new interest, when associated with the names of Strong and Steward.

The reader will find, inserted in this volume, a few of the psalms and hymns to which it is designed as a supplement. But he is desired to recollect, that Dwight's edition of Watts is in extensive circulation. In his edition, some of Watts' psalms and hymns were omitted; and those which I have inserted are principally of this character.

I have consulted all the authors and Collections of hymns to which I could gain access. I have availed myself of their labors; and have spent much time in attempts to remodel many of the materials thus collected. In all cases, excepting the hymns of established reputation, wherever abridgments or alterations were deemed conducive to the design of this volume, they have been made without hesitation.

There is a numerous class of hymns which have been sung with much pleasure and profit in seasons of revival, and yet are entirely destitute of poetic merit. Some of my brethren, acquainted with this fact, will probably be disappointed when they find, that so many have been omitted. Others, unacquainted with their beneficial effects at such seasons, would exclude the whole of this class. I am satisfied from observation, as well as from the nature itself of such hymns, that they must be ephemeral. They should be confined to seasons of revival: and even here, they ought to be introduced with discretion; for on this, their principal utility must depend. A book, consisting chiefly of hymns for revivals, however important in its place, would be utterly unfit for the ordinary purposes of devotion—as prescriptions, salutary in sickness, are laid aside on the restoration of health.

With respect to the hymns of a lower grade, I fully unite in the opinion of a much respected correspondent: "That the safest course is to leave them generally out—that the warm heart of a young convert will take a strong hold, and that with pleasure and profit too, of many things, from which, in a more ripened state, he would derive neither."

After selecting a hymn, my first object has been to bring it into a form best adapted to be read or sung in meetings for religious purposes. With this view, some of them have been divided, and others reduced to a stricter unity of thought.

With respect to the arrangement, it has cost me much labor. After all, I have not been able entirely to satisfy my own mind. I am aware that many of the hymns placed under different heads, might have been arranged under the same; and yet all these heads seemed indispensable. The Christian and the Convert, for example, might have been included under one head. But there are so many things peculiar to the commencement of the Christian life, that it was deemed highly proper to collect a number suited to his case, and place them under the eye of the young convert.

This part of my employment has been highly delightful; and I cannot but indulge the hope, that among the many thousands who have commenced their Christian course in the recent revivals, not a few of them will find this volume a pleasant and profitable companion on their way to the heavenly Zion.

The character of some of the hymns is such, that with equal propriety they might have been differently arranged. I have, therefore, distributed them under the several heads where I thought them most needed—recollecting that the intrinsic value of the hymn was not at all affected by the page which it might occupy.

Where the title of a hymn is omitted, it will be found in the next preceding, or in the running title.

Tunes adapted to most of the particular metres will be found in Zion's Harp, a small collection of Music designed to accompany this volume.

The compiler has only to add his grateful acknowledgments that this humble effort has met with such an extensive and welcome reception, and for the many tokens already received, that his labor has not been in vain.

Asahel Nettleton.
New York, May 20, 1825.

Preface to the 1997 Edition

The first edition of *Village Hymns for Social Worship* was published in Hartford, Connecticut in 1824. It was designed to be used as a supplement to the immensely popular psalms and hymns of Isaac Watts. Asahel Nettleton felt there was a great need for a new hymnal wherein hymns expressed the hearts of sinners under awakening influences, conviction of sin, and also reflected the heart of the new convert. A new hymnal would be particularly useful in the current (1820's) atmosphere of revival. During the period of his recovery from his battle with typhus fever, he began working on a hymnal. Reflecting the heart of the one who compiled it, *Village Hymns* is one of the most evangelistic hymnals ever produced.

The reprinting of *Village Hymns for Social Worship* is based on the conviction that what we sing in our public and private worship times affects what we believe. If the songs we sing at these times are doctrinally defective, we are not only influenced by unsound theology ourselves, but we train the next generation inappropriately as well. What we do in every area of life has consequences. If we are ignorant of the character and attributes of the true God, we will substitute a false god in His place. If we do not understand how the Spirit convicts of sin, we may take a simple acknowledgment of sin for true conviction. If our hymns do not warn us of the danger of hypocrisy, we may never consider the possibility that our experience is not genuine. If we eliminate the mention of hell and judgment from our hymns (and anyone who takes the time to scan a modern hymnal will see that we have), we leave the impression that such things are not real or, if they are, that the average church-goer has no need to fear them. If our preaching, teaching, and hymns are stripped of sound doctrinal content the outcome will be destructive to the spread of true religion.

Hymnals in Nettleton's day were usually published in a text only format. Tune books containing collections of tunes for sacred music were published separately. Nettleton made use of these tune books in recommending at least two different tunes for each hymn in *Village Hymns*. Tune books such as *Templi Carmina* and *Musica Sacra* contain many of the tunes Nettleton selected. Nettleton also published a companion tune book to *Village Hymns* entitled *Zion's*

Harp. It contained particular metre tunes which were generally not found as easily in the tune books of the time.

Nettleton drew his hymns from a variety of sources. Nearly 60 of the hymns of John Newton are included, largely, if not wholly taken from Newton's *Olney Hymns.* Close to 50 of the hymns of Isaac Watts are included along with hymns by William Cowper, Philip Doddridge, Samuel Davies, Timothy Dwight, Augustus Toplady, Charles Wesley, and Martin Luther. Some of the hymns were also written by friends of Nettleton like Abbie Hyde, the wife of a Congregational minister in Connecticut, and by others who preferred to remain anonymous.

It was my original intent to publish *Village Hymns* as a text only volume; however, I came under increasing conviction that unless some of the hymns were set to music, the hymnal's use in our day would be limited. In the spring of 1995, shortly after the publication of our volume *Asahel Nettleton: Sermons From the Second Great Awakening,* I began to examine microfilm records of old tune books to try to locate the original tunes that Nettleton had recommended with each hymn. After weeks of searching a number of these tunes were located. I was then ably assisted by Scott Sterner, Minster of Music and Worship at Grand Avenue Baptist Church, who played the tunes into the computer. Musical editing of the tunes was done by Pastor Dave Belford of the First Evangelical Free Church of Ames. Without the help of these two men this volume, in its present form, would have never been published.

I was also assisted in the preliminary text editing by Daria Seda and Jeff and Denise Spahr. Ruth Harris, Music Librarian at the College of William & Mary in Williamsburg, Virginia, allowed me to do extensive photocopying of tunes from their collection of old tune books. Dr. Nola Reed Knouse of The Moravian Music Foundation of Winston-Salem, North Carolina provided copies of hard to locate tunes. I am deeply indebted to all who assisted with this project.

The hymnal is divided into two parts. The first part is the text version of *Village Hymns for Social Worship* as published by Asahel Nettleton. The original spellings have been retained for this portion of the work, so some minor spelling differences will be noted in a few cases. In the second part of the book we have included 183 of the hymns in part one, set to the music recommended by Nettleton. Those hymns in the first part of the book which are also set to music in the second part are marked with an asterisk (*).

It is my hope that by republishing *Village Hymns for Social Worship* with the addition of the music recommended by Nettleton, that many of the hymns contained herein will be rediscovered and used in churches around the world to aid in the teaching of sound doctrine, contribute to the conviction and conversion of sinners, and assist Christians in their public and private worship of the Lord. To that end I dedicate this work.

William C. Nichols
International Outreach, Inc.
Ames, Iowa
November 14, 1997

VILLAGE HYMNS FOR SOCIAL WORSHIP

GOD.

*HYMN 1. L. M.   Watts.
Rothwell. Luther's Hymn.
1 THERE is a God, who reigns above,
Lord of the heav'n, and earth and seas;
I fear his wrath, I ask his love,
And with my lips I sing his praise.

2 There is a law which he has writ,
To teach us all, what we must do;
My soul, to his commands submit,
For they are holy, just, and true.

3 There is a gospel rich in grace,
Whence sinners all their comforts draw;
Lord, I repent and seek thy face,
For I have often broke thy law.

4 There is an hour when I must die,
Nor do I know how soon 'twill come;
How many, younger much than I,
Have pass'd by death to hear their doom.

5 Let me improve the hours I have,
Before the day of grace is fled;
There's no repentance in the grave,
Nor pardon offer'd to the dead.

6 Just as a tree cut down that fell
To north or southward, there it lies;
So man departs to heav'n or hell,
Fixed in the state wherein he dies.

HYMN 2.   C. M.   Watts.
Colchester. St. Ann's.
His condescension. Isaiah lxvi. 2.
1 WHEN the Eternal bows the skies,
To visit earthly things;
With scorn divine he turns his eyes
From towers of haughty kings.

2 He bids his awful chariot roll,
Far downward from the skies,
To visit every humble soul,
With pleasure in his eyes.

3 Why should the Lord, who reigns above,
Disdain so lofty kings?
Say, Lord, and why such looks of love
Upon such worthless things?

4 Mortals, be dumb;—what creature dares
Dispute his awful will?
Ask no account of his affairs
But tremble, and be still.

5 Just like his nature is his grace,
All sovereign and all free;
Great God, how searchless are thy ways!
How deep thy judgments be!

HYMN 3. C. M.   Blacklock
Elgin. Martyr's. Chapel.
Omniscience and Omnipresence. Psalm cxxxix.
1 LORD, thou with an unerring beam
Surveyest all my powers;
My rising steps are watch'd by thee,
By thee, my resting hours.

2 My thoughts, scarce struggling into birth,
Great God, are known to thee;
Abroad, at home, still I'm enclos'd
With thine immensity.

3 To thee the labyrinths of life
In open view appear;
Nor steals a whisper from my lips
Without thy listening ear.

*HYMN 4.   C. M.
Walsal. Plymouth.
Proverbs xv. 3.—Hebrews iv. 13.
1 THE eye of God is every where
To watch the sinner's ways;
He sees who join in humble prayer,
And who in solemn praise.

2 One glance of thine, eternal Lord,
Can pierce and search us through;
Nor heav'n, nor earth, nor hell afford
A shelter from thy view!

3 The universe, in every part,
At once before thee lies;
And every thought of every heart
Is open to thine eyes.

4 Prepare us, Lord, to pray and praise
With fervent, holy love;
And fit us by thy word of grace
To worship thee above.

HYMN 5.   C. M.   Watts.
Cambridge. Swanwick.
His glories in redemption. Isaiah xliv. 23.
1 FATHER, how wide thy glory shines!
How high thy wonders rise!
Known thro' the earth by thousand signs,
By thousands through the skies.

2 But when we view thy strange design,
To save rebellious worms;
Where vengeance and compassion join
In their divinest forms;—

3 Here the whole Deity is known;
Nor dares a creature guess—
Which of the glories brightest shone—
The justice or the grace.

4 Now the full glories of the Lamb
Adorn the heav'nly plains:
Bright seraphs learn Emmanuel's name,
And try their choicest strains.

5 Oh, may I bear some humble part,
In that immortal song!
Wonder and joy shall tune my heart,
And love command my tongue.

HYMN 6. C. M.
Halifax. Braintree.
1 INDULGENT Father, how divine,
How bright thy beauties are!
Through nature's ample round they shine,
Thy goodness to declare.

2 But in thy nobler work of grace,
What brighter mercy smiles
In our benign Redeemer's face,
And every fear beguiles!

3 Such wonders, Lord, while we survey,
To thee our thanks shall rise,
When morning ushers in the day,
Or evening veils the skies.

4 When glimmering life resigns its flame,
Thy praise shall tune our breath;
The dear memorials of thy name
Shall gild the shades of death.

5 But oh, how sweet our song shall rise,
When freed from feeble clay;
And all thy glories meet our eyes
In one eternal day!

*HYMN 7. C. M.
Braintree. York.
Love of God. 1 John iv. 8.
1 COME, ye that know and fear the Lord,
And lift your souls above;
Let every heart and voice accord,
To sing that God is love.

2 This precious truth his word declares,
And all his mercies prove;
Jesus, the gift of gifts, appears
To show, that God is love.

3 Sinai, in clouds, and smoke, and fire,
Thunders his dreadful name
But Zion sings, in melting notes,
The honors of the Lamb.

4 In all his doctrines and commands,
His counsels and designs—
In ev'ry work his hands have fram'd
His love supremely shines.

5 Angels and men the news proclaim,
Through earth and heaven above.
The joyful and transporting news,
That God, the Lord, is love.

HYMN 8.   L. M.   Doddridge.
Antigua. Blendon.
God's goodness. Psalm cvii. 31.
1 YE sons of men, with joy record
The various wonders of the Lord;
And let his power and goodness sound,
Through all your tribes the earth around.

2 Let the high heavens your songs invite,
Those spacious fields of brilliant light;
Where sun, and moon, and planets roll,
And stars, that glow from pole to pole.

3 But Oh! that brighter world above,
Where lives and reigns incarnate love
God's only Son, in flesh array'd,
For man a bleeding victim made.

4 Thither, my soul, with raptures soar,
There, in the land of praise, adore;
The theme demands an angel's lay,
Demands an everlasting day.

HYMN 9. L. M.   Medley.
Blendon. Tallis' Evening Hymn.
Loving-kindness. Isaiah lxiii. 7.
1 AWAKE, my soul, to joyful lays,
And sing the great Redeemer's praise;
He justly claims a song from me,
His loving-kindness, Oh, how free!

2 He saw me ruin'd in the fall,
Yet lov'd me notwithstanding all;
He sav'd me from my lost estate,
His loving-kindness, Oh, how great!

3 Though numerous hosts of mighty foes,
Though earth and hell my way oppose,
He safely leads my soul along,
His loving-kindness, Oh, how strong!

4 When trouble, like a gloomy cloud,
Has gather'd thick, and thunder'd loud,
He near my soul has always stood,
His loving-kindness, Oh, how good!

5 Often I feel my sinful heart,
Prone from my Jesus to depart;
But though I have him oft forgot,
His loving-kindness changes not.

6 Soon shall I pass the gloomy vale,
Soon all my mortal powers must fail;
Oh! may my last expiring breath
His loving-kindness sing in death.

HYMN 10. S. M. Watts.
Peckham Watchman. Pelham.
Love and Mercy.
1 SING—how eternal love
Its chief Beloved chose;
And bade him raise our ruin'd race.
From their abyss of woes.

2 His hand no thunder bears,
No terror clothes his brow;
No bolts to drive our guilty souls
To fiercer flames below.

3 'Twas mercy fill'd the throne,
And wrath stood silent by—
When Christ was sent with pardon down,
To rebels doom'd to die.

4 Now, sinners, dry your tears,
Let hopeless sorrow cease;
Bow to the sceptre of his love,
And take the offer'd peace.

*HYMN 11. C. M.   Watts.
Colchester. Braintree.
Trinity. Ephesians ii. 18.
1 FATHER of glory, to thy name
Immortal praise we give,
Who dost an act of grace proclaim,
And bid us rebels live.

2 Immortal honor to the Son,
Who makes thine anger cease;
Our lives he ransom'd with his own,
And died to make our peace.

3 To thine Almighty Spirit be
Immortal glory given,
Whose influence brings us near to thee,
And trains us up for heaven.

4 Let men, with their united voice,
Adore th' eternal God,
And spread his honors and their joys,
Through nations far abroad.

5 Let faith, and love, and duty join,
One general song to raise:
Let saints in earth and heaven combine,
In harmony and praise.

*HYMN 12. C. M. Cowper.
Abridge. St. Ann's.
The Mysteries of Providence.
1 GOD moves in a mysterious way,
His wonders to perform;
He plants his footsteps in the sea,
And rides upon the storm.

2 Deep in unfathomable mines
Of never-failing skill,
He treasures up his bright designs,
And works his sov'reign will.

3 Ye fearful saints, fresh courage take,
The clouds ye so much dread,
Are big with mercy, and shall break
In blessings on your head.

4 Judge not the Lord by feeble sense,
But trust him for his grace;
Behind a frowning providence
He hides a smiling face.

5 His purposes will ripen fast,
Unfolding every hour;
The bud may have a bitter taste,
But sweet will be the flower.

6 Blind unbelief is sure to err,
And scan his work in vain;
God is his own interpreter,
And he will make it plain.

*HYMN 13 C. M.   Addison.
Mear. Rochester.
Servants of God always safe.
1 HOW are thy servants bless'd, O Lord,
How sure is their defence!
Eternal wisdom is their guide,
Their help, Omnipotence.

2 In foreign realms, and lands remote,
Supported by thy care;
Through burning climes they pass unhurt
And breathe in tainted air.

3 When by the dreadful tempest borne,
High on the broken wave,
They know thou art not slow to bear,
Nor impotent to save.

4 The storm is laid—the winds retire,
Obedient to thy will:
The sea that roars at thy command,
At thy command is still.

5 In midst of dangers, fears, and deaths,
Thy goodness we'll adore;
We'll praise thee for thy mercies past;
And humbly hope for more.

UNIVERSAL PRAISE.

HYMN 14. 6, 4.   Madan's Col.
Trinity. St Clemen's.
1 COME, thou Almighty King,
Help us thy name to sing,
Help us to praise
Father all glorious,
O'er all victorious,
Come and reign over us,
Ancient of days.

2 Jesus, our Lord, arise,
Scatter our enemies,
And make them fall!
Let thine almighty aid
Our sure defence be made:
Our souls on thee be stay'd
Lord, hear our call!

3 Come, thou incarnate Word,
Gird on thy mighty sword;
Our prayer attend!
Come, and thy people bless,
And give thy word success;
Spirit of holiness,
On us descend!

4 Come, holy Comforter,
Thy sacred witness bear,
In this glad hour!
Thou, who almighty art,
Now rule in ev'ry heart,
And ne'er from us depart,
Spirit of power.

5 To the great ONE in THREE,
The highest praises be,
Hence evermore!
His sovereign majesty,
May we in glory see,
And to eternity
Love and adore.

*HYMN 15. L. M.   Watts.
Wells. Old Hundred.
God exalted above all praise.
1 ETERNAL power! whose high abode
Becomes the grandeur of a God;
In vain the tallest angel tries
To reach the height with wond'ring eye.

2 Earth, from afar, has heard thy fame,
And worms have learn'd to lisp thy name
But oh, the glories of thy mind
Leave all our soaring thoughts behind.

3 God is in heaven, but man below:
Be short our tunes, our words be few:
A sacred rev'rence checks our songs,
And praise sits silent on our tongues.

HYMN 16. 5, 6.   Madan's Col.
Locke. Devonshire.
God's servants should praise him.
1 YE servants of God,
Your Master proclaim,
And publish abroad
His wonderful Name;
The Name all victorious
Of Jesus extol;
His kingdom is glorious,
And rules over all.

2 God ruleth on high,
Almighty to save;
And still he is nigh,
His presence we have:
The great congregation
His triumph shall sing,
Ascribing salvation
To Jesus our king.

3 Salvation to God
Who sits on the throne—
Let all cry aloud
And honor the Son:
Of Jesus's praises
The angels proclaim;

Fall down on your faces
And worship the Lamb.

4 Then let us adore,
And give him his right;
All glory and power,
And wisdom and might:
All honor and blessing,
With angels above;
And thanks never ceasing,
And infinite love.

*HYMN 17. 8, 7.　　　Taylor.
Sicilian Hymn. Northampton Chapel.
1 SAINTS, with pious zeal attending,
Now a grateful tribute raise;
Solemn songs to heav'n ascending,
Join the universal praise.

2 Round Jehovah's footstool kneeling,
Lowly bend with contrite souls;
Here his milder grace revealing,
Here his wrath no thunder rolls.

3 Every secret fault confessing,
Deed unrighteous, thought of sin,
Seize, O seize the proffer'd blessing,
Grace from God and peace within.

4 Heart and voice with rapture swelling,
Still the song of glory raise;
On the theme immortal dwelling,
Join the universal praise.

HYMN 18. L. M.　　　Doddridge.
Portugal. Chatham. Bicester.
1 GOD of my life, through all its days,
My grateful powers shall sound thy praise;
The song shall wake with opening light,
And warble to the silent night.

2 When anxious cares would break my rest,
And grief would tear my throbbing breast,
Thy tuneful praise I'll raise on high,
And check the murmur and the sigh.

3 When death o'er nature shall prevail,
And all its powers of language fail,
Joy through my swimming eyes shall break,
And mean the thanks I cannot speak.

4 But Oh! when that last conflict's o'er,
And I am chain'd to flesh no more
With what glad accents shall I rise,
To join the music of the skies!

SCRIPTURES

*HYMN 19. C. M.
Barby. Wareham.
1 HOW precious is the book divine,
By inspiration given!
Bright as a lamp its doctrines shine
To guide our souls to heaven.

2 It sweetly cheers our drooping hearts,
In this dark vale of tears;
Life, light, and joy, it still imparts,
And quells our rising fears.

3 This lamp, through all the tedious night
Of life, shall guide our way,
Till we behold the clearer light
Of an eternal day.

*HYMN 20. C. M.   Steele.
St. Ann's. Canterbury.
1 FATHER of mercies, in thy word,
What endless glory shines!
For ever be thy name ador'd
For these celestial lines.

2 Here, the Redeemer's welcome voice,
Spreads heavenly peace around,
And life, and everlasting joys
Attend the blissful sound.

3 Oh, may these heavenly pages be
My ever dear delight;
And still new beauties may I see,
And still increasing light!

4 Divine instructer, gracious Lord,
Be thou for ever near,
Teach me to love thy sacred word,
And view my Saviour there.

*HYMN 21. C. M.   Watts.
Plymouth. Abridge.
1 LADEN with guilt and full of fears,
I fly to thee, my Lord,
And not a glimpse of hope appears,
But in thy written word.

2 The volume of my Father's grace
Does all my grief assuage;
Here I behold my Saviour's face
Almost in every page.

3 This is the field where hidden lies
The pearl of price unknown;
That merchant is divinely wise,
Who makes the pearl his own.

4 This is the Judge that ends the strife
Where wit and reason fail;
My guide to everlasting life,
Through all this gloomy vale.

HYMN 22. L. M. Watts.
Angel's Hymn. Kent. Old Hundred.
The power of the Gospel.
1 JESUS, thy witness speaks within;
The mercy which thy words reveal,
Refines the heart from sense and sin,
And stamps its own celestial seal.

2 'Tis God's renewing, gracious hand,
That moulds and forms the earth anew;
Transgressors can no more withstand,
But bow and own his doctrine true.

3 The guilty wretch, that trusts thy blood,
Finds peace and pardon at the cross;
The soul, that was averse to God,
Believes and loves his Maker's laws.

4 Let proud opposers cease their strife,
And own, O Lord, the work is thine:
The voice, that calls the dead to life,
Must be almighty and divine.

HYMN 23. L. M.   Beddome.
Italy. Bicester. Truro.
1 GOD, in the gospel of his Son,
Makes his eternal counsels known;
'Tis here his richest mercy shines,
And truth is drawn in fairest lines.

2 Here sinners of an humble frame
May taste his grace and learn his name;
'Tis writ in characters of blood,
Severely just, immensely good.

3 Here Jesus, in ten thousand ways,
His soul-attracting charms displays,
Recounts his poverty and pains,
And tells his love in melting strains.

4 Wisdom its dictates here imparts,
To form our minds, to cheer our hearts;
Its influence makes the sinner live,
It bids the drooping saint revive.

5 Our raging passions it controls,
And comfort yields to contrite souls;
It brings a better world in view,
And guides us all our journey through.

6 May this bless'd volume ever lie
Close to my heart, and near my eye,
Till life's last hour my soul engage,
And be my chosen heritage!

HYMN 24. C. M.   Cowper.
Abridge. Barby.
The glory of the word.
1 THE Spirit breathes upon the word,
And brings the truth to sight:
Precepts and promises afford
A sanctifying light.

2 A glory gilds the sacred page,
Majestic like the sun;
It gives a light to every age,
It gives—but borrows none.

3 The hand that gave it still supplies
The gracious light and heat;
His truths upon the nation rise,
They rise, but never set.

4 Let everlasting thanks be thine,
For such a bright display,
As makes a world of darkness shine
With beams of heavenly day.

ALARMING

*HYMN 25. S. M.   Newton.
Wirksworth. Orange.
Few saved. Luke xiii. 23.
1 DESTRUCTION'S dangerous road
What multitudes pursue!
While that which leads the soul to God,
Is known or sought by few.

2 Believers find the way
Through Christ the living gate;
But those who hate this holy way
Complain it is too strait.

3 If self must be denied,
And sin no more caress'd,
They rather choose the way that's wide,
And strive to think it best.

4 Encompass'd by a throng,
On numbers they depend;
They say, so many can't be wrong,
And miss a happy end.

5 But hear the Saviour's word,
"Strive for the heav'nly gate,
Many will call upon the Lord,
And find their cries too late."

6 Obey the gospel call,
And enter while you may;
The flock of Christ is always small,
And none are safe but they.

7 Lord, open sinners' eyes,
Their awful state to see;
And make them, ere the storm arise,
To thee for safety flee.

HYMN 26. C. M. Dobell.
Windsor. Buckingham. Lebanon.
Matthew vii. 13, 14.
1 SINNERS, behold that downward road
Which leads to endless wo;
What multitudes of thoughtless souls,
The road to ruin go!

2 But yonder see that narrow way
Which leads to endless bliss;
There see a happy chosen few,
Redeem'd by sovereign grace.

3 They from destruction's city came,
To Zion upward tend:
The bible is their precious guide,
And God himself their friend.

4 Lord, I would now a pilgrim be—
Guide thou my feet aright;
I would not for ten thousand worlds
Be banish'd from thy sight.

*HYMN 27. L. M. Doddridge.
Bath. Luther's Hymn.
The sinner weighed and found wanting. Daniel v. 27.
1 RAISE, thoughtless sinner, raise thine eye—
Behold God's balance lifted high!
There shall his justice be display'd,
And there thy hope and life be weigh'd.

2 See in one scale his perfect law;
Mark with what force its precepts draw:
Wouldst thou the awful test sustain?
Thy works how light! thy thoughts how vain!

3 Behold, the hand of God appears
To trace in dreadful characters;
"Sinner—thy soul is wanting found,
And wrath shall smite thee to the ground."

4 Let sudden fear thy nerves unbrace;
Let horror change thy guilty face;
Through all thy thoughts let anguish roll,
Till deep repentance melt thy soul.

5 One only hope may yet prevail;—
Christ hath a weight to turn the scale;
Still doth the gospel publish peace,
And show a Saviour's righteousness.

6 Great God, exert thy power to save;
Deep on the heart these truths engrave;
The pond'rous load of guilt remove,
That trembling lips may sing thy love.

*HYMN 28. C. M.
Funeral Hymn. Elgin.
Hell. Isaiah xxx. 33. Mark ix. 43, 44.
1 FAR from the utmost verge of day
Those gloomy regions lie,
Where flames amid the darkness play—
The worm shall never die.

2 The breath of God—his angry breath
Supplies and fans the fire;
There sinners taste the second death,
And would—but can't expire.

3 Conscience, the never dying worm,
With torture gnaws the heart;
And wo and wrath, in every form,
Is now the sinner's part.

4 Sad world indeed! ah, who can bear
For ever there to dwell—
For ever sinking in despair
In all the pains of hell!

*HYMN 29. C. M.   Watts.
Elgin. Funeral Hymn
The Scoffer.
1 ALL ye who laugh and sport with death,
And say, there is no hell;
The gasp of your expiring breath
Will send you there to dwell.

2 When iron slumbers bind your flesh,
With strange surprise you'll find
Immortal vigor spring afresh,
And tortures wake the mind!

3 Then you'll confess, the frightful names
Of plagues, you scorn'd before,
No more shall look like idle dreams,
Like foolish tales no more.

4 Then shall ye curse that fatal day,
With flames upon your tongues,
When you exchang'd your souls away
For vanity and songs.

HYMN 30. L. M
Bath. Monmouth.
To-day. Hebrews iv. 7.
1 HASTEN, O sinner, to be wise,
And stay not for the morrow's sun;
The longer wisdom you despise
The harder is she to be won.

2 Oh, hasten, mercy to implore,
And stay not for the morrow's sun,
For fear thy season should be o'er
Before this evening's course be run.

3 Hasten, O sinner, to return,
And stay not for the morrow's sun,
For fear thy lamp should fail to burn
Before the needful work is done.

4 Hasten, O sinner, to be blest,
And stay not for the morrow's sun,
For fear the curse should thee arrest,
Before the morrow is begun.

*HYMN 31. L. M. Newton.
Winchester. Bath. Wells.
The fig-tree. Mark xi. 20.
1 ONE awful word which Jesus spoke
Against the tree that bore no fruit,
More dreadful than the lightning's stroke,
Blasted and dried it to the root.

2 How many, who the gospel hear,
Whom Satan blinds, and sin deceives,
May with this wither'd tree compare?—
They yield no fruit, but only leaves.

3 Knowledge, and zeal, and gifts, and talk,
Unless combin'd with faith and love,
And witness'd by a gospel walk,
Will not a true profession prove.

4 Without such fruit as God expects,
Knowledge will make our state the worse;
The fruitless sinners he rejects,
And soon will blast them with his curse.

HYMN 32. S. M. Doddridge.
Dunbar. Orange. Bridgeport.
Preparation for the Judgment. Revelation xx. 11.
1 HOW will my heart endure
The terrors of that day;
When earth and heav'n, before the judge
Astonish'd shrink away!

2 But ere that trumpet shakes
The mansions of the dead;
Hark! from the gospel's cheering sound,
What joyful tidings spread!

3 Ye sinners, seek his grace,
Whose wrath ye cannot bear;
Fly to the shelter of his cross,
And find salvation there.

4 So shall that curse remove,
By which the Saviour bled;
And the last awful day shall pour
His blessings on your head.

*HYMN 33. S. M.   Dwight.
Bridgeport. Wirksworth.
The harvest is past. Jeremiah viii. 20.
1 I SAW, beyond the tomb,
The awful Judge appear,
Prepar'd to scan with strict account,
My blessings wasted here.

2 His wrath like flaming fire,
Burn'd to the lowest hell—
And in that hopeless world of wo,
He bade my spirit dwell.

3 Ye sinners, fear the Lord,
While yet 'tis call'd to-day;
Soon will the awful voice of death
Command your souls away.

4 Soon will the harvest close—
The summer soon be o'er—
And soon, your injur'd, angry God
Will hear your prayers no more.

*HYMN 34. C. M.   Newton.
Elim. Barby.
The rich worldling. Luke xii. 16-21.
1 "MY barns are full, my stores increase;
And now for many years,
Soul, eat and drink, and take thine ease,
Secure from wants and fears."

2 Thus, while a worldling boasted once,
As many now presume,
He heard the Lord himself pronounce
His sudden, awful doom:

3 "This night, vain fool, thy soul must pass,
Into a world unknown;
And who shall then the stores possess,
Which thou hast call'd thine own?"

4 Thus blinded mortals fondly scheme
For happiness below;
Till death destroys the pleasing dream,
And they awake to wo.

HYMN 35. C. M.   Part II.
Elgin. Martyrs.
1 AH! who can speak the vast dismay
That fills the sinners mind,
When torn by death's strong hand away,
He leaves his all behind!

2 Worldlings, who cleave to earthly things,
But are not rich to God,
Will feel that death is full of stings,
And hell a dark abode.

3 Dear Saviour, make us timely wise,
Thy gospel to attend;
That we may live above the skies,
When time and life shall end.

*HYMN 36. C. M.   Newton.
York. Mear. Walsal.
Trust of the wicked. Jeremiah xvii. 5, 6.
1 SEE how the worthless bramble stands
Beneath the burning sky;
Wither'd and parch'd in barren sands,
And only grows to die.

2 Such is the sinner's awful case,
Who makes the world his trust;
And dares his confidence to place
In vanity and dust.

3 A secret curse destroys his root,
And dries its moisture up
He lives a while, but bears no fruit,
Then dies without a hope.

HYMN 37. H. M.   Lee
Bethesda. Eagle-Street.
Romans iii. 16.
1 WHEN frowning death appears,
And points his fatal dart,
What dark foreboding fears
Distract the sinner's heart!
    The dreadful blow
    No arm can stay,

But torn away
He sinks to wo.

2 Now every hope denied,
Bereft of every good,
He must the wrath abide
Of an avenging God;
    No mercy there
    Will greet his ear,
    Nor wipe the tear
    Of black despair.

3 Sinners, awake, attend,
And flee the wrath to come;
Make Christ, the Judge, your friend,
And heav'n shall he your home.
    His mercy nigh,
    Now points the path
    That leads from death
    To joys on high.

*HYMN 38. C. M. Doddridge.
St. Martin's. Dundee. Barby.
Acts xvii. 30.

1 REPENT, the voice celestial cries,
Nor longer dare delay:
The wretch that scorns the mandate dies,
And meets a fiery day.

2 No more the sov'reign eye of God
O'erlooks the crimes of men;
His heralds are despatch'd abroad
To warn the world of sin.

3 Together in his presence bow,
And all your guilt confess;
Accept the offer'd Saviour now,
Nor trifle with his grace.

4 Bow, ere the awful trumpet sound,
And call you to his bar:
For mercy knows th' appointed bound,
And turns to vengeance there.

5 Amazing love, that yet will call,
And yet prolong our days!
Our hearts, subdu'd by goodness, fall,
And weep, and love, and praise.

*HYMN 39. L. M. Pres. Davies.
Luther's Hymn. Old Hundred.
The wreck of nature. Isaiah xxiv. 18-20.
1 HOW great, how terrible that God,
Who shakes creation with his nod!
He frowns—earth, sea, all nature's frame
Sink in one universal flame.

2 Where now, oh, where shall sinners seek
For shelter in the general wreck!
Shall falling rocks be o'er them thrown?
See rocks, like snow dissolving down.

3 In vain for mercy now they cry;
In lakes of liquid fire they lie;
There on the flaming billows toss'd,
For ever—oh, for ever lost!

4 But saints, undaunted and serene,
With calmness view the dreadful scene;
Their Saviour lives, the worlds expire;
And earth and skies dissolve in fire.

5 Jesus, the hopeless creature's friend,
To thee my all I dare commend;
Thou canst preserve my feeble soul,
When lightnings blaze from pole to pole.

*HYMN 40. 7s. Newton.
Middleton. Pleyel's.
Sinner, prepare to meet God.
1 SINNER, art thou still secure?
Wilt thou still refuse to pray?
Can thy heart or hands endure
In the Lord's avenging day?

2 See, his mighty arm is bar'd!
Awful terrors clothe his brow
For his judgment stand prepar'd,
Thou must either break or bow.

3 At his presence nature shakes,
Earth affrighted hastes to flee;
Solid mountains melt like wax,
What will then become of thee?

4 Who his advent may abide?
You that glory in your shame,
Will you find a place to hide,
When the world is wrapt in flame?

5 Lord, prepare us by thy grace!
Soon we must resign our breath,
And our souls be call'd to pass
Through the iron gate of death.

6 Let us now our day improve,
Listen to the gospel voice;
Seek the things that are above;
Scorn the world's pretended joys.

*HYMN 41. L. M. Lee.
Surry. Putney.
God angry with the wicked. Psalm vii. 11.
1 AN angry God—a Judge severe—
How just, how holy is the Lord!
While christians hope with humble fear,
Let sinners tremble at his word.

2 His law condemns the wicked now,
And goodness seals their awful doom;
But wrath, though here unseen, and slow,
Will burst, and burn beyond the tomb.

3 Then, how may hope and peace be found?
My trembling, anxious heart inquires;—
A hope secure on gospel ground,
No phantom which the world inspires?

4 Dear Saviour, friend of sinners, hear,
And lift on me thy smiling face;
Chase from my soul each doubt and fear,
And bid me taste thy cheering grace.

*HYMN 42. S. M.   Hyde.
Oulney. Wirksworth.
Apostacy. 2 Peter ii. 22.
1 YE, who in former days,
Were found at Zion's gate;
Who seem'd to walk in wisdom's ways,
And told your happy state;

2 But now to sin draw back,
And love again to stray,
The narrow path of life forsake,
And choose the beaten way;

3 Think not your names above
Are written with the saints
The promise of unchanging love
Is his who never faints.

4 Your transient joy and peace
Your deeper doom have seal'd,
Unless you wake to righteousness,
Ere judgment is reveal'd.

HYMN 43. 7, 6.   Newton.
Brighthelmstone. Amsterdam. Margate.
The Alarm.
1 STOP, poor sinners, stop and think,
Before you further go;
Will you sport upon the brink
Of everlasting wo?
On the verge of ruin stop—
Now the friendly warning take—
Stay your footsteps—ere you drop
Into the burning lake.

2 Say, have you an arm like God,
That you his will oppose?
Fear ye not that iron rod
With which he breaks his foes?
Can you stand in that dread day,
Which his justice shall proclaim,
When the earth shall melt away
Like wax before the flame?

3 Ghastly death will quickly come,
And drag you to his bar;
Then to hear your awful doom,
Will fill you with despair!
All our sins will round you crowd;
You shall mark their crimson dye;
Each for vengeance crying loud,
And what can you reply?

4 Though your heart were made of steel,
Your forehead lined with brass;
God at length will make you feel,
He will not let you pass;
Sinners then in vain will call,
Those who now despise his grace,
"Rocks and mountains on us fall,
And hide us from his face."

INVITING.

*HYMN 44. C. M.   Steele.
Clifford. Bray. Herman.
The Saviour's invitation. John vii. 37.
1 THE Saviour calls— let every ear
Attend the heav'nly sound;
Ye doubting souls, dismiss your fear,
Hope smiles reviving round.

2 For ev'ry thirsty, longing heart,
Here streams of bounty flow,
And life, and health, and bliss impart
To banish mortal wo.

3 Ye sinners, come, 'tis mercy's voice;
The gracious call obey;
Mercy invites to heav'nly joys—
And can you yet delay?

4 Dear Saviour, draw reluctant hearts
To thee let sinners fly,
And take the bliss thy love imparts
And drink, and never die.

HYMN 45. C. M.   Medley.
Barby. Clarendon.
1 OH, what amazing words of grace
Are in the gospel found!
Suited to ev'ry sinner's case,
Who knows the joyful sound.

2 Come then, with all your wants and wounds,
Your ev'ry burden bring;
Here love, eternal love abounds,
A deep celestial spring.

3 This spring with living water flows,
And living joy imparts;
Come, thirsty souls, your wants disclose,
And drink with thankful hearts.

HYMN 46. C. M.   Watts.
Wantage. Buckingham.
1 THERE is a voice of sovereign grace
Sounds from the sacred word;
"Ho! ye despairing sinners, come,
And trust upon the Lord."

2 My soul obeys th' Almighty call,
And runs to this relief;
I would believe thy promise, Lord,
Oh! help my unbelief.

3 To the dear fountain of thy blood,
Incarnate God, I fly;
Here let me wash my spotted soul
From crimes of deepest dye.

4 Stretch out thine arm, victorious King,
My reigning sins subdue;
Drive the old dragon from his seat
With his apostate crew.

5 A guilty, weak, and helpless worm
On thy kind arms I fall;
Be thou my strength and righteousness,
My Jesus, and my all!

HYMN 47. 8,7. Newton.
Northampton-Chapel. Drummond.
John iii. 14.
1 AS the serpent, rais'd by Moses,
Heal'd the burning serpent's bite;
Jesus thus himself discloses
To the wounded sinner's sight.

2 Hear his gracious invitation:
"I have life and peace to give;
I have wrought out full salvation:
Sinner, look to me and live.

3 You had been for ever wretched,
Had I not espous'd your part;
Now, behold my arms outstretched,
To receive you to my heart.

4 Well may shame, and joy, and wonder,
All your inward passions move;
I could crush you with my thunder,
But I speak to you in love."

5 Dearest Saviour, we adore thee
For thy precious life and death,
Melt each stubborn heart before thee,
Give us all the eye of faith.

HYMN 48. L. M.
Kingsbridge. Darwent.
Behold, I stand at the door. Revelation iii. 20
1 BEHOLD a stranger at the door!
He gently knocks, has knock'd before;
Hath waited long—is waiting still;
You treat no other friend so ill.

2 Oh, lovely attitude, he stands
With melting heart and loaded hands!
Oh, matchless kindness! and he shows
This matchless kindness to his foes.

3 But will he prove a friend indeed?
He will; the very friend you need;
The friend of sinners—yes, 'tis He,
With garments dy'd on Calvary.

4 Rise, touch'd with gratitude divine;
Turn out his enemy and thine,
That soul—destroying monster sin,
And let the heavenly stranger in.

5 Admit him, ere his anger burn,
His feet departed ne'er return
Admit him, or the hour's at hand,
You'll at his door rejected stand.

HYMN 49. C. M.
Clarendon. Newmark.
1 AMAZING sight, the Saviour stands
And knocks at every door!
Ten thousand blessings in his hands
To satisfy the poor.

2 "Behold," he saith, "I bleed and die
"To bring you to my rest
"Hear, sinners, while I'm passing by,
"And be for ever blest.

3 "Will you despise my bleeding love,
"And choose the way to hell?
"Or in the glorious realms above,
"With me for ever dwell?

4 "Not to condemn your wretched race
"Have I in judgment come
"But to display unbounded grace,
"And bring lost sinners home.

5 "Will you go down to endless night,
"And bear eternal pain?
"Or in the glorious realms of light
"With me for ever reign ?

6 "Say—will you hear my gracious voice,
"And have your sins forgiven?
"Or will you make that wretched choice,
"And bar yourselves from heaven?"

*HYMN 50. C. M.   Steele.
Springfield. Bray. Newmark.
1 AND will the Lord thus condescend
To visit sinful worms ?
Thus at the door shall mercy stand
In all her winning forms?

2 Surprising grace— and shall my heart
Unmov'd and cold remain?
Has this hard rock no tender part?
Must mercy plead in vain?

3 Shall Jesus for admission sue—
His charming voice unheard?
And this vile heart, his rightful due,
Remain for ever barr'd?

4 'Tis sin, alas, with tyrant pow'r,
The lodging has possess'd
And crowds of traitors bar the door
Against the heav'nly guest.

5 Ye dang'rous inmates, hence depart;
Dear Saviour, enter in,
And guard the passage to my heart,
And keep out every sin.

*HYMN 51. C. M.   Cowper.
Tunbridge. Keene.
1 NOW is the time, th' accepted hour,
O sinners, come away
The Saviour's knocking at your door,
Arise without delay.

2 Oh! don't refuse to give him room,
Lest mercy should withdraw
He'll then in robes of vengeance come
To execute his law.

3 Then where, poor mortals, will you be,
If destitute of grace,
When you your injur'd Judge shall see,
And stand before his face.

4 Oh! could you shun that dreadful sight,
How would you wish to fly
To the dark shades of endless night,
From that all-searching eye?

5 The dead awak'd must all appear,
And you among them stand,
Before the great impartial bar,
Arraign'd at Christ's left hand.

6 Let not these warnings be in vain,
But lend a list'ning ear
Lest you should meet them all again,
When wrapp'd in keen despair.

HYMN 52. C. M. Heginbothom.
Walsal. Elgin. Windsor.
He beheld the city, etc. Luke, xix. 41, 42.
1 "UNHAPPY city! hadst thou known—
Then were thy peace secure;
But now the day of grace is gone,
And thy destruction sure."

2 Thus to the Jews the Saviour calls,
As near their gates he stood,
His eyes beheld their guilty walls,
And wept a sacred flood.

3 And can mine eyes, without a tear,
A weeping Saviour see?
Shall I not weep his groans to hear,
Who groan'd and died for me?

4 Blest Jesus let those tears of thine
Subdue each stubborn foe;
Come, fill my heart with love divine,
And bid my sorrows flow.

HYMN 53. C. M.
Wednesbury. Dundee.
1 JESUS, Redeemer of mankind,
Thy saving power display;
Thy mercy now may sinners find,
And know their gracious day.

2 Ah, give them, Lord, a longer space;
Nor suddenly consume;—
But let them take the proffer'd grace,
And flee the wrath to come.

3 Open their eyes thy cross to view,
Their ears to hear thy cries—
Sinners, the Saviour weeps for you,
For you he weeps and dies.

4 All the day long he meekly stands,
The rebels to receive;
And shows his wounds, and spreads his hands,
And bids you turn, and live.

HYMN 54. C. M.　　　Steele.
Springfield. Bray. Colchester.
And yet there is room. Luke xiv. 22.
1 YE wretched, hungry, starving poor,
Behold a royal feast!
Where mercy spreads her bounteous store,
For every humble guest.

2 See, Jesus stands with open arms;
He calls, he bids you come;
Guilt holds you back, and fear alarms;
But see, there yet is room.

3 Room in the Saviour's bleeding heart,
There love and pity meet;
Nor will he bid the soul depart,
That trembles at his feet.

4 In him the Father, reconcil'd,
Invites your souls to come;
The rebel shall be call'd a child,
And kindly welcom'd home.

HYMN 55. C. M.　　　Watts.
Barby. Wareham.
1 JESUS, thy blessings are not few,
Nor is thy gospel weak;
Thy grace can melt the stubborn Jew,
And heal the dying Greek.

2 Wide as the reach of Satan's rage,
Does thy salvation flow;
'Tis not confin'd to sex or age,
The lofty or the low.

3 While grace is offer'd to the prince,
The poor may take their share,
No mortal has a just pretence
To perish in despair.

4 Come, all ye wretched sinners, come,
He'll form your souls anew;
His gospel and his heart have room
For rebels such as you.

HYMN 56. H. M.   Boden.
Eagle-Street. Bethesda.
1 YE dying sons of men,
Immerg'd in sin and wo,
The gospel's voice attend,
While Jesus sends to you:
Ye perishing and guilty, come,
In Jesus' arms there yet is room,

2 No longer now delay;
No vain excuses frame;
He bids you come to-day,
Though poor, and blind, and lame:
All things are ready, sinners, come!
For every trembling soul there's room.

3 Compell'd by bleeding love,
Ye wand'ring souls, draw near;
Christ calls you from above—
His charming accents hear!
Let whosoever will, now come;
In mercy's arms there still is room.

HYMN 57. 8, 7, 4.   Hart.
Littleton. Jordan.
Sinners invited to Christ. Matthew x. 28-30.
1 COME, ye weary, heavy laden,
Lost and ruin'd by the fall;
If you tarry till you're better
You will never come at all:

Not the righteous—
Sinners Jesus came to call.

2 Let not conscience make you linger,
Nor of fitness fondly dream;
All the fitness he requireth,
Is to feel your need of him:
This he gives you—
'Tis the Spirit's rising beam.

3 Agonizing in the garden,
Lo ! your Maker prostrate lies!
On the bloody tree behold him;
Hear him cry before he dies,
"It is finish'd:"
Sinners, will not this suffice?

4 Lo ! th' incarnate God ascended,
Pleads the merit of his blood
Venture on him, venture wholly,
Let no other trust intrude:
None but Jesus
Can do helpless sinners good.

5 Saints and angels, join'd in concert,
Sing the praises of the Lamb
While the blissful seats of heaven,
Sweetly echo with his name:
Hallelujah!
Sinners here may sing the same.

HYMN 58. L. M. Steele.
Portugal. Bath.
1 COME, weary souls, with sin's distress,
Come, and accept the promis'd rest;
The Saviour's gracious call obey,
And cast your gloomy fears away.

2 Oppress'd with guilt, a painful load,
O, come, and spread your woes abroad;
Divine compassion, mighty love,
Will all the painful load remove.

3 Here mercy's boundless ocean flows,
To cleanse your guilt and heal your woes;

Pardon and life, and endless peace;
How rich the gift, how free the grace!

4 Lord, we accept, with thankful heart,
The hope thy gracious words impart;
We come with trembling, yet rejoice,
And bless the kind inviting voice.

HYMN 59. 5,6.
Devonshire. Locke.
1 COME, sinners, attend,
And make no delay;
Good news from a friend,
I bring you to-day;
Glad news of salvation
Come now and receive;
There's no condemnation
To them that believe.

2 I AM THAT I AM
Hath sent me to you;
Glad news to proclaim,
Your sins to subdue:
To you, O distressed,
Afflicted, forlorn,
Whose sins are increased,
And cannot be borne.

3 But still if you cry,
Oh, what is his name?
You have the reply,
I AM THAT I AM:
Though blind, lame, and feeble,
And helpless you lie,
He's willing and able
Your wants to supply.

4 Then only believe,
And trust in his name;
He will not deceive,
Nor put you to shame;
But fully supply you
With all things in store;
Nor will he deny you
Because you are poor.

*HYMN 60. L. M.
Blendon. Bath. Portugal.
Luke xv. 20-24.
1 LO! what a rapt'rous joy possess'd
The tender parent's throbbing breast,
To see his spendthrift son return,
And all his former follies mourn!

2 So Jesus never will despise
The contrite heart for sacrifice;
The deep-fetch'd sigh, the secret groan
Will rise accepted to the throne.

3 He meets, with tokens of his grace,
The trembling lip, the blushing face;
His bowels yearn when sinners pray,
And mercy bears their sins away.

HYMN 61. L. M.   C. Wesley.
St. Peter's. PortugaL
1 SINNERS, obey the gospel word,
Haste to the supper of your Lord;
Be wise to know your gracious day,
All things are ready, come away.

2 Ready the Father is to own
And welcome his returning son,
Ready the gracious Saviour stands,
And spreads for you his bleeding hands.

3 Ready the Spirit from above
To fill the broken heart with love,
T' apply and witness Jesus' blood,
And wish and seal you sons of God.

4 Ready for you the angels wait,
To triumph in your blest estate
Turning their harps by which they praise
The wonders of Redeeming grace.

HYMN 62.   L. M.
Surry. Warwick.
1 SINNERS, approach your dying Lord,
And find your happiness restor'd:

His proff'er'd benefits embrace,
The plenitude of gospel grace:

2 A pardon written with his blood,
The favor and the peace of God;
The seeing eye, the feeling sense,
The trembling joys of penitence:

3 The godly fear, the pleasing smart,
The meltings of a broken heart;
The tears that tell your sins forgiv'n;
The sighs that waft your souls to heav'n.

4 Oh, quit this world's delusive charms,
And quickly fly to Jesus' arms;
Wrestle, until your God is known,
Till you can call the Lord your own.

*HYMN 63. C. M.
Rochester. Braintree. Brighton.
Isaiah lv. 1, 2.
1 LET every mortal ear attend,
And every heart rejoice!
The trumpet of the gospel sounds,
With an inviting voice.

2 Ho! all ye hungry, starving souls,
Who feed upon the wind,—
And vainly strive, with earthly toys,
To fill an empty mind:—

3 Eternal wisdom has prepar'd
A soul-reviving feast;
And bids your longing appetites
The rich provision taste.

4 Ho! ye who pant for living streams,
And pine away and die;
Here, you may quench your raging thirst,
With springs that never dry.

5 The happy gates of gospel grace
Stand open all the day;
Lord, we are come to seek supplies,
And drive our wants away.

HYMN 64. L. M.
Bicester. China.
1 HO! every one that thirsts, draw nigh,
'Tis God invites the fallen race;
Mercy and free salvation buy,
Buy wine, and milk, and gospel grace.

2 Ye nothing in exchange can give,
Leave all ye have and are behind;
Freely the gift of God receive,
Pardon and peace in Jesus find.

3 Come to the living waters, come!
Sinners, obey your Makers voice;
Return, ye weary wanderers, home,
And in redeeming love rejoice.

HYMN 65. L. M.
Carthage. Surry.
Compel them.—Luke xiv. 23.
1 COME, all ye souls, by sin oppress'd,
Ye weary wanderers after rest;
Ye poor and maim'd and halt and blind,
In Christ a hearty welcome find.

2 See him set forth before your eyes;
Behold the bleeding sacrifice!
His offer'd love with joy embrace,
Bow to the sceptre of his grace.

3 This message from your God receive,
Nor longer dare his spirit grieve—
Yield to his love's constraining pow'r.
And fight against your God no more.

HYMN 66. 8s. Maxwell.
Consolation. Lambeth. New-Jerusalem.
Excellencies of Christ.
1 HOW shall I my Saviour set forth?
How shall I his beauties declare?
Oh, how shall I speak of his worth,
Or what his chief dignities are?
His angels can never express,
Nor saints who sit nearest his throne,

How rich are his treasures of grace;—
No! this is a myst'ry unknown.

2 In him all the fulness of God
For ever transcendently shines
Though once like a mortal he stood,
To finish his gracious designs:
Though once he was nail'd to the cross,
Vile rebels like me to set free;
His glory sustained no loss,
Eternal his kingdom shall be.

3 O sinner, believe and adore
The Saviour so rich to redeem:
No creature can ever explore
The treasures of goodness in him:
Come, all ye, who see yourselves lost,
And feel yourselves burden'd with sin,
Draw near while with terror you're toss'd,
Believe—and your peace shall begin.

HYMN 67. L. M.   Watts.
Quito. Kent. Portugal.
The wonderful love of Christ.
1 COME, let me love, or is my mind
Harden'd to stone, or froze to ice?
I see the blessed fair one bend,
And stoop t' embrace me from the skies.

2 Oh! 'tis a thought would melt a rock,
And make a heart of iron move,
That those sweet lips, that heav'nly look
Should seek and wish a mortal love!

3 I was a traitor doom'd to fire,
Bound to sustain eternal pains;
He flew on wings of strong desire,
Assum'd my guilt and took my chains.

4 Infinite grace! almighty charms!
Stand in amaze, ye rolling skies!
Jesus, the God, extends his arms,
Hangs on a cross of love, and dies.

5 Did pity ever stoop so low,
Dress'd in divinity and blood?
Was ever rebel courted so,
In groans of an expiring God?

6 Again he lives, and spreads his hands,
Hands that were nail'd to torturing smart;
"By these dear wounds," says he; and stands,
And prays to clasp me to his heart.

7 Sure I must love; or are my ears
Still deaf, nor will my passions move?
Lord! melt this stubborn heart to tears;
This heart shall yield to death or love.

HYMN 68. L. M.   Collyer.
Armley. Surry.
Jeremiah xxxi. 18-20.
1 RETURN, O wanderer, return,
And seek an injur'd Father's face;
Those warm desires that in thee burn,
Were kindled by reclaiming grace.

2 Return, O wanderer, return,
And seek a Father's melting heart;
His pitying eyes thy grief discern,
His hand shall heal thine inward smart.

3 Return, O wanderer, return,
Thy Saviour bids thy spirit live;
Go to his bleeding feet, and learn
How freely Jesus can forgive.

4 Return, O wanderer, return,
And wipe away the falling tear;
'Tis God who says, "No longer mourn,"
'Tis mercy's voice invites thee near.

*HYMN 69. C. M. Fawcett.
Mear. Plymouth. Bangor.
Let the wicked forsake, etc. Isaiah lv. 7.
1 SINNERS, the voice of God regard;
His mercy speaks to-day;
He calls you by his sov'reign word,
From sin's destructive way.

2 Like the rough sea that cannot rest,
You live devoid of peace:
A thousand stings within your breast,
Deprive your souls of ease.

3 Your way is dark, and leads to hell;
Why will you persevere?
Can you in endless torments dwell,
Shut up in black despair?

4 Why will you in the crooked ways
Of sin and folly go?
In pain you travel all your days,
To reap immortal wo!

*HYMN 70. C. M.   Part II.
Rochester. York. St. Ann's.
1 NOW, he who turns to God shall live,
Through his abounding grace:
His mercy will the guilt forgive.
Of those who seek his face.

2 Bow to the sceptre of his word,
Renouncing every sin;
Submit to him, your sov'reign Lord,
And learn his will divine.

3 His love exceeds your highest thoughts;
He pardons like a God;
He will forgive your num'rous faults,
Through a Redeemer's blood.

HYMN 71. 8,7,4.   Allen.
Littleton. Helmsley.
1 SINNERS, will you scorn the message,
Sent in mercy from above?
Every sentence—Oh, how tender!
Every line is full of love;
Listen to it—
Every line is full of love.

2 Hear the heralds of the Gospel,
News from Zion's king proclaim,
To each rebel sinner—"Pardon,
"Free forgiveness in his name."

How important!
Free forgiveness in his name!

3 Tempted souls, they bring you succour;
Fearful hearts, they quell your fears;
And with news of consolation,
Chase away the falling tears:
Tender heralds—
Chase away the falling tears.

4 False professors, grov'ling worldlings,
Callous hearers of the word,
While the messengers address you,
Take the warnings they afford;
We entreat you,
Take the warnings they afford.

5 Who hath our report believed?
Who receiv'd the joyful word?
Who embrac'd the news of pardon,
Offer'd to you by the Lord?
Can you slight it—
Offer'd to you by the Lord!

6 O, ye angels, hovering round us,
Waiting spirits, speed your way,
Hasten to the court of heaven,
Tidings bear without delay:
Rebel sinners
Glad the message will obey.

HYMN 72. L. M.
Blendon. Winchester.
Come and see. John i. 39.
1 JESUS, dear name, how sweet the sound!
Replete with balm for every wound!
His word declares his grace is free;
Come, needy sinner, come and see.

2 He left the shining courts on high,
Came to our world to bleed and die:
Jesus, the God, hung on the tree;
Come, careless sinner, come and see.

3 Your sins did pierce his bleeding heart,
Till death had done its dreadful part:
Yet his dear love still burns to thee;
Come, anxious sinner, come and see.

4 His blood can cleanse the foulest stain,
And make the filthy leper clean;
His blood at once avail'd for me;
Come, guilty sinner, come and see.

*HYMN 73. L. M.   Steele.
Shoel. Leyden.
Healing virtue in Christ. Luke vi. 19.
1 YE mourning sinners, here disclose
Your deep complaints, your various woes;
Approach—'tis Jesus, he can heal
The pain which mourning sinners feel.

2 Dear Lord, extend thy healing hand;
Diseases fly at thy command;
O, let thy sov'reign touch impart
Life, strength, and health to every heart.

3 Then shall the sick, the blind, the lame,
Adore their great Physician's name;
Then dying souls shall bless their God,
And spread his wondrous praise abroad.

HYMN 74. C. M.   Newton.
Springfield. Clarendon.
The leper healed. Matthew viii. 2, 3.
1 WHEN the poor leper's case I read,
My own describ'd I feel;
Sin is a leprosy indeed,
Which none but CHRIST can heal.

2 What anguish did my soul endure,
Till hope and patience ceas'd?
The more I strove myself to cure,
The more the plague increas'd.

3 While thus I lay distress'd,
I saw The Saviour passing by;
To him, though fill'd with shame and awe
I rais'd my mournful cry:

4 "Lord, thou canst heal me, if thou wilt,
Oh, pity to me show;
Oh, cleanse my leprous soul from guilt;
My filthy heart renew."

5 He heard, and with a gracious look,
Pronounc'd the healing word:
"I will—be clean," and while he spoke
I felt my health restor'd.

6 Come, sinners, seize the present hour
The Saviour's grace to prove;
He can relieve, for he is pow'r—
He will, for he is love.

HYMN 75.   C. M.   Montgomery.
Barby. Springfield.
The soul. Mark viii. 2, 3.
1 WHAT is the thing of greatest price,
The whole creation round?—
That which was lost in Paradise,
That which in Christ is found:

2 The soul of man—Jehovah's breath—
That keeps two worlds at strife;
Hell moves beneath to work its death,
Heaven stoops to give it life.

3 God, to redeem it, did not spare
His well beloved Son;
Jesus, to save it, deign'd to bear
The sins of all in one.

4 And is this treasure borne below,
In earthen vessels frail ?
Can none its utmost value know,
Till flesh and spirit fail?

5 Then let us gather round the cross,
That knowledge to obtain;
Not by the soul's eternal loss,
But everlasting gain.

*HYMN 76. C. M.   Rippon.
Newmark. Colchester.

1 LORD, shall we part with gold for dross,
With solid good for show!
Outlive our bliss, and mourn our loss
In everlasting wo!

2 Let us not lose the living God,
For one short dream of joy:
With fond embrace cling to a clod,
And fling all heav'n away.

3 Vain world, thy weak attempts forbear,
We all thy charms defy;
And rate our precious souls too dear
For all thy wealth to buy.

*HYMN 77. C. M.   E. Jones.
Reading. Windsor.
Resolve. Esther iv. 16.

1 COME, humble sinner, in whose breast,
A thousand thoughts revolve;
Come, with your guilt and fear oppress'd
And make this last resolve:

2 "I'll go to Jesus, though my sin
"Hath like a mountain rose;
"I know his courts, I'll enter in,
 "Whatever may oppose.

3 "Prostrate I'll lie before his throne,
"And there my guilt confess,
"I'll tell him, I'm a wretch undone
"Without his sov'reign grace.

4 "Perhaps he will admit my plea,
"Perhaps will hear my pray'r;
"But, if I perish, I will pray,
"And perish only there.

5 "I can but perish if I go;
"I am resolv'd to try
"For if I stay away,
"I know I must for ever die."

*HYMN 78. L. M.   Lee.
Bath. Carthage. Armley.
Religion. Proverbs iv. 7.
1 TEACH us, O Lord, the great concern,
To know thy will, thy name to love;
Our duty from thy word to learn,
And gain the wisdom from above.

2 Religion, richest blessing given,
Fountain of all our joys below,
Bids mortals lift their eyes to heaven,
In scenes of darkness and of wo.

3 Religion must be all in all,
Would we th' immortal prize obtain,
Retrieve the ruins of the fall,
And scape the death of endless pain.

4 Send thy good Spirit, Lord, we pray,
To sanctify and cleanse our heart:
May we repent, believe, obey,
And from thy service ne'er depart.

HYMN 79. C. M.
Chapel Walsal.
The woman of Samaria. John iv.
1 LIKE her who in Samaria's bound,
Beneath a sultry sky,
Oft at the Patriarch's well was found,
Her weary toil to ply:—

2 Thus we our measur'd span employ
In labors, long and vain—
We try each boasted fount of joy,
And drink—and thirst again.

3 O thou, who with a pitying heart,
Didst hear her earnest tale,
To us that living stream impart,
Whose waters never fail.

4 So shall our broken cisterns here,
By fickle dew-drops fed,
No more awake the bitter tear,
Or bow the sorrowing head—

5 A holy fountain in the soul,
Eternally shall rise,
Supplied by those pure streams that roll,
Where pleasure never dies.

HYMN 80. C. M.
Newmark. Barby.
1 AT Jacob's well a stranger sought
His drooping frame to cheer:
Samaria's daughter little thought
That Jacob's God was near.

2 This had she known, her fainting mind
For richer draughts had sigh'd;
Nor had Messiah, ever kind,
Those richer draughts denied.

3 The man, who came on earth to die
How few appear to know
The friend of sinners, passing by,
Is still esteem'd a foe.

4 The sinner must the stranger know,
Or soon his loss deplore;
Behold! the living waters flow;
Come—drink, and thirst no more.

HYMN 81. S. M.   Dobell.
Durham. St. Thomas.
The accepted time. 2 Corinthians vi. 2.
1 NOW is th' accepted time,
Now is the day of grace;
Now, sinners, come without delay,
And seek the Saviour's face.

2 Now is th' accepted time,
The Saviour calls to-day;
To-morrow it may be too late—
Then why should you delay?

3 Now is th' accepted time,
The gospel bids you come;
And every promise in his word
Declares there yet is room.

4 Lord, draw reluctant souls,
And feast them with thy love
Then will the angels clap their wings,
And bear the news above.

HYMN 82. L. M.   Dwight.
Psalm 88th. Carthage. Darwent.
1 WHILE life prolongs its precious light
Mercy is found and peace is given;
But soon, ah soon! approaching night
Shall blot out every hope of heav'n.

2 While God invites, how blest the day!
How sweet the gospel's charming sound—
"Come, sinners, haste, Oh, haste away,
While yet a pard'ning God he's found."

3 "Soon, borne on time's most rapid wing,
Shall death command you to the grave,
Before his bar your spirits bring,
And none be found to hear, or save."

4 "In that lone land of deep despair,
No sabbath's heav'nly light shall rise;
No God regard your bitter pray'r,
Nor Saviour call you to the skies."

HYMN 83. L. M.
Blendon. China.
1 To-day, if ye will hear his voice,
Now is the time to make your choice;
Say, will you to Mount Zion go?
Say, will you have this Christ, or no?

2 Ye wand'ring souls, who find no rest,
Say, will you be for ever blest?
Will you be sav'd from sin and hell?
Will you with Christ in glory dwell?

3 Come now, dear youth, for ruin bound,
Obey the gospel's joyful sound;
Come, go with us, and you shall prove
The joy of Christ's redeeming love.

4 Once more we ask you in his name—
For yet his love remains the same—
Say, will you to Mount Zion go?
Say, will you have this Christ, or no?

5 Leave all your sports and glittering toys,
Come share with us eternal joys;
Or must we leave you bound to hell—
Then dear young friends, a long farewell.

*HYMN 84. S. M.　　Doddridge.
Little Marlboro'. Aylesbury.
James iv. 13,14.
1 TOMORROW, Lord, is thine,
Lodg'd in thy sov'reign hand;
And, if its sun arise and shine,
It shines by thy command.

2 The present moment flies,
And bears our life away;
Oh, make thy servants truly wise,
That they may live to-day.

3 Since on this winged hour
Eternity is hung,
Waken by thy almighty power
The aged and the young.

4 One thing demands our care;
Oh, be it still pursu'd—
Lest, slighted once, the season fair
Should never be renew'd.

5 To Jesus may we fly,
Swift as the morning light,
Lest life's young golden beam should die
In sudden, endless night.

*HYMN 85. L. M. Heginbothom.
Leyden. Luton. Nantwich.
The night cometh. John ix. 4.
1 AWAKE, awake, my sluggish soul,
Awake, and view the setting sun;
See how the shades of death advance,
Ere half the task of life is done.

2 Death!—'tis an awful, solemn sound;
Oh, let it wake the slumb'ring ear!
Apace the dreadful conqueror comes,
With all his pale companions near.

3 Thy drowsy eyes will soon be clos'd,—
These friendly warnings heard no more;
Soon will the mighty Judge approach,
E'en now he stands before the door.

4 To-day attend his gracious voice;
This is the summons that he sends:
"Awake,—for on this transient hour
Thy long eternity depends."

PENITENTIAL.

HYMN 86. C. M. Watts.
Wantage. Bangor.
Repentance. Zechariah xii. 10.
1 ALAS! and did my Saviour bleed!
And did my Sov'reign die?
Would he devote that sacred head
For such a worm as I?

2 Was it for crimes, that I had done—
He groan'd upon the tree?
Amazing pity! grace unknown!
And love beyond degree!

3 Well might the sun in darkness hide,
And shut his glories in,
When God, the mighty Maker, dy'd
For man, the creature's sin.

4 Thus might I hide my blushing face,
While his dear cross appears;
Dissolve, my heart, in thankfulness,
And melt, my eyes, to tears.

5 But drops of tears can ne'er repay
The debt of love I owe;
Here, Lord, I give myself away—
'Tis all that I can do.

HYMN 87. C. M.   Steele.
Funeral Hymn. Buckingham.

1 O THOU, whose tender mercy hears
Contrition's humble sigh;
Whose hand, indulgent, wipes the tears
From sorrow's weeping eye;—

2 See, low before thy throne of grace,
A wretched wanderer mourn;
Hast thou not bid me seek thy face?
Hast thou not said—"Return?"

3 And shall my guilty fears prevail
To drive me from thy feet?
Oh, let not this dear refuge fail,
This only safe retreat!

4 Oh, shine on this benighted heart,
With beams of mercy shine!
And let thy healing voice impart
A taste of joys divine.

HYMN 88. C. M.   Watts.
Wantage. Standish.

1 OH, the sharp pangs of smarting pain
My dear Redeemer bore;
When knotty whips, and ragged thorns
His sacred body tore!

2 'Twere you, my sins, my cruel sins,
His chief tormentors were;
Each of my crimes became a nail,
And unbelief the spear.

3 'Twere you that pull'd the vengeance down
Upon his guiltless head;
Break, break, my heart, oh, burst mine eyes,
And let my sorrows bleed.

4 Strike, mighty grace, my stubborn soul,
Till melting waters flow,
And deep repentance drown mine eyes,
In undissembled wo.

HYMN 89. L. M.   Steele.
Surry. Carthage.
1 THE Lord of life, the Saviour dies,
For mortal crimes, a sacrifice:
What love, what mercy, how divine!
Jesus, and can I call thee mine?—

2 Be all my heart, and all my days
Devoted to my Saviour's praise;
And let my glad obedience prove,
How much I owe, how much I love.

3 Let humble, penitential wo,
With painful, pleasing anguish flow:
And thy forgiving smiles impart
Life, hope, and joy to every heart.

HYMN 90. C. M.   B.
Walsal. Wantage.
The Penitent. Luke vii. 36-50.
1 AS once the Saviour took his seat—
Attracted by his fame,
And lowly bending at his feet,
An humble suppliant came.

2 Asham'd to lift her streaming eyes
His holy glance to meet,
She pour'd her costly sacrifice
Upon the Saviour's feet.

3 Oppress'd with sin and sorrow's weight,
And sinking in despair,
With tears she wash'd his sacred feet,
And wip'd them with her hair.

4 "Depart in peace," the Saviour said,
"Thy sins are all forgiv'n!"
The trembling sinner rais'd her head,
In peaceful hope of heav'n.

HYMN 91. C. M.   Stennett.
Bangor. Windsor.
1 PROSTRATE, dear Jesus, at thy feet
A guilty rebel lies;
And upwards to the mercy-seat
Presumes to lift his eyes.

2 Oh, let not justice frown me hence;
Stay, stay the vengeful storm:
Forbid it, that omnipotence
Should crush a feeble worm.

3 If tears of sorrow would suffice
To pay the debt I owe,
Tears should from both my weeping eyes,
In ceaseless currents flow.

4 But no such sacrifice I plead
To expiate my guilt;
No tears, but those which thou hast shed,
No blood, but thou hast spilt.

HYMN 92. L. M.
Antworth. Surry. Darwent.
Prayer of a Penitent. Psalm 6.
1 OH, that the Lord would hear my cry,
And stay his anger lest I die!
Thy wrath is just—yet, oh, forgive!
And let a mourning sinner live.

2 In all my frame, without, within,
I feel the sad effects of sin
How long, my God, must I complain,
And deprecate thy wrath in vain?

3 Oh, should I die depriv'd of thee!
What being else can succour me?
Thy frowns would rend my soul in death,
And sink it to the depths beneath.

4 Ye darling sins, that plague me so,
The greatest enemies I know,
Depart—for God hath heard my pray'r,
And will not let me long despair.

5 No;—I shall yet his goodness bless
And when this transient life shall pass,
Then, full of glory, I shall prove
He can be just, and sinners love.

HYMN 93. L. M.   Merrick.
Kingsbridge. Armley.
Psalm li. 9-13.
1 OH, turn, great Ruler of the skies,
Turn from my sin thy searching eyes,
Nor let th' offences of my hand,
Within thy book recorded stand.

2 Give me a will to thine subdu'd,
A conscience pure, a soul renew'd;
Nor let me, wrapp'd in endless gloom,
An outcast from thy presence roam.

3 Oh, let thy Spirit to my heart
Once more his quick'ning aid impart;
My mind from every fear release,
And sooth my troubled thoughts to peace.

4 So shall the souls, whom error sway
Has urg'd from thee, blest Lord, to stray,
From me thy heavenly precepts learn,
And, humbled, to their God return.

HYMN 94. C. M.
Springfield. Clarendon. Coventry.
1 ALMIGHTY God of truth and love,
In me thy power exert—
The mountain from my soul remove—
The hardness from my heart.

2 Do thou in mercy wake within,
A jealous, godly fear,
A sensibility to sin,
A pain to feel it near.

3 Teach me the first approach to feel
Of pride, or fond desire;
To catch the wand'rings of my will,
And quench the kindling fire.

4 The filial awe, the contrite heart,
The tender conscience give;
That I from thee no more may part—
No more thy goodness grieve.

*HYMN 95.   7s.   Raffles.
Pleyel's. Epiphany. Pastoral Duet.
1 SOV'REIGN Ruler, Lord of all,
Prostrate at thy feet I fall:
Hear, oh, hear my ardent cry,
Frown not, lest I faint and die.

2 Vilest of the sons of men,
Worst of rebels I have been!
Oft abused thee to thy face,
Trampled upon thy richest grace!

3 Justly might thy vengeful dart
Pierce this bleeding, broken heart;
Justly might thy kindled ire
Blast me in eternal fire.

4 But with thee there's mercy found,
Balm to heal my every wound;
Sooth, oh, sooth the troubled breast,
Give the weary wanderer rest.

*HYMN 96. S. M.
Orange. Bridgeport.
1 LORD, help me to repent—
With sin for ever part;
And to thy gracious eye present
An humble, contrite heart.

2 A heart with grief oppress'd,
For having griev'd thy love;
A troubled heart that cannot rest,
Till cleansed from above.

3 Jesus, on me bestow
The penitent desire;
With true sincerity of wo,
My aching breast inspire;

4 With soft'ning pity look,
And melt my hardness down;
Strike, with thy love's resistless stroke,
And break this heart of stone.

HYMN 97. L. M.   Hillhouse.
Surry. Darwent. Warwick.
1 TREMBLING before thine awful throne,
O Lord, in dust, my sins I own:
Justice and Mercy for my life
Contend!—Oh, smile and heal the strife.

2 The Saviour smiles! upon my soul
New tides of hope tumultuous roll—
His voice proclaims my pardon found—
Seraphic transport wings the sound.

3 Earth has a joy unknown in heaven—
The new-born joy of sin forgiven!
Tears of such pure and deep delight,
Ye angels! never dimm'd your sight.—

HYMN 98. L. M.
Surry. Kingsbridge.
1 FRIEND of the friendless and the faint!
Where can I lodge my deep complaint?
Where, but with thee, whose open door
Invites the helpless sinner, poor!

2 Did ever mourner plead with thee,
And thou refuse that mourner's plea?
Does not the word still fix'd remain,
That none shall seek thy face in vain?

3 That were a grief I could not bear,
Didst thou not hear and answer prayer:
O thou, prayer-hearing, answering God,
Take from my heart this painful load.

HYMN 99.   L. M.
Surry. Kingsbridge. Carthage.
1 WITH conscious guilt and bleeding heart,
Near to thy throne of grace I fly;
O! friend of friendless sinners, deign
To hear my penitential cry.

2 My first, my only cry shall be,
"Thy sanctifying grace impart,
And form my soul alike to thee,
And dwell for ever in my heart."

*HYMN 100. L. M
Truro. Kent. Bath.
Hosea xiv. 1, 2.
1 O JESUS, full of truth and grace,
More full of grace than I of sin;
I now would flee to thine embrace;
Open thine arms and take me in!

2 The stone to flesh do thou convert;
And all my guilt and sin remove;
Sprinkle thy blood upon my heart,
And melt it by thy dying love.

3 Give to mine eyes refreshing tears,
And kindle my relentings now;
Fill all my soul with filial fears:
To thy sweet yoke my spirit bow.

4 O, give me, Lord, the tender heart,
That trembles at the approach of sin;
A godly fear of sin impart;
Implant and root it deep within!

HYMN 101. L. P. M.   Raffles.
Harlington. Eaton.
1 FATHER of mercies, God of love!
Oh, hear an humble suppliant's cry
Bend from thy lofty seat above,
Thy throne of glorious majesty:
Oh, deign to listen to my voice,
And bid this drooping heart rejoice.

2 I urge no merits of my own,
For I, alas, am all that's vile
No—when I bow before thy throne,
Dare to converse with God awhile,
Thy name, blest Jesus, is my plea,
That dearest, sweetest name to me!

3 Within this heart of mine, I feel
The weight of sin's oppressive load;
Oh, help! or else I sink to hell,
Crush'd by thine arm, avenging God!
Entomb'd within that dread abyss,
And exil'd from the realms of bliss!

4 But ah! the thought alone is hell—
That prospect drives me to despair;
For who can 'mid those horrors dwell?
Or who those dreadful torments bear?
Where not a ray of hope appears,
Or beam of joy the bosom cheers!

5 Yet, mighty God! thy powerful arm
Can snatch me from that dread abode;
Can shield me from th' impending harm,
And ease me of my heavy load:
One pard'ning word can make me whole,
And sooth the anguish of my soul!

6 Father of Mercies, God of Love
Then hear thy humble suppliant's cry,
Bend from thy lofty seat above,
Thy throne of glorious majesty:
Oh ! listen to a sufferer's voice,
Then shall this bleeding heart rejoice!

CHRIST.

HYMN 102. C. M.   Medley.
Braintree. Colchester.
His Nativity.
1 MORTALS, awake, with angels join,
And chant the solemn lay:
Joy, love, and gratitude, combine
To hail th' auspicious day.

2 In heaven the rapt'rous song began,
And sweet seraphic fire
Through all the shining legions ran,
And strung and tun'd the lyre.

3 Swift, through the vast expanse, it flew,
And loud the echo roll'd;
The theme, the song, the joy was new,
'Twas more than heaven could hold.

4 Down through the portals of the sky
Th' impetuous torrent ran;
And angels flew with eager joy,
To bear the news to man.

5 Hark! the cherubic armies shout,
And glory leads the song;
Good will and peace are heard throughout
Th' harmonious heavenly throng.

HYMN 103. C. M.   Watts.
Abridge. Barby.
Angels' song. Luke ii. 8-14.
1 "SHEPHERDS, rejoice; lift up your eyes,
And send your fears away;
News from the region of the skies—
Salvation's born today.

2 *"Jesus,* the God, whom angels fear,
Comes down to dwell with you;
To-day he makes his entrance here,
But not as monarchs do.

3 "No gold, nor purple swaddling bands,
Nor royal shining things
A manger for his cradle stands,
And holds the King of kings!

4 "Go, shepherds, where the infant lies,
And see his humble throne;
With tears of joy in all your eyes,
Go, shepherds, kiss the Son."

5 Thus Gabriel sang—and straight around
The heav'nly armies throng:
They tune their harps to lofty sound,
And thus conclude the song:

6 "Glory to God, who reigns above,
Let peace surround the earth;
Mortals shall know their Maker's love,
At their Redeemer's birth."

HYMN 104. 7s.
Redemption. Hampton.
1 HARK!—the herald angels sing,
"Glory to the new-born King!
Peace on earth, and mercy mild,
God and sinners reconcil'd."

2 Mild he lays his glory by;
Born, that man no more may die;
Joyful, all ye nations, rise,
Join the triumph of the skies.

3 "Glory to the new-born King"—
Let us all the anthem sing—
"Peace on earth, and mercy mild,
God and sinners reconcil'd."
Repeat.

HYMN 105.   C. M.   Doddridge.
Arundel. St. Asaph's.
The Redeemer's Message.
1 HARK, the glad sound, the Saviour comes,
The Saviour, promis'd long!
Let every heart prepare a throne,
And every voice a song.

2 On him, the Spirit, largely pour'd,
Exerts his sacred fire;
Wisdom, and might, and zeal, and love
His holy breast inspire.

3 He comes, from thickest films of vice
To clear the mental ray;
And, on the eyes, oppress'd with night,
To pour celestial day.

4 Our glad hosannas, Prince of Peace,
Thy welcome shall proclaim;
And heaven's eternal arches ring
With thy beloved name.

HYMN 106. L. M.   Steele.
Islington. Portugal.
Our Example.
1 AND is the gospel peace and love?
Such let our conversation be;
The serpent blended with the dove—
Wisdom and meek simplicity.

2 Whene'er the angry passions rise,
And tempt our thoughts and tongues to strife;
To Jesus let us lift our eyes,
Bright pattern of the christian life.

3 Dispensing good where'er he came,
The labors of his life were love;.
Then, if we bear the Saviour's name,
By his example let us move.

4 Oh, how benevolent and kind!
How mild—how ready to forgive!
Be this the temper of our mind,
And these the rules by which we live.

*HYMN 107. L. M.   Watts.
Blendon. China. Luton.
1 MY dear Redeemer, and my Lord,
I read my duty in thy word;
But in thy life the law appears,
Drawn out in living characters.

2 Cold mountains, and the midnight air,
Witness'd the fervor of thy prayer:
The desert thy temptations knew,
Thy conflict, and thy vict'ry too.

3 Such was thy truth, and such thy zeal,
Such def'rence to thy Father's will,
Thy love and meekness so divine,
I would transcribe, and make them mine.

*HYMN 108. C. M.   Collyer.
Moreton. Luton. Malmsbury.
Transfiguration. Luke ix. 28-31.
1 ON Tabor's top the Saviour stands,
His alter'd face resplendent shines;
And, while he elevates his hands,
Lo, glory marks its gentle lines!

2 Two heavenly forms descend to wait
Upon their suffering Prince below;
But while they worship at his feet,
They talk of fast approaching wo.

3 Amid the lustre of the scene,
To Calvary he turns his eyes;
And, with submission, all serene,
He marks the future tempest rise,

4 Then let us climb the mount of prayer,
Where all his beaming glories shine;
And, gazing on his brightness there,
Our woes forget in joys divine.

5 Oh, that on yonder heavenly hills,
Where now the risen Saviour stands,
And peace, like softest dew, distils—
I too may elevate my hands.

HYMN 109. L. M.   Tappan.
Munich. Armley.
Gethsemane.
1 'TIS midnight—and on Olive's brow,
The star is dimm'd that lately shone;
'Tis midnight—in the garden now,
The suff'ring Saviour prays alone.

2 'Tis midnight—and from all remov'd,
Immanuel wrestles lone, with fears;
E'en the disciple that he lov'd
Heeds not his Master's grief and tears.

3 'Tis midnight—and for others' guilt
The man of sorrows weeps in blood;
Yet be that hath in anguish knelt,
Is not forsaken by his God.

4 'Tis midnight—and from ether plains,
Is borne the song that angels know;
Unheard by mortals are the strains
That sweetly sooth the Saviour's wo.

*HYMN 110. L. M.   Steele.
Armley. Bath.
Sufferings and Death.
1 STRETCH'D on the cross, the Saviour dies;
Hark! his expiring groans arise:
See from his hands, his feet, his side,
Runs down the sacred crimson tide.

2 But life attends the deathful sound,
And flows from every bleeding wound;
The vital stream how free it flows,
To save and cleanse his rebel foes!

3 Can I survey this scene of wo,
Where mingling grief and wonder flow;
And yet my heart unmov'd remain,
Insensible to love, or pain?

4 Come, dearest Lord, thy grace impart,
To warm this cold, this stupid heart!
'Till all its pow'rs and passions move
In melting grief, and ardent love.

HYMN 111. L. P. M.
Carolans. Harlington. Clapton.
1 O LOVE divine, what hast thou done!
The Lord of life hath died for me!
The Father's co-eternal Son
Bore all my sins upon the tree;
Th' incarnate God for me hath died;
The Lord, my love, was crucified.

2 Sinners, behold, as ye pass by,
The bleeding Prince of life and peace;
Come, sinners, see your Saviour die,
And say, was ever grief like his?
Come, feel with me his blood applied,
The Lord, my love, was crucified:

3 Is crucified for you and me,
To bring us, rebels, back to God;
Salvation now for us is free
His church is purchas'd with his blood
Pardon and life flow from his side;
The Lord, my love, is crucified.

4 Then let us sit beneath his cross,
And gladly catch the healing stream;
All things for him account but dross,
And give up all our hearts to him;
Of nothing speak, or think beside,
The Lord, my love, was crucified.

HYMN 112.   C. M.   Stennett.
Buckingham. Elgin. Plymouth.
1 YONDER— amazing sight— I see
Th' incarnate Son of God,
Expiring on th' accursed tree,
And welt'ring in his blood.

2 Behold the purple torrent run
Down from his hands and head:
The crimson tide puts out the sun;
His groans awake the dead.

3 The trembling earth, the darken'd sky,
Proclaim the truth aloud;
And with the amaz'd centurion cry,
"This is the Son of God."

4 So great, so vast a sacrifice
May well my hope revive
If God's own Son thus bleeds and dies,
The sinner sure may live.

HYMN 113.   8, 7, 4.   F.
Littleton. Helmsley.
It is finished. John xix. 30.
1 HARK! the voice of love and mercy!
Sounds aloud from Calvary;
See, it rends the rocks asunder—
Shakes the earth and veils the sky!
"It is finish'd!"—
Hear the Saviour—dying—cry.

2 It is finish'd!—Oh, what pleasure
Do these precious words afford!
Heav'nly blessings without measure,
Flow to us from Christ, the Lord:
It is finish'd!—
Saints, the dying words record.

3 Finish'd—all the types and shadows
Of the ceremonial law;
Finish'd—all that God had promis'd;
Death and hell no more shall awe:
It is finish'd—
Saints, from hence your comforts draw.

4 Tune your harps anew, ye seraphs,—
Join to sing the pleasing theme;
All on earth, and all in heaven,
Join to praise Immanuel's name:
Hallelujah!
Glory to the bleeding Lamb!

HYMN 114. L. M.   Stennett.
Munich. German.
1 'TIS finish'd! so the Saviour cried,
And meekly bow'd his head and died
'Tis finish'd—yes, the race is run,
The battle fought, the victory won.

2 'Tis finish'd—all that heaven decreed,
And all the ancient prophets said
Is now fulfill'd, as was design'd,
In me, the Saviour of mankind.

3 'Tis finish'd—this my dying groan
Shall sins of every kind atone:
Millions shall be redeem'd from death,
By this my last expiring breath.

4 'Tis finish'd—heaven is reconcil'd,
And all the powers of darkness spoil'd;
Peace, love, and happiness again
Return, and dwell with sinful men.

HYMN 115. L. M.   Watts.
Norfolk. Dresden.
Dying, rising, and reigning.
1 HE dies—the Friend of sinners dies!
Lo! Salem's daughters weep around!
A solemn darkness veils the skies!
A sudden trembling shakes the ground.

2 Come, saints, and drop a tear or two,
For him who groan'd beneath your load;
He shed a thousand drops for you—
A thousand drops of richer blood.

3 Here's love and grief beyond degree—
The Lord of glory dies for men!
But lo! what sudden joys we see!
Jesus, the dead—revives again!

4 The rising God forsakes the tomb!
Up to his Father's court he flies!
Cherubic legions guard him home,
And shout him welcome to the skies!

5 Break off your tears, ye saints, and tell
How high our great Deliv'rer reigns;
Sing, how he spoil'd the hosts of hell,
And led the tyrant, death—in chains.

6 Say, "live for ever, glorious King,
Born to redeem, and strong to save!"
Then ask—"O death, where is thy sting?
And where thy vict'ry, boasting grave!"

HYMN 116. 7s.   Collver.
Hotham. Epiphany.
1 TO the cross where Jesus dies,
Where my Lord resigns his breath,
Where affliction veils his eyes,
Swimming in the tears of death:
Thither bringing all my guilt,
From avenging wrath I flee,
To the blood of sprinkling spilt—
Spilt to let the sinner free.

2 'Mid convulsive agonies,
Peace his quivering lips impart;
Pardon seal'd by broken sighs
Issuing from a bursting heart;
Let me feel this healing power,
Let this harden'd heart of stone,
Melt beneath this purple shower,
From his body trickling down.

3 On those temples, crown'd with thorns,
Suff'ring majesty appears;
Love that dying face adorns,
Stain'd with blood and soil'd with tears;
Pierce the shadows of the heart,
With the light'ning of that eye;
Smiles of peace to me impart,
Let me feel, or I must die!

HYMN 117. 7s.　　　Gibbons.
Redeeming Love. Hampton.
Resurrection.
1 ANGELS! roll the rock away!
Death! yield up the mighty prey;
See! he rises from the tomb,
Glowing with immortal bloom.

2 'Tis the Saviour! angels, raise
Fame's eternal trump of praise!
Let the earth's remotest bound
Hear the joy-inspiring sound.

3 Now, ye saints, lift up your eyes!
Now to glory see him rise,
In long triumph, up the sky—
Up to waiting worlds on high.

4 Praise him, all ye heavenly choirs!
Praise, and sweep your golden lyres!
Shout, O earth in rapt'rous song,
Let the strains be sweet and strong!

HYMN 118. 7s.   Madan.
Middleton. Epiphany. Hotham.
Ascension.
1 HAIL, the day that saw him rise,
Ravish'd from our wishful eyes;
Christ, awhile to mortals giv'n,
Reascends his native heaven;
There the pompous triumph waits;
Lift your heads eternal gates!
Wide unfold the radiant scene,
Take the King of glory in!"

2 Him though highest heav'n receives,
Still he loves the earth he leaves
Though returning to his throne,
Still he calls mankind his own:
Still for us he intercedes,
Prevalent his death he pleads;
Next himself prepares a place,
Harbinger of human race.

3 Master, (may we ever say),
Taken from the world away,
See thy faithful servants, see,
Ever gazing up to thee:
Grant, though parted from our sight,
High above yon azure height,—
Grant our souls may thither rise—
Foll'wing thee beyond the skies.

4 Ever upward let us move,
Wasted on the wings of love;
Looking when our Lord shall come—
Looking for a happier home:
There we shall with thee remain,
Partners of thy endless reign;
There thy face unclouded see—
Find a heav'n of heav'ns in thee.

*HYMN 119. C. M. Colliver
Colchester. Clarendon.
Luke xxiv. 50, 51.
1 IT is the voice of love divine,
That strikes the list'ning ear,

That sooths his mourning follower's grief,
And wipes the falling tear.

2 "Because I leave this world"— he cries,
"Your weeping eyes o'erflow;
But though I seek my native skies,
My heart remains below."

3 "My Spirit shall descend, and rest
Upon each faithful head,
Till I, your Lord, return to call
My servants from the dead."

4 He said—and lifting up his hands,
Pronounc'd his parting prayer;
When lo, a bright descending cloud
Convey'd him through the air.

5 With solemn awe his followers view'd
The splendor of the scene,
While the unfolding gates of light
Receiv'd the Saviour in.

6 Burning with holy zeal, they spread,
Through distant lands, his word;
And we, like them, with faith and joy
Expect our risen Lord.

HYMN 120. L. M.   Watts.
Antigua. Portugal.
Philippians ii. 8, 9. Colossians ii. 15.
1 THE mighty frame of glorious grace,
That brightest monument of praise,
That e'er the God of love design'd,
Employs and fills my lab'ring mind.

2 Begin, my soul, the heav'nly song,
A burden for an angel's tongue:
When Gabriel sounds these awful tidings,
He tunes and summons all his strings.

3 Proclaim inimitable love;
Jesus, the *Lord* of worlds above,
Puts off the beams of bright array,
And veils the God in mortal clay.

4 He that distributes crowns and thrones
Hangs on a tree, and bleeds and groans;
The prince of life resigns his breath,
The King of glory bows to death!

5 But see the wonders of his power,
He triumphs in his dying hour;
And, while by Satan's rage he fell,
He dash'd the rising hopes of hell.

6 Thus were the hosts of death subdu'd;
And sin was drown'd in *Jesus'* blood;
Then he arose, and reigns above,
And conquers sinners by his love.

*HYMN 121. H. M.   Stennett.
Jubilee. Eagle Street.
1 COME, every pious heart
That loves the Saviour's name,
Your noblest power exert
To celebrate his fame:
Tell all above, and all below
The debt of love to him you owe.

2 He left his starry crown,
And laid his robes aside;
On wings of love came down,
And wept, and bled, and died:
What he endur'd, oh, who can tell?
To save our souls from death and hell.

3 From the dark grave he rose,
The mansion of the dead;
And thence his mighty foes
In glorious triumph led:
Up through the sky the conqueror rode,
And reigns on high, the Saviour God.

4 Jesus, we ne'er can pay
The debt we owe thy love;
Yet tell us how we may
Our gratitude approve:
Our hearts—our all to thee we give:
The gift, though small, do thou receive.

*HYMN 122. L. M.   Steele.
Kent. Bath.
Intercession Hebrews vii. 25.
1 He lives, the great Redeemer lives,
(What joy the blest assurance gives!)
And now, before his Father God,
Pleads the full merit of his blood.

2 Repeated crimes awake our fears,
And justice arm'd with frowns appears;
But in the Saviour's lovely face
Sweet mercy smiles, and all is peace.

3 Hence then, ye black despairing thoughts;
Above our fears, above our faults
His powerful intercessions rise,
And guilt recedes, and terror dies.

4 In every dark distressful hour,
When sin and Satan join their power,
Let this dear hope repel the dart,
That Jesus bears us on his heart.

5 Great Advocate, Almighty Friend—
On him our humble hopes depend:
Our cause can never, never fail,
For Jesus pleads and must prevail.

HYMN 123. C. M.   Duncan.
Harborough. Exeter.
Coronation. Canticles iii. 11.
1 All hail the power of Jesus' name!
Let angels prostrate fall;
Bring forth the royal diadem,
And crown him—Lord of all.

2 Crown him, ye martyrs of our God,
Who from his altar call;
Extol the stem of Jesse's rod,
And crown him—Lord of all.

3 Hail him, ye heirs of David's line,
Whom David, Lord did call;
The God incarnate! Man Divine!
And crown him—Lord of all.

4 Ye chosen seed of Israel's race,
Ye ransom'd from the fall,
Hail him who saves you by his grace,
And crown him—Lord of all.

5 Sinners, whose love can ne'er forget
The wormwood and the gall,
Go, spread your trophies at his feet,
And crown him—Lord of all.

6 Let every kindred, every tribe,
On this terrestrial ball,
To him all majesty ascribe,
And crown him—Lord of all.

HYMN 124. H. M. Rippon.
1 REJOICE, the *Lord* is king,
Your *God* and king adore;
Mortals, give thanks, and sing,
And triumph evermore:
Lift up the heart, lift up the voice,
Rejoice aloud, ye saints, rejoice.

2 Rejoice, the Saviour reigns,
The *God* of truth and love;
When he had purg'd our stains,
He took his seat above:
Lift up the heart, lift up the voice,
Rejoice aloud, ye saints, rejoice.

3 His kingdom cannot fail,
He rules o'er earth and heav'n;
The keys of death and hell
Are to our *Jesus* giv'n.
Lift up the heart, lift up the voice,
Rejoice aloud, ye saints, rejoice.

4 He all his foes shall quell,
Shall all our sins destroy;
And every bosom swell
With pure seraphic joy:
Lift up the heart, lift up the voice,
Rejoice aloud, ye saints, rejoice.

5 Rejoice in glorious hope,
Jesus, the Judge, shall come,
And take his servants up
To their eternal home:
We soon shall hear th' archangel's voice,
The trump of God shall sound, rejoice.

CHARACTERS OF CHRIST.
IN ALPHABETICAL ORDER.

HYMN 125. L. M. Steele.
Surry. Armley. Warwick.
Advocate. 1 John ii. 1.
1 WHERE is my God?—does he retire
Beyond the reach of humble sighs?
Are these weak breathings of desire
Too languid to ascend the skies?

2 Look up, my soul, with cheerful eye,
See where the great Redeemer stands,
The glorious advocate on high,
With precious incense in his hands!

3 He sweetens every humble groan,
He recommends each broken prayer;
The softest call before his throne,
May rise, and find acceptance there.

4 Teach my weak heart, O gracious Lord,
With stronger faith to call thee mine;
Bid me pronounce the blissful word,
My *Father, God,* with joy divine.

*HYMN 126. 8, 7.   Newton.
Northampton Chapel. Sicilian Hymn.
Friend. Proverbs xviii. 24.
1 One there is, above all others,
Well deserves the name of Friend,
His is love, beyond a brother's,
Costly, free, and knows no end.

2 Which of all our friends to save us,
Could or would have shed his blood?
But this Saviour died to have us
Reconcil'd in him to God.

3 When he liv'd on earth abased,
Friend of sinners was his name;
Now, above all glory raised,
He rejoices in the same.

4 Oh, for grace our hearts to soften!
Teach us, Lord, at length to love;
We, alas! forget too often,
What a Friend we have above.

HYMN 127. C. M. S.
Clifford. Springfield.
Canticles v. 10.
1 MAJESTIC sweetness sits enthron'd
Upon the Saviour's brow;
His head with radiant glories crown'd,
His lips with grace o'erflow.

2 No mortal can with him compare
Among the sons of men;
Fairer is He than all the fair
Who fill the heavenly train.

3 He saw me plung'd in deep distress,
And flew to my relief;
For me He bore the shameful cross,
And carried all my grief.

4 Since from his bounty I receive
Such proofs of love divine,
Had I a thousand hearts to give,
Lord, they should all be thine.

HYMN 128. C. M.   Cowper.
Tunbridge. St. Asaph's
Fountain. Zechariah xiii. 1.
1 THERE is a fountain fill'd with blood,
Drawn from Emmanuel's veins;
And sinners, plung'd beneath that flood,
Lose all their guilty stains.

2 The dying thief rejoic'd to see
That fountain in his day;
And there may I, as vile as he,
Wash all my sins away.

3 Dear dying Lamb, thy precious blood
Shall never lose its power,
Till all the ransom'd church of God
Be sav'd to sin no more.

4 E'er since, by faith, I saw the stream,
Thy flowing wounds supply,
Redeeming love has been my theme,
And shall be—till I die.

5 Then in a nobler, sweeter song,
I'll sing thy pow'r to save;
When this poor, lisping, stamm'ring tongue
Lies silent in the grave.

HYMN 129. L. M. Brewer.
Carthage. Armley.
Hiding place. Isaiah xxxii. 2.
1 HAIL, sov'reign love, that first began
The scheme to rescue fallen man!
Hail, matchless, free, eternal grace,
That gave my soul a hiding place.

2 Against the God that rules the sky,
I fought with hands uplifted high;
Despis'd the offers of his grace,
Too proud to seek a hiding place.

3 Enwrapp'd in dark Egyptian night,
And fond of darkness more than light,
Madly I ran the sinful race,
Secure without a hiding place.

4 But thus the eternal counsel ran:
"Almighty love! arrest the man;"—
I felt the arrows of distress,
And found I had no hiding place.

5 Vindictive justice stood in view;
To Sinai's fiery mount I flew;
But justice cried with frowning face:
"This mountain is no hiding place."

6 But lo! a heavenly voice I heard—
And mercy's angel soon appear'd;
Who led me on a pleasing pace,
To Jesus Christ, my hiding place.

7 On him Almighty vengeance fell,
Which must have sunk a world to hell;
He bore it for his chosen race,
And now he is my hiding place.

*HYMN 130. C. M.   Newton.
Clarendon. Wareham.
1 HE who on earth as man was known,
And bore our sins and pains,
Now seated on th' eternal throne—
The God of glory reigns!

2 His righteousness to faith reveal'd,
Wrought out for guilty worms,
Affords a hiding place, and shield,
From enemies and storms.

3 When troubles, like a burning sun,
Beat heavy on their head,
To this high rock his people run,
And find a pleasing shade.

4 How glorious He!—how happy they!
In such a glorious Friend!
Whose love secures them all the way,
And crowns them at the end.

*HYMN 131. S. M.   Watts.
St. Thomas. Shirland.
Lamb of God. John i. 29.
1 NOT all the blood of beasts,
On Jewish altars slain,
Could give the guilty conscience peace,
Or wash away the stain.

2 But Christ, the heav'nly Lamb,
Takes all our sins away;
A sacrifice of nobler name,
And richer blood than they.

3 My faith would lay her hand
On that dear head of thine—
While like a penitent I stand,
And there confess my sin.

4 My soul looks back to see
The burdens thou didst bear,
When hanging on the cursed tree,
And hopes her guilt was there.

5 Believing, we rejoice
To see the curse remove;
We bless the Lamb with cheerful voice,
And sing his bleeding love.

HYMN 132. 8,7. Utica Col.
Carlisle. Love Divine.
Light. Isaiah ix. 2.
1 LIGHT of those whose dreary dwelling
Borders on the shades of death,
Come, and by thy love's revealing,
Dissipate the clouds beneath:
The new heav'n and earth's Creator
In our deepest darkness rise,
Scatt'ring all the night of nature,
Pouring eye-sight on our eyes.

2 Still we wait for thine appearing;
Life and joy thy beams impart,
Chasing all our fears, and cheering
Every poor, benighted heart:
Come, and manifest the favor
Thou hast for the ransom'd race;
Come, thou glorious God and Saviour!
Come, and bring the gospel grace.

3 Save us, in thy great compassion,
O thou mild, pacific Prince!
Give the knowledge of salvation,
Give the pardon of our sins;
By thine all-sufficient merit,
Every burden'd soul release;
Every weary, wand'ring spirit,
Guide into thy perfect peace.

*HYMN 133. C. M.   Steele.
Parma. Springfield. Rochester.
Pearl of great price. Matthew xiii. 46.
1 YE glittering toys of earth, adieu;
A nobler choice be mine;
A real prize attracts my view,
A treasure all divine.

2 Begone, unworthy of my cares,
Ye specious baits of sense;
Inestimable worth appears,
The pearl of price immense!

3 Jesus, to multitudes unknown,
O name divinely sweet!
Jesus, in thee, in thee alone,
Wealth, honor, pleasure meet.

4 Should both the Indies at my call,
Their boasted stores resign;
With joy I would renounce them all,
For leave to call thee mine.

5 Should earth's vain treasures all depart,
Of this dear gift possess'd,
I'd clasp it to my joyful heart,
And think myself most bless'd.

6 Dear sov'reign of my soul's desires,
Thy love is bliss divine;
Accept the wish that love inspires,
And bid me call thee mine.

HYMN 134. L. M.   Steele.
Portugal. German.
Physician of souls. Jeremiah viii. 22.
1 DEEP are the wounds which sin has made;
Where shall the sinner find a cure?
In vain, alas, is nature's aid—
The work exceeds all nature's pow'r.

2 And can no sov'reign balm be found?
And is no kind physician nigh,
To ease the pain and heal the wound,
Ere life and hope for ever fly?

3 There is a great physician near, Look up,
O fainting soul, and live;
See, in his heav'nly smiles, appear
Such ease as nature cannot give!

4 See, in the Saviour's dying blood,
Life, health, and bliss abundant flow!
'Tis only this dear sacred flood
Can ease thy pain and heal thy wo.

HYMN 135. 7, 6.   Newton.
Brighthelmstone. Margate.
1 HOW lost was my condition,
Till Jesus made me whole!
There is but one physician,
Can cure a sin-sick soul!—
The worst of all diseases
Is light compar'd with sin;
On ev'ry part it seizes,
But rages most within.

2 From men great skill professing,
I thought a cure to gain;
But this prov'd more distressing,
And added to my pain—
Some said that nothing ail'd me,
Some gave me up for lost,
Thus every refuge failed me,
And all my hopes were cross'd.

3 At length this great Physician—
How matchless is his grace!
Accepted my petition,
And undertook my case—
Next door to death he found me,
And snatch'd me from the grave;
To tell to all around me,
His wond'rous power to save.

4 A dying, risen JESUS,
Seen by the eye of faith,
At once from danger frees us,
And saves the soul from death—

Come then to this Physician,
His help he'll freely give,
He makes no hard condition,
'Tis only—look—and live.

HYMN 136. 8, 7.
Gethsemane. Northampton Chapel. Love Divine.
Priest.
1 GREAT High Priest, we view thee stooping,
With our names upon thy breast;
In the garden, groaning, drooping,
To the ground with sorrow press'd.

2 Weeping angels stood confounded
To beheld their Maker thus!
And can we remain unwounded,
When we know 'twas all for us?

3 On the cross thy body broken,
Cancels ev'ry penal tie—
Tempted souls, produce this token
All demands to satisfy.

4 All is finish'd, do not doubt it,
But believe your dying Lord;
Never reason more about it,
Only take him at his word.

5 Lord, we fain would trust thee solely,
Since for us thy blood was spilt:
Gracious Saviour, take us wholly—
Take and make us what thou wilt.

*HYMN 137. C. M.   Steele.
St. Ann's. Barby.
Saviour. John iv. 42.
1 THE Saviour! Oh, what endless charms
Dwell in the blissful sound!
Its influence every fear disarms,
And spreads sweet peace around.

2 Here pardon, life, and joys divine,
In rich effusion flow,
For guilty rebels, lost in sin,
And doom'd to endless wo.

3 Oh, the rich depths of love divine,
Of bliss, a boundless store!
Dear Saviour, let me call thee mine;
I cannot wish for more.

4 On thee alone my hope relies,
Beneath thy cross I fall;
My Lord, my life, my sacrifice,
My Saviour, and my all.

HYMN 138. L. M. H. K. White.
Kent. Blendon.
Star of Bethlehem. Matthew ii. 1, 2.
1 ONCE on the raging seas I rode,
The storm was loud, the night was dark,
The ocean yawn'd and rudely blow'd
The wind that toss'd my found'ring bark.

2 Deep horror then my vitals froze,
Death-struck, I ceas'd the tide to stem:
When suddenly a Star arose,
It was the Star of Bethlehem.

3 It was my guide, my light, my all,
It bade my dark forebodings cease;
And through the storm and danger's thrall,
It led me to the port of peace.

4 Now safely moor'd—my perils o'er,
I'll sing, first in night's diadem;
For ever and for evermore,
The Star—the Star of Bethlehem.

HYMN 139. L. M.   Cennick.
Portugal. Blendon.
Way to Canaan. John xiv. 6.
1 JESUS, my all, to heaven is gone,
He whom I fix'd my hopes upon;
His track I see, and I'll pursue
The narrow way till him I view.

2 The way the holy prophets went,
The road that leads from banishment,
The King's highway of holiness
I'll go, for all his paths are peace.

3 This is the way I long have sought,
And mourn'd because I found it not;
My grief, my burden long has been,
Because I could not cease from sin.

4 The more I strove against his pow'r,
I sinn'd and stumbled but the more,
Till late I heard my Saviour say,
Come hither, soul, "I am the way."

5 Lo! glad I come, and thou, blest Lamb,
Shalt take me to thee as I am;
Nothing but sin I thee can give,
Nothing but love shall I receive.

6 Then will I tell to sinners round,
What a dear Saviour I have found;
I'll point to thy redeeming blood,
And say, "Behold the way to God."

HYMN 140. 8s. Newton.
Uxbridge. New Jerusalem.
Matthew xxii. 42. John xx. 28.
1 "WHAT think ye of Christ?" is the test,
To try both your state and your scheme;
You cannot be right in the rest,
Unless you think rightly of him;
As Jesus appears in your view,
As he is beloved or not;
So God is disposed to you,
And mercy or wrath is your lot.

2 Same call him a Saviour in word,
But mix their own works with the plan;
And hope he his help will afford,
When they have done all that they can;
If doings prove rather too light—
A little they own they may fail—
They purpose to make up full weight,
By casting his name in the scale.

3 Some take him a creature to be—
A man, or an angel at most;
Sure these have no feelings like me,
Nor know themselves wretched and lost;

So guilty—so helpless am I,
I could not confide in his word,
Unless I could make the reply,
That Christ is "My Lord and my God."

DOCTRINES OF THE GOSPEL
IN ALPHABETICAL ORDER.

*HYMN 141. L. M.　　Stennett.
Portugal. Shoel.
Adoption. John i. 12. 1 John iii. 1.
1 NOT all the nobles of the earth,
Who boast the honors of their birth,
Such real dignity can claim,
As those who bear the Christian name.

2 To them the privilege is giv'n
To be the sons and heirs of heav'n;
Sons of the God who reigns on high,
All heirs of joys beyond the sky.

3 His will he makes them early know,
And teaches their young feet to go;
Whispers instruction to their minds,
And on their hearts his precepts binds.

4 When, through temptation, they rebel,
His chast'ning rod he makes them feel;
Then, with a Father's tender heart,
He sooths the pain, and heals the smart.

5 Their daily wants his hands supply,
Their steps he guards with watchful eye,
Leads them from earth to heav'n above,
And crowns them with eternal love.

HYMN 142.　　L. M.　　Stennett.
Surry. Armley.
Atonement.　　John xiv. 6.
1 HOW shall the sons of men appear,
Great God, before thine awful bar?
How may the guilty hope to find
Acceptance with th' eternal mind?

2 Not vows, nor groans, nor broken cries,
Not the most costly sacrifice,
Nor infant blood, profusely spilt,
Will expiate a sinner's guilt.

3 The blood of Jesus Christ alone,
Hath sov'reign virtue to atone;
Here we will rest our only plea,
When we approach, Great God, to thee.

HYMN 143. C. M.   Cowper.
Elgin. Martyrs.
Communion with God.   Genesis v. 24.
1 OH! for a closer walk with God,
A calm and heav'nly frame;
A light to shine upon the road
That leads me to the Lamb!

2 Where is the blessedness I knew
When first I saw the Lord?
Where is the soul-refreshing view
Of Jesus, and his word?

3 What peaceful hours I once enjoy'd!
How sweet their mem'ry still!
But they have left an aching void,
The world can never fill.

4 Return, O holy Dove, return,
Sweet messenger of rest;
I hate the sins that made thee mourn,
And drove thee from my breast.

5 The dearest idol I have known,
Whate'er that idol be,
Help me to tear it from thy throne,
And worship only thee.

6 So shall my walk be close with God,
Calm and serene my frame
So purer light shall mark the road
That leads me to the Lamb.

HYMN 144.   C. M.   Watts.
Bedford. Abridge.
Job xxiii. 3.
1 OH, that I knew the secret place,
Where I might find my God
I'd spread my wants before his face,
And pour my woes abroad.

2 I'd tell him how my sins arise,
What sorrows I sustain
How grace decays, and comfort dies,
And leaves my heart in pain.

3 He knows what arguments I'd take
To wrestle with my God;
I'd plead for his own mercy's sake,
And for my Saviour's blood.

4 My God will pity my complaints,
And heal my broken bones;
He takes the meaning of his saints,
The language of their groans.

5 Arise, my soul, from deep distress,
And banish every fear;
He calls thee to his throne of grace,
To spread thy sorrows there.

*HYMN 145.   C. M.
Walsal. Chapel.
1 OH, could I find from day to day,
A nearness to my God:
Then should my hours glide sweet away,
And lean upon his word.

2 Lord, I desire with thee to live
Anew from day to day;
In joys the world can never give,
Nor ever take away.

3 O Jesus, come and rule my heart,
And make me wholly thine,
That I may never more depart,
Nor grieve thy love divine.

4 Thus till my last expiring breath,
Thy goodness I'll adore;
And when my flesh dissolves in death,
My soul shall love thee more.

*HYMN 146. C. M.   Watts.
Canterbury. St. Ann's. Bedford.
Decrees of God.
1 KEEP silence, all created things,
And wait your Maker's nod:
My soul stands trembling, while she sings
The honors of her God.

2 Life, death, and hell, and worlds unknown
Hang on his firm decree;
He sits on no precarious throne,
Nor borrows leave—*to be.*

3 Chain'd to his throne, a volume lies,
With all the fates of men:
With ev'ry angel's form and size,
Drawn by th' eternal pen.

4 His providence unfolds the book,
And makes his counsels shine;
Each op'ning leaf, and every stroke,
Fulfils some deep design.

5 Here, he exalts neglected worms
To sceptres and a crown;
And there, the following page he turns,
And treads the monarch down.

6 Not Gabriel asks the reason why,
Nor God the reason gives;
Nor dares the fav'rite angel pry
Between the folded leaves.

7 In thy fair book of life and grace,
Oh, may I find my name,
Recorded in some humble place,
Beneath my Lord— the Lamb.

HYMN 147. L. M.　　Beddome.
Warwick. Armley.
1 WAIT, O my soul, thy Maker's will!
Tumultuous passions, all be still!
Nor let a murm'ring thought arise,
His ways are just, his counsels wise.

2 He in the thickest darkness dwells,
Performs his work, the cause conceals;
But though his methods are unknown,
Judgment and truth support his throne.

3 In heav'n, and earth, and air, and seas,
He executes his firm decrees;
And by his saints it stands confess'd,
That what he does is ever best.

4 Wait then, my soul, submissive wait,
Prostrate before his awful seat:
And 'midst the terrors of his rod,
Trust in a wise and gracious God.

*HYMN 148. L. M. Steward.
Bath. Leydon. Truro.
Depravity.
1 GOD, from his throne, with piercing eye,
Naked does every heart behold;
But never, till we come to die,
Will he to us the view unfold.

2 Should sin, in naked form appear,
Just as it rises in the heart,
And others know and see it there
In ev'ry feeling, every thought;

3 The fire of hell must kindle soon,
How envy and revenge would flame!
One heart would urge another on,
Till rage and vengeance want a name!

4 Sin in its nature would appear
A living death, to form a hell;
The worst of mis'ries creatures fear,
The worst of plagues the tongue can tell.

5 Unveil'd and naked ev'ry heart
Before the judgment seat must stand,
Sin act no more a double part,
But meet a death from its own hand.

6 The fiery lake will hotter grow
From the fierce clash of sinful souls;
Each bosom like a furnace glow,
Nor God the rage, or fire control.

*HYMN 149.   L. M.   J. Steward.
Armley. Sheerness.
Sin and misery connected.
1 AH, wretched souls are they, who hear
With scorn, the sound of gospel grace;
For sorrow walks along with sin,
Although they keep not equal pace.

2 How blindly sinners grasp their chains,
And yet of freedom vainly boast;
They look for happiness and peace,
Nor think by sin their peace is lost.

3 Approaching vice is deck'd in charms,
And smiles with promises of gain;
No sooner past—Its joys are fled,
And all its pleasures chang'd to pain.

4 Sinners may for a time rejoice—
Till storms of threaten'd wrath arise—
Till justice grasp th' avenging sword;
And then the wretch, the sinner dies.

HYMN 150. 7s.
Mount Calvary. Montpelier.
1 HEARTS of stone, relent, relent,
Break, by Jesus' cross subdu'd;
See his body, mangled—rent,
Cover'd with a gore of blood;
Sinful soul, what hast thou done!
Murder'd God's eternal Son.

2 Yes, our sins have done the deed,
Drove the nails that fixed him there;
Crown'd with thorns his sacred head,

Pierc'd him with a soldier's spear,
Made his soul a sacrifice,
For a sinful world he dies.

3 Will you let him die in vain,
Still to death pursue your Lord;
Open tear his wounds again,
Trample on his precious blood?
No! with all my sins I'll part,
Saviour, take my broken heart.

HYMN 151. 11, 8.   K.
Zion's Pilgrim. Solicitude.
Election. Jer. xxxi. 3. 1 Cor. iv. 7.
1 IN songs of sublime adoration and praise;
Ye pilgrims, for Zion who press,
Break forth and extol the great Ancient of days,
His rich and distinguishing grace.

2 His love from eternity fix'd upon you,—
Broke forth and discover'd its flame,
When each with the cords of his kindness he drew,
And brought you to love his great name.

3 O, had not he pitied the state you were in,
Your bosoms his love had ne'er felt;
You all would have liv'd, would have died too in sin,
And sunk with the load of your guilt.

4 What was there in you, that could merit esteem,
Or give the Creator delight?
'Twas "Even so, Father," you ever must sing,
"Because it seem'd good in thy sight."

5 Then give all the glory to his holy name,
To him all the glory belongs
Be yours the high joy still to sound forth his fame,
And crown him in each of your songs.

HYMN 152. C. M.   Newton.
Mear. St. Martin's.
The Lord's call. 2 Corinthians vi. 17, 18.
1 LET us adore the grace that seeks
To draw our hearts above!

Attend, 'tis God, the Saviour, speaks,
And every word is love.

2 "Come forth," he says, "no more pursue
The path that leads to death;
Look up, a bleeding Saviour view,
Look, and be sav'd by faith.

3 "My sons and daughters you shall be,
Through my atoning blood;
And you shall claim and find in me,
A Father and a God."

4 Lord, speak these words to ev'ry heart,
By thine Almighty voice;
That we may now from sin depart,
And make thy love our choice.

HYMN 153. C. M.   Newton.
Barby. Abridge.
Grace reigning. Romans v. 21.
1 NOW may the Lord reveal his face,
And teach our stamm'ring tongues
To make his sov'reign, reigning grace,
The subject of our songs!

2 Grace reigns to pardon crimson sins,
To melt the hardest hearts
And, from the work it once begins,
It never more departs.

3 'Twas grace that call'd our souls at first,
By grace thus far we're come,
And grace will help us through the worst,
And lead us safely home.

HYMN 154. S. M.   Doddridge.
Northampton. Shirland. Pelham.
Salvation by grace. Ephesians ii. 5.
1 GRACE! 'tis a charming sound;
Harmonious to the ear!
Heav'n with the echo shall resound,
And all the earth shall hear.

2 Grace first contriv'd the way
To save rebellious man;
And all the steps that grace display,
Which drew the wond'rous plan.

3 Grace led my roving feet
To tread the heavenly road;
And new supplies each hour, I meet,
While pressing on to God.

4 Grace all the work shall crown,
Through everlasting days;
It lays in heav'n the topmost stone,
And well deserves the praise.

HYMN 155. C. M.   Newton.
Arlington. Springfield. Keene.
1 AMAZING grace! how sweet the sound,
That sav'd a wretch like me!
I once was lost, but now am found—
Was blind, but now I see.

2 'Twas grace that taught my heart to fear,
And grace my fears reliev'd;
How precious did that grace appear,
The hour I first believ'd.

3 Through many dangers, toils, and snares,
I have already come;
'Tis grace that brought me safe thus far,
And grace will lead me home.

4 And when this flesh and heart shall fail,
And mortal life shall cease;
I shall possess within the veil,
A life of joy and peace.

HYMN 156. 7s.   Newton.
Pleyel's. Somerset.
1 SOV'REIGN grace hath power alone
To subdue a heart of stone;
And the moment grace is felt,
Then the hardest heart will melt.

2 When the Lord was crucified,
Two transgressors with him died;
One, with vile blaspheming tongue,
Scoff'd at Jesus as he hung.

3 Thus be spent his wicked breath
In the very jaws of death;
Perish'd, as too many do,
With the Saviour in his view.

4 But the other touch'd with grace,
Saw the danger of his case;
Faith receiv'd to own the Lord,
Whom the scribes and priests abhorr'd.

5 "Lord," he pray'd, "remember me,
When in glory thou shalt be."
"Soon with me," the Lord replies,
"Thou shalt rest in paradise."

6 This was wondrous grace indeed,
Grace bestow'd in time of need!
Sinners, trust in Jesus' name,
You shall find him still the same.

HYMN 157. C. M.   Steele.
Plymouth. Chapel. Windsor.
Pardon. Jeremiah iii. 22. Hosea xiv. 4.
1 HOW oft, alas this wretched heart
Has wander'd from the Lord!
How oft my roving thoughts depart,
Forgetful of his word.

2 Yet sov'reign mercy calls, "Return:"
Dear Lord, and may I come?
My vile ingratitude I mourn
Oh, take the wand'rer home.

3 And canst thou, wilt thou yet forgive,
And bid my crimes remove?
And shall a pardon'd rebel live
To speak thy wondrous love?

4 Almighty grace, thy healing power
How glorious, how divine!
That can to bliss and life restore
So vile a heart as mine.

5 Thy pard'ning love, so free, so sweet,
Dear Saviour, I adore;
Oh, keep me at thy sacred feet,
And let me rove no more.

HYMN 158. C. M.   Stennett.
Springfield. Windsor.
The converted thief. Luke xxiii. 39-43.
1 AS on the cross the Saviour hung,
And wept, and bled, and died,
He pour'd salvation on a wretch,
That languish'd at his side.

2 His crimes, with inward grief and shame,
The penitent confess'd
Then turn'd his dying eyes to Christ,
And thus his prayer address'd:

3 "Jesus, thou Son and heir of heaven,
Thou spotless Lamb of God!
I see thee bath'd in sweat and tears,
And welt'ring in thy blood.

4 "Yet quickly from these scenes of wo,
In triumph shalt thou rise,
Burst through the gloomy shades of death,
And shine above the skies.

5 "Amid the glories of that world,
Dear Saviour, think on me,
And in the vict'ries of thy death
Let me a sharer be."

6 His prayer the dying Jesus hears,
And instantly replies:
"Today thy parting soul shall be
With me in paradise."

HYMN 159.   L. M.   Gibbons.
Cumberland. Stirling. Moreton.
Luke vii. 47.
1 FORGIVENESS! 'tis a joyful sound
To anxious souls, condemn'd to die;
Publish the bliss, the world around;
Ye seraphs, shout it from the sky.

2 O'er sins unnumber'd as the sand,
And like the mountains for their size,
The seas of sov'reign grace expand,
The seas of sov'reign grace arise.

3 For this stupendous love of heav'n,
What grateful honors shall we show?
Where much transgression is forgiv'n,
Let love in equal ardor glow.

HYMN 160. L. M.   Watts.
Armley. Kingsbridge.
Perseverance. Philippians i. 6.
1 TO God I cried, when troubles rose;
He heard me and subdu'd my foes;
He did my rising fears control,
And strength diffus'd through all my soul.

2 Amid a thousand snares I stand,
Upheld and guarded by thy hand;
Thy words my fainting soul revive,
And keep my dying faith alive.

3 Grace will complete what grace begins,
To save from sorrows and from sins;
The work that wisdom undertakes,
Eternal mercy ne'er forsakes.

HYMN 161. 11s.   Kennady.
Walsal. Idumea.
Precious promises. 2 Peter 1. 4.
1 HOW firm a foundation, ye saints of the Lord,
Is laid for your faith in his excellent word!
What more can he say than to you he hath said,
Who unto the Saviour for refuge have fled:

2 "Fear not, I am with thee, O be not dismay'd,
For I am thy God, and will still give thee aid;
I'll strengthen thee, help thee, and cause thee to stand,
Upheld by my righteous, omnipotent hand.

3 "When through the deep waters I call thee to go,
The rivers of sorrow shall not overflow;
For I will be with thee thy troubles to bless,
And sanctify to thee thy deepest distress.

4 When thro' fiery trials thy pathway shall lie,
My grace all-sufficient shall be thy supply;
The flame shalt not hurt thee, I only design
Thy dross to consume, and thy gold to refine.

5 E'en down to old age, all my people shall prove
My sov'reign, eternal unchangeable love;
And then, when grey hairs shall their temples adorn,
Like lambs they shall still in my bosom be borne.

6 The soul that on Jesus hath lean'd for repose,
I will not, I will not desert to his foes;
That soul, though all hell should endeavor to shake,
I'll never—no never—no never forsake."

*HYMN 162. L. M.   Doddridge.
Angel's Hymn. Blendon.
Christ, the Believer's Ark. 1 Peter iii. 20.
1 THE deluge, at th' Almighty's call,
In what impetuous streams it fell!
Swallow'd the mountains in its rage,
And swept a guilty world to hell.

2 How dire the wreck! how loud the roar!
How shrill the universal cry—
Of millions in the last despair—
Re-echo'd from the low'ring sky!—

3 Yet Noah, humble, happy saint,
Surrounded with the chosen few,
Sat in his ark, secure from fear,
And sang the grace that steer'd him thro'.

4 So may I sing, in Jesus safe,
While storms of vengeance round me fall;

Conscious how high my hopes are fix'd,
Beyond what shakes this earthly ball.

5 Enter thine ark, while patience waits,
Nor ever quit that sure retreat;
Then the wide flood, that buries earth,
Shall waft thee to a fairer seat.

HYMN 163. 7s. Madan's Col.
Redeeming Love. Bath Abbey.
Redeemer.
1 NOW begin the heav'nly theme,
Sing aloud in Jesus name;
Ye, who Jesus' kindness prove;
Triumph in redeeming love.

2 Ye, who see the Father's grace,
Beaming in the Saviour's face,
As to Canaan on ye move,
Praise and bless redeeming love.

3 Mourning souls, dry up your tears,
Banish all your guilty fears,
See your guilt and curse remove,
Cancell'd by redeeming love.

4 Ye, alas! who long have been
Willing slaves of death and sin!
Now from bliss no longer rove,
Stop, and taste redeeming love.

5 Welcome, all by sin oppress'd—
Welcome to his sacred rest:
Nothing brought him from above,
Nothing—but redeeming love.

6 Hither, then, your music bring,
Strike aloud each joyful string;
Mortals, join the hosts above—
Join to praise redeeming love.

*HYMN 164. C. M.   Watts.
Stade. Braintree.

1 PLUNG'D in a gulf of dark despair,
We wretched sinners lay—
Without one cheerful beam of hope,
Or spark of glimm'ring day!

2 With pitying eyes the prince of grace
Beheld our helpless grief;
He saw—and (Oh amazing love!)
He ran to our relief.

3 Down from the shining seats above,
With joyful haste he fled;
Enter'd the grave in mortal flesh,
And dwelt among the dead.

4 He spoil'd the powers of darkness thus,
And brake our iron chains;
Jesus has freed our captive souls
From everlasting pains.

5 Oh, for this love, let rocks and hills
Their lasting silence break;
And all harmonious, human tongues
The Saviour's praises speak.

*HYMN 165. S. M.   Newton.
Cambridge. St. Thomas.

1 PREPARE a thankful song
To the Redeemer's name;
Let his high praise employ our tongue,
And every heart inflame.

2 He laid his glory by,
And bitter pains endur'd;
That rebels such as you and I,
From wrath might be secur'd.

3 The Holy Ghost he sends,
Our stubborn souls to move:
To make his enemies his friends,
And conquer them by love.

4 Assur'd that Christ our King,
Will put our foes to flight;
We on the field of battle sing,
And triumph while we fight.

HYMN 166. C. M.   Hoskins.
Bray. Dundee.
Regeneration. John iii. 5, 7.
1 SINNERS, this solemn truth regard,
Hear, all ye sons of men:
For Christ the Saviour hath declar'd,
"Ye must be born again."

2 Whate'er might be your birth or blood,
The sinner's boast is vain;
Thus saith the glorious Son of God,
"Ye must be born again."

3 Our nature's totally deprav'd—
The heart a sink of sin;
Without a change we can't be sav'd;
"Ye must be born again."

4 Spirit of life, thy grace impart,
And breathe on sinners slain;
Bear witness, Lord, in ev'ry heart,
That we are born again.

HYMN 167. C. M.   Watts.
Braintree. Irish.
1 ATTEND, while God's exalted Son
Doth his own glories shew;
Behold him seated on his throne,
Creating all things new.

2 Mighty Redeemer! set me free
From my old state of sin;
Oh, make my soul alive to thee,
Create new powers within.

3 Open mine eyes, unstop mine ears,
And form my heart afresh;
Give me new passions, joys, and fears,
And turn the stone to flesh.

4 Far from the regions of the dead,
From sin, and earth, and hell
In the new world that grace has made,
I would for ever dwell.

*HYMN 168. C. M.
Windsor. Bangor.
1 CAN aught beneath a power divine
The stubborn will subdue?
'Tis thine, eternal Spirit, thine
To form the heart anew.

2 'Tis thine the passions to recall,
And upward bid them rise;
And make the scales of error fall
From reason's darken'd eyes.

3 To chase the shades of death away,
And bid the sinner live,
A beam of heav'n, a vital ray—
'Tis thine alone to give.

4 Oh, change these wretched hearts of ours
And give them life divine;
Then shall our passions and our pow'rs,
Almighty Lord, be thine.

*HYMN 169. C. M.   Wallis.
Mear. Colchester.
Efficacious grace. Psalm xlv. 3, 5.
1 HAIL! mighty Jesus; how divine
Is thy victorious sword!
The stoutest rebel must resign,
At thy commanding word.

2 Deep are the wounds thine arrows give;
They pierce the hardest heart:
Thy smiles of grace the slain revive,
And joy succeeds to smart.

3 Still gird thy sword upon thy thigh,
Come with majestic sway,
Down from thy glorious throne on high,
And make thy foes obey.

4 And when thy vict'ries are complete;
When all the chosen race
Shall round the throne of glory meet,
To sing thy conquering grace;

5 Oh, may my humble soul be found
Among that favor'd band!
And I, with them, thy praise will sound
As round the throne we stand.

*HYMN 170. C. M.   Watts.
Buckingham. Windsor.
Sanctification and pardon.
1 WHERE shall we sinners hide our heads!
Can rocks or mountains save?
Or shall we wrap us in the shades
Of midnight and the grave?

2 Is there no shelter from the eye
Of an avenging God?
Jesus, to thy dear wounds we fly,
Bedew us with thy blood.

3 Those guardian drops our souls secure,
And wash away our sins:
Eternal justice frowns no more,
And conscience smiles within.

4 We bless that wond'rous purple stream,
That cleanses every stain:
Our souls are yet but half redeem'd,
If sin, the tyrant, reign.

5 Lord, blast his empire with thy breath,
That cursed throne must fall;
Ye flatt'ring plagues, that work our death,
Fly, for we hate you all.

LAW AND GOSPEL.

HYMN 171. L. M.   Watts.
Carthage. Green's Hundredth.
The Law and Gospel.
1 WHILE Sinai roars, and round the earth,
Thunder, and fire, and vengeance flings—

Jesus, thy dear, expiring breath,
And Calvary, speak gentler things.

2 Pardon, and grace, and boundless love,
Streaming along a Saviour's blood;
And life, and joys, and crowns above,
Purchas'd by our redeeming God.

3 Hark! how he prays (the charming sound
Dwells on his dying lips)—Forgive!
And every groan, and gaping wound,
Cries, "Father let the rebels live!"

4 Go, ye that rest upon the law,
And toil and seek salvation there;
Look to the flames that Moses saw,
And shrink, and tremble, and despair.

5 But I'll retire beneath the cross;
Saviour, at thy feet I'll lie:
And the keen sword that justice draws,
Flaming and red, shall pass me by.

HYMN 172 C. M. Cowper.
St. Ann's. York.
1 HOW long beneath the law I lay
In bondage and distress!
I toil'd the precept to obey,
But toil'd, without success.

2 Then, all my servile works were done,
A righteousness to raise;
Now, freely chosen in the Son,
I freely choose his ways.

3 To see the law by Christ fulfill'd,
And hear his pard'ning voice,
Will change a slave into a child,
And duty, into choice.

HYMN 173 L. M. Watts.
Carthage. Blendon.
Power of the gospel. Romans i. 16.
1 WHAT shall the dying sinner do,
That seeks relief from all his wo?

Where shall the guilty conscience find
Ease for the torment of the mind?

2 How shall we get our crimes forgiv'n,
Or form our natures fit for heav'n?
Can souls, all o'er defil'd with sin,
Make their own powers and passions clean;

3 In vain we search, in vain we try,
Till Jesus brings his gospel nigh;
'Tis there that power and glory dwell,
Which save rebellious souls from hell.

4 This is the pillar of our hope
That bears our fainting spirits up,
We read the grace and trust the word,
And find salvation in the Lord.

HOLY SPIRIT

HYMN 174 C. M. Doddridge
Bedford. Dundee.
Insensibly withdrawn. Judges xvi. 20.
1 A PRESENT God is all our strength,
And all our joy and hope;
When he withdraws, our comforts die,
And every grace must droop.

2 But flatt'ring trifles charm our hearts,
To court their false embrace,
Till justly this neglected friend
Averts his angry face.

3 He leaves us, and we miss him not;
But go presumptuous on,
Till baffled, wounded, and enslav'd,
We learn, that God is gone.

4 And what, my soul, can then remain
One ray of light to give?
Sever'd from him, their better life,
How can his children live?

5 Hence, all ye painted forms of joy,
And leave my heart to mourn:
I would devote these eyes to tears,
Till cheer'd by his return.

6 Look back, my Lord, and own the place,
Where once thy temple stood;
For lo, its ruins bear the mark
Of rich atoning blood.

HYMN 175. L. M.   Steele.
Hinton. Moreton.
His influences. John xiv. 16, 17.
1 SURE the blest Comforter is nigh,
'Tis he sustains my fainting heart;
Else would my hope for ever die,
And every cheering ray depart.

2 When some kind promise glads my soul,
Do I not find his healing voice
The tempest of my fears control,
And bid my drooping pow'rs rejoice?

3 Whene'er to call the Saviour mine,
With ardent wish my heart aspires;
Can it be less than pow'r divine,
Which animates these strong desires.

4 What less than thine almighty word
Can raise my heart from earth and dust,
And bid me cleave to thee, my Lord,
My life, my treasure, and my trust?

5 And when my cheerful hope can say,
I love my God, and trust his grace,
Lord, is it not thy blissful ray,
Which brings this dawn of sacred peace?

6 Let thy kind Spirit in my heart
For ever dwell, O God of love,
And light and heavenly peace impart,
Sweet earnest of the joys above.

HYMN 176. S. M.
St. Thomas. Shirland.
Invocation to the Holy Spirit.
1 BLEST Comforter Divine!
Whose rays of heavenly love
Amid our gloom and darkness shine,
And point our souls above;

2 Thou—who with "still small voice"
Dost stop the sinner's way,
And bid the mourning saint rejoice,
Though earthly joys decay;—

3 Thou—whose inspiring breath
Can make the cloud of care,
And e'en the gloomy vale of death
A smile of glory wear;—

4 Thou—who dost fill the heart
With love to all our race,
Blest Comforter!—to us impart
The blessings of thy grace.

*HYMN 177. C. M.   Watts
Barby. Zion. Turner.
Breathing after the Holy Spirit.
1 COME, Holy Spirit, heav'nly Dove,
With all thy quick'ning pow'rs,—
Kindle a flame of sacred love
In these cold hearts of ours.

2 In vain we tune our formal songs,
In vain we strive to rise;
Hosannas languish on our tongues,
And our devotion dies.

3 Dear Lord! and shall we ever live
At this poor dying rate?
Our love so faint, so cold to thee,
And thine to us so great.

4 Come Holy Spirit, heav'nly Dove,
With all thy quick'ning pow'rs,—
Come, shed abroad a Saviour's love,
And that shall kindle ours.

HYMN 178. 8, 7.
Ingatestone. Tabernacle.
To the blessed Spirit.
1 HOLY GHOST, disperse our sadness,
Pierce the clouds of sinful night;
Come, thou source of sweetest gladness,
Breathe thy life and spread thy light;
Loving Spirit, God of peace,
Great distributer of grace,
Rest upon this congregation!
Hear, Oh, hear our supplication.

2 From that height which knows no measure,
As a gracious shower descend:
Bringing down the richest treasure
Man can wish, or God can send.
O thou Glory shining down
From the Father and the Son,
Grant us thy illumination!
Rest on all this congregation.

3 Come, thou best of all donations
God can give, or we implore;
Having thy sweet consolations,
We need wish for nothing more;
HOLY SPIRIT, heavenly DOVE,
Now descending from above,
Rest on all this congregation!
Make our hearts thy habitation.

*HYMN 179. S. M.   Hart.
Shirland. Watchman.
John xiv. 26.
1 COME, Holy Spirit, come,
Let thy bright beams arise;
Dispel the sorrow from our minds,—
The darkness from our eyes.

2 Convince us of our sin;
Then lead to Jesus' blood;
And to our wond'ring view reveal
The secret love of God.

3 'Tis thine to cleanse the heart—
To sanctify the soul—

To pour fresh life in every part,
And new create the whole.

4 Revive our drooping faith;
Our doubts and fears remove;
And kindle in our breasts the flame
Of never-dying love.

HYMN 180.   8s.   Rippon.
Consolation. Dismission.
1 DESCEND, Holy Spirit, the Dove,
And visit a sorrowful breast;
My burden of guilt to remove,
And bring me assurance of rest;
Thou only hast power to relieve
A sinner o'erwhelm'd with his load;
The sense of redemption to give,
And sprinkle his heart with thy blood.

2 With me, if of old thou hast strove,
And kindly withheld me from sin;
Resolv'd by the strength of thy love,
My worthless affections to win;
The work of thy mercy revive,
Invincible mercy exert,
And keep my weak graces alive,
And set up thy rest in my heart.

3 If when I have put thee to grief,
And madly to folly return'd,
Thy goodness has been my relief,
And lifted me up as I mourn'd:
O spirit of pity and grace,
Relieve me again and restore;
My spirit in holiness raise,
To fall, and to grieve thee, no more.

4 If now I lament after God,
And pant for a taste of his love,—
If Jesus, who pour'd out his blood,
Obtain'd me a mansion above ;—
Come, heavenly Comforter, come,
Sweet witness of mercy divine!
And make me thy permanent home,
And seal me eternally thine.

HYMN 181. L. P. M. Pres. Davies.
Eaton. Claybury. Harlington.
1 ETERNAL Spirit, source of light,
Enliv'ning, consecrating fire,
Descend, and with celestial heat
Our dull, our frozen hearts inspire:
Our souls refine, our dross consume!
Come, condescending Spirit, come!

2 In our cold breasts, O strike a spark
Of the pure flame, which seraph's feel,
Nor let us wander in the dark,
Or lie benumb'd and stupid still:
Come, vivifying Spirit, come,
And make our souls thy constant home.

3 Let pure devotion's fervor rise;
Let every pious passion glow:
O let the raptures of the skies
Kindle in our cold hearts below!
Come, condescending Spirit, come,
And make our souls thy constant home!

HYMN 182. L. M.   C. Wesley.
Surry. Armley. Warwick.
Take not thy Holy Spirit, & c. Psalm li. 11.
1 STAY, thou insulted Spirit, stay,
Tho' I have done thee such despite,
Cast not the sinner quite away,
Nor take thine everlasting flight:

2 Though I have most unfaithful been
Of all, whoe'er thy grace receiv'd,
Ten thousand times thy goodness seen,
Ten thousand times thy goodness griev'd:

3 Yet Oh, the chief of sinners spare,
In honor of my great High Priest;
Nor in thy righteous anger swear,
I shall not see thy people's rest.

4 If yet thou canst my sins forgive,
E'en now, O Lord, relieve my woes;
Into thy rest of love receive,
And bless me with a calm repose.

5 E'en now my weary soul release,
And raise me by thy gracious hand!
Guide me into thy perfect peace,
And bring me to the promis'd land.

GRACES OF THE SPIRIT.
IN ALPHABETICAL ORDER.

*HYMN 183.   C. M.   Kirkham.
Clarendon. Bray.
Bearing the Cross. Mark viii. 38.
1 DIDST thou, dear Jesus, suffer shame,
And bear the cross for me?
And shall I fear to own thy name,
Or thy disciple be?

2 Forbid it, Lord, that I should dread
To suffer shame or loss;
Oh, let me in thy footsteps tread,
And glory in thy cross.

3 Inspire my soul with life divine,
And holy courage bold;
Let knowledge, faith, and meekness shine,
Nor love, nor zeal grow cold.

4 Say to my soul, "Why dost thou fear
The face of feeble clay?
Behold thy Saviour ever near,
Will guard thee in the way."

5 Oh, how my soul would rise and run,
At this reviving word:
Nor any painful suff'rings shun,
To follow thee, my Lord.

6 Let sinful men reproach, defame,
And call thee what they will,
If I may glorify thy name,
And be thy servant still.

HYMN 184.   C. M.   Barbauld.
Buckingham. Plymouth.
Charity.
1 BLEST is the man whose soft'ning heart
Feels all another's pain;
To whom the supplicating eye
Was never rais'd in vain:

2 Whose breast expands with gen'rous warmth,
A stranger's woes to feel;
And bleeds in pity o'er the wound
He wants the power to heal.

3 He spreads his kind supporting arms
To every child of grief:
His secret bounty largely flows,
And brings unmask'd relief.

4 To gentle offices of love
His feet are never slow:
He views, through mercy's melting eye,
A brother in a foe.

5 He, from the bosom of his God,
Shall present peace receive—
And when he kneels before the throne,
His trembling soul shall live.

*HYMN 185. C. M.   Cowper.
Canterbury. Colchester.
Comforts—true and false.
1 O GOD, whose favorable eye
The sin-sick soul revives;
Holy and heav'nly is the joy,
Thy shining presence gives.

2 This hypocrites have ne'er believ'd,
They judge with graceless hearts;
Swell'd with their pride, they are deceiv'd
By Satan's wily arts.

3 Unholy, selfish joys are theirs;
And while they boast their light,
And seem to soar above the stars,
They're plunging into night.

4 Lull'd in a soft and formal sleep,
They sin, and yet rejoice;
Were they indeed the Saviour's sheep,
They sure would hear his voice.

5 Be mine the comforts that reclaim
The soul from Satan's pow'r;
That make me blush for what I am,
And hate my sin the more.

6 'Tis joy enough, my All in All,
At thy dear feet to lie
Thou wilt not let me lower fall,
And none can higher fly.

HYMN 186. L. P. M.   D. R.
Carolan's. Cumberland.
Confidence in the Mediator. Hebrews iv. 15.
1 WHEN gathering clouds around I view,
And days are dark and friends are few,
On him I lean, who not in vain,
Experienc'd every human pain;
He sees my wants, allays my fears,
And counts and treasures up my tears.

2 If aught should tempt my soul to stray
From heav'nly virtue's narrow way,
To fly the good I would pursue,
Or do the sin I would not do,
Still he who felt temptation's pow'r
Shall guard me in that dang'rous hour.

3 When sorrowing o'er some stone I bend,
Which covers all that was a friend;
And from his voice, his hand, his smile
Divides me—for a little while,—
Thou, Saviour, seest the tears I shed,
For thou didst weep o'er Lazarus dead.

4 And Oh, when I have safely past
Through every conflict—but the last,
Still, still unchanging, watch beside
My painful bed,—for thou hast died
Then point to realms of cloudless day,
And wipe the latest tear away.

HYMN 187. C. M.   Ryland.
Barby. Bray.
Delight in God. Psalm xxxvii. 4.
1 GRANT, Lord, I may delight in thee,
And on thy care depend
To thee in every trouble flee,
My best, my only friend.

2 No good in creatures can be found,
But all is found in thee;
I must be blessed and abound,
While thou art God to me.

3 Oh, that I had a stronger faith,
To look within the veil,
To credit what my Saviour saith,
Whose word can never fail.

4 O Lord, I cast my care on thee,
I triumph and adore
Henceforth my great concern shall be,
To love and please thee more.

*HYMN 188. C. M.   Cowper.
Plymouth. Walsal.
Contrite heart. Isaiah lvii. 15.
1 THE Lord will happiness divine
On contrite hearts bestow;
Then tell me, gracious God, is mine
A contrite heart or no?

2 I hear, but seem to hear in vain,
Insensible as steel;
If aught is felt, 'tis only pain,
To find I cannot feel.

3 I sometimes think myself inclin'd
To love thee, if I could;
But often feel another mind,
Averse to all that's good.

4 My best desires are faint and few,
I fain would strive for more;
But, when I cry, "My strength renew,"
Seem weaker than before.

5 Thy saints are comforted, I know,
And love thy house of pray'r;
I therefore go where others go,
But find no comfort there.

6 Oh, make this heart rejoice or ache—
Decide this doubt for me;
And if it be not broken, break,
And heal it, if it be.

HYMN 189. 8s.   Hart.
Lambeth. Uxbridge. Bethany.
Faith conquering. Romans i. 17.
1 THE moment a sinner believes,
And trusts in his crucify'd God,
His pardon at once he receives—
Redemption in full through his blood.
'Tis faith that still leads us along,
And lives under pressure and load,
That makes us in weakness more strong,
And draws the soul upward to God.

2 It treads on the world and on hell,
It vanquishes death and despair;
And Oh! let us wonder to tell,
It wrestles and conquers by pray'r:
Permits a vile worm of the dust,
With God to commune as a friend;
To hope his forgiveness as just,
And look for his love to the end.

3 It says to the mountains, "Depart,"
That stand between God and the soul;—
It binds up the broken in heart,
And makes wounded consciences whole;
Bids sins of a crimson-like dye
Be spotless as snow, and as white;
And raises the sinner on high,
To dwell with the angels of light.

*HYMN 190. L. .M.   Watts.
Portugal. Kent.
Faith connected with salvation.
1 NOT the best deeds that we have done,
Can make a wounded conscience whole;

Faith is the grace,—and faith alone,
That flies to Christ, and saves the soul.

2 Lord, I believe thy heav'nly word,
Fain would I have my soul renew'd;
I mourn for sin and trust the Lord,
To have it pardon'd and subdu'd.

3 Oh may thy grace its power display,
Let guilt and death no longer reign,
Save me in thine appointed way,
Nor let my humble faith be vain.

*HYMN 191. L. M.   Cowper.
Bath. Kent.
A living and a dead Faith.
1 THE Lord receives his highest praise,
From humble minds and hearts sincere
While all the loud professor says,
Offends the righteous Judge's ear.

2 To walk as children of the day,
To mark his precepts' holy light,
To wage the warfare, watch and pray,
Show who are pleasing in his sight.

3 Not words alone it cost the Lord,
To purchase pardon for his own;
Nor will a soul by grace restor'd,
Rest in mere forms and words alone.

4 Easy indeed it were to reach
A mansion in the courts above,
If wat'ry floods and fluent speech
Might serve instead of faith and love.

5 But none shall gain that blissful place,
Or God's unclouded glory see;
Who talk of rich and sov'reign grace;
Unless from sin they are made free.

HYMN 192. C. M.   Turner.
Dundee. Colchester.
The power of Faith.
1 FAITH adds new charms to earthly bliss,
And saves me from its snares;
Its aid in ev'ry duty brings,
And softens all my cares:

2 Extinguishes the thirst of sin,
And lights the sacred fire
Of love to God and heav'nly things,
And feeds the pure desire.

3 The wounded conscience knows its pow'r,
The healing balm to give;
That balm the saddest heart can cheer,
And make the dying live.

4 Wide it unveils celestial worlds,
Where deathless pleasures reign;
And bids me seek my portion there,
Nor bids me seek in vain.

*HYMN 193. C. M.   Watts.
Braintree. Arlington.
Holy Fortitude.
1 AM I a soldier of the cross;
A foll'wer of the Lamb;
And shall I fear to own his cause,
Or blush to speak his name?

2 Shall I be carry'd to the skies,
On flow'ry beds of ease,
While others fought to win the prize,
And sail'd through bloody seas?

3 Are there no foes for me to face,
Must I not stem the flood
Is this vain world a friend to grace,
To help me on to God?

4 Sure I must fight, if I would reign
Increase my courage, Lord,
To bear the cross, endure the shame,
Supported by thy word.

5 The saints, in all this glorious war,
Shall conquer, though they die;
They see the triumph from afar,
With faith's discerning eye.

HYMN 194. C. M.   Taylor.
Bray. Braintree.
Humble Gratitude.
1 SINCE we, and all our treasures too,
Are his who reigns above;
Then is there nothing we can do,
To prove our grateful love?

2 A broken heart he'll not despise—
It is his chief delight;
This is an humble sacrifice,
Well pleasing in his sight.

3 Tho' treasures brought before his throne
Would no acceptance find,
He kindly condescends to own
A meek and lowly mind.

4 This is an off'ring we may bring,
However mean our store
The poorest child, the greatest king,
Can give him nothing more.

HYMN 195. L. M.   Watts.
Portugal. Winchester.
Gravity and Decency.
1 BEHOLD the sons the heirs of God
So dearly bought with Jesus' blood;
Are they not born to heav'nly joys,
And shall they stoop to earthly toys?

2 Doth vain discourse, or empty mirth,
Well suit the honors of their birth?
Shall they be fond of gay attire,
Which children love, and fools admire?

3 Lord, with a heaven-directed eye
We'll pass these glitt'ring trifles by;
Oh, raise our hearts and passions higher,
Touch our vain souls with sacred fire.

4 We'll look on all the toys below
With such disdain as angels do;
And wait the call that bids us rise
To mansions promis'd in the skies.

*HYMN 196. L. M.   Steele.
Quercy. Blendon.
Happy Poverty. Matthew v. 3.
1 YE humble souls, complain no more ;
Let faith survey your future store;
How happy, how divinely blest,
The sacred words of truth attest.

2 When conscious grief laments sincere,
And pours the penitential tear:
Hope points to your dejected eyes,
The bright reversion in the skies.

3 In vain the sons of wealth and pride
Despise your lot, your hopes deride
In vain they boast their little stores;
Trifles are *theirs,* a kingdom *yours:*

4 A kingdom of immense delight,
Where health and peace and joy unite;
Where undeclining pleasures rise,
And every want hath full supplies.

HYMN 197. L. M.   Cowper.
Bath. Leeds. Portugal.
Hatred of Sin.
1 HAD I a throne above the rest,
Where angels and archangels dwell,
One sin, unslain within my breast,
Would make that heav'n as dark as hell.

2 The pris'ner, sent to breathe fresh air
And bless'd with liberty again,
Would mourn were he condemn'd to wear
One link of all his former chain.

3 But Oh! no foe invades the bliss,
When glory crowns the christian's head;
One view of Jesus as he is,
Will strike all sin for ever dead.

*HYMN 198.   L. M.   Harrison.
Warwick. Surry.
1 OH, could I find some peaceful bow'r,
Where sin has neither place nor pow'r;
This traitor vile I fain would shun,
But cannot from his presence run.

2 When to the throne of grace I flee,
He stands between my God and me;
Where'er I rove, where'er I rest,
I feel him working in my breast.

3 When I attempt to soar above,
To view the heights of Jesus' love;
This monster seems to mount the skies,
And veils his glory from my eyes.

4 Lord, free me from this deadly foe,
Which keeps my faith and hope so low;
I long to dwell in heav'n my home,
Where not one sinful thought can come.

*HYMN 199. L. M.   Watts.
Islington. Truro.
The Christian's Hope.
1 WHAT sinners value I resign;
Lord, 'tis enough that thou art mine:
I shall behold thy blissful face,
And stand complete in righteousness.

2 This life's a dream, an empty show;
But the bright world to which I go—
Hath joys substantial and sincere;
When shall I wake and find me there?

3 O glorious hour! O blest abode!
I shall be near and like my God!
And flesh and sin no more control
The sacred pleasures of the soul.

HYMN 200. 8, 7, 4.
Fawcett. Jordan. Littleton.
Hope encouraged. Psalm xlii. 5.
1 O MY soul, what means this sadness?

Wherefore art thou thus cast down?
Let thy griefs be turn'd to gladness;
Bid thy restless fears begone;
Look to Jesus,
And rejoice in his dear name.

2 What though Satan's strong temptations
Vex and grieve thee day by day;
And thy sinful inclinations
Often fill thee with dismay;
Thou shalt conquer—
Through the Lamb's redeeming blood.

3 Though ten thousand ills beset thee,
From without and from within;
Jesus saith he'll ne'er forget thee,
But will save from hell and sin:
He is faithful
To perform his gracious word.

4 Though distresses now attend thee,
And thou treadst the thorny road;
His right hand shall still defend thee;
Soon he'll bring thee home to God!
Therefore praise him—
Praise the great Redeemer's name.

5 Oh, that I could now adore him,
Like the heav'nly host above,
Who for ever bow before him,
And unceasing sing his love!
Happy songsters!
When shall I your chorus join?

HYMN 201. L. M.   Steele.
Armley. Darwent.
1 Samuel xxx. 6.
1 WHY sinks my weak desponding mind?
Why heaves my heart the anxious sigh?
Can sov'reign goodness be unkind?
Am I not safe, if God is nigh?

2 He holds all nature in his hand:
That gracious hand, on which I live,

Does life, and time, and death command,
And has immortal joys to give.

3 'Tis he supports this fainting frame,
On him alone my hopes recline;
The wond'rous glories of his name,
How wide they spread! how bright they shine!

4 My God, if thou art mine indeed,
Then I have all my heart can crave;
A present help in times of need,
Still kind to hear, and strong to save.

*HYMN 202.　C. M.　　J. Steward.
Standish. Elgin.
Hoping, yet trembling.
1 MY soul would fain indulge a hope
To reach the heavenly shore;
And when I drop this dying flesh,
That I shall sin no more.

2 I hope to hear, and join the song,
That saints and angels raise;
And while eternal ages roll,
To sing eternal praise.

3 But Oh—this dreadful heart of sin!
It may deceive me still;
And while I look for joys above,
May plunge me down to hell.

4 The scene must then for ever close,
Probation at an end;
No gospel grace can reach me there,
No pardon there descend.

5 Come then, O blessed Jesus, come,
To me thy Spirit give;
Shine through a dark, benighted soul,
And bid a sinner live.

HYMN 203. L. M.   Enfield.
Warwick. Carthage. Surry.
Humility.
1 WHEREFORE should man, frail child of clay,
Who from the cradle to the shroud,
Lives but the insect of a day—
Oh, why should mortal man be proud?

2 His brightest visions just appear,
Then vanish, and no more are found;
The stateliest pile his pride can rear,
A breath may level with the ground.

3 Follies and crimes, a countless sum,
Are crowded in life's little span:
How ill, alas, does pride become
That erring, guilty creature, man!

4 God of my life, Father divine!
Give me a meek and lowly mind:
In modest worth, Oh, let me shine,
And peace in humble virtue find.

*HYMN 204. C. M.
Mear. St. Martin's.
Joy in the Holy Ghost. Luke i. 46.
1 MY soul doth magnify the Lord,
My Spirit doth rejoice
In God, my Saviour, and my God;
I hear his joyful voice.

2 I need not go abroad for joy,
Who have a feast at home;
My sighs are turned into songs,—
The Comforter is come.

3 Down from on high, the blessed Dove
Is come into my breast;
To witness God's eternal love;
This is my heav'nly feast.

4 There is a stream that issues forth
From God's eternal throne,
And from the Lamb, a living stream,
Clear as the crystal stone.

5 That stream doth water paradise;
It makes the angels sing;
One cordial drop revives my heart;
Hence all my joys do spring.

*HYMN 205. S. M.   Watts.
Newton. Silver Street. St. Thomas.
Heavenly joy on earth.
1 COME, we who love the Lord,
And let our joys be known;
Join in a song with sweet accord,
And thus surround the throne.

2 Let those refuse to sing,
Who never knew our God;
But fav'rites of the heav'nly King
Should speak their joys abroad.

3 The men of grace have found
Glory begun below:
Celestial fruits on earthly ground,
From faith and hope may grow.

4 The hill of Zion yields
A thousand sacred sweets,
Before we reach the heav'nly fields,
Or walk the golden streets.

5 Then let our songs abound,
And every tear be dry;
We're marching thro' Immanuel's ground
To fairer worlds on high.

HYMN 206. L. M.   Watts.
Portugal. Shoel.
Justice and equity. Matthew vii. 12.
1 BLESSED Redeemer! how divine,
How righteous is this rule of thine,
"Never to deal with others worse
Than we would have them deal with us!"

2 This golden lesson, short and plain,
Gives not the mind nor memory pain,
And every conscience must approve
This universal law of love.

3 Is reason ever at a loss?—
Call in self-love to judge the cause;
Let our own fondest passion show
How we should treat our neighbor too.

4 How bless'd would every nation prove,
Thus rul'd by equity and love!
All would be friends, without a foe,
And form a paradise below.

*HYMN 207. C. M.   Watts.
York. Braintree
Love to God. 1 Cor. xiii. 8. Ps. cxxxvii. 5, 6.
1 HAPPY the heart where graces reign,
Where love inspires the breast;
Love is the brightest of the train,
And strengthens all the rest.

2 This is the grace that lives and sings,
When faith and hope shall cease;
'Tis this shall strike our joyful strings
In the sweet realms of bliss.

3 Before we quite forsake our clay,
Or leave this dark abode,
The wings of love bear us away
To see our smiling God.

HYMN 208. C. M.
Dundee. Zion.
1 Corinthians ii. 9.
1 EYE hath not seen, nor ear hath heard,
From fancy 'tis conceal'd,
What thou, my Lord, hast laid in store,
And hast to me reveal'd.

2 I see thy face, I hear thy voice,
And taste thy sweetest love;
My soul doth leap; but Oh, for wings,
The wings of Noah's dove!

3 Then should I fly far hence away,
And leave this world of sin;
Then should my Lord put forth his hand,
And kindly take me in.

4 Then should my soul with angels feast
On joys that always last;
Bless'd be my God, the God of joy,
Who gives me here a taste.

HYMN 209. L. M.   Tappan.
Haverhill. Philadelphia.
1 THE ransom'd spirit to her home,
The clime of cloudless beauty, flies;
No more on stormy seas to roam,
She hails her haven in the skies
But cheerless are those heav'nly fields,
The cloudless clime no pleasure yields,
There is no bliss in bow'rs above,
If thou art absent, HOLY LOVE!

2 The cherub near the viewless throne
Hath smote the harp with trembling hand;
And One with incense-fire hath flown,
To touch with flame the angel-band:
But tuneless is the quiv'ring string,
No melody can Gabriel bring,
Mute are its arches, when above
The harps of heav'n wake not to LOVE!

3 Earth, sea, and sky one language speak,
In harmony that sooths the soul;
'Tis heard when scarce the zephyrs wake,
And when on thunders, thunders roll:
That voice is heard and tumults cease,
It whispers to the bosom peace;
O, speak, Inspirer! from above,
And cheer our hearts, CELESTIAL LOVE!

HYMN 210. 8s.   Francis.
Consolation. Dismission.
Love to Christ.
1 MY gracious Redeemer I love,
His praises aloud I'll proclaim;
And join with the armies above,
To shout his adorable name:
To gaze on his glories divine,
Shall be my eternal employ
To see them incessantly shine,
My boundless, ineffable joy.

2 He freely redeem'd, with his blood,
My soul from the confines of hell,
To live on the smiles of my God,
And in his sweet presence to dwell;
To shine with the angels in light,
With saints and with seraphs to sing;
To view with eternal delight,
My Jesus, my Saviour, my King.

3 Ye palaces, sceptres, and crowns,
Your pride with disdain I survey;
Your pomps are but shadows and sounds;
And pass in a moment away:
The crown that my Saviour bestows,
You permanent sun shall outshine;
My joy everlastingly flows—
My God, my Redeemer is mine,

HYMN 211. L. M.   Watts.
Bath. Leeds.
Love to Christ present or absent.
1 OF all the joys we mortals know,
Jesus, thy love exceeds the rest;
Love, the best blessing here below,
The highest rapture of the blest.

2 While we are held in thine embrace,
There's not a thought attempts to rove;
Each smile that's seen upon thy face,
Fixes, and charms, and fires our love.

3 When of thine absence we complain,
And long, and weep, and humbly pray;
There's a strange pleasure in the pain,—
Those tears are sweet which mourn thy stay.

4 When round thy courts by day we rove,
Or ask the watchmen of the night,
For some kind tidings from above,
Thy very name creates delight.

5 Jesus, our God, descend and come;
Our eyes would dwell upon thy face;
Heav'n to see our Lord at home,
And feel the presence of his grace.

*HYMN 212. 7s.   Newton.
Pleyel's. Bath Abbey.
Lovest thou me? John xxi. 15.

1 'TIS a point I long to know,
Oft it causes anxious thought
Do I love the Lord, or no?
Am I his, or am I not?

2 If I love, why am I thus?
Why this dull, this lifeless frame?
Hardly, sure, can they be worse,
Who have never heard his name.

3 Could my heart so hard remain,
Pray'r a task and burden prove—
Ev'ry trifle give me pain—
If I knew a Saviour's love?

4 When I turn mine eyes within,
All is dark, and vain, and wild;
Fill'd with unbelief and sin—
Can I deem myself a child?

5 If I pray, or hear, or read,
Sin is mix'd with all I do;
You who love the Lord indeed,
Tell me—is it thus with you?

6 Yet I mourn my stubborn will,
Find my sin a grief and thrall;
Should I grieve for what I feel,
If I did not love at all!

7 Lord decide the doubtful case!
Thou who art thy people's Sun:
Shine upon thy work of grace,
If it be indeed begun.

8 Let me love thee more and more,
If I love at all, I pray;
If I have not lov'd before,
Help me to begin to-day.

HYMN 213. C. M. Stennett.
Clarendon. Springfield.
Without love I am nothing. 1 Corinthians xii. 1-3.
1 DID I possess the gift of tongues,
Great God, without thy grace,
My loudest words, my loftiest songs
Would be but sounding brass.

2 Tho' thou should'st give me heav'nly skill,
Each myst'ry to explain,
Had I no heart to do thy will,
My knowledge would be vain.

3 Had I so strong a faith, my God,
As mountains to remove,
No faith could do me real good,
That did not work by love.

4 Oh, grant me then this one request,
And I'll be satisfied,
That love divine may rule my breast,
And all my actions guide.

HYMN 214. S. M. Toplady.
Watchman. Froome.
Christian love. Galatians iii. 28.
1 LET party names no more
The Christian world o'erspread;
Gentile and Jew, and bond and free,
Are one in Christ their head.

2 Among the saints on earth,
Let mutual love be found;
Heirs of the same inheritance,
With mutual blessings crown'd.

3 Let discord—child of hell!
Be banish'd far away;
Those should in strictest friendship dwell,
Who the same Lord obey.

4 Thus will the church below
Resemble that above,
Where streams of pleasure ever flow,
And every heart is love.

HYMN 215. C. M.   Swain.
Springfield. Newmark. Barby.
1 HOW sweet, how heav'nly is the sight,
When those who love the Lord,
In one another's peace delight,
And so fulfil his word:—

2 When each can feel his brother's sigh,
And with him bear a part:
When sorrows flow from eye to eye,
And joy from heart to heart:—
3 When free from envy, scorn, and pride,
Our wishes all above,
Each can his brother's failings hide,
And show a brother's love!

4 Let love in one delightful stream,
Through every bosom flow;
And union sweet, and dear esteem,
In every action glow.

5 Love is the golden chain that binds
The happy souls above;
And he's an heir of heaven who finds
His bosom glow with love.

HYMN 216. L. M. Heginbothom.
Winchester. Portugal.
Peace of Conscience. Acts xxiv. 16.
1 SWEET peace of conscience, heav'nly guest!
Come, fix thy mansion in my breast;
Dispel my doubts, my fears control,
And heal the anguish of my soul.

2 Come, smiling hope, and joy sincere,
Come, make your constant dwelling here;
Still let your presence cheer my heart
Nor sin compel you to depart.

3 Thou God of hope, and peace divine,
O, make these sacred pleasures mine!
Forgive my sins, my fears remove,
And send the tokens of thy love.

4 Then, should mine eyes, without a tear,
See death, with all his terrors, near;
My heart should then in death rejoice,
And raptures tune my falt'ring voice.

HYMN 217. 6, 8.　　　Raffles
Bethesda. Edwin's.
1 COME, heavenly peace of mind,
I sigh for thy return;
I seek, but cannot find
The joys for which I mourn;
Ah! where's the Saviour now,
Whose smiles I once possess'd?
Till he return, I bow,
By heaviest grief oppress'd;
My days of happiness are gone,
And I am left to weep alone.

2 I tried each earthly charm—
In pleasure's haunts I stray'd—
I sought its soothing balm—
I ask'd the world its aid;
But ah! no balm it had
To heal a wounded breast,
And I, forlorn and sad,
Must seek another rest;
My days of happiness are gone,
And I am left to weep alone.

3 Where can the mourner go,
And tell his tale of grief?
Ah! who can sooth his wo,
And give him sweet relief?
Thou, Jesus! canst impart,
By thy long wish'd return,
Ease to this wounded heart,
And bid me cease to mourn;
Then shall this night of sorrow flee,
And I rejoice, my Lord, in thee.

*HYMN 218. S. M.　　　Doddridge.
Dover. Peckham. Shirland.
Rejoicing. Psalm cxxxviii 5.
1 NOW let our voices join
To form a sacred song;

Ye pilgrims, in Jehovah's ways,
With music pass along.

2 How straight the path appears
How open and how fair!
No lurking gins t' entrap our feet,
No fierce destroyer there.

3 But flowers of paradise
In rich profusion spring;
The Sun of glory gilds the path,
And dear companions sing.

4 All honor to his name,
Who marks the shining way,—
To him who leads the wand'rers on
To realms of endless day.

HYMN 219. C. M. Beddome.
Abridge. Barby.
Resignation.
1 MY times of sorrow and of joy,
Great God, are in thy hand;
My choicest comforts come from thee,
And go at thy command.

2 If thou should'st take them all away,
Yet would I not repine;
Before they were possess'd by me,
They were entirely thine.

3 Nor would I drop a murm'ring word,
Though the whole world were gone,
But seek enduring happiness
In thee, and thee alone.

*HYMN 220. C. M. Young.
Chapel. Georgia. Walsal.
1 OUR hearts are fasten'd to this world
By strong and num'rous ties,
And every sorrow breaks a string,
And urges us to rise.

2 When heav'n would kindly set us free,
And earth's enchantment end,

It takes the most effectual means,
And robs us of a friend.

3 Resign— and all the load of life
That moment you remove;
Its heavy tax, ten thousand cares
Devolve on ONE above.

*HYMN 221. C. M.   Rippon.
Bray. Rochester.
Self-denial. Mark viii. 34.
1 AND must I part with all I have,
My dearest Lord, for thee?
It is but right, since thou hast done
Much more than this for me.

2 Yes, let it go—one look from thee
Will more than make amends,
For all the losses I sustain
Of credit, riches, friends.

3 Ten thousand worlds, ten thousand lives,
How worthless they appear,
Compar'd with thee, supremely good,
Divinely bright and fair!

4 Saviour of souls, could I from thee
A single smile obtain,
Though destitute of all things else,
I'd glory in my gain.

HYMN 222. C. M.   Watts.
Barby. Abridge.
Sincerity and Truth. Philippians iv. 8.
1 LET those who bear the Christian name
Their holy vows fulfil;
The saints, the foll'wers of the Lamb,
Are men of honor still.

2 True to the solemn oaths they take,
Though to their hurt they swear:
Constant and just to all they speak;
For God and angels hear.

3 Still with their lips their hearts agree,
Nor flatt'ring words devise:
They know the God of truth can see
Through every false disguise.

4 From all deceit they swiftly fly,
Whatever shape it wears,
They love the truth and when they die,
Eternal life is theirs.

*HYMN 223. C. M.   Cowper.
St. Ann's. Barby.
Submission.
1 O LORD, my best desires fulfil,
And help me to resign
Life, health, and comfort to thy will,
And make thy pleasure mine.

2 Why should I shrink at thy command,
Whose love forbids my fears?
Or tremble at the gracious hand
That wipes away my tears?

3 No—let me rather freely yield
What most I prize to thee;
Who never has a good withheld,
Or wilt withhold from me.

4 Thy favor, all my journey thro'
Thou art engag'd to grant;
What else I want, or think I do,
'Tis better still to want.

5 Wisdom and mercy guide my way,
Shall I resist them both?
A poor, blind creature of a day,
And crush'd before the moth!

6 But ah! my inward spirit cries,
Still bind me to thy sway;
Else the next cloud that veils my skies,
Will drive these thoughts away.

HYMN 224. C. M.
Chapel. Walsal.
Submission to Christ.
1 JESUS once left his throne on high,
Left the bright realms of bliss,
And came on earth to bleed and die—
Was ever love like this?

2 Is there a heart that will not bend
To his divine control?
Descend, O sov'reign love, descend,
And melt that stubborn soul.

3 Come, dearest Lord, we will confess
Thy sweet, thy gentle sway:
Our willing hearts, constrain'd by grace,
Thy pleasing rule obey.

4 Though we, for bounty so divine,
No equal honors raise;
Yet, Lord, may all our hearts be thine,
Our tongues proclaim thy praise.

HYMN 225. C. M.   Tate.
Swanwick. Hanover.
Trust and love God. Psalm xxxiv.
1 THROUGH all the changing scenes of life,
In trouble and in joy,
The praises of my God shall still
My heart and tongue employ.

2 Of his deliv'rance I will boast
Till all who are distress'd,
From my example, comfort take,
And charm their griefs to rest.

3 Oh, make but trial of his love—
Experience will decide,
How blest are they, and only they,
Who in his truth confide.

4 Fear him, ye saints, and you will then
Have nothing else to fear:
Come, make his service your delight,
He'll make your wants his care.

*HYMN 226. L. M.   Steele.
Bath. Luton. Wells.
Trust in God. Habakkuk iii. 17, 18.
1 THE God of my salvation lives;
My nobler life he will sustain;
His word immortal vigor gives,
Nor shall my glorious hopes be vain.

2 Thy presence, Lord, can cheer my heart,
Though every earthly comfort die;
Thy smile can bid my pains depart,
And raise my sacred pleasures high.

3 Oh, let me hear thy blissful voice,
Inspiring life and joy divine!
The barren desert shall rejoice;
'Tis paradise, if thou art mine!

*HYMN 227. S. M.
St. Thomas. Shirland.
1 GIVE to the winds thy fears;
Hope, and be undismay'd;
God hears thy sighs, and counts thy tears;
He shall lift up thy head.

2 Through waves, and clouds, and storms,
He gently clears the way;
Wait thou his time; so shall this night
Soon end in joyous day.

3 Still heavy is thy heart?—
Still sink thy spirits down?
Cast off this weight, let fear depart,
And every care be gone.

4 What though thou rulest not
Yet heav'n, and earth, and hell
Proclaim, that "God is on the throne,
And ruleth all things well."

HYMN 228. 5,6.   Newton.
Newcastle. Devonshire.
I will trust. Isaiah xii. 2.
1 BEGONE, unbelief!
My Saviour is near;

And for my relief
Will surely appear:
By pray'r let me wrestle,
And he will perform
With Christ in the vessel,
I smile at the storm.

2 Determin'd to save,
He watch'd o'er my path,
When Satan's blind slave,
I sported with death:
And can he have taught me
To trust in his name,
And thus far have brought me
To put me to shame?

3 Why should I complain
Of want or distress,
Temptation or pain?
He told me no less:
The heirs of salvation,
I know from his word,
Through much tribulation,
Must follow the Lord.

4 Though dark be my way,
Since he is my guide,
'Tis mine to obey,
'Tis his to provide;
His way was much rougher,
And darker than mine
Did Jesus thus suffer,
And shall I repine?

5 His love, in time past,
Forbids me to think
He'll leave me at last
In trouble to sink:
Though painful at present,
'Twill cease before long,
And then, Oh, how pleasant
The conquerer's song!

HYMN 229. L. M.
Green's Hundredth. Islington.
True wisdom. Proverbs iii. 13.
1 HAPPY the man, who finds the grace,
The blessings of God's chosen race,
The wisdom coming from above,
And faith that sweetly works by love.

2 Her ways are ways of pleasantness,
And all her flow'ry paths are peace;
Wisdom to silver we prefer.
And gold is dross compar'd with her.

3 Happy the man who wisdom gains,
In whose obedient heart she reigns;
He owns, and will for ever own,
Wisdom and Christ, and heav'n are one.

*HYMN 230. C. M.   Newton
Mear. Abridge.
Zeal—true and false.
1 ZEAL is that pure and heav'nly flame,
The fire of love supplies;
While that which often bears the name,
Is self in a disguise.

2 True zeal is merciful and mild,
Can pity and forbear;
The false is headstrong, fierce and wild,
And breathes revenge and war.

3 While zeal for truth the Christian warms,
He knows the worth of peace;
But self contends for names and forms,
Its party to increase.

4 Zeal has attain'd its highest aim,
Its end is satisfy'd,
If sinners love the Saviour's name,
Nor seeks it aught beside.

5 But self, however well employ'd,
Has its own ends in view;
And says, as boasting Jehu cried,
"Come, see what I can do."

6 Dear Lord, the idol self dethrone,
And from our hearts remove:
And let no zeal by us be shown,
But that which springs from love.

CHRISTIAN.

HYMN 231. L. M.   Stennett.
Vanhall's Hymn. Leeds.
Warfare. Ephesians vi. 13-17.
1 JESUS, my King, proclaims the war;
"Awake, the powers of hell are near!
To arms, to arms!" I hear him cry,
"Tis yours to conquer or to die."

2 Rous'd by the animating sound,
I cast my eager eyes around
Make haste to gird my armor on,
And bid each trembling fear be gone.

3 Hope is my helmet, faith my shield,
The word of God the sword I wield:
With sacred truth my loins are girt,
And holy zeal inspires my heart.

4 Thus arm'd, I venture on the fight,
Resolv'd to put my foes to flight:
While Jesus kindly deigns to spread
His conq'ring banner o'er my head.

5 In him I hope, in him I trust;
His bleeding cross is all my boast;
Through troops of foes he'll lead me on
To vict'ry and the victor's crown.

HYMN 232. L. M.   Barbauld.
Truro. Blendon.
1 AWAKE, my soul lift up thine eyes;
See where thy foes against thee rise,
In long array, a num'rous host
Awake, my soul! or thou art lost.

2 See where rebellious passions rage,
And fierce desires and lusts engage;
The meanest foe of all that train
Has thousands and ten thousands slain.

3 Thou tread'st upon enchanted ground;
Perils and shares beset thee round
Beware of all, guard every part,
But most the traitor in thy heart.

4 Clad in the armor, from above,
Of heav'nly truth, and heav'nly love,
Come now, my soul, the charm repel,
And pow'rs of earth and pow'rs of hell.

HYMN 233. L. M. Cruttenden
Armley. Bath.
1 WHAT jarring natures dwell within,
Imperfect grace, remaining sin!
Nor this can reign, nor that prevail,
Though each by turns my heart assail.

2 Now I complain, and groan and die,—
Now raise my songs of triumph high;
Sing a rebellious passion slain,
Or mourn to feel it live again.

3 One happy hour beholds me rise,
Borne upward to my native skies
While faith assists my soaring flight
To realms of joy, and worlds of light.

4 Great God, assist me thro' the fight;
Make me triumphant in thy might;
Thou the desponding heart canst raise,
The vict'ry mine, and thine the praise.

*HYMN 234. C. M.   Stennett.
Windsor. Plymouth.
Indwelling sin lamented.
1 WITH tears of anguish I lament,
Here at thy feet, my God,
My passion, pride, and discontent,
And vile ingratitude.

2 Sure there was ne'er a heart so base,
So false as mine has been;
So faithless to its promises,
So prone to every sin.

3 How long, dear Saviour, shall I feel
These struggles in my breast?
When wilt thou bow my stubborn will,
And give my conscience rest?

4 Break, sov'reign grace, O break the charm,
And set the captive free:
Reveal, Almighty God, thine arm,
And haste to rescue me.

*HYMN 235. L. M.
Kingsbridge. Putney.
1 LORD, I'm defil'd in every part,
Barren my life, and cold my heart,
Yet sometimes thro' thy sov'reign grace,
I catch a glimpse at Jesus' face.

2 This gives my drowsy heart a spring,
I fain would rise, and fain would sing;
But soon a cloud rolls in between,
All black with some indwelling sin.

3 My notes then falter on my tongue,
The foul contagion spoils my song;
But Thou, who dost the world control,
Speak but the word—I shall be whole.

*HYMN 236. C. M.
Clarendon. Colchester.
Self- examination. 2 Corinthians xiii. 5.
1 'TIS first of all thyself to know,
To feel the plague of sin,
Expos'd to everlasting wo,
And nothing good within:

2 To know thy wretched sinful state,
Averse to all that's good;
To feel thy guilt exceeding great,
Thy heart oppos'd to God:

3 To know thy law-condemned case,
And own thy sentence just;
Thy heart subdu'd by sov'reign grace,
And humbled in the dust:

4 To know the pangs of pious grief,
For sins against the Lord;
To know that nought can give relief,
But trusting in his word

5 To know that thou art born of God,
Thy num'rous sins forgiven,
Thy soul redeem'd by Jesus' blood,
And thou an heir of heav'n.

HYMN 237. L. M. Pres. Davies.
Carthage. Kingsbridge.
1 AND what am I ?—My soul, awake,
And an impartial survey take:
Does no dark sign, no ground of fear,
In practice or in heart appear?

2 What image does my spirit bear!
Is Jesus form'd, and living there?
Say, do his lineaments divine
In thought, and, word, and action shine?

3 Searcher of hearts, O search me still;
The secrets of my soul reveal ;
Scatter the clouds which o'er my head
Thick glooms of dubious terrors spread.

4 May I at that blest world arrive,
Where Christ thro' all my soul shall live;
And give full proof that he is there,
Without one gloomy doubt of fear.

HYMN 238. 7s. Newton.
Montpelier. Finedon.
In darkness.
1 ONCE I thought my mountain strong,
Firmly fix'd no more to move;
Then my Saviour was my song,
Then my soul was fill'd with love;

Those were happy, golden days,
Sweetly spent in pray'r and praise.

2 Little then myself I knew,
Little thought of Satan's pow'r;
Now I feel my sins anew;
Now I feel the stormy hour!
Sin has put my joys to flight;
Sin has turn'd my day to night.

3 Saviour, shine and cheer my soul,
Bid my dying hopes revive;
Make my wounded spirit whole,
Far away the tempter drive;
Speak the word and set me free,
Let me live alone to thee.

HYMN 239. 8s.   Newton.
Lambeth. Uxbridge.
1 HOW tedious and tasteless the hours
When Jesus no longer I see!
Sweet prospects, sweet birds, and sweet flow'rs,
Have lost all their sweetness to me.

2 His name yields the richest perfume,
And sweeter than music his voice
His presence disperses my gloom,
And makes all within me rejoice.

3 Dear Lord, if indeed I am thine,
And thou art my sun and my song;
Say, why do I languish and pine,
And why are my winters so long?

4 Oh, drive these dark clouds from the sky
Thy soul-cheering presence restore,
Or take me up to thee on high,
Where winter and clouds are no more.

HYMN 240.   8, 7.
Love Divine. Tabernacle.
1 WHERE is now our boasted Saviour,
Where our rapture of delight?
Thou hast, Lord, withdrawn thy favor,
Thou art vanish'd from our sight,

Once thy blissful love we tasted,
Cheer'd by thee with living bread;
Oh, how short a time it lasted,
Oh, how soon the joy is fled!

2 Yet thou hast the cause unfolded,
Could we but the truth receive;
Thou in humbling love hast told it,
Needful 'tis for us to grieve—
Son of God, for thee we languish,
Still thy presence we bemoan,
Overwhelm'd with grief and anguish,
Poor, forsaken, and alone.

3 Stripp'd of that excess of pleasure,
Fondly we the loss deplore,
Till we find again our treasure,
Find, and never lose thee more.
Oh, cut short the night of mourning
May we glory in thy grace,
Triumph in thy full returning,
See again thy smiling face.

HYMN 241.   8s.   Toplady.
Bethany. Lambeth.
Faith fainting.
1 ENCOMPASS'D with clouds of distress,
Just ready all hope to resign,
I pant for the light of thy face,
And fear it will never be mine;
Dishearten'd with waiting so long,
I sink at thy feet with my load:
All-plaintive I pour out my song,
And stretch forth my hands unto God.

2 If sometimes I strive, as I mourn,
My hold on thy promise to keep,
The billows more fiercely return,
And plunge me again in the deep:
While harass'd and cast from thy sight,
The tempter suggests with a roar,
"The Lord has forsaken thee quite:
Thy God will be gracious no more."

3 Shine, Lord, and my terrors shall cease;
The blood of atonement apply;
And lead me to Jesus for peace,
The rock that is higher than I.
Almighty to rescue thou art;
Thy grace is my shield and my tow'r;
Come, succor and gladden my heart,
Let this be the day of thy pow'r.

HYMN 242.   L. M.   Watts.
Armley. Carthage. Warwick.
Forsaken, yet hoping.
1 HAPPY the hours, the golden days,
When I could call my Jesus mine
And sit, and view his smiling face,
And melt in pleasures all divine.

2 Near to my heart, within my arms
He lay, till sin defil'd my breast:
Till broken vows, and earthly charms,
Tir'd and provok'd my heav'nly guest.

3 But now he's gone, (0 mighty wo!)
Gone from my soul, and hides his love!
I hate the sins that griev'd him so;
The sins that forc'd him to remove.

*HYMN 243.   C. M.   Newton.
Canterbury. York.
O that I were as in months past. Job xxix. 2
1 SWEET was the time, when first I felt
The Saviour's pard'ning blood
Applied to cleanse my soul from guilt,
And bring me home to God.

2 Soon as the morn the light reveal'd,
His praises tun'd my tongue;
And when the ev'ning shades prevail'd,
His love was all my song.

3 In pray'r my soul drew near the Lord,
And saw his glory shine;
And when I read his holy word,
I call'd each promise mine.

4 But now when ev'ning shade prevails,
My soul in darkness mourns
And when the morn the light reveals,
No light to me returns.

5 My pray'rs are now an empty noise,
For Jesus hides his face
I read—the promise meets my eyes,
But will not reach my case.

6 Rise, Lord, now help me to prevail,
And make my soul thy care;
I know thy mercy cannot fail—
Let me that mercy share.

*HYMN 244.   L. M.   Newton
Portugal. Luton.
Prayer answered by crosses.
1 I ASK'D the Lord, that I might grow
In faith, and love, and every grace;
Might more of his salvation know,
And seek more earnestly his face.

2 'Twas he who taught me thus to pray,
And he, I trust, has answer'd pray'r;
But it has been in such a way,
As almost drove me to despair.

3 I hop'd that in some favor'd hour,
At once he'd answer my request;
And by his love's restraining pow'r,
Subdue my sins, and give me rest.

4 Instead of this, he made me feel
The hidden evils of my heart,
And let the angry pow'rs of hell
Assault my soul in ev'ry part.

5 Yea more, with his own hand he seem'd
Intent to aggravate my wo;
Cross'd all the fair designs I schem'd,
Blasted my hopes, and laid me low.

6 "Lord, why is this," I trembling cried,
"Wilt thou pursue thy worm to death?"

"'Tis in this way," the Lord replied,
"I answer pray'r for grace and faith:

7 "These inward trials I employ,
From self, and pride, to set thee free;
And break thy schemes of earthly joy,
That thou may'st seek thy all in me."

*HYMN 245.   C. M.
Elgin. Chapel.
Backsliding and returning.
1 HOW far, alas, in sinful ways,
How far from God I've gone;
And now I mourn in painful lays—
Ah! Lord, what have I done!

2 To sin and Satan's bold demand,
I was a willing prey;
He was not readier to command,
Than I was to obey.

3 Perchance the tempter left my heart,
Yet still his work went on;
I acted o'er his dreadful part—
Ah! Lord, what have I done!

4 Saviour, Almighty and divine,
I've slighted all thy charms;
Restore me from this sad decline,
Nor thrust me from thy arms.

HYMN 246.   C. M.
Wantage. Martyr's.
1 DEAR Jesus, let thy pitying eye
Call back a wand'ring sheep;
False to my vows, like Peter,
I would fain, like Peter, weep.

2 Now let me be by grace restor'd,
To me thy mercy shown;
Oh, turn and look upon me, Lord,
And break my heart of stone.

3 Almighty Prince, enthron'd above,
Repentance to impart,

Grant, through the greatness of thy love,
The humble, contrite heart.

4 Give, what I should have long implor'd,
A taste of love unknown;
Oh, turn and look upon me, Lord,
And break my heart of stone.

5 Behold me, Saviour, from above,
Nor suffer me to die;
For life, and happiness, and love,
Smile in thy gracious eye.

6 Speak but the reconciling word
Let mercy melt me down:
Oh, turn and look upon me, Lord,
And break my heart of stone.

HYMN 247. C. M. Newton.
Bangor. Wantage.
1 BLEST Saviour, by thy pow'rful word,
Once night was turn'd to day;
And thy salvation joy restor'd,
Which I had sinn'd away.

2 'Twas then I wonder'd and ador'd
To see thy grace divine;
I felt thy love, I prais'd the Lord,
Who made such blessings mine.

3 Wilt thou not still vouchsafe to own
A wretch so vile as I?
May I not still approach thy throne,
And, Abba Father, cry?

4 Lord, speak that gracious word again,
And cheer my drooping heart;
No voice but thine can sooth my pain,
Or bid my fears depart.

*HYMN 248. S. M. Beddome.
Orange. Wirksworth.
Luke xix. 41.
1 DID Christ o'er sinners weep?
And shall our cheeks be dry?

Let floods of penitential grief
Burst forth from ev'ry eye.

2 The Son of God in tears,
Angels with wonder see
Be thou astonish'd, O my soul
He shed those tears for thee.

3 He wept, that we might weep;
Each sin demands a tear:
In heav'n alone no sin is found,
And there's no weeping there.

HYMN 249.   7s.   Madan's Col.
Finedon. Bloxham. St. John's.
Adieu to the vain world.
1 WORLD, adieu! thou real cheat;
Oft have thy deceitful charms
Fill'd my heart with fond conceit,
Foolish hopes and false alarms:
Now I see, as clear as day,
How thy follies pass away.

2 Vain, thy entertaining sights;
False, thy promises renew'd;
All the pomp of thy delights
Does but flatter and delude:
Thee I quit for heav'n above,
Object of the noblest love.

3 Let not, Lord, my wand'ring mind
Follow after fleeting toys;
Since in thee alone I find
Solid and substantial joys:—
Joys that, never overpast,
Through eternity shall last.

*HYMN 250.   C. M.   Watts.
Wareham. Braintree.
1 HOW false this earth in all its forms,
How big with flatt'ring lies!
We seek to catch her airy charms,
And straight the phantom dies.

2 There's nothing round these painted skies,
Or on this earthly clod;
Nothing, my soul, that's worth thy joys,
Or lovely as thy God.

3 'Tis heav'n on earth to taste his love,
To feel his quick'ning grace:
And all the heav'n I hope above,
Is but to see his face.

4 No—'tis in vain to seek for bliss,
For bliss can ne'er be found,
Till we arrive where Jesus is,
And tread on heav'nly ground.

HYMN 251. L. M. Watts.
Blendon. Armley. Moreton.
1 DEAD be my heart to all below,
To mortal joys and mortal cares;
To sensual bliss that charms us so,
Be dark mine eyes and deaf mine ears.

2 All earthly joys are overweigh'd,
With mountains of vexatious care:
And where's the sweet that is not laid,
A bait to some destructive snare?

3 Lord, I renounce my carnal taste
Of the fair fruit that sinners prize;
Their Paradise shall never waste
One thought of mine, but to despise.

4 Come, heav'n, and fill my vast desires;
My soul pursues the sov'reign good:
She was all made of heav'nly fires,
Nor can she live on meaner food.

*HYMN 252. C. M. Stennett.
Clarendon. Braintree.
Psalm iv. 6.
1 IN vain the giddy world inquires—
Forgetful of their God—
"Who will supply our vast desires,
Or show us any good?"

2 Through the wide circuit of the earth,
Their eager wishes rove,
In chase of honor, wealth, and mirth,
The phantoms of their love.

3 But oft these shadowy joys elude
Their most intense pursuit;
Or, if they seize the fancied good,
There's poison in the fruit.

4 Lord, from this world call off my love.
Set my affections right;
Bid me aspire to joys above,
And walk no more by sight.

*HYMN 253.   L. M.   Watts.
Evening Hymn. Kingsbridge.
Parting with carnal joys.
1 SEND the joys of earth away;
Away, ye tempters of the mind,
False as the smooth deceitful sea,
And empty as the whistling wind.

2 Your streams were floating me along,
Down to the gulf of black despair;
And whilst I listen'd to your song,
Your streams had e'en convey'd me there.

3 Lord, I adore thy matchless grace,
That warn'd me of that dark abyss;
That drew me from those treach'rous seas,
And bade me seek superior bliss.

4 Now to the shining realms above,
I stretch my hands, and glance my eyes;
Oh, for the pinions of a dove,
To bear me to the upper skies.

HYMN 254.   C. M.   Steele.
Canterbury. Bedford.
A refuge from the storm. Deuteronomy xxxiii. 27.
1 DEAR refuge of my weary soul,
On thee, when sorrows rise,
On thee, when waves of trouble roll,
My fainting hope relies.

2 To thee I tell each rising grief,
For thou alone canst heal;
Thy word can bring a sweet relief
For every pain I feel.

3 But O! when gloomy doubts prevail,
I fear to call thee mine;
The springs of comfort seem to fail,
And all my hopes decline.

4 Yet, gracious God, where shall I flee?
Thou art my only trust;
And still my soul would cleave to thee,
Though prostrate in the dust.

HYMN 255. 7s.　　　　C. Wesley.
Hotham. Middleton.
1 JESUS, lover of my soul,
Let me to thy bosom fly,
While the billows near me roll,
While the tempest still is high;
Hide me, O my Saviour, hide,
Till the storm of life be past;
Safe into the haven guide,
Oh, receive my soul at last!

2 Other refuge have I none,
Lo! I, helpless, hang on thee:
Leave, Oh, leave me not alone,
Lest I basely shrink and flee:
Thou art all my trust and aid,
All my help from thee I bring;
Cover my defenceless head
With the shadow of thy wing!

3 Thou, O Christ, art all I want;
Boundless love in thee I find:
Raise the fallen, cheer the faint,
Heal the sick, and lead the blind.
Just and holy is thy name;
I am all unrighteousness,
Vile and full of sin I am;
Thou art full of truth and grace.

4 Plenteous grace with thee is found,
Grace to pardon all my sin;
Let the healing streams abound,
Make and keep me pure within.
Thou of life the fountain art,
Freely let me take of thee:
Reign, o Lord, within my heart,
Reign to all eternity.

HYMN 256.   L. M.   Stennett
Portugal. Sterling.
Our bodies God's temple. 1 Corinthians vi. 19
1 AND will th' offended God again
Return and dwell with sinful men?
Will he within this bosom raise
A living temple to his praise?

2 The joyful news transports my breast,
All hail! I cry, thou heav'nly guest!
Lift up your heads, ye pow'rs within,
And let the King of glory in.

3 Enter with all thy heav'nly train,
Here live, and here for ever reign;
Thy sceptre o'er my passions sway;
Let love command, and I'll obey.

4 Reason and conscience shall submit,
And pay their homage at thy feet;
To thee I'll consecrate my heart,
And bid each rival thence depart.

HYMN 257. L. M.
German. Armley. Kingsbridge.
Prayer for grace.
1 O THOU, to whose all-searching sight,
The darkness shineth as the light,
Search, prove my heart, and let it be
Freed from these bonds and join'd to thee.

2 Wash out its stains, refine its dross,
Nail my affections to the cross!
Hallow each thought; let all within
Be clean, as thou, my Lord, art clean.

3 If in this darksome wild I stray,
Be thou my light, be thou my way;
No foes, no violence I fear,
No fraud, while thou, my God, art near.

4 When rising floods my soul o'erflow,
When sinking deep in waves of wo,
Jesus, thy timely aid impart,
And raise my head, and cheer my heart.

5 Oh, let thy hand support me still,
And lead me to thy holy hill!
Where toil and grief, and pain shall cease,
Where all is calm, and all is peace.

HYMN 258. C. M.   Steele.
Plympton. Buckingham.
Pleasures unseen. 2 Corinthians iv. 18.
1 OH, could our thoughts and wishes fly,
Above these gloomy shades,
To those bright worlds beyond the sky,
Which sorrow ne'er invades!

2 There joys, unseen by mortal eyes,
Or reason's feeble ray,
In ever blooming prospects rise,
Unconscious of decay.

3 Lord, send a beam of light divine,
To guide our upper aim!
With one reviving touch of thine,
Our languid hearts inflame.

4 Then shall, on faith's sublimest wing,
Our ardent wishes rise
To those bright scenes, where pleasures spring,
Immortal in the skies.

*HYMN 259. S. M.   Heath.
Watchman. Cambridge.
Watch and pray. Matthew xxvi. 41.
1 MY soul, be on thy guard;
Ten thousand foes arise;
And hosts of sins are pressing hard,
To draw thee from the skies.

2 Oh, watch, and fight, and pray,
The battle ne'er give o'er,
Renew it boldly every day,
And help divine implore.

3 Ne'er think the vict'ry won,
Nor once at ease sit down:
The arduous work will not be done,
Till thou hast got thy crown.

HYMN 260. C. M. Steele.
Wantage. Windsor.
1 ALAS, what hourly dangers rise!
What snares beset my way
To heav'n, Oh, let me lift my eyes,
And hourly watch and pray.

2 O Lord, increase my faith and hope,
When foes and fears prevail;
And bear my fainting spirit up,
Or soon my strength will fail.

3 Oh, keep me in thy heav'nly way,
And bid the tempter flee;
And let me never, never stray
From happiness and thee.

HYMN 261. S. M.
Wirksworth. Berkley.
1 SAVIOUR, we wait the day,
The awful day unknown,
To quit our house, this tent of clay,
And lay our bodies down.

2 Come, and our souls prepare
For such a solemn day;
And fill us now with watchful care,
And stir us up to pray—

3 Oh, may we all ensure
A lot among the blest;
And watch a moment to secure
An everlasting rest.

HYMN 262. L. M.   Watts.
Richmond. Bicester. Leyden.
Crucifixion to the world. Galatians vi. 14.
1 WHEN I survey the wond'rous cross,
On which the prince of glory died,
My richest gain I count but loss,
And, mourning, weep o'er all my pride.

2 Forbid it, Lord, that I should boast,
Save in the death of Christ, my God
All the vain things that charm me most,
I sacrifice them to his blood.

3 See, from his head, his hands, his feet,
Sorrow and love flow mingled down!
Did e'er such love and sorrow meet;
Or thorns compose so rich a crown?

4 Were the whole realm of nature mine,
That were a present far too small;
Love, so amazing, so divine,
Demands my soul, my life, my all.

HYMN 263. L. M.   Newton.
Virginia. Surry Kingsbridge.
1 WHEN I the blest Redeemer see,
All bleeding on th' accursed tree;
Satan and sin no more can move,
For I am all transformed to love.

2 His thorns and nails pierce thro' my heart,
In ev'ry groan I hear a part;
I view his wounds with streaming eyes;
But see! he bows his head and dies!

3 Come, sinners, view the Lamb of God,
Wounded and dead, and bath'd in blood;
Behold his side, and venture near—
The spring of endless life is here.

4 Here I forget my cares and pains;
I drink, yet still my thirst remains;
Only the fountain head above
Can satisfy the thirst of love.

*HYMN 264.   C. M.   Newton.
New Cambridge. Rochester.
Christ precious. 1 Peter ii. 7.
1 HOW sweet the name of Jesus sounds
In a believer's ear!
It sooths his sorrows, heals his wounds,
And drives away his fear.

2 It makes the wounded spirit whole,
And calms the troubled breast;
'Tis manna to the hungry soul,
And to the weary, rest.

3 By him, my pray'rs acceptance gain,
Although with sin defil'd;
Satan accuses me in vain,
And I am own'd a child.

4 Weak is the effort of my heart,
And cold my warmest thought
But when I see thee as thou art,
I'll praise thee as I ought.

5 Till then, I would thy love proclaim,
With every fleeting breath;
And may the music of thy name
Refresh my soul in death.

HYMN 265. 8, 7.   Robinson.
Love Divine. Tabernacle.
Sitting at Jesus' feet.
1 SWEET the moments, rich in blessing,
Which before the cross I spend;
Life, and health, and peace possessing,
From the sinner's dying Friend
Love and grief my heart dividing,
With my tears his feet I'll bathe;
Constant still in faith abiding,
Life deriving from his death.

2 Truly blessed is this station—
Low before his cross I'll lie;
While I see divine compassion
Floating in his languid eye;

Here I'll sit—for ever viewing
Mercy streaming in his blood:
Precious drops, my soul bedewing,
Plead and claim my peace with God.

*HYMN 266.   L. M.   Fawcett.
Armley. Warwick.
The Christian Pilgrim. Deuteronomy viii. 2.
1 THROUGH this wide wilderness I roam,
Far distant from my blissful home;
My earthly joys are from me torn,
And oft an absent God I mourn.

2 My soul with various tempests toss'd,
Her fairest hopes and projects cross'd,
Sees ev'ry day new straits attend,
And wonders where the scene will end.

3 Is this, dear Lord, that thorny road,
Which leads us to the mount of God?—
Are these the toils thy people know,
While in the wilderness below?

4 'Tis even so—thy faithful love
Doth all thy children's graces prove;
'Tis thus our pride and self must fall,
That Jesus may be all in all.

*HYMN 267.   C. M.
Walsal. Standish.
Hebrews xii. 22-24.
1 CHILDREN of God, who, trav'ling slow,
Your pilgrim path pursue,
In strength, and weakness, joy and wo,
To God's high calling true;—

2 Why move ye thus with ling'ring tread,
A doubtful, mournful band?
Why faintly hangs the drooping head?
Why fails the feeble hand?

3 Was the full orb that rose in light
To cheer your early way,
A treach'rous meteor, falsely bright,
That blaz'd, and pass'd away?

4 Was the rich vale that proudly shone
Beneath the morning beam,
A soft illusion, swiftly gone—
A fair and faithless dream?

5 Oh! weak to know a Saviour's pow'r,
To feel a father's care:
A moment's toil, a passing show'r,
Is all the grief ye share.

*HYMN 268.   C. M.   Part II.
Keene. Abridge.
1 THE Lord of light, though veil'd awhile
He hide his noon tide ray,
Shall soon in lovelier beauty smile
To gild the closing day:

2 And, bursting thro' the dusky shroud
That dar'd his pow'r invest,
Ride thron'd in light o'er every cloud,
Triumphant to his rest:

3 And there, beneath his beam renew'd,
That glorious vale shall shine,
So long by trembling hope pursu'd,
And now for ever thine.

4 Then, Christian, dry the falling tear;
The faithless doubt remove;
Redeem'd at last from guilt and fear,
Oh! wake thy heart to love.

*HYMN 269.   L. M.   Newton.
Bath. Kent
1 AS when the weary trav'ler gains
The height of some o'erlooking hill,
His heart revives, if, cross the plains,
He eyes his home though distant still;

2 So when the Christian pilgrim views,
By faith his mansion in the skies;
The sight his fainting strength renews,
And wings his speed to reach the prize.

3 'Tis there, he says, I am to dwell,
With Jesus in the realms of day:
Then I shall bid my cares farewell,
And he will wipe my tears away.

HYMN 270.   7s.
Condolence. Hotham.
1 PILGRIM, burden'd with thy sin,
Haste to Zion's gate to-day;
There, till mercy let thee in,
Knock, and weep, and watch, and pray.

2 Knock—for mercy lends an ear;
Weep—she marks the sinner's sigh;
Watch—till heavenly light appear;
Pray—she hears the mourner's cry.

3 Mourning Pilgrim! what for thee
In this world can now remain?
Seek that world from which shall flee
Sorrow, shame, and tears and pain.

4 Sorrow shall for ever fly;
Shame shall never enter there;
Tears be wip'd from every eye;
Pain in endless bliss expire.

HYMN 271.   L. M.
Kent. Clarendon.
In thy light shall we see light. Psalm xxxvi. 9.
1 FOUNTAIN of light, whose copious stream
Supplies the sun with every beam;
Night fades before thy kindling ray,
Till all within is perfect day.

2 A beam of life and light impart,
To quicken and to warm my heart,
And bid the lucid current roll,
Through all the channels of the soul;—

3 Till to its source above the skies,
The tributary stream shall rise;
And, ceasing in this world to be,
Rejoice to lose itself in thee.

HYMN 272.   7, 6.   Newton.
Fairfax. Margate.
1 SOMETIMES a light surprises
The Christian while he sings;
It is the Lord who rises,
With healing on his wings;
When comforts are declining,
He grants the soul again
A season of clear shining,
To cheer it after rain.

2 In holy contemplation,
We sweetly then pursue
The theme of God's salvation,
And find it ever new:
Set free from present sorrow,
We cheerfully can say,
Let the unknown to-morrow
Bring with it what it may.

3 It can bring with it nothing,
But he will bear us through,—
Who gives the lilies clothing,
Will clothe his people too:
Beneath the spreading heavens,
No creature but is fed;
And he who feeds the ravens,
Will give his children bread.

4 Though vine nor fig-tree neither,
Their wonted fruit should bear,
Though all the fields should wither,
Nor flocks nor herds be there;
Yet God the same abiding,
His praise shall tune my voice;
For while in him confiding,
I cannot but rejoice.

*HYMN 273.   C. M.   Watts.
Stade. Abridge.
1 O HAPPY soul, that lives on high,
While men lie grov'ling here!
His hopes are fix'd above the sky,
And faith forbids his fear.

2 His conscience knows no secret stings,
While grace and joy combine,
To form a life whose holy springs
Are hidden and divine.

3 He waits in secret on his God,
His God in secret sees;
Let earth be all in arms abroad,
He dwells in heav'nly peace.

4 His pleasures rise from things unseen,
Beyond this world of time,
Where neither eyes nor ears have been,
Nor thoughts of mortals climb.

5 He wants no pomp nor royal throne,
To raise his figure here,
Content and pleas'd to live alone,
Till Christ his life appear.

HYMN 274.   C. M.   Watts.
Edinburgh. Canterbury.
The hope of heaven our support.
1 WHEN I can read my title clear
To mansions in the skies,
I bid farewell to every fear,
And wipe my weeping eyes.

2 Should earth against my soul engage,
And hellish darts be hurl'd,
Then I can smile at Satan's rage,
And face a frowning world.

3 Let cares, like a wild deluge come,
And storms of sorrow fall;
May I but safely reach my home,
My God, my heav'n, my all;

4 There shall I bathe my weary soul
In seas of heav'nly rest;
And not a wave of trouble roll
Across my peaceful breast.

*HYMN 275.   C. M.   Doddridge.
Clifford. York. Braintree.
The fear of God. Proverbs xxiii. 17.
1 THRICE happy souls, who, born of heav'n,
While yet they sojourn here,
Humbly begin their days with God,
And spend them in his fear.

2 So may our eyes with holy zeal
Prevent the dawning day;
And turn the sacred pages o'er,
And praise thy name and pray.

3 Midst hourly cares may love present
Its incense to thy throne;
And, while the world our hands employs,
Our hearts be thine alone.

4 At night we lean our weary heads
On thy paternal breast;
And, safely folded in thine arms,
Resign our powers to rest.

5 In solid, pure delights, like these,
Let all my days be past;
Nor shall I then impatient wish,
Nor shall I fear the last.

HYMN 276.   8, 7,4.   Robinson.
Tamworth. Littleton. Helmsley.
The Pilgrim's Guide. Psalm xlviii. 14.
1 GUIDE me, O thou great Jehovah,
Pilgrim, through this barren land;
I am weak, but thou art mighty,
Hold me with thy powerful hand:
Bread of heaven, Feed me till I want no more.

2 Open thou the crystal fountain,
Whence the healing streams do flow:
Let the fiery, cloudy pillar
Lead me all my journey through:
Strong Deliv'rer,
Be thou still my strength and shield.

3 When I tread the verge of Jordan,
Bid my anxious fears subside;
Death of death, and hell's destruction,
Land me safe on Canaan's side:
Songs of praises
I will ever give to thee.

HYMN 277.　　7, 6.　　Whitefield.
Amsterdam. Hymn 5th.
Pilgrim's Song.
1 RISE, my soul, and stretch thy wings,
Thy better portion trace;
Rise from transitory things,
Tow'rds heav'n, thy native place.
Sun, and moon, and stars decay—
Time shall soon this earth remove,
Rise, my soul, and haste away
To seats prepar'd above.

2 Rivers to the ocean run,
Nor stay in all their course:
Fires ascending seek the sun,
Both speed them to their source;
So a soul that's born of God,
Pants to view his glorious face;
Upward tends to his abode,
To rest in his embrace.

3 Fly me riches, fly me cares,
While I that coast explore,
Flatt'ring world, with all thy snares,
Solicit me no more.
Pilgrims fix not here their home,
Strangers tarry but a night;
When the last dear morn is come,
They'll rise to joyful light.

4 Cease, ye pilgrims, cease to mourn,
Press onward to the prize;
Soon the Saviour will return,
Triumphant in the skies:
There we'll join the heav'nly train,
Welcom'd to partake the bliss;
Fly from sorrow and from pain,
To realms of endless peace.

*HYMN 278.   L. M.   Gibbons.
Hinton. Blendon. Shoel.
Rising to God.
1 NOW let our souls, on wings sublime,
Rise from the vanities of time
Draw back the parting veil, and see
The glories of eternity.

2 Born by a new celestial birth,
Why should we grovel here on earth?
Why grasp at transitory toys,
So near to heaven's eternal joys?

3 Shall aught beguile us on the road,
When we are walking back to God?
For, strangers, into life we come,
And dying is but going home.

4 Welcome, sweet hour of full discharge,
That sets our longing souls at large;
Unbinds our chains, breaks up our cell,
And gives us with our God to dwell.

5 To dwell with God, to feel his love,
Is the full heav'n enjoy'd above;
And the sweet expectation now
Is the young dawn of heav'n below.

WORSHIP.

HYMN 279.   C. M.   Doddridge.
Windsor. Wantage.
Private devotion. Matthew vi. 6.
1 FATHER Divine, thy piercing eye
Sees through the darkest night,
In deep retirement thou art nigh,
With heart-discerning sight.

2 There may thy piercing eye survey
My solemn homage paid,
With ev'ry morning's dawning ray,
And ev'ry evening's shade.

3 Oh, let thy own celestial fire
The incense still inflame;
While my warm vows to thee aspire,
Through my Redeemer's name.

4 So shall the visits of thy love
My soul in secret bless;
So shalt thou deign in worlds above,
Thy suppliant to confess.

HYMN 280.　　L. M.　　Doddridge.
Gouldbourn. Cumberland.
1 RETURN, my roving heart, return,
And chase these shadowy forms no more;
Seek out some solitude to mourn,
And thy forsaken God implore.

2 Wisdom and pleasure dwell at home:
Retir'd and silent seek them there:
This is the way to overcome—
The way to break the tempter's snare.

3 O thou, great God, whose piercing eye
Distinctly marks each deep recess,
In these sequester'd hours draw nigh,
And with thy presence fill the place.

4 Through all the windings of my heart,
My search let heav'nly wisdom guide,
And still its radiant beams impart,
Till all be search'd and purified.

5 Then, with the visits of thy love,
Vouchsafe my inmost soul to cheer;
Till ev'ry grace shall join to prove,
That God hath fix'd his dwelling there.

HYMN 281.　　C. M.　　Williams.
Retirement. Clarendon.
1 WHILST thee I seek, protecting Power!
Be my vain wishes still'd;
And may this consecrated hour
With better hopes be fill'd.

2 Thy love the pow'r of thought bestow'd,
To thee my thoughts would soar:
Thy mercy o'er my life has flow'd;
That mercy I adore.

3 In each event of life, how clear
Thy ruling hand I see!
Each blessing to my soul most dear,
Because conferr'd by thee.

4 In every joy that crowns my days,
In every pain I bear,
My heart shall find delight in praise,
Or seek relief in prayer.

5 When gladness wings my favor'd hour,
Thy love my thoughts shall fill:
Resign'd, when storms of sorrow low'r,
My soul shall meet thy will.

6 My lifted eye, without a tear,
The gath'ring storm shall see;
My steadfast heart shall know no fear;
That heart will rest on thee.

HYMN 282.   C. M.   Cowper.
Springfield. Chapel.
1 FAR from the world, O Lord, I flee,
From strife and tumult far;
From scenes where Satan wages still
His most successful war.

2. The calm retreat, the silent shade,
With pray'r and praise agree:
And seem by thy sweet bounty made,
For those who follow thee.

3 Then if thy Spirit touch the soul,
And grace her mean abode,
Oh, with what peace and joy and love,
She there communes with God!

4 There, like the nightingale, she pours
Her solitary lays;

Nor asks a witness of her song,
Nor thirsts for human praise.

HYMN 283.   C. M.   Steele.
St. Mary's. Walsal.
The request.
1 FATHER, whate'er of earthly bliss,
Thy sov'reign will denies,
Accepted at thy throne of grace,
Let this petition rise:—

2 "Give me a calm, a thankful heart,
From ev'ry murmur free;
The blessings of thy grace impart,
And make me live to thee.

3 "Let the sweet hope that I am thine,
My life and death attend;
Thy presence through my journey shine,
And crown my journey's end."

HYMN 284.   C. M.
Clarendon. Newmark.
1 COME, Holy Ghost, my soul inspire—
This one great gift impart—
What most I need—and most desire,
A humble, holy heart.

2 Bear witness that I'm born again,
My many sins forgiv'n:
Nor let a gloomy doubt remain
To cloud my hope of heav'n.

3 More of myself grant I may know,
From sin's deceit be free,
In all the Christian graces grow,
And live alone to thee.

*HYMN 285.   C. M.   B.
Barby. Plymouth.
Evening twilight.
1 I LOVE to steal awhile away
From every cumb'ring care,
And spend the hours of setting day,
In humble, grateful prayer.

2 I love in solitude to shed
The penitential tear,
And all His promises to plead,
Where none but God can hear.

3 I love to think on mercies past,
And future good implore,
And all my care and sorrows cast
On him whom I adore.

4 I love by faith to take a view
Of brighter scenes in heav'n;
The prospect doth my strength renew
While here by tempests driv'n.

5 Thus, when life's toilsome day is o'er,
May its departing ray
Be calm as this impressive hour,
And lead to endless day.

*HYMN 286.   L. M.   Cowper.
Armley. Bath.
Social prayer.
1 WHAT various hind'rances we meet,
In coming to a mercy-seat!
Yet who that knows the worth of pray'r,
But wishes to be often there.

2 Pray'r makes the darken'd cloud withdraw;
Pray'r climbs the ladder Jacob saw—
Gives exercise to faith and love—
Brings every blessing from above.

3 Restraining pray'r—we cease to fight;
Pray'r makes the Christian's armor bright;
And Satan trembles when he sees
The weakest saint upon his knees.

4 Have you no words?—Ah, think again;
Words flow apace when you complain,
And fill your fellow-creature's ear,
With the sad tale of all your care.

5 Were half the breath thus vainly spent,
To heav'n in supplication sent—
Your cheerful song would oft'ner be,
"Hear what the Lord hath done for me."

HYMN 287.   S. M.   Newton.
Durham. St. Thomas.
Importunate. Luke xviii. 1-7.
1 JESUS, who knows full well
The heart of every saint,
Invites us all our griefs to tell,
To pray, and never faint.

2 He bows his gracious ear—
We never plead in vain;
Then let us wait till he appear,
And pray, and pray again.

3 Though unbelief suggest,
"Why should we longer wait?"
He bids us never give him rest,
But knock at mercy's gate.

4 Jesus, the Lord, will hear
His chosen when they cry;
Yes, though he may a while forbear,
He'll help them from on high.

5 Then let us earnest cry,
And never faint in pray'r:
He sees, he hears, and from on high,
Will make our cause his care.

HYMN 288.   C. M.   Montgomery.
Clarendon. Brighton.
Behold he prayeth. Acts ix. 11.
1 PRAY'R is the soul's sincere desire,
Unutter'd or express'd,
The motion of a hidden fire
That trembles in the breast.

2 Pray'r is the burden of a sigh,
The falling of a tear;
The upward glancing of an eye,
When none but God is near.

3 Pray'r is the simplest form of speech
That infant lips can try;
Pray'r the sublimest strains that reach
The majesty on high.

4 Pray'r is the Christian's vital breath,
The Christian's native air,
His watchword at the gate of death—
He enters heav'n with pray'r.

5 Pray'r is the contrite sinner's voice
Returning from his ways,
While angels in their songs rejoice,
And say,—" Behold he prays."

*HYMN 289.   L M.   Hart.
Bath. Blendon.
Pray without ceasing. 1 Thessalonians v. 17.
1 PRAY'R was appointed to convey
The blessings God designs to give;
Long as they live should Christians pray,
For only while they pray they live.

2 If pain afflict, or wrongs oppress—
If cares distract or fears dismay—
If guilt deject—if sin distress,
The remedy's before thee—pray.

3 'Tis pray'r supports the soul that's weak;
Tho' thought be broken—language lame;
Pray, if thou canst, or canst not speak,
But pray with faith in Jesus' name.

HYMN 290.   L. M.   Doddridge.
Truro. Bath.
Family worship. Genesis xviii. 19.
1 FATHER of all, thy care we bless,
Which crowns our families with peace;
From thee they spring, and by thy hand,
They have been, and are still sustain'd.

2 To God, most worthy to be prais'd,
Be our domestic altars rais'd;
Who, Lord of heav'n, scorns not to dwell
With saints, in their obscurest cell.

3 To thee may each united house,
Morning and night present its vows;
Our servants there, and rising race,
Be taught thy precepts and thy grace.

4 Oh, may each future age proclaim
The honors of thy glorious name;
While pleas'd and thankful, we remove
To join the family above.

*HYMN 291.   S. M.   Hoskins.
Maryland. Little Marlboro'.
Formal.   Job xxvii. 8.
1 RELIGION'S form is vain,
While we deny its power!
What will the hypocrite obtain,
In death's tremendous hour?

2 Now he may credit gain,
And in his affluence roll;
But all his profit will be pain,
When God shall take his soul.

3 Then, O what dread surprise,
What horror and dismay,
When death shall open wide his eyes,
And tear his mask away!

4 Lord, search and know my heart,
And make my soul sincere;
And bid hypocrisy depart,
And keep my conscience clear.

HYMN 292.   C. M.   Doddridge.
Abridge. Christmas.
Ministers watch for souls.   Hebrews xiii. 17.
1 LET Zion's watchmen all awake,
And take th' alarm they give;
Now let them, from the mouth of God,
Their awful charge receive.

2 'Tis not a cause of small import
The pastor's care demands;
But what might fill an angel's heart—
It fill'd a Saviour's hands.

3 They watch for souls, for which the Lord
Did heav'nly bliss forego;—
For souls, which must for ever live,
In raptures, or in wo.

4 May they that Jesus, whom they preach
Their own Redeemer, see;
And watch thou daily o'er their souls,
That they may watch for Thee.

HYMN 293.   H. M.   Doddridge.
Bethesda. Eagle Street.
A sweet savor. 2 Corinthians ii. 15, 16.
1 PRAISE to the Lord on high,
Who spreads his triumphs wide!
While Jesus' fragrant name
Is breath'd on every side:
Balmy and rich the odours rise,
And fill the earth, and reach the skies.

2 Ten thousand dying souls
Its influence feel—and live;
Sweeter than vital air
The incense they receive:
They breathe anew, and rise and sing
Jesus, the Lord, their conq'ring King.

3 But sinners scorn the grace,
That brings salvation nigh:
They turn their face away,
And faint, and fall, and die.
So sad a doom, ye saints, deplore—
For Oh! they fall to rise no more.

HYMN 294. 8, 7, 4.   Kelly.
Tamworth. Helmsley.
Cry aloud. Isaiah lviii. 1.
1 MEN of God, go take your stations;
Darkness reigns throughout the earth;
Go, proclaim among the nations,
Joyful news of heav'nly birth;
Bear the tidings
Of the Saviour's matchless worth.

2 What though earth and hell united,
Should oppose the Saviour's plan?
Plead his cause, nor be affrighted:
Fear ye not the face of man:
Vain their tumult,
Stop his work they never can.

3 When expos'd to fearful dangers,
Jesus will his own defend
Borne afar 'midst foes and strangers,
Jesus will appear your friend:
And his presence
Shall he with you to the end

HYMN 295. L. M.
Carthage. Armley.
Prayer for a sick Minister.
1 O THOU, before whose gracious throne,
We bow our suppliant spirits down;
Avert thy swift descending stroke,
Nor smite the shepherd of the flock.

2 Restore him, sinking to the grave;
Stretch out thine arm, make haste to save;
Back to our hopes and wishes give,
And bid our friend and father live.

3 Bound to each soul by tend'rest ties,
In every breast his image lies;
Thy pitying aid, O God, impart,
Nor rend him from each bleeding heart.

4 Yet, if our supplications fail,
And pray'rs and tears cannot prevail;
Be thou his strength, be thou his stay,
And guide him safe to endless day.

HYMN 296. C. M. Doddridge.
Buckingham. Plympton

Comfort under the loss of Ministers.
1 WHAT—tho' the arm of conquering death
Does God's own house invade;
What—though the Prophet and the Priest
Be number'd with the dead!

2 Though earthly shepherds dwell in dust,
The aged and the young;
The watchful eye in darkness clos'd,
And mute th' instructive tongue

3 Th' *Eternal Shepherd* still survives,
New comforts to impart;
His eye still guides us, and his voice
Still animates our heart.

4 Then let our drooping hearts revive,
And all our tears be dry;
Why should those eyes be drown'd in grief,
Which view a Saviour nigh?

HYMN 297. S. M.   Dwight.
Shirland. Watchman.
Love to the Church
1 I LOVE thy kingdom, Lord,
The house of thine abode,
The church our blest Redeemer sav'd,
With his own precious blood.

2 If e'er to bless thy sons,
My voice, or hands deny,
These hands let useful skill forsake,
This voice in silence die.

3 If e'er my heart forget
Her welfare, or her wo,
Let every joy this heart forsake,
And every grief o'erflow.

4 For her my tears shall fail;
For her my prayers ascend;
To her my cares and toils be giv'n,
Till toils and cares shall end.

*HYMN 298. 8, 7.   Newton.
Sicilian Hymn. Northampton Chapel.
Declension lamented.
1 ONCE, O Lord, thy garden flourish'd,
Ev'ry part look'd gay and green;
Then thy word our spirits nourish'd,
Happy seasons we have seen!—

2 But a drought has since succeeded,
And a sad decline we see;
Lord, thy help is greatly needed,
Help can only come from thee.

3 Some, in whom we once delighted,
We shall meet no more below;
Some, alas! we fear are blighted,
Scarce a single leaf they show.

4 Dearest Saviour, hasten hither,
Thou canst make them bloom again.;
Oh, permit them not to wither,
Let not all our hopes be vain!

HYMN 299. L. M.
Leeds. St. Catherine's.
1 O SUN of Righteousness divine,
On us with beams of mercy shine,
Chase the dark clouds of guilt away,
And turn our darkness into day.

2 While mourning o'er our guilt and shame,
And asking mercy in thy name,
Dear Saviour, cleanse us with thy blood,
And be our Advocate with God.

3 Sustain, when sinking in distress,
And guide us through this wilderness;
Teach our low thoughts from earth to rise,
And lead us onward to the skies.

*HYMN 300. C. M.
Colchester. Clarendon.
Isaiah liii. 1.
1 HOW few the word of God regard,
Or seek their Maker's face!
In vain the gospel is proclaim'd,
If not enforc'd by grace.

2 Almighty God, exert thy power,
And melt the stony breast;
Then shall thy justice be ador'd,
Thy mercy stand confess'd.

3 The scorner then shall mourn in dust,
And put his sins away;
No more resist his Maker's hands,
But lift his own to pray.

HYMN 301. L. P. M.
Eaton. St. Helen's.
1 LOST in a labyrinth of sin,
Long have we wander'd to and fro,
The wilderness hath shut us in,
And only faith the way can show;
And only pray'r can lend the clue,
And guide our weary footsteps through.

2 Jesus, thou sov'reign Lord of all,
The same through one eternal day,
Attend thy feeble followers' call,
And Oh, instruct us how to pray:
Pour out the supplicating grace,
And stir us up to seek thy face.

HYMN 302. C. M. Kelly.
Arlington. Bray.
Amos vii. 2.
1 BY whom shall Jacob now arise?
For Jacob's friends are few
And, what should fill us with surprise,
They seem divided too.

2 By whom shall Jacob now arise?
For Jacob's foes are strong,
I read their triumph in their eyes,
They think he'll fall ere long.

3 By whom shall Jacob now arise?
Can any tell by whom?
Say, shall this branch that wither'd lies,
Again revive and bloom?

4 Lord, thou canst tell—the work is thine,
The help of man is vain—
On Jacob now arise and shine,
And he shall live again.

HYMN 303. L. M. Hyde.
Moreton. Bath. Chatham
Prayer for the children of the Church.
1 DEAR Saviour, if these lambs should stray,
From thy secure enclosure's bound,
And, lur'd by worldly joys away,
Among the thoughtless crowd be found;

2 Remember still that they are thine,
That thy dear sacred name they bear,
Think that the seal of love divine,—
The sign of cov'nant grace they wear,

3 In all their erring, sinful years,
Oh, let them ne'er forgotten be;
Remember all the pray'rs and tears,
Which made them consecrate to thee.

4 And when these lips no more can pray,
These eyes can weep for them no more,
Turn thou their feet from folly's way,
The wand'rers to thy fold restore.

*HYMN 304. L. M. Newton.
Bath. Armley.
Wheat and tares. Matthew xiii. 37-42.
1 THOUGH in the earthly church below,
The wheat and tares together grow;
Jesus ere long will weed the crop,
And pluck the tares in anger up.

2 Will it relieve their horrors there,
To recollect their stations here?
How much they heard how much they knew,
How long among the wheat they grew!

3 Oh! this will aggravate their case!
They perish under means of grace;
To them the word of life and faith
Became an instrument of death.

4 We seem alike when thus we meet,—
Strangers might think we all were wheat;
But to the Lord's all-searching eyes,
Each heart appears without disguise.

5 The tares are spar'd for various ends,
Some for the sake of praying friends;
Others, the Lord against their will,
Employs his counsel to fulfil.

6 But though they grow so tall and strong,
His plan will not require them long;
 In harvest when he saves his own,
The tares shall into hell be thrown.

HYMN 305. 8, 7, 4.   Newton.
Jordan. Littleton.
Prayer for a Revival. Psalm lxxxv. 37
1 SAVIOUR, visit thy plantation:
Grant us, Lord, a gracious rain!
All will come to desolation,
Unless thou return again.
Lord, revive us;
All our help must come from thee.

2 Keep no longer at a distance;
Shine upon us from on high,
Lest, for want of thine assistance,
Every plant should droop and die.

3 Let our mutual love be fervent,
Make us prevalent in pray'rs;
Let each one esteem'd thy servant,
Shun the world's bewitching snares.

4 Break the tempter's fatal power;
Turn the stony heart to flesh;
And begin from this good hour
To revive thy work afresh.

HYMN 306. L. M. Doddridge.
Derby. Carthage. Darwent
Ezekiel xxxvi. 37.
1 COME, sacred Spirit, from above,
And fill the coldest heart with love;
Soften to flesh the flinty stone,
And let thy godlike pow'r be known.

2 Speak, Thou, and from the haughtiest eyes,
Shall floods of pious sorrow rise;
While all their glowing souls are borne,
To seek that grace which now they scorn.

3 Oh, let a holy flock await,
Num'rous around thy temple gate,
Each pressing on with zeal to be,
A living sacrifice to thee.

4 In answer to our fervent cries,
Give us to see thy church arise;
Or, if that blessing seem too great,
Give us to mourn its low estate.

HYMN 307. L. M.
Chatham. New Hundredth.
1 AS in soft silence, vernal show'rs
Descend and cheer the fainting flow'rs;
So in the secrecy of love,
Falls the sweet influ'nce from above.

2 May we this heav'nly influ'nce find,
In holy silence of the mind,
And every grace maintain its bloom,
Diffusing wide the rich perfume:

3 And lands beneath the burning sky,
Which now are desolate and dry,
Ere long the blest effusions share,
And sudden greens and herbage wear.

HYMN 308. L. M. Doddridge.
Limerick. Darwent. Armley.
Beholding transgressors. Psalm cxix. 158.
1 SEE human nature sunk in shame;
See scandals pour'd on Jesus' name;
The Father wounded through the Son;
The world abus'd, the soul undone.

2 See the short course of vain delight,
Closing in everlasting night;
In flames that no abatement know,
Kindled by sin the source of wo.

3 My God, I feel the mournful scene;
My bowels yearn o'er dying men;
And fain my pity would reclaim,
And snatch the fire-brands from the flame.

4 But feeble my compassion proves,
And can but weep where most it loves;
Thy own all-saving arm employ,
And turn these drops of grief to joy.

HYMN 309. L. M. Doddridge.
Geneva. Green's Hundredth.
Vision of the dry bones. Ezekiel xxxvii. 3.
1 LOOK down, O Lord, with pitying eye,
See Adam's race in ruin lie;
Sin spreads its trophies o'er the ground,
And scatters slaughter'd heaps around.

2 And can these mould'ring corpses live ?
And can these perish'd bones revive?
That, mighty God, to thee is known;
That wondrous work is all thine own.

3 Thy ministers are sent in vain,
To prophesy upon the slain;
In vain they call, in vain they cry.
Till thine almighty aid is nigh.

4 But if thy Spirit deign to breathe,
Life spreads thro' all the realms of death:
Dry bones obey thy pow'rful voice;
They move—they waken—they rejoice.

HYMN 310. C. M. Davis.
Braintree. Barby. Rochester.
As the Rain, &c. Isaiah lv. 10, 11.
1 BEHOLD the genial showers descend
Upon the fruitful field;
What blessings in their train attend,
What kind effects they yield.

2 'Tis God himself the ground prepares.
His Spirit sows the land;
And ev'ry pleasant fruit it bears,
Is nurtur'd by his hand.

3 In vain the husbandman would toil,
And scatter seed in vain;
Did not the Lord refresh the soil,
With gentle show'rs of rain.

4 Spirit of influence! now descend
Like rain upon the ground!
Through the wide world the gospel send,
And make its fruits abound.

HYMN 311. L. M.
Luther's Hymn. Nantwich.
1 O SUN of Righteousness, arise,
With gentle beams on Zion shine;
Dispel the darkness from our eyes,
And souls awake to life divine.

2 On all around let grace descend,
 Like heav'nly dew, or copious show'rs,
That we may call our God our friend
That we may hail salvation ours.

HYMN 312. H. M. Scott.
Allerton. Eagle Street. Weymoutb.
1 GIRD on, great God, thy sword,
Ascend thy conq'ring car,
While justice, truth, and love,
Maintain the holy war;
Victorious thou, thy foes shalt tread,
And sin and hell in triumph lead.

2 Make bare thy potent arm,
And wing th' unerring dart,
With salutary pangs,
To each rebellious heart;
Then dying souls for life shall sue,
 Num'rous as drops of morning dew.

3 Then shall the spacious earth
Beneath thy sceptre bend;
And peace her olive-branch,
And balmy wings extend:
The dews of heav'n enrich the ground,
And Paradise shall bloom around.

HYMN 313. L. M. Strong.
Kingsbridge. Armley.
Prayer for opposers of revivals.
1 BLEST Lord, behold the guilty scorn
Of those who hate and mock our praise;
Pity their state and make them turn,
No more to walk in sinful ways.

2 Anxious we see their wretched state,
Who never think of heav'n or hell;
They laugh and sport and court the gate,
Which opes where endless terrors dwell.

3 Lead them to view a sinful heart,
A soul all enmity to thee,
Destroy'd, defil'd in every part,
Too proud to bow, too blind to see.

4 Lead them to view a holy law,
Which justly dooms to endless death,
To feel that guilt which Jesus saw,
And pray'd 'Forgive,' with dying breath.

5 Open their eyes, unstop their ears,
To hear condemning justice sound;
Lord, change their hearts and then their tears
Will witness grief to all around.

6 Once we were blind, like them we strove,
Till sov'reign mercy chang'd our ways;
Lord, bow their wills, and make them love,
Then they will join our songs of praise.

HYMN 314. 8s.
Uxbridge. Lambeth.
1 ALL glory to God in the sky,
And peace upon earth be restor'd:
O Jesus, exalted on high,
Appear our omnipotent Lord!
Who, meanly in Bethlehem born,
Didst stoop to redeem a lost race,
Once more to thy creatures return,
And reign in thy kingdom of grace.

2 Oh, wouldst thou again be made known,
Again in thy Spirit descend,
And set up, in each of thine own,
A kingdom that never shall end!
Thou only art able to bless,
And make the glad nations obey,
And bid the dire enmity cease,
And bow the whole world to thy sway.

3 Come then to thy servants again,
Who long thy appearing to know;
Thy quiet and peaceable reign
In mercy establish below:
Appeas'd by the charms of thy grace,
We all shall in amity join,
And kindly each other embrace,
And love with affection like thine.

*HYMN 315. C. M.　　　Newton.
St. Ann's. Barby.
For Christian Conference.
1 O LORD, our languid souls inspire,
　For here we trust thou art
Send down a coal of heav'nly fire,
To warm each waiting heart.

2 Show us some tokens of thy love,
Our fainting hope to raise;
And pour thy blessing from above,
That we may render praise.

3 Within these walls let holy praise,
And love and concord dwell:
Here give the troubled conscience ease,
The wounded spirit heal.

4 The feeling heart, the melting eye,
The humble mind bestow;
And shine upon us from on high,
To make our graces grow.

5 May we in faith receive thy word,
In faith present our pray'rs;
And in the presence of our Lord,
Unbosom all our cares.

6 And may the gospel's joyful sound,
Enforc'd by mighty grace,
Awaken sinners all around
To come and fill the place.

HYMN 316. L. M. B.
Portugal. Blendon.
Romans viii. 14.
1 COME, gracious Spirit, heav'nly Dove,
With light and comfort from above,
Be thou our guardian, thou our guide,
O'er ev'ry thought and step preside.

2 Conduct us safe, conduct us far
From ev'ry sin and hurtful snare;
Lead to thy word that rules must give,
And teach us lessons how to live.

3 The light of truth to us display,
And make us know and choose thy way;
Plant holy fear in ev'ry heart,.
That we from God may ne'er depart.

4 Lead us to holiness, the road
That we must take to dwell with God;
Lead us to Christ, the living way,
Nor let us from his pastures stray.

5 Lead us to God, our final rest,
In his enjoyment to be bless'd;
Lead us to heav'n, the seat of bliss,
Where pleasure in perfection is.

HYMN 317. L. M. Fawcett.
Portugal. Sabbaoth.
Beginning of worship.
1 THY presence, gracious God, afford
Prepare us to receive thy word;
Now let thy voice engage our ear,
And faith be mix'd with what we hear.

2 Distracting thoughts and cares remove,
And fix our hearts and hopes above;
With food divine may we be fed,
And satisfied with living bread.

3 To us thy sacred word apply,
With sov'reign power and energy;
And may we in true faith and fear,
Reduce to practice what we hear.

HYMN 318. L. M.   Steele.
Rothwell. Wells. Shoel.
Prayer for the presence of Christ.
1 LORD, in the temples of thy grace,
Thy saints behold thy smiling face;
And oft have seen thy glories shine
With pow'r and majesty divine:

2 But soon, alas! thy absence mourn,
And pray, and wish thy kind return;
Without thy life-inspiring light,
'Tis all a scene of gloomy night.

3 Come, dearest Lord, thy children cry,
Our graces droop, our comforts die;
Return, and let thy glories rise
Again, to our admiring eyes;

4 Till fill'd with light, and joy, and love,
Thy courts below, like those above,
Triumphant hallelujahs raise,
And heav'n and earth resound thy praise.

HYMN 319. C. M. Steele.
Bray. Colchester.
1 COME, Lord, and warm each languid heart—
Inspire each lifeless tongue;
And let the joys of heav'n impart
Their influ'nce to our song.

2 Come, Lord, thy love alone can raise
In us the heav'nly flame;
Then shall our lips resound thy praise,
Our hearts adore thy name.

3 Dear Saviour, let thy glory shine,
And fill thy dwellings here,
Till life, and love, and joy divine
A heav'n on earth appear.

HYMN 320. L. M. Tappan.
Armley. Darwent.
1 HOLY be this, as was the place,
To him of Padan-aram known,
Where Abram's God reveal'd his face,
And caught the pilgrim to the throne.

2 Oh, how transporting was the glow
That thrill'd his bosom, mix'd with fear:
"Lo, the Eternal walks below,
The Highest tabernacles here!"

3 Be ours, when faith and hope grow dim,
The glories which the Patriarch saw;
And when we faint, may we, like him,
Fresh vigor from the vision draw.

4 Heav'n's lightning hover'd o'er his head,
And flash'd new splendors on his view;
Break forth, O Sun! and freely shed
Glad rays upon our Bethel too.

HYMN 321. L. M. Part II.
1 'TIS ours to sojourn in a waste,
Barren and cold as Shinar's ground;
No fruits of Eschol charm the taste,
No streams of Meribah are found.—

2 But Thou canst bid the desert bud.
With more than Sharon's rich display;
But thou canst bid the cooling flood,
Gush from the rock and cheer the way.

3 We tread the path thy people trod,
Alternate sunshine, bitter tears;
Go Thou before, and with thy rod
Divide the Jordan of our fears.

4 Be ours the song of triumph giv'n,
Angelic themes to lips of clay;
And ours the holy harp of heav'n,
Whose strain dissolves the soul away.

HYMN 322. L. M. Watts.
Moreton. Portugal.
1 FAR from my thoughts, vain world, be gone,
Let my religious hours alone:
Fain would my eyes my Saviour see;—
I wait a visit, Lord, from thee!

2 My heart grows warm with holy fire,
And kindles with a pure desire:
Come, my dear Jesus, from above,
And feed my soul with heav'nly love.

3 Bless'd Jesus, what delicious fare!
How sweet thine entertainments are!
Never did angels taste above
Redeeming grace, and dying love.

HYMN 323. C. M. Hoskins.
Bray. Newmark. St. Martin's.
1 IN thy great name, O Lord, we come
To worship at thy feet;
Oh, pour thy Holy Spirit down
On all that now shall meet.

2 We come to hear Jehovah speak
To hear the Saviour's voice;
Thy face and favor, Lord, we seek,
Now make our hearts rejoice.

3 Teach us to pray, and praise—to hear,
And understand thy word;
To feel thy blissful presence near,
And trust our living Lord.

4 Let sinners now thy goodness prove,
And saints rejoice in thee;
Let rebels be subdu'd by love,
And to the Saviour flee.

HYMN 324. L. M. Newton.
Sterling. Bath.
1 HAPPY the saints whose lot is cast,
Where oft is heard the gospel sound;
The word is pleasant to their taste,
A healing balm for every wound.

2 With joy they hasten to the place,
Where they their Saviour oft have met,
And while they feast upon his grace,
Their burdens and their griefs forget.

3 This favor'd lot, my friends, is ours;
May we the privilege improve,
And find these consecrated hours,
Sweet earnests of the joys above.

HYMN 325. L. M. Doddridge.
Blendon. Leyden.
On opening a place of worship.
1 GREAT God, we to thy honor raise
These walls to echo forth thy praise;
Do thou, descending, fill the place
With choicest tokens of thy grace.

2 Here let the great Redeemer reign,
With all the graces of his train,
While power divine his word attends,
To conquer foes and cheer his friends.

3 And, in the great decisive day,
When God the nations shall survey,
May it before the world appear,
That crowds were born to glory here.

HYMN 326. 8, 7, 4. Rippon.
Littleton. Jordan. Tamworth.
Dismission
1 LORD, dismiss us with thy blessing—
Fill our hearts with joy and peace;
Let us each, thy love possessing,
Triumph in redeeming grace;
Oh, refresh us!
Trav'ling through this wilderness.

2 Thanks we give, and adoration,
For thy gospel's joyful sound;
May the fruits of thy salvation
In our hearts and lives abound:
May thy presence
With us evermore be found.

3 So, whene'er the signal's giv'n,
Us from earth to call away;
Borne on angels' wings to heav'n,
Glad to leave our cumb'rous clay,
May we, ready,
Rise and reign in endless day!

HYMN 327. L. M. Hart.
Chatham. Portugal.
1 DISMISS us with thy blessing, Lord—
Help us to feed upon thy word;
All that has been amiss forgive,
And let thy truth within us live.

2 Though we are guilty, thou art good—
Wash all our works in Jesus' blood;
Give ev'ry fetter'd soul release,
And bid us all depart in peace.

HYMN 328. 8s. Hart
Dismission. Lambeth.
1 THIS God is the *God* we adore,
Our faithful, unchangeable friend;
Whose love is as large as his pow'r,
And neither knows measure nor end;

2 'Tis *Jesus*, the first and the last.
Whose Spirit shall guide us safe home;
We'll praise him for all that is past,
And trust him for all that's to come.

HYMN 329. S. M. Hart.
Cambridge. Sicily.
1 ONCE more, before we part,
We'll bless the Saviour's name,
Record his mercies, every heart;
Sing, every tongue, the same.

2 Receive his sacred word,
And feed thereon and grow;
Go on to seek, to know the Lord,
And practise what you know.

HYMN 330. C. M.
Colchester. Barby. Braintree.
Numbers vi. 25, 26.
1 ETERNAL Sun of Righteousness,
Display thy beams divine;
Now may the glory of thy face
Upon our darkness shine.

2 Light, in thy light, Oh, may we see—
Thy grace and mercy prove—
Reviv'd, and cheer'd, and bless'd by thee,
The God of pard'ning love.

3 Lift up thy countenance serene,
And let each happy child
Behold, without a cloud between,
His Father reconcil'd.

4 On us the blessing now bestow,
The joy of sins forgiv'n,
Sweet peace and holiness below,
And then the joys of heav'n.

HYMN 331. 6, 4.   Hill's Col.
Bermondsey Bridgeton.
1 GLORY to God on high,
Let heav'n and earth reply,
Praise ye his name!
Angels his love adore,
Who all our sorrows bore,
And saints sing, evermore,
"Worthy the Lamb."

2 Ye, who surround the throne,
Cheerfully join in one,
Praising his name!
Ye, who have felt his blood,
Sealing your peace with God,
Sound his dear name abroad;
"Worthy the Lamb."

3 Soon must we change our place,
Yet will we never cease
Praising his name!
Still will we tribute bring,

Hail him our gracious King,
And through all ages sing,
"Worthy the Lamb."

THE SINNER AWAKENED.

*HYMN 332. L. M. Strong.
Kingsbridge. Armley.
1 ALAS, alas, how blind I've been,
How little of myself I've seen!
Sportive I sail'd the sensual tide,
Thoughtless of God, whom I defied.

2 Oft have I heard of heav'n, and hell,
Where bliss and wo eternal dwell;
But mock'd the threats of truth divine,
And scorn'd the place where angels shine.

3 My heart has long refus'd the blood
Of Jesus, the descending God;
And guilty passion boldly broke
The holy law which heav'n had spoke.

4 Th' alluring world controll'd my choice;
When conscience spake, I hush'd its voice;
Securely laugh'd along the road,
Which hapless millions first had trod.

5 But now, th' Almighty God comes near
And fills my soul with awful fear—
Perhaps I sink to endless pain,
Nor hear the voice of joy again.

*HYMN 333. L. M.   Hyde.
Blendon. Armley. Warwick.
My Spirit shall not always strive. Genesis vi. 3.
1 SAY, sinner, hath a voice within,
Oft whisper'd to thy secret soul,
Urg'd thee to leave the ways of sin,
And leave thy heart to God's control?

2 Hath something met thee in the path
Of worldliness and vanity,
And pointed to the coming wrath,
And warn'd thee from that wrath to flee?

3 Sinner, it was a heav'nly voice,
It was the Spirit's gracious call,
It bade thee make the better choice,
And haste to seek in Christ thine all.

4 Spurn not the call to life and light;
Regard in time the warning kind;
That call thou may'st not always slight,
And yet the gate of mercy find.

5 God's Spirit will not always strive
With harden'd, self-destroying man;
Ye, who persist his love to grieve,
May never hear his voice again.

6 Sinner—perhaps this very day,
Thy last accepted time may be;
Oh, should'st thou grieve him now away,
Then hope may never beam on thee.

HYMN 334. C. M.
Walsal. Buckingham.
1 AND does the Spirit kindly move
To wake my drowsy heart;
And shall I slight and grieve his love,
And bid him hence depart?

2 Shall I the tempter's voice believe,
And still refuse to pray,
And thus the Holy Spirit grieve,
And bid him go his way?—

3 This solemn warning, once receiv'd,
I dare no longer slight;
The Holy Spirit often griev'd,
May take its final flight.

HYMN 335. S. M. Hyde.
Shirland. St. Thomas.
Grieve not the Spirit. Ephesians iv. 30.
1 AND canst thou, sinner, slight
The call of love divine?
Shall God, with tenderness invite,
And gain no thought of thine?

2 Wilt thou not cease to grieve
The Spirit from thy breast,
Till he thy wretched soul shall leave
With all thy sins oppress'd?

3 To-day, a pard'ning God
Will hear the suppliant pray;
To-day, a Saviour's cleansing blood
Will wash thy guilt away.

4 But, grace so dearly bought,
If yet thou wilt despise,
Thy fearful doom with vengeance fraught,
Will fill thee with surprise.

HYMN 336. C. M.
Elgin. Martyr's. Aldridge.
What must I do?
1 MY conscious guilt is now so great,
If I attempt to pray,
The tempter tells me yet to wait,
Or frights my soul away.

2 In painful doubt what course to try,—
I fear this long delay,—
And must I linger here and die,
Asham'd to ask the way?

3 Ye Christian pilgrims, can ye tell
A stranger to the road,
The way that leads to Zion's hill,
To find a pard'ning God?

HYMN 337. C. M.   Hyde.
Bangor. Windsor.
1 AH, what can I, a sinner, do,
With all my guilt oppress'd?
I feel the hardness of my heart,
And conscience knows no rest.

2 Great God, thy good and perfect law
Does all my life condemn;
The secret evils of my soul
Fill me with grief and shame.

3 How many precious Sabbaths gone,
I never can recall;
And Oh, what cause have I to mourn,
Who misimprov'd them all!

4 How long, how often have I heard
Of Jesus, and of heav'n
Yet scarcely listen'd to his word,
Or pray'd to be forgiv'n!

5 Constrain me, Lord, to turn to thee,
And grant renewing grace;
For thou this flinty heart canst break,
And thine shall be the praise.

HYMN 338. C. M.
Standish. Buckingham.
Hardness of heart.
1 THE voice, that bids us all repent,
I hear with terror oft:
But never will this heart relent,
Till Jesus make it soft.

2 The charming voice of bleeding love
I hear from lips divine;
Yet melting strains can never move
A soul so base as mine.

3 Almighty God, do then renew
This sinful heart of stone;
Sweetly my stubborn will subdue—
Conform it to thy own.

HYMN 339. L. M. Hart.
Bath. Moreton.
1 OH, for a glance of heav'nly day
To take the stubborn stone away;
And thaw, with beams of love divine,
This heart, this frozen heart of mine.

2 The rocks can rend, the earth can quake;
The sea can roar, the mountains shake;
Of feeling, all things show some sign,
But this unfeeling heart of mine.

3 To hear the sorrow thou hast felt,
Dear Lord, an adamant would melt,
But I can read each moving line,
And nothing move this heart of mine.

4 But pow'r divine can do the deed,
And much to feel that pow'r I need;—
Come, Holy Spirit, and refine,
And move, and melt this heart of mine.

HYMN 340. C. M. Newton.
Martyr's. Lucan.
Belshazzar. Daniel v. 5, 6.
1 POOR sinners! little do they think
With whom they have to do!
They stand securely on the brink
Of everlasting wo.

2 Chaldea's king, profanely bold,
The Lord of hosts defied;
But vengeance soon his boasts control'd,
And humbled all his pride.

3 He saw a hand upon the wall,
And trembled on his throne,
Which wrote his sudden, dreadful fall,
In characters unknown.

4 His pomp and music, guests and wine,
No more delight afford:
O sinner, ere this case be thine,
Begin to seek the Lord.

5 The law, like this handwriting, stands,
And speaks the wrath of God;
But Jesus answers its demands,
And cancels it with blood.

*HYMN 341. C. M. Strong.
Wantage. Standish.
The sinner's complaint.
1 LONG have I walk'd this dreary road,
Beset with darkness round;
Nor seen, nor heard a smiling God,
Nor one bright moment found.

2 Others, who once did join my speech,
And mourn'd in painful lay,
Now, mounting up with rapture, stretch
To seize a heav'nly day.

3 Far left behind to feel my wo,
With harden'd heart to groan,
Each pray'r, each struggle sinks me low,
Each breath repeats my moan.

4 The lengthen'd day, the gloomy night,
Draw fast the bands of grief:
Sometimes despair o'erclouds my sight,
And says, "There's no relief."

5 Then conscience thunders, Sinai flames—
I try again to rise;
The trial fails, and conscience blames
My pray'rs, my tears, my cries.

6 'Tis thus perplex'd, forlorn, and lost,
I spend my weary days;
No Jesus comes, my hopes are cross'd,
While other's sing, and praise.

*HYMN 342. L. M. Strong.
Limehouse. Wells.
God's answer.
1 SINNER, behold, I've heard thy groan,
I know thy heart, thy life I've known;
I've seen thy hope from grace proclaim'd,
Thy trembling fear when Sinai flam'd.

2 To me, the mighty God, attend,
In me, behold the sinner's friend;
'Twas I who gave thy conscience voice,
Thou hast oppos'd by sinful choice.

3 Think not to bribe my sov'reign grace,
Nor move me by a sorrowing face;
'Tis thine own heart makes grace delay,
And hides a pard'ning glorious day.

4 Mov'd by thy fear, and not by love,
Thy daily pray'rs are sent above;
Thou hast not wish'd my will to meet,
Nor lain submissive at my feet.

5 Should thy proud will at length submit,
With holy sorrow deeply smit,
Thy voice would be the first to say,
I'm glorious in this long delay.

6 Stay, sinner, cease my grace to chide,
Nor think thy moan such sin can hide,
Delay no more, repent and live,
Or meet the death my wrath must give.

*HYMN 343.　　H. M.
Eagle Street. Bethesda.
Who can tell? Jonah iii. 9
1 GREAT God, to thee I make
My sins and sorrows known;
And with a trembling heart
Approach thine awful throne;
Though by my sins deserving hell,
I must repent for who can tell?—

2 O thou, who by a word
My drooping soul canst cheer,
And by thy Spirit form
Thy glorious image there—
My heart subdue, my fears dispel,
I must repent—for who can tell?—

3 While conscience thunders loud,
To thee alone I fly—
Fall down before thy face
And mightily will cry—
Though fears prevail that I shall dwell
In endless flames—yet who can tell?

4 God hath an ear to hear,
While I've a heart to pray—
To him I will submit,
And give myself away
If he be mine, all will be well,
For ever so—and who can tell?

CONVICTION.

*HYMN 344. S. M.   Cowper.
Bridgeport. Wirkswortb.
1 MY former hopes are fled,
My terror now begins;
I feel, alas! that I am dead
In trespasses and sins.

2 Ah, whither shall I fly?
I hear the thunder roar
The law proclaims destruction nigh,
And vengeance at the door.

3 When I review my ways,
I dread impending doom;
But sure, a friendly whisper says,
"Flee from the wrath to come.

4 I see, or think I see,
A glimm'ring from afar
A beam of day that shines for me,
To save me from despair.

5 Forerunner of the sun,
It marks the pilgrim's way;
I'll gaze upon it while I run,
And watch the rising day.

*HYMN 345. S. M.   Toplady.
Shirland. St. Thomas
The heart. Jeremiah xvii. 9. Matthew xv. 19.
1 ASTONISH'D and distress'd,
I turn mine eyes within
My heart with loads of guilt oppress'd,
The seat of ev'ry sin.

2 What crowds of evil thoughts,
What vile affections there!
Distrust, presumption, artful guile,
Pride, envy, slavish fear.

3 Almighty King of saints,
These tyrant lusts subdue;

Expel the darkness of my mind,
And all my pow'rs renew.

4 This done, my cheerful voice
Shall loud hosannas raise;
My soul shall glow with gratitude,
My lips proclaim thy praise.

HYMN 346.　　　L. M.
Carthage. Darwent.
1 OH, that my load of sin were gone!
Oh, that I could at last submit!
At Jesus' feet to lay me down—
To lay my soul at Jesus' feet.

2 Rest for my soul I long to find—
Saviour, if mine indeed thou art,
Give me thy meek and lowly mind,
and stamp thine image on my heart.

3 Break off the yoke of inbred sin,
And fully set my spirit free;
I cannot rest till pure within—
Till I am wholly lost in thee.

*HYMN 347. S. M.　　　Newton.
Guilford. Little Marlboro'.
1 O LORD, how vile am I,
Unholy and unclean!
How can I dare to venture nigh
With such a load of sin!

2 Is this polluted heart
A dwelling fit for thee?
Swarming, alas! in ev'ry part,
What evils do I see!

3 If I attempt to pray,
And raise my soul on high,
My thoughts are hurried fast away,
For sin is ever nigh.

4 If in thy word I look,
Such darkness fills my mind,

I only read a sealed book,
But no relief can find.

5 Thy gospel oft I hear,
But hear it still in vain:
Without desire, or love, or fear,
Harden'd I still remain.

6 And must I then indeed
Sink in despair and die?
Fain would I hope that thou didst bleed
For such a wretch as I.

HYMN 348. C. M.
Dundee. Barby.
Luke vii. 37-50.
1 BEHOLD the tears that Mary shed—
Her many sins forgiv'n!
Her doubts and darkness all are fled
In peaceful hope of heav'n.

2 When o'er the Saviour's feet in pray'r
She pour'd a flood of grief,
And dried them with her flowing hair,
How soon she found relief!

3 Say, burden'd soul, whose num'rous sins
In dark array are set;
What canst thou do to mitigate
The terrors of thy debt?

4 Canst thou not love the friend, who died
That burden to assume?
Who shrunk not from the crown of thorns,
The scourge—the cross—the tomb?

5 If heavy is thy weight of guilt,
Thy love must greater be—
Then He, whose blood for man was spilt,
Will shed his peace on thee.

*HYMN 349. C. M.　　　Haweis.
St. Ann's. Tempest.
God our hiding-place Psalm xxxii. 7.
1 WHEN low'ring clouds deform the sky,
And darkness thickens round,
Sudden the forked lightnings fly,
Loud thunders rock the ground.

2 The howling blasts, impetuous, sweep
The desolated plain;
The frighted beasts to covert creep;
Home flies the trembling swain!

3 But louder thunders o'er my head,
My heart with terror fill;
And storms of wrath divine I dread,
Which soul and body kill!

4 See, on the whirlwind's rapid wing,
The King of terrors ride,
And with him desolation bring
Myself where can I hide?

5 "Haste, sinner! haste," the Saviour cried,
"Behold my wounded form!
The cleft of my deep-pierced side
Shall hide thee from the storm."

HYMN 350. 7s.
Magdalen. Pastoral Duet.
Matthew xi. 28.
1 COME, ye weary sinners, come,
All, who feel your heavy load;
Jesus calls the wand'rers home;
Hasten to your pard'ning God,
Come, ye guilty souls oppress'd,
Answer to the Saviour's call:
"Come, and I will give you rest;
Come, and I will save you all."

2 Jesus,—full of truth and love,
We thy kindest call obey,
Faithful let thy mercies prove,
Take our load of guilt away,

Weary of this war within,
Weary of this endless strife,
Weary of ourselves and sin,
Weary of a wretched life.

3 Burden'd with a world of grief,
Burden'd with our sinful load,
Burden'd with this unbelief,
Burden'd with the wrath of God,
Lo, we come to thee for ease,
True and gracious as thou art;
Now our weary souls release,
Write forgiveness on our heart.

HYMN 351. 7s.   Newton.
Middleton. Hotham.
Sin bewailed.
1 COME, my soul, thy suit prepare,
Jesus loves to answer pray'r;
He himself has bid thee pray,
Rise and ask without delay.

2 With my burden I begin;
Lord! remove this load of sin!
Let thy blood for sinners spilt,
Set my conscience free from guilt.

3 Lord! I come to thee for rest,
Take possession of my breast;
There thy sov'reign right maintain,
And without a rival reign.

4 Shew me what I have to do,
Ev'ry hour my strength renew;
Let me live a life of faith,
Let me die thy people's death.

HYMN 352. C. M. Newton.
Windsor. Standish.
Prayer for spiritual healing.
1 THOU great Physician of the soul,
To thee I bring my case;
My raging malady control,
And heal me by thy grace.

2 Help me to state my whole complaint;
But where shall I begin ?
Nor words, nor thoughts can fully paint
That worst distemper—sin.

3 It lies not in a single part,
But through my soul is spread;
And all th' affections of my heart
By sin are captive led.

4 A thousand evil thoughts intrude,
Tumultuous in my breast;
Which indispose me for my food,
And rob me of my rest.

5 Thou great Physician, hear my cry,
And set my spirit free;
Let not a trembling sinner die,
Who longs to live to thee.

HYMN 353. C. M.   Cowper.
York. Walsal.
1 HEAL us, Immanuel, here we stand,
Waiting to feel thy touch;
To wounded souls stretch forth thy hand,
Blest Saviour, we are such.

2 Remember him who once applied,
With trembling for relief;
"Lord, I believe," with tears, he cried,
"Oh, help my unbelief."

3 She too, who touch'd thee in the press,
 And healing virtue stole,
Was answer'd, "Daughter, go in peace,
Thy faith hath made thee whole."

4 Like her, with hopes and fears we come,
To touch thee if we may;
Oh, send us not despairing home,
Send none unheal'd away.

HYMN 354. C. M. Brown.
Bangor. Wantage.
Sinners pleading for mercy.
1 LORD, at thy feet we sinners lie,
And knock at mercy's door;
With heavy heart and downcast eye,
Thy favor we implore.

2 Without thy grace, we sink opprest
Down to the gates of hell;
Oh, give our troubled spirit rest,
Our gloomy fears dispel.

3 'Tis mercy, mercy we implore;
 Oh, may thy bowels move:
Thy grace is an exhaustless store,
And thou thyself art love.

4 In mercy now, for Jesus' sake,
Our many sins forgive;
Thy grace our rocky hearts can break,
And breaking soon relieve.

5 Thus melt us down, thus make us bend,
And thy dominion own;
Nor let a rival more pretend
To repossess thy throne.

HYMN 355. 8,7. Turner.
Sicilian Hymn. Love Divine.
1 JESUS, full of all compassion,
Hear thy humble suppliant's cry;
Let me know thy great salvation,
See, I languish, faint, and die.

2 Guilty, but with heart relenting,
Overwhelm'd with helpless grief—
Prostrate at thy feet repenting—
Send, O send me quick relief!

3 Whither should a wretch be flying,
But to him who comfort gives?
Whither, from the dread of dying,
But to him who ever lives?

4 Sav'd—the deed shall spread new glory
Through the shining realms above;
Angels sing the pleasing story,
All enraptur'd with thy love.

HYMN 356. L. M. Parnell.
Brunswick. Putney.
1 WITH kind compassion hear my cry
O Jesus, Lord of life, on high!
And on thy servant's drooping head,
The dews of blessing sweetly shed.

2 Change all my sad complaints to ease,
To cheerful notes of endless praise;
A sense of pard'ning favor give,
And raise my mind and bid me live.

3 My fears of danger while I breathe,
My dread of endless hell beneath,
My sense of sorrow for my sin,
To springing comfort change within;

4 Be not to me a Judge severe,
For so thy presence who can bear?
But Oh, regard my mournful cry,
And look with mercy's gracious eye.

5 Then grant, O Lord, that I may burn
To make my Saviour some return;
And be my heart inspir'd to rise,
On wings of love to yonder skies.

*HYMN 357.   L. M.
Armley. Surry.
A sinner submitting to God.
1 WEARY of struggling with my pain,
Hopeless to burst this sinful chain,
At length I give the contest o'er,
And seek to free myself no more.

2 From my own works at last I cease—
God that creates must seal my peace;
Fruitless my toil, and vain my care,
Unless thy sov'reign grace I share.

3 Lord, I despair myself to heal;
I see my sin but do not feel;
Nor shall I till thy Spirit blow,
And bid th' obedient waters flow;

4 'Tis thine a heart of flesh to give,
Thy gifts I only can receive;
Here then to thee I all resign,—
To draw, redeem, and seal is thine.

HYMN 358. L. M. Cruttenden.
Kingsbridge. Darwent.
1 OWN my guilt, my sins confess;
Can men or devils make them more?
Of crimes already numberless,
Vain the attempt to swell the score.

2 Were the black list before my sight,
While I remember thou hast died,
'Twill only urge my speedier flight,
To seek salvation at thy side.

3 Low at thy feet I'll cast me down,
To thee reveal my guilt and fear,
And, if thou spurn me from thy throne,
I'll be the first who perish'd there.

CONVICTION AND CONVERSION

HYMN 359. C. M.   Strong.
Wantage. Martyr's.
Slain and reviving. Romans vii. 9.
1 SMOTE by the law, I'm justly slain;
Great God, behold my case;
Pity a sinner fill'd with pain,
Nor drive me from thy face.

2 Dread terrors fright my guilty soul—
Thy justice, all in flames,
Gives sentence on this heart so foul,
So hard, so full of crimes.

3 'Tis trembling hardness that I feel;
I fear, but don't relent,—

Perhaps of endless death the seal:
Oh, that I could repent!

4 My pray'rs, my tears, my vows are vile;
My duties black with guilt;
On such a wretch can mercy smile,
Though Jesus' blood was spilt?

5 Speechless I sink—to endless night,
I see an op'ning hell;
But lo! what glory strikes my sight!
Such glory who can tell!

6 Enrapp'd in these bright beams of peace,
I feel a gracious God:
Swell, swell the note: Oh, tell his grace;
Sound his high praise abroad!

HYMN 360. 8, 7, 4.
Tamworth. Jordan. Littleton.
The surrender.
1 WELCOME, welcome, dear Redeemer,
Welcome to this heart of mine:
Lord, I make a full surrender,
Ev'ry pow'r and thought be thine,
Thine entirely,
Through eternal ages thine.

2 Known to all to be thy mansion,
Earth and hell will disappear;
Or in vain attempt possession,
When they find the Lord is near—
Shout, O Zion!
Shout, ye saints, the Lord is here!

*HYMN 361. L. M. Livingstone.
Luther's Hymn. Bath.
Conviction and conversion. Psalm cvii. 17-20.
1 THE sinner's flatt'ring dreams are fled,
Destruction hovers o'er his head;
And conscience throws her darts around,
And poison rankles in each wound.

2 Despair and death his heart assail,
And all his hopes of comfort fail;

Till, deeply humbled in the dust,
He owns his punishment is just.

3 Then Penitence beside him stands,
With brow severe, but healing hands;
The wounds she probes, the balm applies,
To heav'n directs the mourner's sighs.

4 To heav'n his streaming eyes he rears,
And Mercy's radiant form appears;
She whispers peace and hope within,
His sorrows cease—his joys begin.

HYMN 362.　　C. M.　Hoskins.
Buckingham. Wantage.
The Jailor. Acts xvi. 30, 31.
1 "WHAT must I do," the jailor cries,
 "To save my sinking soul!"
"Believe in Christ," the word replies,
 "Thy faith shall make thee whole."

2 Our works are all the works of sin,
Our nature quite deprav'd:
Jesus alone can make us clean;—
By grace are sinners sav'd.

3 Come, sinners, then, the Saviour trust,
To wash you in his blood;
To change your hearts, subdue your lust,
And bring you home to God.

*HYMN 363. C. M.　　Newton.
Barby. Mear.
Heart taken. Luke xi. 21, 22.
1 THE castle of the human heart,
Strong in its native sin,
Is guarded well in every part,
By him who dwells within.

2 For Satan there in arms resides,
And calls the place his own;
With care against assaults provides,
And rules as on a throne.

3 But Jesus, stronger far than he,
In his appointed hour,
Appears to set his people free
From the usurper's pow'r.

4 "This heart I bought with blood," he cries,
"And now it shall be mine;"
His voice the strong man arm'd dismays;
He knows he must resign.

5 In spite of unbelief and pride,
And self and Satan's art,
The gates of brass fly open wide,
And Jesus wins the heart.

*HYMN 364. S. M.   S.
St. Thomas. Dover.
1 BENEATH the pois'nous dart
Of Satan's rage I fell—
How narrowly my feet escap'd
The snares of death and hell!

2 Darkness, and shame, and grief
Oppress'd my gloomy mind;
I look'd around me for relief,
But no relief could find.

3 At length, to God I cried;
He heard my plaintive sigh;
He heard, and instantly he sent
Salvation from on high.

4 Oh, may I ne'er forget
The mercy of my God!
Nor ever want a tongue to spread
His loudest praise abroad.

HYMN 365. 8, 7.   Newton.
Northampton Chapel. Sicilian Hymn.
Bartimeus. Mark x. 48.
1 "MERCY, O thou son of David!"
Thus the blind Bartim'us pray'd;
"Others by thy word are saved,
Now to me afford thine aid."

2 Many for his crying chid him,
But he call'd the louder still;
Till the gracious Saviour bid him,
"Come, and ask me what you will."

3 Money was not what he wanted,
Though by begging us'd to live;
But he ask'd, and Jesus granted
Alms which none but he could give.

4 "Lord, remove this grievous blindness,
"Let my eyes behold the day!"
Straight he saw, and won by kindness,
Follow'd Jesus in the way.

5 Oh! methinks, I hear him praising,
Publishing to all around;
"Friends, is not my case amazing?
What a Saviour I have found!

6 "Oh that all the blind but knew him,
And would be advised by me!
Surely they would hasten to him,
He would cause them all to see."

HYMN 366. L. M. Newton.
Blendon. Bath.
The happy change.
1 IN sin by blinded passions led,
In search of fancied good we range;
The paths of disappointment tread,
To nothing fix'd—but love of change.

2 But, when the Holy Ghost imparts
The knowledge of the Saviour's love;
Our wand'ring, weary, restless hearts,
Are then renew'd, no more to rove.

3 Now a new principle takes place,
Which guides and animates the will;
This love, another name for grace,
Constrains to good and bars from ill.

4 By love's pure light we soon perceive
Our noblest bliss and proper end;
And gladly ev'ry idol leave,
To love and serve our Lord and Friend.

HYMN 367. C. P. M.   Ockum.
Ganges. Chapel. Willoughby.
1 AWAK'D by Sinai's awful sound,
My soul in bonds of guilt I found,
And knew not where to go;
Eternal truth did loud proclaim,
"The sinner must be born again,
Or sink to endless wo."

2 When to the law I trembling fled,
It pour'd its curses on my head,
I no relief could find
This fearful truth increas'd my pain,
"The sinner must be born again,"
And whelm'd my tortur'd mind.

3 Again did Sinai's thunders roll,
And guilt lay heavy on my soul,
A vast, oppressive load;
Alas, I read, and saw it plain,
"The sinner must be born again,"
Or drink the wrath of God.

4 The saints I heard with rapture tell,
How Jesus conquer'd Death and Hell,
And broke the fowler's snare;
Yet, when I found this truth remain,
"The sinner must be born again,"
I sunk in deep despair.

5 But while I thus in anguish lay,
The gracious Saviour pass'd this way,
And felt his pity move;
The sinner, by his justice slain,
Now by his grace is born again,
And sings redeeming love.

*HYMN 368. C. M.
Colchester. Barby.
The Prodigal. Luke xv. 11-24.
1 THANKLESS—the Prodigal receives
The bounty of his Sire,
Rejoicing only in the hope
To have his own desire.

2 And far from home, in climes of vice,
He joins the heedless throng;
Begins in pleasure to rejoice,
And chants the mirthful song.

3 But lo, the famine coming on,
Now dies the song profane;—
The youth beholds his substance gone,
And begs the husk in vain.

4 The terrors of the world to come
Have struck his pleasures dead—
And far from God—and far from home,
His every friend has fled.

*HYMN 369. C. M.   Part II.
Wantage. Buckingham
Returning
1 THE Prodigal, with streaming eyes,
From folly just awake,
Reviews his wand'rings with surprise;
His heart begins to break.

2 I starve, he cries, nor can I bear
The famine in this land;
While servants of my Father share
The bounty of his hand.

3 With deep repentance I'll return
And seek my Father's face;
Unworthy to be call'd a son,
I'll ask a servant's place.

4 Far off He saw him slowly move,
In pensive silence mourn;
The Father ran with arms of love
To welcome his return.

5 Through all the courts the tidings flew,
And spread the joy around;
The angels tune their harps anew;
The Prodigal is found!

HYMN 370. C. M. Part III. H.
Clarendon. Barby.
1 MY soul!—thy hasty censure spare,
Repress the bitter tone,—
Forbear thy brother's faults to judge,—
And watchful, scan thy own.

2 Hast thou th' unwearied gifts of heaven
Beheld with thoughtless pride?
Ungratefully their blessings shar'd,
Or madly misapplied?

3 In the "far country" of thy sin,
Hast thou perceiv'd with pain,
The evils of thy wayward course,
And sought thy God again?

4 And was thy penitence receiv'd,
And was the rebel lov'd?—
Then, with the Prodigal, adore
The mercy thou hast prov'd.

HYMN 371. S. M.
Shirland. Orange. Wirksworth.
The sinner cured. John v. 2-9.
1 BESIDE the gospel pool,
Appointed for the poor,
From year to year a sinful soul
Had waited for a cure.

2 The voice of one unknown,
Advancing where he lay,
Bespoke him in a gentle tone,
And thus it seem'd to say:

3 "Poor, sinful, dying soul,
Why linger here and die?
Only consent to be made whole
You need no longer lie.

4 "The Saviour passing by,
Well knows your sinking state,
And while the Saviour is so nigh,
The sinner need not wait."

5 That voice dispell'd the charm,
His fatal slumbers broke;
He saw his sins with fresh alarm,
And fear'd the vengeful stroke.

6 Unable to endure,
He call'd for aid divine—
The great Physician wrought the cure;
That guilty soul was mine.

THE CONVERT.

*HYMN 372. L. M. Tatlock.
Surry. Armley.
1 FAR from thy fold, O God, my feet
Once mov'd in error's devious maze,
Nor found religious duties sweet,
Nor sought thy face, nor lov'd thy ways.

2 With tend'rest voice thou bad'st me flee
The paths which thou could'st ne'er approve;
And gently drew my soul to thee,
With cords of sweet, eternal love.

3 Now to thy footstool, Lord, I fly,
And low in self-abasement fall;
A vile, a helpless worm, I lie,
And thou, my God, art all in all.

4 Dearer, far dearer to my heart,
Than all the joys that earth can give;
From fame, from wealth, from friends I'd part,
Beneath thy countenance to live.

5 And when, in smiling friendship dress'd
Death bids me quit this mortal frame,
Gently reclin'd on Jesus' breast,
My latest breath shall bless his name.

6 Then my unfetter'd soul shall rise,
And soar above yon starry spheres,
Join the full chorus of the skies,
And sing thy praise thro' endless years.

HYMN 373. C. M. Newton.
Clifford. Bradford.
Old things passed away. 2 Corinthians v. 17.
1 LET carnal minds the world pursue,
It has no charms for me;
Once, I admir'd its trifles too,
But grace has set me free.

2 Its fading charms no longer please,
No more content afford
Far from my heart be joys like these,
Now I have seen the Lord.

3 As by the light of op'ning day,
The stars are all conceal'd
So earthly pleasures fade away,
When Jesus is reveal'd.

4 Creatures no more divide my choice—
I bid them all depart
His name, and love, and gracious voice,
Have fix'd my roving heart.

5 Now, Lord, I would be thine alone,
And wholly live to thee;
But may I hope that thou wilt own
A worthless worm like me!

6 Yes, though of sinners I'm the worst,
I cannot doubt thy will;
For, if thou had'st not lov'd me first,
I had refus'd thee still.

*HYMN 374. L. M. Cowper.
Kent. Bath. Truro.
1 NO more I ask, or hope to find,
Delight or happiness below:
Sorrow may well possess the mind,
That feeds where thorns and thistles grow.

2 The joy that fades is not for me,
I seek immortal joys above;
There, glory without end shall be
The bright reward of faith and love.

3 Cleave to the world, ye sordid worms,
Contented, lick your native dust;
But God shall fight, with all his storms,
Against the idol of your trust.

HYMN 375. S. M. Hammond.
Nativity. Peckham.
Song of Moses and the Lamb. Revelation xv. 3
1 AWAKE, and sing the song
Of Moses and the Lamb;
Wake, ev'ry heart and ev'ry tongue,
To praise the Saviour's name.

2 Sing of his dying love;
Sing of his rising pow'r;
Sing, how he intercedes above,
For those whose sins he bore.

3 Sing, till we feel our heart
Ascending with our tongue;
Sing, till the love of sin depart,
And grace inspire our song.

4 Sing on your heavn'ly way,
Ye ransom'd sinners, sing;
Sing on, rejoicing every day,
In Christ, th' eternal King.

5 Soon shall we hear him say,
"Ye blessed children come;"
Soon will he call us hence away,
And take his wand'rers home.

6 Soon shall our raptur'd tongue
His endless praise proclaim;
And sweeter voices tune the song
Of Moses and the Lamb.

HYMN 376. C. M.
Clifford. St. Martin's.
1 OH, for a thousand tongues to sing
My dear Redeemer's praise;
The glories of my God and King,
The triumphs of his grace!

2 My gracious Master, and my God,
Assist me to proclaim,
To spread through all the earth abroad
The honors of thy name.

3 JESUS, the name that calms our fears,
That bids our sorrows cease;
'Tis music in the sinner's ears;
'Tis life, and health, and peace.

4 He breaks the pow'r of reigning sin,
He sets the pris'ner free;
His blood can make the foulest clean;
His blood avail'd for me.

5 Let us obey, we then shall know,
Shall feel our sins forgiv'n:
Anticipate our heav'n below,
And own that love is heav'n.

HYMN 377. C. M. Doddridge.
York. St. Ann's.
Returning to Zion. Isaiah xxxv. 10.
1 SING, ye redeemed of the Lord,
Your great Deliv'rer sing:
Pilgrims, for Zion's city bound,
Be joyful in your King.

2 A hand divine shall lead you on,
Through all the blissful road:
Till to the sacred mount you rise,
And see your smiling God.

3 The garlands of immortal joy
Shall bloom on ev'ry head;
While sorrows, sighing, and distress,
Like shadows, all are fled.

4 March on in your Redeemer's strength;
Pursue his footsteps still
And let the prospect cheer your eye,
While lab'ring up the hill.

HYMN 378.   7s.   Cennick.
Pilgrim's Hymn. Somerset. Middleton.
1 CHILDREN of the heav'nly King,
As ye journey, sweetly sing;
Sing your Saviour's worthy praise,
Glorious in his works and ways.

2 Ye are trav'ling home to God,
In the way the fathers trod,
They are happy now, and ye
Soon their happiness shall see.

3 Shout, ye little flock, and blest,
You near Jesus' throne shall rest;
There your seats are now prepar'd,
There your kingdom and reward.

4 Fear not, brethren, joyful stand
On the borders of your land:
Jesus Christ, your Father's son,
Bids you undismay'd, GO ON.

5 LORD! submissive make us go,
Gladly leaving all below:
Only thou our Leader be
And we still will follow thee.

HYMN 379.   L. M.   Livingstone.
Blendon. Portugal.
Psalm ciii. 1-4.
1 MY soul, with humble fervor raise
To God the voice of grateful praise,
And every mental power combine,
To bless his attributes divine.

2 Deep on my heart let mem'ry trace
His acts of mercy and of grace;
Who with a Father's tender care,
Sav'd me when sinking in despair:

3 Gave my repentant soul to prove
The joy of his forgiving love;
Pour'd balm into my bleeding breast,
And led my weary feet to rest.

HYMN 380. 8, 7. Wingrove.
Sicilian. Love Divine.
1 HAIL, my ever blessed Jesus,
Only thee I wish to sing;
To my soul thy name is precious,
Thou my Prophet, Priest, and King.

2 Oh, what mercy flows from heav'n,
Oh, what joy and happiness!
Love I much?—I've much forgiv'n—
I'm a miracle of grace.

3 Once, with Adam's race in ruin,
Unconcern'd in sin I lay
Swift destruction still pursuing,
Till my Saviour pass'd that way.

4 Witness, all ye hosts of heav'n,
My Redeemer's tenderness!
Love I much?—I've much forgiv'n—
I'm a miracle of grace.

5 Shout, ye bright angelic choir;
Praise the Lamb enthron'd above;
While astonish'd, I admire
God's free grace, and boundless love.

6 That blest moment I receiv'd him,
Fill'd my soul with joy and peace;
Love I much ?—I've much forgiv'n—
I'm a miracle of grace.

HYMN 381. L. M. Kelly.
St. Catharine's. Portugal.
1 I HEAR a voice that comes from far;
From Calvary it sounds abroad;
It sooths my soul, and calms my fear:
It speaks of pardon bought with blood.

2 And is it true, that many fly
The sound that bids my soul rejoice;
And rather choose in sin to die,
Than turn an ear to mercy's voice!

3 Alas, for those!—the day is near,
When mercy will be heard no more;
Then will they ask in vain to hear
The voice they would not hear before.

4 With such, I own, I once appear'd,
But now I know how great their loss;
For sweeter sounds were never heard,
Than mercy utters from the cross.

5 But let me not forget to own,
That if I differ aught from those,
'Tis due to sov'reign grace alone,
That oft selects its proudest foes.

HYMN 382. C. M. Collyer.
St. Martin's. Colchester.
Herein is love. 1 John iv. 10.
1 YE saints, assist me in my song—
Let all your passions move;
To Jesus all the notes belong—
I sing redeeming love.

2 Opposing spirits 'gainst his cross,
Their force united prove;
But quit the field with mighty loss,
Crush'd by redeeming love.

3 Around the circle of his friends
His tender passions move;
And while he liv'd his constant theme
Was still redeeming love.

4 Gently he rais'd his sacred hands,
Before his last remove:
And the last whispers of his tongue,
Sigh'd forth redeeming love.

5 Through life's wide waste, with weary feet
In darkness I may rove;

But never can my heart forget
Redeeming, dying love.

6 Oh, that before his sacred throne,
I all its sweets may prove
Still as my pleasures rise, my song
Shall be redeeming love.

HYMN 383. L. M.
Portugal. Chatham.
1 SURROUNDED by a frightful gloom,
And dreading fiercer ills to come;
From chains of wo, and haunts of vice,
To liberty and life we rise.

2 Thanks to the hand that set us free;
Eternal Spirit, thanks to thee
Whose pow'r resistless, unconfin'd,
Subdues the passions of the mind.

3 Religion like a sun appears,
And shines upon our dawning years;
We follow still the guiding ray,
That kindles into perfect day.

4 Conducted safe along the road,
That leads to peace—that leads to God;
With active feet, with ardent eyes,
We seek our home above the skies.

5 Subdu'd by love, and taught of God,
 Rejoicing in redeeming blood,
We press to find that happy shore,
Where sin and sorrow reign no more.

HYMN 384. C. P. M.
Chapel. Chilton. Abby
The heavenly prospect. Numbers xiii.
1 REJOICING now in glorious hope,
We stand, and from the mountain top,
View all the land below;
Rivers of milk and honey rise,
And all the fruits of Paradise
In endless plenty flow.

2 A land where sin shall ne'er invade,
Nor doubt shall cast a gloomy shade,
With every blessing crown'd;
There dwells the Lord our righteousness,
And keeps his own in perfect peace;
And all his praise resound.

3 May we this better land possess,
When in this howling wilderness,
No longer we shall rove,—
Lord, help us humbly to rejoice,
In hope we there shall hear thy voice,
And sing redeeming love.

HYMN 385. 5, 6, 9.
Feversham. Salem.
1 HOW happy are they
Who the Saviour obey,
And have laid up their treasure above!
Oh, what tongue can express
The sweet comfort and peace
Of a soul in its earliest love!

2 'Twas heaven below
My Redeemer to know,
And the angels could do nothing more
Than to fall at his feet,
And the story repeat,
And the lover of sinners adore.

3 Then, all the day long,
Was my Jesus my song
And redemption through faith in his name;
Oh, that all might believe,
And salvation receive,
And their song and their joy be the same.

HYMN 386. L. M. Collyer.
Chatham. Moreton St. Catharine's.
1 SOFT be the gently breathing notes,
That sing the Saviour's dying love;
Soft as the ev'ning zephyr floats,
Soft as the tuneful lyres above.

2 Soft as the morning dews descend,
While the sweet lark exulting soar's;
So soft to your Almighty Friend,
Be every sigh your bosom pours:

3 Pure as the sun's enliv'ning ray
That scatters life and joy abroad;
Pure as the lucid ear of day,
That wide proclaims its Maker, God.

4 True as the magnet to the pole,
So true let your contrition be—
So true let all your sorrows roll,
To him who bled upon the tree.

HYMN 387. C. M. Dwight.
Chapel. Walsal.
Deliverance from evil companions.
1 THE giddy world, with flatt'ring tongue,
Had charm'd my soul astray,
And lur'd my heedless feet to death
Along the flow'ry way.

2 My heart, with agonizing pray'r,
Besought the Lord to save;
Unseen he seiz'd my trembling hand,
And brought me from the grave.

3 He broke the charm, which drew my feet
To darkness and the dead:
From lips profane, and tongues impure,
With quiv'ring steps I fled.

4 Homeward I flew to find my God,
And seek his face divine,
Restor'd to peace, to hope, to life,
To Zion's friends, and mine.

HYMN 388. L. M. Collyer.
China. Nantwich. Bath.
1 I LEAVE the world with willing feet,
Great God, to find repose in thee:
Once its enchantments soft and sweet,
Threw silken fetters over me.

2 Vice pointed to a flow'ry vale,
Where streams of pleasure seem'd to roll,
And every sweet, on every gale,
Press'd through the senses to the soul.

3 Imagination lent her aid
To strengthen ev'ry dang'rous snare;
But soon the flatt'ring vision fled,
And gave its victim to despair.

4 My youth restor'd from fatal wiles,
Has learn'd temptation's pow'r to fear;
To dread the world's delusive smiles,
And 'scape the fowler's cruel snare.

HYMN 389. L. M. .   Cowper.
Carthage. Armley.
The new convert humbled.
1 THE new-born child of gospel grace
Like some fair tree when summer's nigh
Beneath Immanuel's shining face,
Lifts up his blooming branch on high.

2 No fear he feels, he sees no foes;
No conflict yet his faith employs;
Nor has he learnt to whom he owes
The strength and peace his soul enjoys.

3 But sin soon darts its cruel sting,
And comforts sink from day to day:
What seem'd his own, a self-fed spring,
Proves but a brook that glides away.

4 When Gideon arm'd his num'rous host,
The Lord soon made his numbers less;
And said—lest Israel vainly boast—
"My arm procur'd me this success,"

5 Thus will he bring our spirits down,
And draw our ebbing comforts low,
That, sav'd by grace, but not our own,
We may not claim the praise we owe.

*HYMN 390. C. M.   Newton.
Barby. Colchester

1 ANXIOUS, I strove to find the way,
Which to salvation led;
I listen'd long, I tried to pray,
And heard what many said.

2 When some of joys and comforts told,
I fear'd that I was wrong;
For I was stupid, dead, and cold,
Had neither joys nor song.

3 The Lord my lab'ring heart reliev'd,
And made my burden light;
Then for a moment I believ'd,
And thought that all was right.

4 Of fierce temptations others talk'd,
Of anguish and dismay;
Through what distresses they had walk'd
Before they found the way.

5 Ah! then I thought my hopes were vain,
For I had liv'd at ease;
I wish'd for all my fears again,
To make me more like these.

6 I had my wish, the Lord disclos'd
The evils of my heart;
And left my naked soul expos'd
To Satan's fiery dart.

7 Alas! I cried in deep despair,
Borne down with fearful pain!
How can I these fierce terrors bear,
And who will now sustain?

8 Again my Saviour brought me aid,
And when he set me free,
"Trust simply on my word," he said,
"And leave the rest to me."

HYMN 391. C. M. Swain.
Springfield. Barby.
In darkness.
1 "REJOICE in God," the word commands,
And fain would I obey;
Yet still my spirit ling'ring stands,
While doubts impede my way.

2 How can my soul exalt for joy,
Which feels this load of sin?
And how can praise my tongue employ,
While darkness reigns within?

3 If falling tears and rising sighs
In triumph share a part;
Then, Lord, behold these streaming eyes,
And search this bleeding heart!

4 My soul forgets to use her wings;
My harp neglected lies,
For sin has broken all its strings,
And guilt shuts out my joys.

5 The pow'r, the sweetness of thy voice,
Alone my heart can move;
Make me in Christ, my Lord, rejoice,
And melt my soul to love.

HYMN 392. C. M. H.
Colchester. Barby.
2 Corinthians iv. 6. Psalm xliii. 5.
1 WHEN renovating grace begins
To move the heart of stone,
A holy joy illumes the soul,
As light from darkness shone.

2 High songs of praise with dawn begin,
Exulting close the day;
And e'en the silent watch of night
Is vocal with their lay.

3 But cares arise—temptations throng—
The world prepares her dart—
A "Horror of great darkness" falls,
And whelms the shudd'ring heart.

4 Yet why cast down, sad mourner, say?
Behold the glorious Sun—
Full oft he gilds the kindling morn,
Yet fades ere day is done.

5 But still his unextinguish'd beam
Behind the cloud survives—
Still his appointed course he runs,
And at the goal arrives.

6 Hope thou in God! and he shall make
Thy path like noontide glow:
Obey him with a steadfast mind,
And thou his smile shalt know.

*HYMN 393. L. M.
Brentford. Sterling Shoel.
1 LIKE Israel, safe upon the shore,
Who thought the conflict all was o'er,
Young converts view the frightful train
Of all their foes for ever slain.

2 But soon, with sick'ning heart, survey
The perils of the desert way;
The pow'r of sin revives again,
And all their hopes seem false and vain.

3 The morning sun that shone so bright
Is shrouded in the gloom of night;
Hopeless the victor's crown to win,
They yield ere they the fight begin.

4 But Jesus calls them to the field:
"Come, gird on harness, sword and shield;
Stand fast in faith, fight for your King,
My grace shall strength and vict'ry bring."

HYMN 394. C. M.
Wantage. Chapel.
The Desert.   1 Peter v. 8.
 1 WHEN night descends in sable guise,
And spreads her gloom around,
To close the weary trav'ler's eyes,
And rest him on the ground;

2 Amidst the dreary desert wide,
The wand'rer faints to hear
The wide alarm on ev'ry side,
Which speaks some danger near;

3 So, in this wilderness of life,
Whene'er afflictions come,
We sink, as in a night of grief,
Far from our shelt'ring home.

4 The tempter's, like a lion's roar,
Sounds through the vale abroad;
Then let us watch, and ever more
Depend upon our God.

5 From ev'ry other help afar,
And left without a friend,
God is a helper ever near,
And faithful to the end.

*HYMN 395. L. M.   Luther.
Luther's Hymn. Old Hundred. Bath.
1 NATURE will raise up all her strife,
Foe to the flesh-abasing life,
Loath in a Saviour's death to share,
Her daily cross compell'd to bear.

2 But grace omnipotent at length
Shall arm the saint with saving strength;
Through the sharp war with aid attend,
And the dire conflict safely end.

3 Act but the infant's gentle part;
Give up to love thy willing heart;
And grace will then the vict'ry claim,
And light it with a purer flame.

*HYMN 396. L. M.   Luther.
Putney. Warwick.
1 THE sov'reign Father, good and kind,
Wants but to have his child resign'd;
Wants but the healing heart, no more—
With his rich gifts of grace to store.

2 He to thy soul no anguish brings;
From thine own stubborn will it springs;
That foe subdue, the foe within—
Then shall thy peace and joy begin.

3 Let faith exert its conqu'ring pow'r,
Say, in thy fearing, trembling hour,
"Father!—thy pitying help impart"—
'Tis done—a sigh can reach his heart.

4 But if corruption's strength prevail,
And if thy pilgrim footsteps fail;
Lift for his grace thy louder cries,
So shalt thou cleans'd, and stronger rise.

HYMN 397. 8s.
Lambeth. Uxbridge.
1 THE happy in Jesus may sleep,
But Oh, till in me he appears,
Be this my employment, to weep,
And water my couch with my tears.
Ye watchmen of Israel, declare,
If ye my Beloved have seen,
And point to that heav'nly fair,
Surpassing the children of men:

2 My Lover and Lord from above,
Who only can quiet my pain,
Whom only I languish to love,
Oh, where shall I find him again?
Once more if he show me his face,
He never again shall depart.
Detain'd in my closest embrace,
Eternally held in my heart.

HYMN 398. C. M. Cotton.
Buckingham. Windsor.
Faith in suffering. Psalm xiii.
1 LET thy returning Spirit, Lord!
Dispel the shades of night;
Smile on this poor, benighted soul,
For Oh! thy smiles are light.

2 While scoffers at thy sacred word
Deride the pangs I feel,

Deem my religion insincere,
Or call it useless zeal;

3 Yet will I ne'er repent my choice,
I'll ne'er withdraw my trust;
I know thee, Lord, a powerful friend,
And kind, and wise, and just.

4 Then, O my soul, why thus depress'd,
And whence this anxious fear?
In God, the refuge, fix thy trust,
And check the rising tear.

HYMN 399. L. M. Kelly.
Moreton. Luther's Hymn.
Mariner. Matthew viii. 24. Psalm cvii. 30.
1 THE christian voy'ger strikes the rock
That lies conceal'd beneath the wave!
Yet safely he survives the shock;
For Jesus is at hand to save.

2 His destin'd land he sometimes sees,
And thinks his toils will soon be o'er,
Expects some favorable breeze
Will waft him quickly to the shore.

3 But hark!—the midnight tempest roars!
He seems forsaken, and alone:
But Jesus, whom he then implores,
Unseen preserves and leads him on.

4 Though fear his heart should overwhelm,
He'll reach the port to which he's bound;
For Jesus holds and guides the helm,
And soon the haven will be found.

HYMN 400. H. M. Toplady.
Allerton. Whitchurch. Jubilee.
Jesus, the Pilot.
1 JESUS, at thy command,
I launch into the deep;
And leave my native land,
Where sin lulls all asleep:
For thee I fain would all resign,
And sail to heav'n with thee and thine;

2 Thou art my Pilot wise;
My compass is thy word;
My soul each storm defies,
While I have such a Lord!
I trust thy faithfulness and pow'r,
To save me in the trying hour.

3 Though rocks and quicksands deep,
Through all my passage lie;
Yet thou wilt safely keep,
And guide me with thine eye:
My anchor, hope, shall firm abide,
And I each boist'rous storm outride.

4 By faith I see the land,
The port of endless rest:
My soul, thy sails expand,
And fly to Jesus' breast.
Oh, may I reach the heav'nly shore,
Where winds and waves distress no more!

5 Whene'er becalm'd I lie,
And storms and winds subside;
Lord, to my succor fly,
And keep me near thy side:
For more the treach'rous calm I dread,
Than tempests bursting o'er my head.

6 Come, heav'nly Wind, and blow
A prosp'rous gale of grace,
To waft me from below,
To heav'n, my destin'd place:
Then in full sail, my port I'll find,
And leave the world, and sin behind.

HYMN 401. 8s.
Lambeth. Uxbridge.
1 AH! why this disconsolate frame?
Though earthly enjoyments decay,
My Jesus is ever the same,
A Sun in the gloomiest day:
Though molten awhile in the fire,
'Tis only the gold to refine;
And be it my simple desire
Though suffering, not to repine.

2 What can be the pleasures to me,
Which earth in its fulness can boast?
Delusive, its vanities flee,
A flash of enjoyment at most:
And if the Redeemer could part
For me, with his throne in the skies,
Ah! why is so dear to my heart,
What he in his wisdom denies?

3 Then let the rude tempest assail,
The blast of adversity blow,
The haven, though distant, I hail,
Beyond this rough ocean of wo:
When safe on its beautiful strand,
I'll smile on the billows that foam,
Kind angels to hail me to land,
And Jesus to welcome me home.

HYMN 402. C. M. Newton.
Colchester. St Ann's. Stade.
The storm hushed.
1 'TIS past—the dreadful stormy night
Is gone, with all its fears!
And now I see returning light,
The Lord, my Sun, appears.

2 Oh, wond'rous change! but just before,
Despair beset me round;
I heard the lion's horrid roar,
And trembled at the sound.

3 Before corruption, guilt, and fear,
My former comforts fell;
And I discover'd, standing near,
The dreadful depths of hell.

4 But Jesus pitied my distress;
He heard my feeble cry,
Reveal'd his blood and righteousness,
And brought salvation nigh.

5 Dear Lord, since thou hast broke my bands
And set the captive free,
I would devote my tongue, my hands,
My heart, my all to thee.

*HYMN 403. C. M. Madan's Col.
Stade. Braintree. Abridge.
1 OUR little bark on boist'rous seas,
By cruel tempest toss'd,
Without one cheerful beam of hope,
Expecting to be lost;

2 We to the Lord, in humble prayer,
Breath'd out our sad distress;
Though feeble, yet with contrite hearts,
We begg'd return of peace.

3 The stormy winds did cease to blow,
The waves no more did roll;
And soon again a placid sea
Spoke comfort to each soul.

4 Oh! may our grateful, trembling hearts
Sweet hallelujahs sing,
To him who hath our lives preserv'd,
Our Saviour, and our King.

5 Let us proclaim to all the world,
With heart and voice, again,
And tell the wonders he hath done
For us, the sons of men.

HYMN 404. C. P. M.   Brown.
Ganges. Penitent. Chapel.
True convert. 2 Corinthians v. 17.
1 WHEN with my mind devoutly press'd,
Dear Saviour, my revolving breast
Would past offences trace;
Trembling I make the black review,
Yet pleas'd behold, admiring too,
The pow'r of changing grace.

2 This tongue with blasphemies defil'd,
These feet to erring paths beguil'd,
In heav'nly league agree:
Who would believe such lips could praise,
Or think from dark and winding ways,
I e'er should turn to thee?

3 These eyes that once abus'd the light,
Now lift to thee their wat'ry sight,
And weep a silent flood;
These hands are rais'd in ceaseless pray'r,
Oh, wash away the stains they wear,
In pure redeeming blood.

4 These ears, that once could entertain
The midnight oath, the festive strain,
Around the sinful board;
Now deaf to all th' enchanting noise,
Avoid the throng, detest their joys,
And long to hear thy word.

5 Thus art thou serv'd in ev'ry part;
Go on, bless'd Lord, to cleanse my heart,
That drossy thing refine;
That grace may nature's pow'rs control,
And a new creature, body, soul,
Be all and wholly thine.

HYMN 405. C. P. M. Newton.
Chilton. Kew. Aithlone. Ganges.
1 IF God had bid his thunders roll,
And lightnings flash to blast my soul,
I still had stubborn been:
But mercy has my heart subdu'd—
A bleeding Saviour I have view'd,
And now I hate my sin.

2 Now, Lord, I would be thine alone;
Come take possession of thine own,
For thou hast set me free;
Releas'd from Satan's hard command,
See all my pow'rs in waiting stand,
To be employ'd by thee.

3 My will conform'd to thine would move;
On thee my hope, desire, and love,
In fix'd attention join:
My hands, my eyes, my ears, my tongue,
Have Satan's servants been too long,
But now they shall be thine.

4 And can I be the very same,
Who lately durst blaspheme thy name,
And on thy gospel tread?
Surely each one, who hears my case,
Will praise thee, and confess thy grace
Invincible indeed!

HYMN 406. C. M. Newton.
Newmark. Abridge.
Will ye go away ? John vi. 67-69.
1 WHEN any turn from Zion's way,
(As numbers often do),
Methinks I hear my Saviour say,
"Wilt thou forsake me too?"

2 Ah, Lord! with such a heart as mine,
Unless thou hold me fast,
My faith will fail, I shall decline,
And prove like them at last.

3 'Tis thou alone hast power and grace,
To save a wretch like me;
To whom then shall I turn my face,
If I depart from thee.

4 Beyond a doubt I rest assur'd,
Thou art the CHRIST of GOD;
Who hast eternal life secur'd,
By promise and by blood.

5 The help of men and angels join'd,
Could never reach my case!
Nor can I hope relief to find,
But in thy boundless grace.

6 No voice but thine can give me rest,
And bid my fears depart;
No love but thine can make me blest,
And satisfy my heart.

HYMN 407. L. M. Steele.
Armley. Kingsbridge.
1 THOU only Sov'reign of my heart,
My refuge, my almighty Friend;

And can my soul from thee depart,
On whom alone my hopes depend?

2 Whither, ah! whither shall I go—
A wretched wand'rer from my Lord?
Can this dark world of sin and wo,
One glimpse of happiness afford?

3 Thy Name my inmost pow'rs adore;
Thou art my life, my joy, my care;
Depart from thee!—'tis death—'tis more,
'Tis endless ruin— deep despair!

4 Low at thy feet my soul would lie;
Here safety dwells, and peace divine;
Still let me live beneath thine eye,
For life, eternal life is thine.

HYMN 408. C. M.
Standish. Bangor. Walsal.
1 TO whom, my Saviour, shall I go,
If I depart from thee ?
My guide thro' all this vale of wo,
And more than all to me.

2 The world reject thy gentle reign,
And pay thy death with scorn;
Oh, they could plat thy crown again,
And sharpen ev'ry thorn.

3 But I have felt thy dying love
Breathe gently through my heart,
To whisper hope of joys above—
And can we ever part?

4 Ah, no, with thee I'll walk below,
My journey to the grave:
To whom, my Saviour, shall I go,
When only thou canst save?

*HYMN 409. S. M. Cowper.
Orange. Wirksworth.
1 BEWARE of Peter's word,
Nor confidently say,
"I never *will* deny the Lord,"

But "grant I never may."

2 Man's wisdom is to seek
His strength in God alone;
And e'en an angel would be weak,
Who trusted in his own.

3 Retreat beneath his wings,
And in his grace confide;
This more exalts the King of kings
Than all your works beside.

4 In Jesus is our store;
Grace issues from his throne
Whoever says, "I want no more,"
Confesses he has none.

HYMN 410.   L. M.   Gregg.
Portugal. Wells.
Not asham'ed of Jesus. Mark viii. 38.
1 JESUS! and shall it ever be,
A mortal man asham'd of thee!
Asham'd of thee, whom angels praise,
Whose glories shine through endless days.

2 Asham'd of Jesus!—sooner far
Let ev'ning blush to own a star:
He sheds the beams of light divine,
O'er this benighted soul of mine.

3 Asham'd of Jesus!—just as soon
Let midnight be asham'd of noon;
'Tis midnight with my soul, till He,
Bright morning Star, bid darkness flee.

4 Asham'd of Jesus!—that dear friend,
On whom my hopes of heav'n depend!
No! whom I blush, be this my shame,
That I no more revere his name.

5 Asham'd of Jesus—yes I may—
When I've no guilt to wash away—
No tear to wipe—no good to crave—
No fear to quell—no soul to save.

6 Till then—nor is my boasting vain—
Till then I boast a Saviour slain!
And Oh, may this my glory be,
That Christ is not asham'd of me!

*HYMN 411. L. M.
Bath. Kent. Wells.
1 SHALL I, to gain the world's applause,
Or to escape its harmless frown,
Refuse, my Lord, to plead thy cause,
And make thy people's lot my own?—

2 No! let the world cast out my name;
And vile account me if they will;
If to confess the Lord be shame,
I purpose to be viler still.

3 And what is man, or what his smile?
The terrors of his anger, what?
Like grass he flourishes awhile,
And soon his place shall know him not.

HYMN 412. L. M. Pres. Davies.
Armley. Darwent.
Self-dedication to God.
1 LORD, I am thine, entirely thine,
Purchas'd and sav'd by blood divine;
With full consent thine I would be,
And own thy sov'reign right in me.

2 Grant one poor sinner more a place
Among the children of thy grace;
A wretched sinner, lost to God,
But ransom'd by Immanuel's blood.

3 Thee, my new Master, now I call,
And consecrate to thee my all;
Lord, let me live and die to thee—
Be thine through all eternity.

HYMN 413. L. M. Montgomery.
Chatham. Leeds. Bath.
Social dedication to God.
1 JESUS! our best beloved Friend,
On thy redeeming name we call;
Jesus! in love to us descend,
Pardon and sanctify us all.

2 Our souls and bodies we resign,
To fear and follow thy commands;
O take our hearts—our hearts are thine,
Accept the service of our hands.

3 Firm, faithful, watching unto pray'r,
Our Master's voice will we obey,
Toil in thy vineyard here, and bear
The heat and burden of our day.

4 Yet, Lord! for us a resting place,
In heav'n—at thy right hand prepare,
And, till we see thee face to face,
Be all our conversation there.

*HYMN 414. L. M.   Steele.
Kent. Portugal. Sterling.
The noblest resolution. Joshua xxiv. 15.
1 MAY I resolve with all my heart,
With all my pow'rs to serve the Lord;
Nor from his precepts e'er depart,
Whose service is a rich reward.

2 Oh; be his service all my joy!
Around let my example shine,
Till others love the blest employ,
And join in labors so divine.

3 Be this the purpose of my soul,
My solemn, my determin'd choice,
To yield to his supreme control,
And in his kind commands rejoice.

4 Oh, may I never faint, nor tire,
Nor wand'ring, leave his sacred ways;
Great God, accept my soul's desire,
And give me strength to live thy praise.

HYMN 415.   7s.   Montgomery.
Hotham. Middleton.
Ruth i. 16-19.

1 PEOPLE of the living God!
I have sought the world around,
Paths of sin and sorrow trod,
Peace and comfort no where found:
Now to you my spirit turns,
Turns,—a fugitive unblest;
Brethren! where your altar burns,
Oh, receive me into rest.

2 Lonely I no longer roam,
Like the cloud, the wind, the wave,
Where you dwell shall be my home,
Where you die shall be my grave;
Mine the God whom you adore—
Your Redeemer shall be mine;
Earth can fill my soul no more,
Every idol I resign.

*HYMN 416.   C. M.
Colchester. Stade.
Hinder me not. Genesis xxiv. 58.

1 WHEN Jesus bade me leave the world,
My downward steps retrace;
'Twas thus I answer'd every foe,
And fled to his embrace.

2 Stay, said the world, and taste awhile
My ev'ry pleasant sweet;
Hinder me not, my soul replied,
Because the way is great.

3 In all my Lord's appointed ways,
My journey I'll pursue:
Hinder me not, ye much lov'd saints,
For I must go with you.

4 Through duty, and through trials too,
 I go at his command;
Hinder me not, for I am bound
To my Immanuel's land.

HYMN 417. L. M. B.
Blendon. Bath. Portugal.
Welcome to young Converts.
1 WELCOME, ye hopeful heirs of heav'n,
To this rich feast of gospel love—
This pledge is but the prelude giv'n
To that immortal feast above.

2 How great the blessing, thus to meet
Around the sacramental board,
And hold by faith communion sweet,
With Christ our dear and common Lord.

3 And if so sweet this feast below,
What will it be to meet above,
Where all we see, and feel, and know,
Are fruits of everlasting love!

4 Soon shall we tune the heav'nly lyre
Whilst list'ning worlds the song approve;
Eternity itself expire,
Ere we exhaust the theme of love.

HYMN 418. L. M.
Moreton. Blendon.
Strong City. Isaiah xxvi. 1, 2.
1 THE day, the gospel day draws near,
When sinners shall their voices raise,
Sing the New Song with heart sincere,
Triumphant in the land of praise.

2 Glory to God! they all shall cry:
Who is so great a God as ours!
We have a City strong and high,
Salvation is for walls and tow'rs.

3 Secure from danger, as from dread,
We never shall be put to shame,
Who hither have for refuge fled;
For Jesus is our City's name.

4 Open the gates, and open wide,
Let every faithful soul go in;
Open for all the justified,
Who keep the truth that frees from sin.

HYMN 419. C. M. Miller.
Colchester. Clarendon. Washington.
Fellowship. Colossians ii. 2.
1 OUR souls, by love together knit,
Cemented, mix'd in one,
One hope, one heart, one mind, one voice,
'Tis heav'n on earth begun.

2 Our hearts have often burn'd within,
And glow'd with sacred fire,
While Jesus spoke, and fed, and blest,
And fill'd th' enlarg'd desire.

3 The little cloud increases still,
The heav'ns are big with rain;
We haste to catch the teeming show'r,
And all its moisture drain.

4 A rill, a stream, a torrent flows!
But pour a mighty flood;
Oh! sweep the nations, shake the earth,
Till all proclaim thee God.

5 And when thou mak'st thy jewels up,
And set'st thy starry crown;
When all thy sparkling gems shall shine,
Proclaim'd by thee thine own;

6 May we, a little band of love,
We sinners, sav'd by grace,
From glory unto glory chang'd,
Behold thee face to face.

HYMN 420. L. M. Barbauld.
Chatham. Nantwich.
1 HOW blest the sacred tie that binds,
In union sweet, according minds!
How swift the heav'nly course they run,
Whose hearts and faith and hopes are one!

2 To each, the soul of each how dear!
What jealous love, what holy fear!
How doth the gen'rous flame within
Refine from earth, and cleanse from sin!

3 Their streaming eyes together flow,
For human guilt and mortal wo;
Their ardent pray'rs together rise,
Like mingling flames in sacrifice.

4 Together oft they seek the place,
Where God reveals his awful face;—
At length they meet in realms above,
A heav'n of joy—because of love.

HYMN 421. C. M. Doddridge.
St. Martin's. Mear.
Asking the way to Zion. Jeremiah l. 5.
1 INQUIRE, ye pilgrims, for the way,
That lends to Zion's hill,
And thither set your steady face,
With a determin'd will.

2 Invite the strangers all around,
Your pious march to join;
And spread the sentiments you feel
Of faith and love divine.

3 Oh, come, and to his temple haste,
And seek his favor there
Before his footstool humbly bow,
And pour your fervent pray'r!

4 Oh, come, and join your souls to God
In everlasting bands;
Accept the blessings he bestows,
With thankful hearts and hands.

*HYMN 422. L. M. Kelly.
Bath. Portugal.
Hebrews xiii. 14.
1 "WE'VE no abiding city here"—
This may distress the worldly mind;
But should not cost the saint a tear,
Who hopes a better rest to find.

2 "We've no abiding city here"—
Sad truth were this to be our home:
But let this thought our spirits cheer,
"We seek a city yet to come."

3 "We've no abiding city here"—
Then let us live as pilgrims do;
Let not the world our rest appear;
But let us haste from all below.

4 "We've no abiding city here"—
We seek a city out of sight:
Zion its name—the Lord is there,
It shines with everlasting light.

*HYMN 423. C. M. Barbauld.
Barby. Rochester. Clarendon.
1 OUR country is Immanuel's ground,
We seek that promis'd soil:
The songs of Zion cheer our hearts,
While strangers here we toil.

2 Oft do our eyes with joy o'erflow,
And oft are bath'd in tears;
Yet nought but heav'n our hopes can raise,
And nought but sin our fears.

3 Our pow'rs are oft dissolv'd away
In ecstasies of love;
And while our bodies wander here,
Our souls are fix'd above.

4 We purge our mortal dross away,
Refining as we run;
But while we die to earth and sense
Our heav'n is here begun.

REJOICING IN A REVIVAL.

HYMN 424. L. M. Newton.
Bath. Moreton.
1 WHILE I to grief my soul gave way,
To see the work of God decline,
Methought I heard the Saviour say—
"Dismiss thy fears, the ark is mine.

2 "Though for a time I hid my face,
Rely upon my love and pow'r:
Still wrestle at the throne of grace,
And wait for a reviving hour.

3 "Take down thy long neglected harp,
I've seen thy tears and heard thy pray'r,
The winter season has been sharp,
But spring shall all its wastes repair."

4 Lord, I obey,—my hopes revive;
Come, join with me, ye saints, and sing;
Our foes in vain against us strive,
For God will help and triumph bring.

*HYMN 425. C. M. Needham.
Clifford. Clarendon.
Luke xv. 10.
1 OH, how divine, how sweet the joy,
When but one sinner turns,
And with a humble, broken heart,
His sins and errors mourns!

2 Pleas'd with the news the saints below,
In songs their tongues employ;
Beyond the skies the tidings go,
And heav'n is fill'd with joy.

3 Well pleas'd the Father sees and hears
The conscious sinner's moan;
Jesus receives him in his arms,
And claims him for his own.

4 Nor angels can their joys contain,
But kindle with new fire:
"The sinner lost is found," they sing,
And strike the sounding lyre.

HYMN 426. C. M.
Clifford. Springfield.
Great joy in that city. Acts viii. 8.
1 HOW much the drooping hearts revive
Of those who fear the Lord;
When sinners dead are made alive
By his reviving word!

2 The ministers of Christ rejoice,
When souls receive the word—
Then ransom'd sinners hear his voice,
Return and love the Lord.

3 The church of God their praises join,
And of salvation sing;
They glorify the grace divine
Of their victorious King.

4 In heav'n above, th' angelic throng
Around the throne rejoice;
But sinners sav'd should swell the song
With loudest—sweetest voice.

HYMN 427.   C. M.
Rochester. Clarendon.
1 CONVINC'D of sin, men now begin
To call upon the Lord;
Trembling they pray, and mourn the day
In which they scorn'd his word.

2 Young converts sing, and praise their King,
And bless God's holy name;
While older saints leave their complaints,
And joy to join the theme.

3 God's chariot rolls, and frights the souls
Of those who hate the truth:
And saints in pray'r cry, "Lord draw near,
Have mercy on the youth:—

4 "From this glad hour exert thy pow'r,
And melt each stubborn heart;
In those that bleed, let love succeed,
And holy joys impart."

5 Come, sinners, all, hear now God's call,
And pray with one accord:
Saints, raise your songs, with joyful tongues,
To hail th' approaching Lord.

HYMN 428. 8, 7, 4.
Tamworth. Helmsley. Littleton.
1 NOW we hail the happy dawning
Of the Gospel's glorious light,
May it take the wings of morning,
And dispel the shades of night;
Blessed Saviour,
Let our eyes behold the sight.

2 Where, amid the desert dreary,
Plant, nor shrub, nor flow'ret grows,
There refresh the wand'rer weary,
With the sight of Sharon's Rose;
And its beauties
To the longing eye disclose.

3 Where the beasts of prey are prowling,
And the murd'rous serpents hiss,
There exchange the dismal howling
For the pleasing calm of peace;
And for ever
May destruction's empire cease.

4 Oh, let all the world adore thee—
Universal be thy fame;
Kings and subjects fall before thee,
And extol thy matchless name;
All ascribing
Endless praises to the Lamb.

HYMN 429.   8, 7, 4.
Helmsley. Littleton.
Isaiah lii. 10.
1 YES! we trust the day is breaking;
Joyful times are near at hand:
God, the mighty God, is speaking
By his word in ev'ry land:
When he chooses,
Darkness flies at his command.

2 Let us hail the joyful season;
Let us hail the dawning ray:
When the Lord appears, there's reason
To expect a glorious day:
At his presence
Gloom and darkness flee away.

3 While the foe becomes more daring;
While he enters like a flood;
God, the Saviour, is preparing
Means to spread his truth abroad;
Ev'ry language
Soon shall teach the love of God.

4 God of Jacob, high and glorious,
Let thy people see thy hand;
Let the gospel be victorious,
Through the world in ev'ry land:
And the idols
Perish, Lord, at thy command.

HYMN 430.   L. N.   Beddome.
China. Luther's Hymn. Truro.
1 REJOICE, for Christ, the Saviour reigns;
He spreads his triumphs all abroad;
And sinners, freed from endless pains,
Own him their Saviour, and their God.

2 His sons and daughters from afar,
Daily at Zion's gate arrive;
Those who were dead in sin before,
By sov'reign grace are made alive.

3 Oh, may his conquests still increase,
And ev'ry foe his pow'r subdue;
While angels celebrate his praise,
And saints his growing glories show.

4 Loud hallelujahs to the Lamb,
From all below, from all above;
In lofty songs exalt his name;
In songs as lofty as his love.

HYMN 431.   H. M.   Doddridge.
Eagle Street. Psalm 148th. Bethesda.
Isaiah lx. 1.
1 O ZION, tune thy voice,
And raise thy hands on high
Tell all the earth thy joys,
And boast salvation nigh
Cheerful in God,
Arise and shine,
While rays divine
Stream all abroad.

2 He gilds thy mourning face
With beams that cannot fade;
His all resplendent grace
He pours around thy head;

The nations round
Thy form shall view,
With lustre new
Divinely crown'd.

3 In honor to his name
Reflect that sacred light;
And loud that grace proclaim,
Which makes thy darkness bright:
Pursue his praise,
Till sov'reign love
In worlds above
The glory raise.

4 There on his holy hill
A brighter Sun shall rise,
And with his radiance fill
Those fairer, purer skies;
While round his throne,
Ten thousand stars,
In nobler spheres
His influence own.

HYMN 432. H. M. Toplady.
Eagle Street. Bethesda. Jubilee.
1 BLOW ye the trumpet, blow
The gladly solemn sound!
Let all the nations know
To earth's remotest bound;
(Chorus) The year of Jubilee is come;
Return, ye ransom'd sinners, home.

2 Exalt the Lamb of God,
The sin-atoning Lamb;
Redemption by his blood,
Through all the lands proclaim;
(Chorus)

3 Ye slaves of sin and hell,
Your liberty receive;
And safe in Jesus dwell,
And blest in Jesus live.
(Chorus)

4 The gospel trumpet hear,
The news of pard'ning grace;
Ye happy souls, draw near,
Behold your Saviour's face.
(Chorus)

5 Jesus, our great High Priest,
Has full atonement made
Ye weary spirits, rest;
Ye mournful souls be glad!
(Chorus)

HYMN 433. L. P. N. Doddridge.
St. Helen's. Eaton.
Efficacy of God's word. Jeremiah xxiii. 29.
1 WITH rev'rend awe, tremendous Lord
We hear the thunders of thy word;
The pride of Lebanon it breaks,
Swift the celestial fire descends,
The flinty rock in pieces rends,
And earth to its deep centre shakes.

2 Array'd in majesty divine,
Here sanctity and justice shine,
And horror strikes the rebel through;
While loud this awful voice makes known
The wonders which thy sword hath done,
And what thy vengeance yet shall do.

3 So spread the honors of thy name;
The terrors of a God proclaim;
Thick let the pointed arrows fly;
Till sinners, humbled in the dust,
Shall own the execution just,
And bless the hand by which they die.

4 Then clear the dark tempestuous day,
And radiant beams of love display,
Each prostrate soul let mercy raise;
So shall the bleeding captives feel,
Thy word, that gave the wound, can heal,
And change their notes to songs of praise.

HYMN 434. 8, 7, 4.   Kelly.
Littleton. Tamworth.
Isaiah lii. 7.
1 ON the mountain's top appearing,
Lo, the sacred herald stands;
Welcome news to Zion bearing,
Zion long in hostile lands
Mourning captive,
God himself will loose thy bands.

2 Has thy night been long and mournful,
All thy friends unfaithful prov'd?
Have thy foes been proud and scornful,
By thy sighs and tears unmov'd?
Cease thy mourning,
Zion still is well belov'd.

3 God, thy God, will now restore thee!
He himself appears thy friend:
All thy foes shall flee before thee,
Here their boasts and triumphs end:
Great deliv'rance
Zion's King vouchsafes to send.

4 Peace and joy shall now attend thee,
All thy warfare now is past,
God, thy Saviour, shall defend thee,
Peace and joy are come at last;
All thy conflicts
End in everlasting rest.

*HYMN 435. C. M.
St. Ann's. Colchester. St. Martin's.
Sinai and Calvary.
1 HARK! how from Sinai's mount proceed:
The trumpet's awful blast;
While yet the heart with anguish bleeds,
And sinks in wo at last.

2 Behold the sinner's fearless soul,
Which love could ne'er arrest,
With trembling hears the thunder roll,
And death approaching fast.—

3 But lo!—what sounds of heav'nly peace,
Amid the storm I hear;
When howling winds a moment cease,
And love succeeds to fear!

4 Now, on the hill of Calvary,
Where Jesus once was slain,
Sweet peace, and love, and sympathy,
There all unbroken reign.

5 Whene'er the tempest's vengeful voice,
And guilt my soul appal,
I then in Jesus will rejoice,
And mercy's gentle call.

6 And when by care and we oppress'd,
Or storms of sorrow fall,
I'll flee to him and find a rest—
Enjoy in him my all.

HYMN 436. 7s.
Pleyel's Hymn. Hampton.
The little cloud. 1 Kings xviii. 44.
1 SAW ye not the cloud arise,
Little as the human hand!
Now it spreads along the skies,
Hangs o'er all the thirsty land!

2 Lo, the promise of a show'r
Drops already from above;
But the Lord will shortly pour
All the blessings of his love.

3 When he first the work begun,
Small and feeble was his day;
Now the word doth swiftly run,
Now it wins its wid'ning way.

4 Sons of God, your Saviour praise;
He the door hath open'd wide;
He hath giv'n the word of grace;
Jesus' word is glorified.

HYMN 437. S. M.
Cambridge. Silver Street.
Isaiah lx. 8.
1 THE day is drawing nigh,
Still brighter far than this,
When converts like a cloud shall fly
To seek the realms of bliss.

2 What rapt'rous scenes of joy
Shall burst upon our sight,
When sinners up to Zion's hill
Like doves shall speed their flight.

3 Beneath thy balmy wing,
O Sun of righteousness,
These happy souls shall sit and sing
The wonders of thy grace.

HYMN 438. 8, 7.   C. Wesley.
Love Divine. Tabernacle.
1 LOVE divine, all love excelling,
Joy of heav'n to earth come down!
Fix in us thy humble dwelling;
All thy faithful mercies crown;
Jesus, thou art all compassion,
Pure, unbounded love thou art:
Visit us with thy salvation,
Enter ev'ry trembling heart.

2 Breathe, Oh, breathe thy loving Spirit
Into ev'ry troubled breast:
Let us all in thee inherit,
Let us find thy promis'd rest
Take away the love of sinning,
Take our load of guilt away;
End the work of thy beginning,
Bring us to eternal day.

3 Carry on thy new creation,
Pure and holy may we be;
Let us see our whole salvation,
Perfectly secur'd by Thee;
Change from glory into glory,
Till in heav'n we take our place;

Till we cast our crowns before Thee
Lost in wonder, love and praise.

HYMN 439. 8, 7. Robinson.
Love Divine. Good Shepherd.
Grateful recollection 1 Samuel vii. 12.
1 COME, thou Fount of ev'ry blessing,
Tune my heart to sing thy grace;
Streams of mercy, never ceasing,
Call for songs of loudest praise.
Teach me some melodious sonnet,
Sung by flaming tongues above:
Praise the mount—I'm fix'd upon it—
Mount of God's unchanging love.

2 Here I raise my Eben-Ezer,
Hither by thy help I'm come;
And I hope, by thy good pleasure,
Safely to arrive at home.
Jesus sought me when a stranger
Wand'ring from the fold of God;
He to rescue me from danger,
Interpos'd with precious blood.

3 Oh! to grace how great a debtor
Daily I'm constrain'd to be!
Let that grace now, like a fetter,
Bind my wand'ring heart to thee:
Prone to wander, Lord, I feel it—
Prone to leave the God I love
Here's my heart—O take and seal it;
Seal it from thy courts above.

HYMN 440. C. M. Logan.
Braintree. Springfield. Clifford.
Isaiah lv. 12, 13.
1 MESSIAH! at thy glad approach,
The howling winds are still;
Thy praises fill the lonely waste,
And breathe from every hill.

2 The hidden fountains at thy call,
Their sacred stores unlock;
Loud in the desert, sudden streams
Burst living from the rock.

3 The incense of the spring ascends
Upon the morning gale;
Red o'er the hill the roses bloom,
The lilies in the vale.

4 Renew'd, the earth a robe of light,
A robe of beauty wears;
And in new heav'ns a brighter Sun
Leads on the promis'd years.

5 Let Israel to the Prince of Peace
The loud hosanna sing;
With hallelujahs, and with hymns,
O Zion, hail thy King.

HYMN 441. L. M. Tappan.
Shoel. Chatham. Sterling.
1 HARK! from yon wilds is heard the strain
Of joy and praise ascending high;
The song of Zion cheers the plain,
The desert breathes the contrite's sigh.

2 Now true Religion rears her throne,
Where superstition darkly trod;
And where His altar was unknown,
Unnumber'd temples rise to God.

3 Raise your glad songs, ye choirs, on high;
Salvation to the heathen flows;
Let anthems roll along the sky;
The desert blossoms like the rose.

*HYMN 442. L. M.
Moreton. Kent. Luther's Hymn.
John iv. 35.
1 LIFT up your eyes, ye sons of light,
Behold the fields already white!
The glorious harvest now is come;
See ransom'd sinners flocking home.

2 Mov'd by the Spirit's softest wind,
Their hearts are all as one inclin'd;
Their former sins and follies mourn;
They bow, and to their God return.

3 Improve the harvest fleeing fast,
Ere yet the shining season's past,
When all the work of life shall end,
The last—the long dark night descend.

HYMN 443. 8, 7, 4.   Kelly.
Littleton. Jordan.
Zechariah xiii. 1.
1 SEE, from Zion's sacred mountain
Streams of living water flow:
God has open'd there a fountain;
This supplies the plains below:
They are blessed,
Who its sov'reign virtues know.

2 Through ten thousand channels flowing,
Streams of mercy find their way;
Life, and health, and joy bestowing,
Making all around look gay,
O, ye nations!
Hail the long expected day.

3 Gladden'd by the flowing treasure,
All enriching as it goes:
Lo, the desert smiles with pleasure,
Buds and blossoms as the rose,
Ev'ry object
Sings for joy were'er it flows.

4 Trees of life the banks adorning,
Yield their fruit to all around;
Those who eat are sav'd from mourning,
Pleasure comes and hopes abound:
Fair their portion!
Endless life with glory crown'd.

HYMN 444. H. M.
Weymouth. Eagle Street
1 HARK! hark!—the notes of joy
Roll o'er the heav'nly plains,
And seraphs find employ
For their sublimest strains;
Some new delight in heav'n is known;
Loud sing the harps around the throne.

2 Hark! hark!—the sounds draw nigh,
The joyful hosts descend;
Jesus forsakes the sky,
To earth his footsteps bend;
He comes to bless our fallen race;
He comes with messages of grace.

3 Bear, bear the tidings round;
Let every mortal know
What love in God is found,
What pity he can show;
Ye winds that blow, ye waves that roll,
Bear the glad news from pole to pole.

4 Strike, strike the harps again,
To great Immanuel's name;
Arise, ye sons of men,
And all his grace proclaim;
Angels and men, wake ev'ry string,
'Tis God, the Saviour's praise we sing.

HYMN 445. 7, 6. Montgomery.
Brighthelmstone. Margate.
1 HAIL to the Lord's anointed!
Great David's greater Son;
Hail in the time appointed,
His reign on earth begun!
He comes to break oppression,
To set the captive free;
To take away transgression,
And rule in equity.

2 He comes, with succor speedy,
To those who suffer wrong;
To help the poor and needy,
And bid the weak be strong;
To give them songs for sighing,
Their darkness turn to light,
Whose souls condemn'd and dying,
Were precious in his sight.

3 He shall come down, like showers
Upon the fruitful earth,
And love and joy, like flowers,
Spring in his path to birth:

Before him, on the mountains,
Shall peace the herald go,
And righteousness in fountains
From hill to valley flow.

4 For Him shall pray'r unceasing,
And daily vows ascend;
His kingdom still increasing,
A kingdom without end:
The tide of time shall never
His covenant remove;
His name shall stand for ever,
That name to us is—Love.

BAPTISM.

HYMN 446. L. M.
Leyden. Sterling.
Baptism
1 OBEDIENT to our Zion's King,
We to his holy laver bring
These happy converts, who have known
And trusted in his grace alone.

2 Lord, in thy house they seek thy face;
Oh, bless them with peculiar grace;
Refresh their souls with love divine;
Let beams of glory round them shine.

3 Ye, who your native vileness mourn,
And to the great Redeemer turn,
Arise, his gracious call obey,
And be baptiz'd without delay.

HYMN 447. L. M. Collyer.
Bath. Kent.
Household Baptism.
1 UNITED pray'rs ascend to thee,
Eternal parent of mankind;
Smile on this waiting family—
Thy face they seek, and let them find.

2 Let the dear pledges of their love,
Like tender plants around them grew;
Thy present grace, and joys above,
Upon their little ones bestow.

3 Receive, at their believing hand,
The charge which they devote as thine,
Obedient to their Lord's command—
And seal with pow'r the rite divine.

4 To ev'ry member of their house,
Thy grace impart, thy love extend;
Grant ev'ry good that time allows,
With heav'nly joys that never end.

HYMN 448. C. M. Doddridge.
St. Ann's. Arlington.
Mark x. 14.
1 SEE Israel's gentle Shepherd stand
With all engaging charms;
Hark, how he calls the tender Lambs,
And folds them in his arms.

2 "Permit them to approach," he cries,
"Nor scorn their humble name;
"For 'twas to bless such souls as these,
"The Lord of angels came."

3 We bring them, Lord, in thankful hands,
And yield them up to thee;
Joyful that we ourselves are thine,
Thine let our offspring be.

4 Ye little flock, with pleasure hear;
Ye children seek his face;
And fly with transports to receive
The blessings of his grace.

5 If orphans they are left behind,
Thy guardian care we trust;
That care shall heal our bleeding heart,
If weeping o'er their dust.

HYMN 449. C. M. Hyde.
Barby. Clarendon. Chapel.
1 SHEPHERD, who lead'st with tender care,
The feeble of thy fold,—
Who dost regard the weakest there,
And all their steps uphold;

2 This little helpless lamb receive,
In mercy, to thy breast;
And let parental fondness leave
It safely there to rest.

3 Surround it with thy guardian love,
Through all life's dang'rous way;
Ne'er let it from thy pastures rove,
Nor be the lion's prey.

4 In thine eternal, heav'nly home,
Oh, let it find a place;
And be, when life and toils are done,
A trophy of thy grace.

HYMN 450. C. M. Doddridge.
Barby. Bedford. Canterbury.
Practical Improvement. Colossians iii. 1.
1 ATTEND, ye children of your God,
Ye heirs of glory, hear;
For accents, so divine as these,
Might charm the dullest ear.

2 Baptiz'd into your Saviour's death,
Your souls to sin must die:
With Christ, your Lord, ye live anew,
With Christ ascend on high.

3 There, by his Father's side he sits
Enthron'd, divinely fair;
Yet owns himself your Brother still,
And your Forerunner there.

4 Rise from these earthly trifles, rise
On wings of faith and love;
Above, your choicest treasure lies,
And be your hearts above.

MONTHLY CONCERT.

HYMN 451. L. M.
Luton. Leeds. Chatham.
Prayer for the spread of the Gospel.
1 THY people, Lord, who trust thy word,
And wait the smilings of thy face,
Assemble round thy mercy seat,
And plead the promise of thy grace.

2 We consecrate these hours to thee,
Thy sov'reign mercy to entreat;
And feel some animating hope,
We shall divine acceptance meet.

3 Hast thou not promis'd to thy Son,
That his dominion shall extend,
Till ev'ry tongue shall call him Lord,
And ev'ry knee before him bend?

4 Now let the happy time appear,
The time to favor Zion come;
Send forth thy heralds far and near,
To call thy banish'd people home.

HYMN 452. L. M.
Luther's Hymn. Portugal.
1 ETERNAL God! Almighty cause
Of earth, and seas, and worlds unknown;
All things are subject to thy laws,
All things depend on thee alone.

2 Spread thy great name through heathen lands;
Their idol deities dethrone;
Reduce the world to thy commands;
And reign as thou art, God alone.

HYMN 453. C. M.
St. Ann's. Colchester. Bray.
1 O THOU great Monarch, in thy might
Fulfil the long desire;
A thousand ages in thy sight,
Like yesterday retire.

2 Oh, let thy diadem supreme,
Its brightness now display,
And o'er the dying nations beam
With life's immortal day.

3 Then shall the desolations cease,
And earth in sweetest strain,
Through the long Jubilee of peace,
Sing thy unbounded reign.

HYMN 454.   H. M.
Eagle Street. Bethesda.
1 SOV'REIGN of worlds above,
And Lord of all below,
Thy faithfulness and love,
Thy pow'r and mercy show:
Fulfil thy word;
Thy Spirit give;
Let heathens live
And praise the Lord.

2 On lands that lie beneath
Foul superstition's sway,
Whose horrid shades of death
Admit no heav'nly ray,
Blest Spirit! shine,
Their hearts illume;
Dispel the gloom
With light divine.

3 Father, who to thy Son
Thy steadfast word hast giv'n.
That through the earth shall run
The news of peace with heav'n,
Extend his fame;
Thy grace diffuse;
And let the news
The world reclaim.

4 Few be the years that roll,
Ere all shall worship thee;
The travail of his soul,
Soon let the Saviour see;
O God of grace!
Thy pow'r employ,

Fill earth with joy,
And heav'n with praise.

HYMN 455. S. M.
St. Thomas. Shirland.
1 O GOD of sov'reign grace,
We bow before thy throne;
And plead, for all the human race,
The merits of thy Son.

2 Spread through the earth, O Lord,
The knowledge of thy ways;
And let all lands with joy record
The great Redeemer's praise!

HYMN 456. C. M. Gibbons.
Mear. Dundee.
1 GREAT God, the nations of the earth
Are by creation thine;
And in thy works, by all beheld,
Thy radiant glories shine.

2 But, Lord, thy richer love has sent
Thy gospel to mankind,
Unveiling what rich stores of grace
Are treasur'd in thy mind.

3 Lord, when shall these glad tidings spread
The spacious earth around,
Till ev'ry tribe and ev'ry soul
Shall hear the joyful sound.

4 Smile, Lord, on each divine attempt
To spread the gospel rays;
And build, on sin's demolish'd throne,
The temples of thy praise.

HYMN 457. C. M. Part II.
Rochester. Barby.
1 OH, when shall Afric's sable sons
Enjoy the heav'nly word;
And vassals, long enslav'd, become
The freemen of the Lord?

2 When shall th' untutor'd Heathen tribes,
A dark, bewilder'd race,
Sit down at our Immanuel's feet,
And learn and sing his grace?

3 Haste, sov'reign Mercy, and transform
Their cruelty to love
Soften the tiger to a lamb,
The vulture to a dove.

HYMN 458. 8, 7, 4.
Littleton. Helmsley.
Isaiah lx. 2, 3.
1 O'ER the gloomy hills of darkness;
Cheer'd by no celestial ray,
Sun of Righteousness, arising,
Bring the bright, the glorious day;
Send the gospel
To the earth's remotest bound.

2 Kingdoms wide that sit in darkness!
Grant them, Lord, the glorious light;
And from eastern coast to western,
May the morning chase the night;
And redemption
Freely purchas'd, win the day.

3 Fly abroad, thou mighty gospel—
Win and conquer, never cease;
May thy lasting, wide dominions
Multiply and still increase;
Sway thy sceptre,
Saviour, all the world around.

HYMN 459. L. M. Voke.
St. Catharine's. Nantwich. Kent.
1 EXERT thy pow'r, thy rights maintain,
Insulted, everlasting King!
The influence of thy crown increase,
And strangers to thy footstool bring.

2 In one vast symphony of praise,
Gentile and Jew shall then unite;
And infidelity, asham'd,
Sink in th' abyss of endless night.

3 From east to west, from north to south,
Immanuel's kingdom must extend;
And ev'ry man, in ev'ry face,
Shall meet a brother, and a friend.

HYMN 460. C. M. Fawcett.
Colchester. Rochester. Bray.
The desire of all Nations. Haggai ii. 7.
1 INFINITE excellence is thine,
Thou lovely Prince of grace!
Thine uncreated beauties shine,
With never fading rays.

2 Sinners from earth's remotest end,
Come bending at thy feet:
To thee their pray'rs and vows ascend,
In thee their wishes meet.

3 Millions of happy spirits live
On thy exhaustless store;
From thee they all their bliss receive,
And still thou givest more.

4 Thou art their triumph and their joy
They find their all in thee;
Thy glories will their tongues employ,
Through all eternity.

HYMN 461. L. M.
China. Sterling. Truro.
The restoration of Israel. Ezekiel xxxvi. 8.
1 MOUNTAINS of Israel, rear on high
Your summits, crown'd with verdure new,
And spread your branches to the sky,
Refulgent with celestial dew.

2 Fresh cities bloom along the plain;
New temples to Jehovah rise;
The kindling voice of praise again
Wings its sweet anthems to the skies.

3 The bloody sacrifice no more
Shall smoke upon the altars high,
But ardent hearts from hill to shore
Send grateful incense to the sky.

4 The jubilee of man is near
'Tis come, our God's unbounded reign;
Our Jesus wipes the mourner's tear
And Satan's wiles are all in vain.

5 Praise him, ye tribes of Israel, praise
The King that ransom'd you from wo;
Nations! the hymn of triumph raise,
And bid the song of rapture flow.

HYMN 462. 8, 7.   Newton.
Love Divine. Tabernacle.
Psalm lxxxvii. 3. Isaiah xxxiii. 20, 21.
1 GLORIOUS things of thee are spoken,
Zion, city of our God;
He, whose word cannot be broken,
Form'd thee for his own abode:
On the rock of ages founded—
What can shake thy sure repose ?
With salvation's walls surrounded,
Thou may'st smile at all thy foes.

2 See, the streams of living waters,
Springing from eternal love,
Well supply thy sons and daughters,
And all fear of want remove:
Who can faint while such a river
Ever flows thy thirst t' assuage ?
Grace, which, like the Lord, the giver,
Never fails from age to age.

3 Round each habitation hov'ring,
See the cloud and fire appear!
For a glory and a cov'ring,
Showing that the Lord is near:
Thus deriving from their banner
Light by night and shade by day,
Safe they feed upon the manna
Which he gives them when they pray.

HYMN 463. L. M. Hyde.
Chatham. New Hundredth. Bicestor.
Jeremiah xxxi. 6.
1 THE trump of Israel's jubilee
Shall sound aloud from Calvary,
And bid the wand'ring exiles—" Come,
"And find in Zion still a home."

2 Israel shall hear—that thrilling sound
Shall reach to earth's remotest bound,
And gather to that holy place
The fugitives of Jacob's race.

3 Their exil'd tribes shall yet return,
Shall come to Calvary and mourn:
And, bow'd beneath Messiah's sway,
With willing hearts his rule obey.

HYMN 464. L. M.
Kent. Bath. Wells.
Isaiah lx. 2.
1 THOUGH now the nations sit beneath
The darkness of o'erspreading death,
God will arise with light divine
On Zion's holy tow'rs to shine.

2 That light shall glance on distant lands,
And heathen tribes, in joyful bands,
Come with exulting haste to prove
The pow'r and greatness of his love.

3 Lord, may the triumphs of thy grace
Abound, with righteousness and peace,
In mild, and lovely forms, display
The glories of the latter day.

HYMN 465. L. M.
New Hundredth. Shoel. Kent.
The Angel's flight. Revelation xiv. 6.
1 THAT mighty angel, to whose hand
The everlasting word is giv'n,
Waves his broad wing o'er sea and land,
And soaring, cleaves the vault of heav'n.

2 And say—shall aught oppose his flight?—
Aught dim with clouds his flaming scroll?
No!—not till truth with holy light
Shall visit ev'ry heathen soul:

3 Not till blest Peace shall spring to birth;
Till hatred sheath his useless sword;
Not till the nations of the earth
Become the kingdoms of the Lord.

HYMN 466. C. M.
Clifford. Missionary. Keene.
1 BEHOLD, high in the midst of heav'n,
A mighty angel flies;
The gospel, grace, and life are giv'n
By Him who paid their price.

2 Asia receives the word of love,
And wonders as she hears;
The day-spring, dawning from above,
O'er Africa appears.

3 The islands of the sea rejoice,
And sing Immanuel's praise;
With joyful heart, and rapt'rous voice,
They shout his welcome grace.

4 Then—let us shout hosannas too,
To David's princely Son;—
Then let *us* to the nations show
The wonders he has done.

HYMN 467. L. M. Merrick.
Old Hundred. Nantwich,. Leeds.
Prayer for Israel. Romans x. 1.
1 ARISE, great God, and let thy grace
Shed its glad beams on Jacob's race;
Restore the long lost, scatter'd band,
And call them to their native land.

2 Their mis'ry let thy mercy heal,
Their trespass hide, their pardon seal;
O God of Israel, hear our pray'r,
And grant them still thy love to share.

3 How long shall Jacob's offspring prove
The sad suspension of thy love?
Say, shall thy wrath perpetual burn?
And wilt thou ne'er, appeas'd, return?

4 Thy quick'ning Spirit now impart,
And wake to joy each grateful heart,
While Israel's rescu'd tribes in Thee
Their bliss and full salvation see.

HYMN 468. C. M.
Clarendon. Braintree.
1 SHEPHERD of Israel, thou did'st lead
Thy flock the desert through,
And from between the Cherubim
Thy beaming mercy show.

2 And though their sins provok'd thee oft
To give them for a prey,
Yet didst thou for thy mercies' sake
Oft turn thy wrath away.

3 But now for ages they have been
Far banish'd from thy sight,
Wand'ring through all the earth, as those
In whom is no delight.

4 Yet is thy word of promise sure,
That they shall be restor'd,
And with the Gentile church unite
To love and serve the Lord.

5 Our faith in expectation waits
With ever longing eyes;
Oh, bid the shadows flee away—
That glorious morning rise.

HYMN 469. L. M.
Wells. Portugal.
1 FATHER of faithful Abra'm, hear
Our earnest suit for Abra'm's seed;
Justly they claim the softest pray'r
From those adopted in their stead:

2 Outcast from thee, and scatter'd wide
Through ev'ry nation under heav'n,
Rejecting whom they crucified,
Unsav'd, unpitied, unforgiv'n.

3 But hast thou finally forsook,
For ever cast thine own away?
No—thou wilt bid them turn and look
On him they pierc'd, and mourn and pray.

4 Come, then, thou great Deliv'rer, come,
The veil from Jacob's heart remove;
Receive thy ancient people home,
That they may sing redeeming love.

HYMN 470. L. M. Hyde.
Cumberland. Blendon. Chatham.
The restoration of Israel.
1 THE Lord will not forget the grace
Reserv'd for faithful Abra'm's race;
His love their wand'rings shall restore,
And guide them, that they stray no more

2 Israel! 'tis thine accepted day,
Thy God himself prepares the way;—
Behold his ensign from afar—
Behold the light of Jacob's Star.

3 That Star, which once on Bethle'm rose,
A token on thy mountain glows,
The morn of earth's blest jubilee
Sheds its sweet early light on thee.

4 And thou, who once on Israel's ground,
A homeless wanderer was found,
Redeemer, on thy heav'nly throne,
Still call that ancient church thine own,

5 Bid her departed light return,
Thy holy splendor round her burn;
From prostrate Judah's ruins raise
A living temple to thy praise.

HYMN 471. L. M.
Nantwich. Portugal. Moreton.
Prayer for the success of the gospel.
1 INDULGENT God, to thee we pray;
Be with us on this solemn day:
Our brethren bless, their zeal approve,
That zeal which burns to spread thy love.

2 With cheerful steps may they proceed,
Where'er thy providence shall lead:
Let heav'n and earth their work befriend,
And mercy all their paths attend.

3 Let num'rous, solemn crowds be found,
Anxious to hear the gospel sound;
And rude barbarians, bond and free,
In suppliant throngs, resort to thee.

4 Where pagan altars now are built,
And brutal blood, or human, spilt,
There may the bleeding cross be rear'd,
And God, our God, alone rever'd.

*HYMN 472. L. M.
Old Hundred. Bicester. Blendon.
1 O THOU, who from thy glorious throne,
Hast sent thy servants to proclaim
Salvation to a world undone,
And sound through all the earth thy name;

2 Succeed their efforts who invite
The wand'ring, wretched outcasts home;
And let thy sov'reign Spirit's might
Compel the heathen world to come.

3 From Afric's burning, arid sand,
And Asia's mild, resplendent sky;
Let converts, from the heathen lands,
As doves unto their windows fly.

4 With Europe may they join to bless
The Saviour's name, his praise prolong;
And Islands of the Southern seas
Join with America the song.

HYMN 473. L. M.
Blendon. Truro.
1 SOV'REIGN of worlds! display thy pow'r,
Be this thy Zion's favor'd hour;
Bid the bright morning Star arise,
And point the nations to the skies.

2 Set up thy throne where Satan reigns.
On Afric's shore, on India's plains,
On wilds and continents unknown;
And be the universe thine own.

3 Speak! and the world shall hear thy voice;
Speak! and the desert shall rejoice;
Scatter the gloom of heathen night,
And bid all nations hail the light.

HYMN 474. C. M.
Springfield. Barby. St. Martin's.
Matthew xxviii. 18.
1 GREAT Saviour, let thy pow'r divine
O'er all the earth be known;
Let all, to thee, their will resign,
And make thy will their own.

2 Perversion marks the guilty way,
Which heathens madly tread;
From all thy laws they go astray,
And hasten to the dead.

3 Thou, Saviour—God, hast pow'r alone
To turn their wand'ring feet,
To bend their souls before thy throne,
Low at thy mercy seat:—

4 For all the pow'r, beneath, above,
Thy wounded hands sustain;
Then sway the sceptre of thy love,
And let thy mercy reign.

HYMN 475. L. M.
Bath. Chatham.
1 MILLIONS there are on heathen ground,
Who never heard the gospel's sound;

Lord, send it forth, and let it run,
Swift and reviving as the sun.

2 Guide thou their lips, who stand to tell
Sinners the way that leads from hell:
To those who give, do thou impart
A gen'rous, wise, and tender heart.

3 Lord, crown their zeal, reward their care,
That in thy grace they all may share:
And those who now in darkness dwell,
Deliv'rance sing from guilt and hell.

*HYMN 476. L. M.
Kent. Leyden. Luton.
1 LOOK down, O God, with pitying eye,
And view the desolations round;
See what wide realms in darkness lie,
And hurl their idols to the ground.

2 Lord, let the gospel-trumpet blow,
And call the nations from afar;
Let all the isles their Saviour know,
And earth's remotest ends draw near.

3 Let Satan's cruel kingdom shake,—
The realms of darkness, and of sin;
Messiah now his empire take—
In ev'ry soul his reign begin.

HYMN 477. L. M.
Blendon. Bicester.
Isaiah li. 9.
1 ARM of the Lord, awake, awake!
Put on thy strength—the nations shake,
And let the world, adoring, see
Triumphs of mercy wrought by thee.

2 Say to the heathen, from thy throne.
"I am Jehovah-God alone":
Thy voice their idols shall confound,
And cast their altars to the ground.

3 No more let human blood be spilt—
Vain sacrifice for human guilt!

But to each conscience be applied
The blood that flow'd from Jesus' side.

4 Almighty God, thy grace proclaim.
In ev'ry land, of ev'ry name;
Let adverse pow'rs before thee fall,
And crown the Saviour—LORD OF ALL.

HYMN 478. 8, 7, 4.
Jordan. Tamworth.
For the influences of the Spirit.
1 WHO, but thou, almighty Spirit,
Can the heathen world reclaim?
Men may preach, but till thou favor,
Heathens will be still the same:
Mighty Spirit!
Witness to the Saviour's name.

2 Thou hast promis'd by the prophets,
Glorious light in latter days
Come, and bless bewilder'd nations,
Change our pray'rs and tears to praise;
Promis'd Spirit!
Round the world diffuse thy rays.

3 All our hopes, and pray'rs, and labors,
Must be vain without thine aid:
But thou wilt not disappoint us—
All is true that thou hast said:
Faithful Spirit!
O'er the world thine influence shed.

HYMN 479. L. M. Rippon.
Luther's Hymn. Kent. China.
The latter day glory.
1 WHEN will the happy trump proclaim
The judgment of the martyr'd Lamb?
When shall the captive troops be free,
And keep th' eternal jubilee!

2 Hasten it, Lord, in ev'ry land,
Send thou thine angels, and command;
"Go, sound deliv'rance—loudly blow
"Salvation to the saints below!"

3 We long to have the day appear,
The promis'd, great Sabbatic year;
When, far from grief, and sin, and hell,
Israel in ceaseless peace shall dwell.

4 Till then, we will not let thee rest—
Thou still shalt hear our strong request;
And this our daily pray'r shall be,
Lord, sound the trump of jubilee.

HYMN 480. C. M. Tappan.
Colchester. Florence. Wareham.
Arise, shine,— Isaiah lx. 1.
1 HARK! 'tis the Prophet of the skies
Proclaims Redemption near;
The night of death and bondage flies,
The dawning tints appear.

2 Zion, from deepest shades of gloom,
Awakes to glorious day;
Her desert wastes with verdure bloom,
Her shadows flee away.

3 The glad'ning news, convey'd afar,
Remotest nations hear;
To welcome Judah's rising Star,
The ransom'd tribes appear.

4 Fair Lebanon shall hear his voice,
And lands where Jordan flows,
With Sharon's desert shall rejoice,
And blossom as the rose.

*HYMN 481. C. M. Logan.
Braintree. New Cambridge. Keene.
Micah iv. 1-5.
1 BEHOLD! the mountain of the Lord,
In latter days, shall rise
Above the mountains and the hills,
And draw the wond'ring eyes.

2 To this the joyful nations round,
All tribes and tongues, shall flow;
"Up to the hill of God," they say.
"And to his courts we'll go."

3 The beams that shine on Zion's hill
Shall lighten ev'ry land;
The King who reigns in Zion's tow'rs,
Shall all the world command.

4 No longer hosts encount'ring hosts,
Their millions slain deplore;
They hang the trumpet in the hall,
And study war no more.

5 Come then—Oh, come from ev'ry land,
To worship at his shrine:
And walking in the light of God,
With holy beauties shine.

HYMN 482. L. M. Hyde.
Luton. Blendon.
Luke i. 78.
1 BEHOLD the glorious dawning bright
Of the millennial morn arise,
The prelude of the promis'd light
Now gladdens the expecting skies!

2 And shall not those awake, who claim
Their hearts and hopes on high to place;
Who bear the Saviour's sacred name,
While he displays his boundless grace!

3 Lo, Jesus comes! his people know
The goings of their glorious King—
He rends the heav'ns, the mountains flow,
And his redeem'd his triumph sing.

4 How sweet his peaceful reign shall be,
His sway shall all the nations own,
All tongues shall bless him—ev'ry knee
Shall bow submissive to his throne.

HYMN 483. L. M. Beddome.
Old Hundred. Luther's Hymn. Malmsbury.
Thy kingdom come. Matthew vi. 10.
1 ASCEND thy throne, Almighty King,
And spread thy glories all abroad;
Let thy own arm salvation bring,
And be thou known, the gracious God.

2 Let millions bow before thy seat;
Let humble mourners seek thy face;
Bring daring rebels to thy feet,
Subdu'd by thy victorious grace.

3 Oh, let the kingdoms of the world
Become the kingdoms of the Lord;
Let saints and angels praise thy name;
Be thou thro' heav'n and earth ador'd.

*HYMN 484. L. M.
Luther's Hymn. Malmsbury.
1 BRIGHT as the sun's meridian blaze,
Vast as the blessings he conveys,
Wide as his reign from pole to pole,
And permanent as his control:

2 So, Jesus, let thy kingdom come—
Then sin and hell's terrific gloom
Shall, at his brightness, flee away,
The dawn of an eternal day.

HYMN 485. C. M.
Clifford. Steffani's. Keene.
Prince of Peace.
1 LET saints on earth their anthems raise,
Who taste the Savior's grace:
Let heathens too proclaim his praise,
And crown him "Prince of Peace."

2 Praise him, who laid his glory by,
For man's apostate race;
Praise him, who stoop'd to bleed and die,
And crown him "Prince of Peace."

3 Ye nations, lay your weapons down,
Let war for ever cease;
Immanuel for your Sov'reign own,
And crown him "Prince of Peace."

4 We soon shall reach the heav'nly shore,
To view his lovely face;
His name for ever to adore,
And crown him "Prince of Peace."

HYMN 486. 8,7.   Kelly.
Tabernacle. Drummond.
Isaiah ii. 2.
1 HARK! a cry among the nations!
"Come, and let us seek the Lord:
"Vain our former expectations;
"Vain the idols we ador'd:
"Zion's King is God alone:
"Let us bow before his throne."

2 See! from ev'ry quarter flowing,
Joyful crowds assemble round:
Love, in ev'ry heart is glowing:
Praise is heard in ev'ry sound;
While Jehovah shows his face,
Glory fills the sacred place.

3 Weapons meant for mutual slaughter
Now are instruments of peace;
They who taste the living water,
Learn from war and strife to cease:
Jesus reigns—the earth is still—
All the nations do his will.

HYMN 487. 7s.   Montgomery.
Hotham. Middleton.
Revelation xiv. 2, 3.
1 HARK! the song of Jubilee,
Loud as mighty thunders roar,
O'er the fulness of the sea,
When it breaks upon the shore:—
Hallelujah! for the Lord,
God omnipotent, shall reign;
Hallelujah! let the word
Echo round the earth and main.

2 Hallelujah! hark! the sound,
From the depth unto the skies,
Wakes above, beneath, around,
All creation's harmonies:—
See Jehovah's banner furl'd,
Sheath'd his sword: he speaks: 'tis done
And the kingdoms of this world
Are the kingdoms of his Son.

3 He shall reign from pole to pole
With illimitable sway:
He shall reign, when like a scroll,
Yonder heav'ns have pass'd away
Then the end;—beneath his rod,
Man's last enemy shall fall;
Hallelujah! Christ in God,
God in Christ, is all in all.

MISSIONARY MEETINGS.

HYMN 488. L. M. Collyer.
Luther's Hymn. Leeds. Bath.
For Missionary Associations.
1 ASSEMBLED at thy great command,
Before thy face, dread King, we stand;
The voice that marshall'd ev'ry star,
Has call'd thy people from afar.

2 We meet, through distant lands to spread
The truth for which the martyrs bled;
Along the line—to either pole—
The thunder of thy praise to roll.

3 First, bow our hearts beneath thy sway:
Then give thy growing empire way,
O'er wastes of sin—o'er fields of blood—
Till all mankind shall be subdu'd.

4 Our pray'rs assist—accept our praise—
Our hopes revive—our courage raise—
Our counsels aid—and Oh! impart
The single eye—the faithful heart!

5 Forth with thy chosen heralds come,
Recall the wandering spirit home:
From Zion's mount send forth the sound
To spread the spacious earth around.

HYMN 489. L. M. Yoke.
Leyden. China. Leeds.
1 BEHOLD th' expected time draw near,
The shades disperse, the dawn appear;
Behold the wilderness assume
The beauteous tints of Eden's bloom.

2 The untaught heathen waits to know
The joy the gospel will bestow,
The exil'd captive, to receive
The freedom Jesus has to give.

3 Come, let us with a grateful heart
In the blest labor share a part;
Our pray'rs and off'rings gladly bring
To aid the triumphs of our King.

4 Invite the world to come and prove
A Saviour's condescending love;
And humbly fall before his feet,
Assur'd they shall acceptance meet.

HYMN 490. L. M.
Armley. Luton.
1 INDULGENT God of love and pow'r,
Be with us at this solemn hour!
Smile on our souls; our plans approve,
By which we seek to spread thy love.

2 Let each discordant thought be gone,
And love unite our hearts in one;
Let all we *have* and *are* combine,
To forward objects so divine.

HYMN 491. C. M. Doddridge.
Plymouth. Buckingham.
1 THE Lord on mortal worms looks down
From his celestial throne;
And, when the wicked swarm around
He well discerns his own.

2 He sees the tender hearts that mourn
The scandals of the times,
And join their efforts to oppose
The wide-prevailing crimes.

3 Low to the social band he bows
His still attentive ear;
And, while his angels sing around,
Delights their voice to hear.

HYMN 492. 7, 6. Bp. Heber.
Margate. Romain.
1 FROM Greenland's icy mountains,
From India's coral strand;
Where Afric's sunny fountains
Roll down their golden sand;
From many an ancient river,
From many a palmy plain,
They call us to deliver
Their land from error's chain.

2 What though the spicy breezes
Blow soft o'er Ceylon's isle,
Though ev'ry prospect pleases,
And only man is vile;
In vain with lavish kindness
The gifts of God are strown;
The heathen in his blindness
Bows down to wood and stone.

3 Shall we, whose souls are lighted
With wisdom from on high,
Shall we to men benighted
The lamp of life deny?
Salvation! O Salvation!
The joyful sound proclaim,
Till earth's remotest nation
Has learn'd Messiah's name.

4 Waft, waft, ye winds, his story,
And you, ye waters, roll,
Till, like a sea of glory,
It spreads from pole to pole;
Till o'er our ransom'd nature,
The Lamb for sinners slain,
Redeemer, King, Creator,
In bliss returns to reign.

HYMN 493. S. M. Voke.
Shirland. Northampton.
Ordination and departure of Missionaries.
1 YE Messengers of Christ,
His sov'reign voice obey;
Arise! and follow where he leads,
And peace attend your way.

2 The Master, whom you serve,
Will needful strength bestow;
Depending on his promis'd aid,
With sacred courage go.

3 Mountains shall sink to plains,
And hell in vain oppose;
The cause is God's, and must prevail,
In spite of all his foes.

4 Go, spread a Saviour's fame:
And tell his matchless grace
To the most guilty and deprav'd
Of Adam's num'rous race.

5 We wish you in his name,
The most divine success;
Assur'd that he who sends you forth
Will your endeavors bless.

*HYMN 494.   L. M.
New Hundredth. Chatham. Malmsbury.
1 GO, much lov'd brethren, haste and rear
The gospel standard, void of fear:
Go, seek with joy your destin'd shore,
To view your native land no more.

2 Yes—Christian Heroes! go, proclaim
Salvation through Immanuel's name;
To barren climes the tidings bear,
And plant the Rose of Sharon there.

3 He'll shield you with a wall of fire,
With flaming zeal your breasts inspire,
Bid raging winds their fury cease,
And hush the tempests into peace.

4 And when our labors all are o'er,
Then we shall meet to part no more;
Meet with the blood-bought throng to fall
And crown our Jesus Lord of all!

HYMN 495.　　C. M.
Colchester. Clarendon. Keene.
1 GO, and the Saviour's grace proclaim,
Ye messengers of God;
Go, publish, through Immanuel's name,
Salvation bought with blood.

2 What though your arduous track may lie
Through regions dark as death;
What though your faith and zeal to try,
Perils beset your path:

3 Yet, with determin'd courage, go,
And, arm'd with pow'r divine,
Your God will needful aid bestow,
And on your labors shine.

4 He who has called you to the war
Will recompense your pains;
Before Messiah's conq'ring car,
Mountains shall sink to plains.

5 Shrink not though earth, and hell oppose,
But plead your Master's cause;
Nor doubt that e'en your mighty foes
Shalt bow before his cross.

*HYMN 496. C. M.　　　B.
York. Braintree.
1 GO, messenger of love, and bear,
Upon thy gentle wing,
The song which seraphs love to hear,
And angels joy to sing.

2 Go, to the heart with sin oppress'd,
And dry the sorrowing tear;
Extract the thorn that wounds the breast,
The drooping spirit cheer.

3 Go, say to Zion, "Jesus reigns"—
By his resistless pow'r,
He binds his enemies with chains;
They fall to rise no more.

4 Tell how the Holy Spirit flies,
As he from heav'n descends—
Arrests his proudest enemies,
And changes them to friends.

HYMN 497. 6, 4.
Hymn to the Trinity. St Clement's.
1 SOUND, sound the truth abroad,
Bear ye the word of God
Through the wide world;
Tell what our Lord has done,
Tell how the day is won,
And from his lofty throne,
Satan is hurl'd.

2 Far over sea and land,
'Tis our Lord's own command,
Bear ye his name;
Bear it to ev'ry shore,
Regions unknown explore,
Enter at ev'ry door—
Silence is shame.

3 Speed on the wings of love,
Jesus, who reigns above,
Bids us to fly:
They who his message bear,
Should neither doubt nor fear;
He will their friend appear;
He will be nigh.

4 When on the mighty deep,
He will their spirits keep,
Stay'd on his word;
When in a foreign land,
No other friend at hand,
Jesus will by them stand—
Jesus, their Lord.

5 Ye, who forsaking all,
At your lov'd Master's call,
Comforts resign;
Soon will your work be done;
Soon will the prize be won;

Brighter than yonder sun,
Then shall ye shine.

HYMN 498. 7s. J. Marsden.
Middleton. Hotham.
Mark xvi. 15.
1 GO, ye messengers of God,
Like the beams of morning fly;
Take the wonder-working rod,
Wave the banner cross on high!

2 Go to many a tropic isle
On the bosom of the deep;
Where the skies for ever smile,
And the blacks for ever weep.

3 Where the golden gates of day
Open on the palmy East,
Wide the bleeding cross display,
Spread the gospel's richest feast.

4 Visit ev'ry heathen soil,
Ev'ry barren, burning strand,
Bid each dreary region smile,
Lovely as the promis'd land.

5 In yon wilds of stream and shade,
Many an Indian wigwam trace;
And with words of love persuade
Savages to sue for grace.

6 Circumnavigate the Ball—
Visit ev'ry soil and sea;
Preach the cross of Christ to all;
Jesus' love is full and free.

HYMN 499.   8, 7, 4. Baldwin.
Tamworth. Littleton.
Farewell to Missionaries
1 GO, ye heralds of salvation,
Go, proclaim 'Redeeming blood';
Publish to that barb'rous nation,
Peace and pardon from our God:
Tell the heathen,
None but Christ can do them good.

2 While the gospel trump you're sounding
May the Spirit seal the word,
And, through sov'reign grace abounding,
Heathen bow and own the Lord;
Idols leaving,
God alone shall be ador'd.

3 Distant though our souls are blending,
Still our hearts are warm and true;
In our pray'rs to heav'n ascending,
Brethren—we'll remember you;
Heav'n preserve you,
Safely all your journey through.

4 When your mission here is finish'd,
And your work on earth is done,
May your souls, by race replenish'd,
Find acceptance through the Son;
Thence admitted,
Dwell for ever near his throne.

5 Loud hosannas now resounding,
Make the heav'nly arches ring:
Grace to sinful men abounding,
Ransom'd millions sweetly sing;
While, with rapture,
All adore their heav'nly King.

HYMN 500. C. M.
Steffani's. Braintree.
The Missionaries' farewell.
1 KINDRED, and friends, and native land,
How shall we say farewell ?
How, when our swelling sails expand,
How will our bosoms swell!

2 Yes, nature, all thy soft delights,
And tender ties we know;
But love, more strong than death, unites
To him that bids us go.

3 Thus, when our ev'ry passion mov'd,
The gushing tear-drop starts;
The cause of Jesus more belov'd,
Shall glow within our hearts.

4 The sighs we breathe for precious souls,
Where He is yet unknown,
Might waft us to the distant poles,
Or to the burning zone.

5 With the warm wish our bosoms swell,
Our glowing pow'rs expand;
Farewell,—then we can say,—Farewell,
Our friends, our native land!

HYMN 501. L. M.
Kingsbridge. Armley.
1 FAREWELL! and what if next we meet
In yonder world at which we haste,
And join to cast at Jesus' feet
Our crowns, while we his love shall taste.

2 Should sorrow therefore fill our mind?
No; let that hope our bosoms swell,
Then may we smiling look behind
And say to friends and home—Farewell.

COLLECTIONS.

HYMN 502.   L. M.   Gibbons.
Bostock. Bicester. Truro
Acts x. 38.
1 WHEN Jesus dwelt in mortal clay,
What were his works from day to day
But miracles of power and grace,
That spread salvation through our race?

2 Teach us, O Lord, to keep in view
Thy pattern, and thy steps pursue;
Let alms bestow'd, let kindness done,
Be witness'd by each rolling sun.

3 That man may *last,* but never *lives,*
Who much receives, but nothing gives,
Whom none can love, whom none can thank;
Creation's blot, creation's blank.

4 But he, who marks from day to day,
In gen'rous acts his radiant way,
Treads the same path his Saviour trod,
The path to glory and to God.

HYMN 503.   C. M.   Doddridge.
Springfield. York. St. Ann's
The good Samaritan. Luke x. 30-37.
1 FATHER of mercies, send thy grace,
All pow'rful from above,
To form in our obedient souls
The image of thy love.

2 O may our sympathizing breast
That generous pleasure know;
Kindly to share in others' joy,
And weep for others' wo.

3 When the most helpless sons of grief,
In low distress are laid;
Soft be our hearts their pains to feel,
And swift our hands to aid.

4 So Jesus look'd on dying men,
When thron'd above the skies;
And midst th' embraces of thy love,
He felt compassion rise.

5 On wings of love the Saviour flew
To raise us from the ground;
And gave the richest of his blood,
A balm for ev'ry wound.

HYMN 504.   8, 7.   Francis.
Sicilian Hymn. Northampton Chapel.
1 WHILE the heralds of salvation
God's abounding grace proclaim;
Let his friends of ev'ry station,
Gladly join to spread his name.

2 May his kingdom be promoted—
May the world their Saviour know;
Be my all to him devoted—
To my Lord my all I owe.

3 Praise the Saviour, all ye nations—
Praise him, all ye hosts above;
Shout, with joyful acclamations,
His divine—victorious love.

TIMES AND SEASONS.

*HYMN 505.   C. M.
Wareham. Florence.
Morning.
1 WHEN we, with welcome slumber pressed
Had clos'd our weary eyes,
A pow'r unseen secur'd our rest,
And made us joyful rise.

2 Numbers this night have doubtless met
Their long eternal doom;
And lost the joys of morning light,
In death's tremendous gloom.

3 But life to us its light prolongs,—
Let warmest thanks arise;
Great God, accept our morning songs,
Our willing sacrifice.

HYMN 506.   C. M.   Steele.
Braintree. Rochester.
1 GREAT God, preserved by thine arm,
I pass the shades of night;
Serene—and safe from ev'ry harm,
And see returning light.

2 Oh, let the same Almighty care
My wakeful hours defend;
From ev'ry danger, ev'ry snare,
My heedless steps defend.

3 Smile on my minutes as they roll,
And guide my future days;
And let thy goodness fill my soul
With gratitude and praise.

HYMN 507.   C. M.   J. Steward.
Bray. Barby. Clarendon.
1 SHOULD God forbid the sun to rise,
And endless darkness reign
Justice would silence ev'ry mouth,
Nor let a thought complain.

2 Thus had the Sun of Righteousness
Never arose and shone,
The frowning heav'ns had flash'd with wrath,
For crimes which we had done.

3 Then had salvation ne'er appear'd,
Nor angels sung of peace;
The anthem never had begun,
Which now will never cease.

4 But, thanks to God, the nat'ral sun
Does light and heat convey;
The Sun of Righteousness will shine,
An everlasting day.

*HYMN 508.   C. M.
Bray. Colchester.
Mark i. 35.
1 MY lovely Jesus, while on earth,
Arose before 'twas day;
And to a solitary place
Departed, there to pray.

2 I'll do as did my blessed Lord—
His footsteps I will trace
I love to meet him in the grove,
And view his smiling face.

3 Early I'll rise, and sing and pray,
While I the light enjoy;
May this bless'd work, from day to day,
My heart and tongue employ.

HYMN 509.   7s.
Pleyel's. Redeeming Love.
1 NOW the shades of night are gone;
Now the morning light is come;

Lord, may I be thine today—
Drive the shades of sin away.

2 Fill my soul with heav'nly light,
Banish doubt, and cleanse my sight;
In thy service, Lord, today,
Help me labor, help me pray.

3 Keep my haughty passions bound—
Save me from my foes around;
Going out and coming in,
Keep me safe from ev'ry sin.

4 When my work of life is past,
Oh! receive me then at last!
Night of sin will be no more,
When I reach the heav'nly shore.

HYMN 510. C. M.
Colchester. Barby.
Evening.
1 INDULGENT Father, by whose care,
I've pass'd another day.
Let me this night thy mercy share,
And teach me how to pray.

2 Show me my sins, and how to mourn
My guilt before thy face;
Direct me, Lord, to Christ alone,
And save me by thy grace.

3 Let each returning night declare
The tokens of thy love
And ev'ry hour thy grace prepare
My soul for joys above.

4 And when on earth I close mine eyes,
To sleep in death's embrace,
Let me to heav'n and glory rise,
T' enjoy thy smiling face.

*HYMN 511. C. M. H. K. White.
York. Mear.
1 O LORD, another day is flown,
And we, a lonely band
Are met once more before thy throne,
To bless thy fost'ring hand.

2 And wilt thou bend a list'ning ear
To praises low as ours?
Thou wilt! for thou dost love to hear
The song which meekness pours.

3 And, Jesus, thou thy smiles wilt deign,
As we before thee pray;
For thou didst bless the infant train,
And we are less than they.

4 Oh, let thy grace perform its part,
And let contention cease;
And shed abroad in ev'ry heart
Thine everlasting peace.

*HYMN 512. S. M.
Yarmouth. Wirksworth.
1 THE day is past and gone,
The ev'ning shades appear;
Oh, may I ever keep in mind,
The night of death draws near.

2 I lay my garments by,
Upon my bed to rest;
So death will soon remove me hence,
And leave my soul undress'd.

3 Lord, keep me safe this night,
Secure from all my fears;
May angels guard me while I sleep,
Till morning light appears.

4 And when I early rise,
To view th' unwearied sun,
May I set out to win the prize,
And after glory run:

5 That when my days are past,
And I from time remove,
Lord, I may in thy bosom rest,
The bosom of thy love.

HYMN 513.   L. M.   Collyer.
Old Hundred. Kent.
1 THE night shall hear me raise my song.
And in her silent courts my tongue
Shall pour the solitary lay,
For all the mercies of the day.

2 Nor will my God disdain to hear
The sigh I breathe—the fervent pray'r,
When, sinking to oblivious rest,
I seek the pillow of his breast.

3 And when the blushing morn shall rise,
To tinge with gold the eastern skies;
With strength renew'd, my thankful lay
Shall hail the new-born beams of day.

HYMN 514. 8s.   Toplady.
Bethany. Lambeth.
1 INSPIRER and Hearer of pray'r,
Before whom a sinner may bend;
My all to thy covenant care,
I sleeping or waking commend.

2 If thou art my shield and my sun,
The night is no darkness to me;
And fast as my moments roll on,
They bring me but nearer to thee.

3 From evil secure, and its dread,
I rest, if my Saviour be nigh;
And songs his kind presence indeed,
Shall in the night season supply.

4 He smiles, and my comforts abound;
His grace as the dew shall descend;
And walls of salvation surround
The soul he delights to defend.

HYMN 515.   C. M.
Clarendon. Bray.
Saturday night.
1 BE gone, my worldly cares, away,
Nor dare to tempt my sight;
Let me begin th' ensuing day,
Before I end this night.

2 Yes, let the work of pray'r and praise
Employ my heart and tongue;
Begin, my soul;—thy Sabbath days
Can never be too long.

3 Let the past mercies of the week
Excite a grateful frame;
Nor let my tongue refuse to speak
Some good of Jesus' name.

4 On wings of expectation borne,
My hopes to heav'n ascend;
I long to welcome in the morn,
With *thee* the day to spend.

HYMN 516. L. M.   Stennett.
Quercy. Portugal. Blendon.
The Sabbath.
1 ANOTHER six days' work is done,
Another Sabbath is begun;
Return, my soul, enjoy thy rest—
Improve the day thy God has bless'd.

2 Come, bless the Lord, whose love assigns
So sweet a rest to wearied minds:
Provides an antepast of heav'n,
And gives this day the food of sev'n.

3 O, that our thoughts and thanks may rise,
As grateful incense to the skies;
And draw from heav'n that sweet repose,
Which none, but he that feels it, knows.

4 This heav'nly calm, within the breast,
Is the dear pledge of glorious rest,
Which for the church of God remains,
The end of cares, the end of pains.

5 In holy duties let the day,
In holy pleasures, pass away;
How sweet a Sabbath thus to spend,
In hope of one that ne'er shall end!

*HYMN 517.   C. M.
Clarendon. Clifford. Springfield.
1 WHEN, on the third auspicious day,
While yet the blushing dawn
Shed forth its earliest smiling ray
To gild the rising morn;

2 The "holy women" sought the place
Where their belov'd was laid,
And shining angels preach'd the grace
That rais'd him from the dead;

3 They hasted from the hallow'd ground,
Where his dear flesh had lain,
To tell his mourning friends around,
That Jesus lives again.

4 This day, as days of older time,
Is one of heav'nly joy;
Good tidings reach to ev'ry clime,
And ev'ry tongue employ.

*HYMN 518.   C. M.   Brown.
Barby. Mear. York.
Evening of the Lord's day.
1 FREQUENT the day of God returns
To shed its quick'ning beams;
And yet how slow devotion burns;
How languid are its flames!

2 Accept our faint attempts to love—
Our frailties, Lord, forgive;
We would be like thy saints above,
And praise thee while we live.

3 Increase, O Lord, our faith and hope,
And fit us to ascend,
Where the assembly ne'er breaks up,
The Sabbath ne'er shall end;

4 Where we shall breathe in heav'nly air,
With heav'nly lustre shine;
Before the throne of God appear,
And feast on love divine.

HYMN 519. L. M.   Doddridge.
Antigua. Winchester.
The Eternal Sabbath. Hebrews iv. 9.
1 THINE earthly Sabbaths, Lord, we love;
But there's a nobler rest above;
To that our longing souls aspire,
With ardent pangs of strong desire.

2 No more fatigue, no more distress,
Nor sin nor hell shall reach the place;
No groans to mingle with the songs,
Which warble from immortal tongues.

3 No rude alarms of raging foes;
No cares to break the long repose;
No midnight shade, no clouded sun,
Obscures the lustre of thy throne.

4 Around thy throne, grant we may meet,
And give us but the lowest seat;
We'll shout thy praise, and join the song
Of the triumphant, holy throng.

HYMN 520. C. M.
Springfield. Wareham. Barby.
Winter.
1 SEE, how rude winter's icy hand
Has stripp'd the verdant ground
But spring will soon his rage withstand,
And spread new beauties round.

2 My soul a sharper winter mourns;
And fruitless I remain;
When will the gentle spring return,
The graces grow again?

3 Jesus, my glorious Sun, arise—
This frozen heart remove:
O, hush these storms, and clear my skies,
And let me feel thy love!

*HYMN 521. C. M.   Newton.
Colchester. York.
Spring, or return of joy.
1 AT length the wish'd for spring has come;
How alter'd is the scene!
The trees and shrubs are dress'd in bloom,
The earth array'd in green.

2 I see my Saviour from on high,
Break through the clouds and shine;
No creature now more bless'd than I,
No song more loud than mine.

3 Thy word does all my hopes revive;
It overcomes my foes;
It makes my languid graces thrive,
And blossom like the rose.

4 Dear Lord, a monument I stand,
Of what thy grace can do;
Uphold me by thy gracious hand,
Each changing season through.

*HYMN 522. L. M.   Strong.
Old Hundred. Bath. Leeds.
Summer, or the great Harvest. Matthew xiii. 39.
1 THE summer harvest spreads the field,
Mark—how the whitening hills are turn'd!
Behold them to the reapers yield;
The wheat is sav'd—the tares are burn'd.

2 Thus the great Judge with glory crown'd,
Descends to reap the ripen'd earth!
Angelic guards attend him down,
The same who sang his humble birth.

3 In sounds of glory bear him speak,
"Go search around the flaming world;
Haste, call my saints to rise, and take
The seats from which their foes were hurl'd.

4 Go, burn the chaff in endless fire,
In flames unquench'd, consume each tare;
Sinners must feel my holy ire,
And sink in guilt—to deep despair."

5 Thus ends the harvest of the earth:
Angels obey the awful voice;
They save the wheat, they burn the chaff;
All heav'n approves the sov'reign choice.

HYMN 523. L. M. Doddridge.
Malmsbury. Spring. China.
The Seasons. Psalm lxv. 11.
1 THE flow'ry spring at God's command,
Perfumes the air, and paints the land;
The summer rays with vigor shine,
To raise the corn, and cheer the vine.

2 His hand in autumn richly pours,
Through all her coasts, redundant stores:
And winters, soften'd by his care,
No more the face of horror wear.

3 Seasons and months, and weeks, and days,
Demand successive songs of praise;
And be the cheerful homage paid,
With morning light and ev'ning shade.

4 And Oh, may each harmonious tongue
In worlds unknown the praise prolong;
And in those brighter courts adore,
Where days and years revolve no more.

HYMN 524. C. M. Newton.
Lutzen. Bray.
New Year.
1 NOW, gracious Lord, thine arm reveal,
And make thy glory known;
Now let us all thy presence feel,
And soften hearts of stone.

2 From all the guilt of former sin,
May mercy set us free;
And let the year we now begin,
Begin and end with thee.

3 Send down thy Spirit from above,
That saints may love thee more;
And sinners now may learn to love,
Who never lov'd before.

4 And when before thee we appear,
In our eternal home,
May growing numbers worship here,
And praise thee in our room.

*HYMN 525.   C. M.   Cowper.
Chapel. Walsal.
1 COME, Lord, and bless the rising race!
Make this a happy hour,
According to thy richest grace,
And thine almighty pow'r.

2 Dear youth, we know your sinful state—
May God your hearts renew!
We would awhile ourselves forget,
To pour our pray'r for you.

3 We see, though you perceive it not,
Th' approaching awful doom!
Oh, tremble at the solemn thought,
And flee the wrath to come!

4 Dear Saviour, let this new born year
Spread an alarm abroad;
And cry in ev'ry careless ear,
"Prepare to meet thy God!"

HYMN 526. 10,5,11. Har. Sacra.
New Year. Amesbury.
1 COME, let us anew,
Our journey pursue,
Roll round with the year,
And never stand still till the Master appear;
His adorable will
Let us gladly fulfil,
And our talents improve
By the patience of hope, and the labor of love

2 Our life is a dream;
Our time, as a stream,
Glides swiftly away;
And the fugitive moment refuses to stay.
The arrow is flown,
The moment is gone,

The millennial year
Rushes on to our view and eternity's near.

3 Oh, that each in the day
Of his coming may say,
"I have fought my way through,
I have finish'd the work thou didst give me to do!"
Oh, that each from his Lord
May receive the glad word,
Well and faithfully done
Enter into my joy and sit down on my throne!"

HYMN 527. C. M.   Doddridge.
Parma. Braintree. Clifford.
Close of the year. Romans xiii. 11.
1 AWAKE, ye saints, and raise your eyes,
And raise your voices high;
Awake, and praise that sov'reign love,
That shows salvation nigh.

2 On all the wings of time it flies,
Each moment brings it near;
Then welcome each declining day!
Welcome each closing year!

3 Not many years their rounds shall run,
Nor many mornings rise,
Ere all its glories stand reveal'd
To our admiring eyes.

4 Ye wheels of nature, speed your course;
Ye mortal pow'rs, decay;
Fast as ye bring the night of death,
Ye bring eternal day.

HYMN 528. C. M.   Berridge.
Clarendon. Springfield.
Marriage.
1 SINCE Jesus freely did appear
To grace a marriage feast;
O Lord, we ask thy presence here,
To make a wedding guest.

2 Upon the bridal pair look down,
Who now have plighted hands;

Their union with thy favor crown,
And bless the nuptial bands.

3 In purest love these souls unite,
That they with Christian care,
May make domestic burdens light,
By taking mutual share.

4 And when that solemn hour shall come,
And life's short space be o'er,
May they in triumph reach that home,
Where they shall part no more.

HYMN 529. L. M.   Lee.
Olney. Truro. Portugal.
Marriage.
1 WITH grateful hearts and tuneful lays,
We bow before th' Eternal throne,
And offer up our humble praise,
To him whose name is God alone.

2 On this auspicious eve, draw near,
And shed thy richest blessings down;
Fill ev'ry heart with love sincere,
And all thy faithful mercies crown.

3 Grant now thy presence, gracious Lord,
And hearken to our fervent pray'r;
The nuptial vow in heav'n record,
And bless the newly married pair.

4 Oh, guide them safe, this desert through,
Mid all the cares of life and love;
At length with joy thy face to view,
In fairer, better worlds above.

HYMN 530. L. M.   Proud.
Chatham. Sterling.
Marriage.
1 WITH cheerful voices rise and sing
The praises of our God and King;
For he alone can minds unite,
And bless with conjugal delight.

2 Oh, may this pair increasing find
Substantial pleasures of the mind;
Happy together may they be,
And both united, Lord, to thee.

3 So may they live as truly one;
And when their work on earth is done,
Rise, hand in hand, to heav'n, and share
The joys of love for ever there.

HYMN 531. L. M.　　　Newton.
Wells. Bath.
Welcome to Christian friends.
1 BRETHREN, belov'd for Jesus' sake,
A hearty welcome here receive;
May we together now partake
The joys which he alone can give!

2 May he, at whose kind care we meet,
Send his good Spirit from above;
Make our communications sweet,
And cause our hearts to burn with love!

3 Forgotten be each worldly theme,
When thus we meet to pray and praise,
We only wish to speak of him,
And tell the wonders of his grace.

4 We'll talk of all he did and said,
His suff'rings and his dying love,
The path he mark'd for us to tread,
And how he triumphs now above.

5 Thus as the moments pass away,
We'll love, and wonder, and adore;
Then hasten on the glorious day,
When we shall meet to part no more.

HYMN 532. C. M.
Barby. Newmark.
At parting.
1 LORD, when together here we meet,
And taste thy heav'nly grace;
Thy smiles are so divinely sweet,
We're loath to leave the place.

2 But, Father, since it is thy will,
That we must part again;
Oh, may thy special presence still,
With ev'ry one remain.

3 And let us all in Christ be one,
Bound with the cords of love;
Till we, before thy glorious throne,
Shall joyful meet above.

4 All sin and sorrow from each heart,
Shall then for ever fly;
Nor shall a thought that we must part,
Once interrupt our joy.

HYMN 533. S. M.   Fawcett.
Little Marlboro'. Wirksworth.
1 BLEST be the tie that binds
Our hearts in Christian love;
The fellowship of kindred minds,
Is like to that above.

2 Before our Father's throne
We pour our ardent pray'rs;
Our fears, our hopes, our aims are one,
Our comforts and our cares.

3 We share our mutual woes;
Our mutual burdens bear;
And often for each other flows
The sympathizing tear.

4 When we asunder part,
It gives us inward pain;
But we shall still be join'd in heart,
And hope to meet again.

5 This glorious hope revives
Our courage by the way;
While each in expectation
And longs to see the day.

6 From sorrow, toil and pain,
And sin, we shall be free;

And perfect love and friendship reign
Through all eternity.

HYMN 534. C. M.
Springfield. Barby. Newmark
1 THROUGH Christ when we together came.
In singleness of heart,
We met, O Jesus, in thy name;
And in thy name we part.

2 We part in body, not in mind,
Our minds continue one;
And each to each, in Jesus join'd,
We happily go on.

3 Present in spirit still we are,
And intimately nigh;
While on the wings of faith and pray'r
We Abba, Father! cry.

4 Oh, may thy Spirit, dearest Lord,
In all our travels still
Direct and be our constant guard
To Zion's holy hill.

5 Oh! what a joyful meeting there,
Beyond these changing shades;
White are the robes we then shall wear,
And crowns upon our heads.

6 Haste, Lord, and bring us to the day
When we shall dwell at home;
Come, O Redeemer, come away;
O Jesus, quickly come.

HYMN 535. L. M. H. K. White.
Luther's Hymn. Sterling.
1 COME, christian brethren! ere we part
Join every voice and every heart,
One solemn hymn to God we raise.
One final song of grateful praise.

2 Christians, we here may meet no more,
But there is yet a happier shore;

And there, releas'd from toil and pain,
Dear brethren, we shall meet again.

HYMN 536.　C. M.　　C. W.
Barby. Newmark.
1 BLEST be the dear, uniting love,
That will not let us part;
Our bodies may far off remove,
We still are one in heart.

2 Join'd in one Spirit to our Head,
Where he appoints we go;
And still in Jesus' footsteps tread,
And show his praise below.

3 Partakers of the Saviour's grace,
The same in mind and heart,
Nor joy, nor grief, nor time, nor place,
Nor life, nor death can part.

4 But let us hasten to the day,
Which shall our flesh restore;
When death shall all be done away,
And christians part no more!

HYMN 537.　L. M.　　　Watts.
Armley. Darwent. Carthage.
1 FAREWELL, dear friends, a short farewell,
Till we shall meet again above
In the sweet groves where pleasures dwell,
And trees of life bear fruits of love.

2 There glory sits on ev'ry face;—
There friendship smiles in ev'ry eye;
There shall our tongues proclaim the grace,
That led us homeward to the sky.

HYMN 538.　　C. M.　　Taylor.
Walsal. Chapel.
Youth.
1 COME, let us now forget our mirth,
And think that we must die
What are our best delights on earth,
Compar'd with those on high!

2 Our pleasures here will soon be past—
Our brightest joys decay;
But pleasures there for ever last,
And cannot fade away.

3 Here sins and sorrows we deplore,
With many cares distress'd,
But there the mourners weep no more,
And there the weary rest.

4 Our dearest friends, when death shall call,
At once must hence depart;
But there we hope to meet them all,
And never, never part.

5 Then let us love and serve the Lord,
With all our youthful pow'rs;
And we shall gain this great reward,
This glory shall be ours.

HYMN 539. C. M   Logan.
Brighton. Clarendon.
Job xiv. 2.
1 GAY is thy morning;—flattering hope
Thy sprightly step attends
But soon the tempest howls behind,
And the dark night descends!

2 Before its splendid hour, the cloud
Comes o'er the beam of light;
A pilgrim in a weary land,
Man tarries but a night!

3 Determin'd are the days that fly
Successive o'er thy head;
The number'd hour is on the wing,
That lays thee with the dead.

HYMN 540.   S. M.
St. Thomas. Shirland.
1 Chronicles xxviii. 9.
1 MY son, know thou the Lord,
Thy father's God obey;
Seek his protecting care by night,
His guardian hand by day.

2 Call, while he may be found,
And seek him while he's near;
Serve him with all thy heart and mind,
And worship him with fear.

3 If thou wilt seek his face,
His ear will hear thy cry;
Then shalt thou find his mercy sure,
His grace for ever nigh.

4 But if thou leave thy God,
Nor choose the path to heav'n;
Then shalt thou perish in thy sins,
And never be forgiv'n.

HYMN 541.   C. M.   Doddridge.
Springfield. Colchester.
Seek first the kingdom. Matthew vi. 33.
1 NOW let a true ambition rise,
And ardor fire our breast,
To reign in worlds above the skies,
In heav'nly glories dress'd.

2 Behold Jehovah's royal hand
A radiant crown display,
Whose gems with vivid lustre shine,
While stars and suns decay.

3 Away, each grov'ling, anxious care,
Beneath a christian's thought;
Oh, spring to seize immortal joys,
Which your Redeemer bought.

4 Ye hearts, with youthful vigor warm,
The glorious prize pursue;
Nor shall ye want the goods of earth,
While heav'n is kept in view.

*HYMN 542.   C. M.   Fawcett.
Barby. St. Ann's.
1 RELIGION is the chief concern
Of mortals here below;
May I its great importance learn,
Its sov'reign virtue know!

2 More needful this, than glitt'ring wealth,
Or aught the world bestows;
Nor reputation, food, or health,
Can give us such repose.

3 Religion should our thoughts engage,
Amidst our youthful bloom;
Twill fit us for declining age,
And for the awful tomb.

4 O may my heart by grace renew'd,
Be my Redeemer's throne;
And be my stubborn will subdu'd,
His government to own.

5 Let deep repentance, faith, and love,
Be join'd with godly fear;
And all my conversation prove
My heart to be sincere.

HYMN 543.   L. M.   Newton.
Brookfield. Armley.
1 THE God who once to Israel spoke,
From Sinai's top, in fire and smoke,
In gentler strains of gospel grace,
Invites us now to seek his face.

2 Hark! how from Calvary it sounds;
From the Redeemer's bleeding wounds;
"Pardon and grace I freely give,
Poor sinner, look to me—and live.

3 What other arguments can move
The heart that slights a Saviour's love:
Yet till almighty pow'r constrain,
This matchless love is preach'd in vain.

4 O Saviour, let that pow'r be felt,
And cause each stony heart to melt!
Deeply impress upon our youth
The light and force of gospel truth.

5 How will they else thy presence bear,
When as a Judge, thou shalt appear;

When slighted love to wrath shall turn,
And the whole earth like Sinai burn!

HYMN 544.   L. M.
Sterling. Leyden.
1 YE lovely bands of blooming youth,
Warn'd by the voice of heav'nly truth,
Now yield to Christ your youthful prime,
With all your talents and your time.

2 Think on our end—nor thoughtless say,
"I'll put far off the evil day";
Ah! not a moment's in your pow'r,
And death stands ready at the door.

3 Eternity!—how near it rolls!
Count the vast value of your souls!
Beware! and count the awful cost,
What they have gain'd whose souls are lost.

4 Pride, sinful pleasures, lusts and snares,
Beset your hearts, your eyes, your ears—
Take the alarm—the danger fly!
Lord, save me, be your earnest cry.

*HYMN 545.   L. M.   Cowper.
Warwick. Armley.
Vanity of the world.
1 THE joy that vain amusements give,
To him who thoughtless sports and sings,
Is like the honey of a hive,
When guarded by ten thousand stings.

2 'Tis thus the world rewards the fools,
Who live upon her treach'rous smiles:
She leads them blindfold, by her rules,
And ruins all whom she beguiles.

3 'Tis thus that thousands hasten down
From pleasure into endless wo;
And with a long despairing groan,
Blaspheme their Maker as they go.

4 Warn'd by their woes, may we be wise,
Delighting in a Saviour's charms;

Then God will take us to the skies,
Embrac'd in everlasting arms.

HYMN 546.   C. M.   Tappan.
Springfield. Dorset.
1 WE wander in a thorny maze,
A vale of doubts and fears;
A night, illum'd with sickly rays,
A wilderness of tears:
We wander, bound to empty show,
The slaves of boasted will;
We wander, dupes to hope untrue,
And love to wander still.

2 We wander—while unfading joy,
We ne'er with zest approve;
The bliss, that sparkles to destroy,
Secures our warmest love.
Some syren leads our steps astray,
But speaks no peace within;
We wander in a flow'ry way,
We wander, heirs of sin!

3 We wander, but though oft we roam,
Led by allurements strong;
Yet from our heav'nly Father's home,
We would not wander long!
Cleanse us, O Saviour! from this stain,
In mercy's living flood;
Restore the lost, and bring again
The wand'rers back to God.

*HYMN 547.   C. M.   Doddridge.
Clifford. York.
Proverbs viii. 17.
1 YE hearts, with youthful vigor warm,
In smiling crowds draw near,
And turn from ev'ry mortal charm,
A Saviour's voice to hear.

2 He, Lord of all the worlds on high,
Stoops to converse with you;
And lays his radiant glories by,
Your friendship to pursue.

3 "The soul that longs to see my face,
Is sure my love to gain;
And those that early seek my grace,
Shall never seek in vain."

4 What object, Lord, my soul should move,
If once compar'd with thee?
What beauty should command my love,
Like what in Christ I see?

5 Away, ye false, delusive toys,
Vain tempters of the mind!
'Tis here I fix my lasting choice,
And here true bliss I find.

*HYMN 548.   S. M.   Fawcett.
Watchman. Froome.
Prayer of a Youth. Psalm cxix. 9.
1 WITH humble heart and tongue,
My God, to thee I pray;
Oh, make me learn while I am young,
How I may cleanse my way.

2 Make an unguarded youth
The object of thy care;
Help me to choose the way of truth,
And fly from ev'ry snare.

3 My heart, to folly prone,
Renew'd by pow'r divine;
Unite it to thyself alone,
And make me wholly thine.

4 Oh, let thy word of grace
My warmest thoughts employ;
Be this, through all my foll'wing days,
My treasure and my joy.

5 To what thy laws impart,
Be my whole soul inclin'd;
Oh, let them dwell within my heart,
And sanctify my mind.

6 May thy young servant learn,
By these to cleanse his way;

And may I here the path discern
That leads to endless day.

HYMN 549.   C. M.   C. Wesley.
Walsal. Buckingham.
Middle Age. John ix. 4.
1 AND have I measur'd half my days,
And half my journey run,
Nor tasted the Redeemer's grace,
Nor yet my work begun?

2 The morning of my life is past;
The noon is almost o'er;
The night of death approaches fast,
When I can work no more.

3 O Thou who seest and know'st my grief,
Thyself unseen, unknown,
In mercy help my unbelief,
And melt my heart of stone.

4 Regard me with a gracious eye,
The long-sought blessing give,
And bid me, at the point to die,
Behold thy face, and live.

HYMN 550. C. M.
Martyr's. Standish.
Old Age.
1 ETERNAL God! enthron'd on high!
Whom angel hosts adore;
Who yet to suppliant dust art nigh,
Thy presence I implore.

2 Oh, guide me down the steep of age,
And keep my passions cool;
Teach me to scan the sacred page,
And practise ev'ry rule.

3 My flying years time urges on,
What's human must decay:
My friends, my young companions, gone,
Can I expect to stay?

4 Ah! No—then sooth the mortal hour,
On thee my hope depends;
Support me with almighty pow'r,
While dust to dust descends.

*HYMN 551.   C. M.   Steele.
Bangor. Walsal.
Public Fast. Joel i. 14.
1 SEE, gracious Lord, before thy throne,
Thy mourning people bend!
'Tis on thy sov'reign grace alone,
Our humble hopes depend.

2 Tremendous judgments, from thy hand,
Thy dreadful pow'rs display;
Yet mercy spares this guilty land,
And still we live to pray.

3 How chang'd, alas! are truths divine,
For error, guilt, and shame!
What impious numbers, bold in sin,
Disgrace the Christian name.

4 O turn us, turn us, mighty Lord,
By thy resistless grace
Then shall our hearts obey thy word,
And humbly seek thy face.

5 Then, should insulting foes invade,
We shall not sink in fear;
Secure of never failing aid,
When God, our God, is near.

HYMN 552.   C. M.   Newton.
Reading. Plymouth.
Afflictions needful. Hebrews xii. 5-11.
1 BREAK through the clouds, dear Lord, and shine,
Let us perceive thee nigh!
And to each mourning child of thine,
These gracious words apply:

2 "Let not my children slight the stroke
I for chastisement send;
Nor faint beneath my kind rebuke,
For I am still their friend.

3 "The wicked I perhaps may leave
Awhile and not reprove;
But all the children I receive,
I scourge, because I love.

4 "I see your hearts at present fill'd
With grief and deep distress;
But soon these bitter seeds shall yield
The fruits of righteousness."

*HYMN 553.   L. M.
Warwick. Armley.
1 LONG unafflicted, undismay'd,
In pleasure's path, secure I stray'd;
When made to feel thy chast'ning rod,
I straight return'd to thee, my God.

2 What though it pierc'd my fainting heart—
I bless the hand that caus'd the smart;
It taught my tears awhile to flow,
But sav'd me from eternal wo.

3 Oh, hadst thou left me unchastis'd,
Thy precepts I had still despis'd,
With daring rebels been the same,
Or gone where mercy never came.

*HYMN 554. C. M.
Plymouth. Standish.
1 WHY should the Christian waste in sighs
The breath that God hath giv'n;
Whom ev'ry passing hour that flies
Bears onward fast to heav'n?

2 Why should we wish for perfect bliss,
In this dark world forlorn;
Or seek, amidst a wilderness,
A rose without a thorn?

3 Our Father God! be ours the grief,
Which to thy sons belongs;
And let us share in their relief,
Their everlasting songs.

HYMN 555.   C. M.
Plymouth. Buckingham.
1 WERE once our vain desires subdu'd,
The heart resign'd—at rest;
In ev'ry scene we should conclude
The will of heav'n is best.

2 Lord, we expect to suffer here,
Nor would we dare repine;
But give us still to find thee near,
And own us still for thine.

HYMN 556.   C. M.   Toplady.
Elgin. Plymouth.
Affliction sweetened. Psalm civ. 34.
1 WHEN languor and disease invade
This trembling house of clay,
'Tis sweet to look beyond my pains,
And long to fly away.

2 Sweet to look inward and attend
The whispers of his love;
Sweet to look upward to the place
Where Jesus pleads above.

3 Sweet to reflect, how grace divine
My sins on Jesus laid;
Sweet to remember that his blood
My debt of suff'ring paid.

4 Sweet on his faithfulness to rest,
Whose love can never end;
Sweet on his covenant of grace
For all things to depend.

5 Sweet, in the confidence of faith,
To trust his firm decrees;
Sweet to lie passive in his hand,
And know no will but his.

6 If such the sweetness of the streams,
What must the fountain be,
Where saints and angels draw their bliss
Immediately from thee!

*HYMN 557.   C. M.
Standish. Martyr's. Lebanon.
Joy in sorrow
1 AND let this feeble body fail,
And let it faint or die;
My soul shall quit the mournful vale,
And soar to worlds on high;

2 Shall join the disembody'd saints,
And find its long sought rest,
(The only rest for which it pants),
On the Redeemer's breast.

3 In hope of that immortal crown,
I now the cross sustain;
And gladly wander up and down,
And smile at toil and pain.

4 I travel my appointed years,
Till my Deliv'rer come,
And wipe away his servant's tears,
And take his exile home.

HYMN 558.   L. M.   Cowper.
Quercy. Surry.
The billows of temptation.
1 THE billows swell, the winds are high;
Clouds overcast my wintry sky;
Out of the depths to thee I call—
My fears are great, my strength is small.

2 Dangers of ev'ry shape and name,
Attend the foll'wers of the Lamb,
Who leave the world's deceitful shore,
And leave it to return no more.

3 God of my life, to thee I call,
Afflicted at thy feet I fall;
Do thou the pilot's part perform,
And guide and guard me through the storm.

HYMN 559.   8s.
Lambeth. Uxbridge.
Revelation xxi. 4.

1 DISCONSOLATE tenant of clay,
In solemn assurance arise,
Thy treasure of sorrow survey,
And look through it all to the skies:
That heav'nly house is prepar'd
For all who are sufferers here,
And wait the return of their Lord,
And long for his day to appear.

2 There all the tempestuous blast
Of bitter affliction is o'er,
The spirit is landed at last,
And sorrow and shame are no more;
Temptation and trouble are gone,
The trial is all at an end—
And there I shall cease to bemoan
The loss of my brother and friend.

HYMN 560.   C. M.   C. W.
Windsor. Standish.
The Parent's prayer.   John iv. 46-49.

1 JESUS, great healer of mankind,
Who dost our sorrows bear
Let an afflicted parent find
An answer to his pray'r.

2 I look for help in thee alone,
To thee for succour fly;
Come down and heal my darling son,
Now at the point to die.

3 Jesus, if thou pronounce the word,
The gracious answer give,
My dying child shall be restor'd,
And to thy glory live.

4 Oh, save the parent, in the son,
Restore him, Lord, to me;
My heart the miracle shall own,
And give him back to thee.

HYMN 561.   C. M.   M.
Chapel. Buckingham.
Light in darkness. Psalm cxii. 4.
1 O THOU who dry'st the mourner's tear,
How dark this world would be,
If, pierc'd by sins and sorrows here,
We could not fly to thee!

2 The friends, who in our sunshine live.
When winter comes, are flown;
And he who has but tears to give,
Must weep those tears alone.

3 Oh! who could bear life's stormy doom,
Did not thy wing of love
Come brightly wafting through the gloom
Our peace-branch from above?

4 Then sorrow touch'd by thee, grows bright.
With more than rapture's ray;
As darkness shows us worlds of light,
We never saw by day.

HYMN 562. C. M.   Haweis.
Buckingham. Martyr's. Wantage.
Think upon me. Nehemiah v. 19.
1 O THOU, from whom all goodness flows,
I lift my heart to thee;
In all my trials, conflicts, woes,
Dear Lord, remember me.

2 When groaning, on my burden'd heart
My sins lie heavily;
My pardon speak, new peace impart;
In love, remember me.

3 If on my face, for thy dear name,
Shame and reproaches be;
I'll hail reproach, and welcome shame,
If thou remember me.

4 The hour is near—consign'd to death,
I own the just decree;
Saviour, with my last parting breath,
I'll cry—remember me.

*HYMN 563. S. M.   Dwight.
St. Bridges. Orange.
Sick-bed reflections.
1 JUST o'er the grave I hung—
No pardon met my eyes,
As blessings never greet the slain,
And hope shall never rise.

2 Sweet mercy to my soul
Reveal'd no charming ray;
Before me rose a long-dark night,
With no succeeding day.

3 Then—Oh, how vain appear'd
The joys beneath the sky!
Like visions past—like flow'rs that blow
When wint'ry storms are nigh.

4 How mourn'd my sinking soul
The Sabbath's hours divine,
The day of grace, that precious day,
Consum'd in sense and sin.

5 The work—the mighty work
Of life, so long delay'd—
Repentance yet to be begun
Upon a dying bed.

HYMN 564. C. M.
Springfield. Wareham.
1 'TIS hard, from those we love, to go,
Who weep beside our bed,
Whose tears bedew our burning brow,
Whose arm supports our head:

2 When fading from the dizzy view,
I sought their forms in vain;
The bitterness of death I knew,
And groan'd to live again.

3 'Tis dreadful when th' accuser's pow'r
Assails the sinking heart,
Recalling ev'ry wasted hour,
And each unworthy part.

4 Yet, Jesus, in that mortal fray,
Thy blessed comfort stole,
Like sunshine in an autumn day
Across my darken'd soul.

5 When soon, or late, this feeble breath
No more to thee can pray,
Support me through the vale of death,
And in the darksome way.

6 When cloth'd in fleshly weeds again,
I wait thy dread decree;
Judge of the world, remember then,
That thou hast died for me.

FUNERAL.

HYMN 565. C. M.
Martyr's. Lebanon.
Funeral of a faithful Minister.
1 FAR from affliction, toil, and care,
The happy soul is fled;
The breathless clay shall slumber here,
Among the silent dead.

2 The gospel was his joy and song,
E'en to his latest breath;
The truth he had proclaim'd so long
Was his support in death.

3 Now he resides where Jesus is,
Above this dusky sphere;
His soul was ripen'd for that bliss,
While yet he sojourn'd here.

4 The Churches' loss we all deplore,
And shed the falling tear;
Since we shall see his face no more,
Till Jesus shall appear.

5 But we are hasting to the tomb;
Oh, may we ready stand;
Then, dearest Lord, receive us home,
To dwell at thy right hand.

*HYMN 566. L. M.   Collyer.
Kingsbridge. Armley.
Ecclesiastes xii. 7.
1 FROM his low bed of mortal dust,
Escap'd the prison of his clay,
The new inhabitant of bliss,
To heav'n directs his wond'rous way.

2 Ye fields, that witness'd once his tears,
Ye winds, that wafted oft his sighs,
Ye mountains, where he breath'd his pray'rs
When sorrow's shadows veil'd his eyes.

3 No more the weary pilgrim mourns,
No more affliction wrings his heart;
Th' unfetter'd soul to God returns—
For ever he and anguish part!

4 Receive, O earth, his faded form,
In thy cold bosom let it lie;
Safe let it rest from ev'ry storm,
Soon must it rise no more to die!

HYMN 567. L. M.
Norfolk. Armley.
The grave. Job iii. 17.
1 THE grave is now a favor'd spot,—
To saints who sleep, in Jesus bless'd;
For there the wicked trouble not,
And there the weary are at rest.

2 At rest in Jesus' faithful arms;
At rest as in a peaceful bed;
Secure from all the dreadful storms,
Which round this sinful world are spread.

3 Thrice happy souls, who're gone before
To that inheritance divine!
They labor, sorrow, sigh no more,
But bright in endless glory shine.

4 Then let our mournful tears be dry,
Or in a gentle measure flow;
We hail them happy in the sky,
And joyful wait our call to go.

HYMN 568. L. M.   Watts.
Sicilian. Putney. Armley.
1 UNVEIL thy bosom, faithful tomb,
Take this new treasure to thy trust;
And give these sacred relics room,
To seek a slumber in the dust.

2 Nor pain, nor grief, nor anxious fear
Invade thy bounds. No mortal woes
Can, reach the peaceful sleeper here,
While angels watch the soft repose.

3 So Jesus slept;—God's dying Son
Pass'd thro' the grave, and bless'd the bed;
Rest here, blest saint, till from his throne
The morning break, and pierce the shade.

4 Break from his throne, illustrious morn;
Attend, O earth! his sov'reign word;
Restore thy trust—a glorious form—
Call'd to ascend and meet the Lord.

HYMN 569. 8s. C. Wesley.
Lambeth. Mitcham. Franklin.
Death of a Brother.
1 HOW blest is our brother bereft
Of all that could burden his mind:
How easy the soul that hast left
This wearisome body behind!
Of evil incapable thou,
Whose relics with envy I see,
No longer in misery now,
No longer a sinner like me.

2 This earth is affected no more
With sickness, or shaken with pain;
The war in the members is o'er,
And never shall vex him again;
No anger henceforward, or shame,
Shall redden his innocent clay;
Extinct is the animal flame,
And passion is vanish'd away.

3 This languishing head is at rest;
Its thinking and aching are o'er,

This quiet, immoveable breast
Is heav'd by affliction no more;
This heart is no longer the seat
Of trouble and torturing pain;
It ceases to flutter and beat—
It never shall flutter again.

4 The lids he so seldom could close,
By sorrow forbidden to sleep,
Seal'd up in eternal repose,
Have strangely forgotten to weep;
These fountains can yield no supplies
These hollows from water are free;
The tears are all wip'd from these eyes,
And evil they never shall see.

5 To mourn and to suffer is mine,
While bound in a prison I breathe,
And still for deliverance pine,
And press to the issues of death.
What now with my tears I bedew,
Oh, shall I not shortly become!
My spirit created anew,
Ere I am consign'd to the tomb!

HYMN 570. 8s.
Mitcham. Uxbridge. Franklin.
Death of a Sister.
1 'TIS finish'd! the conflict is past,
The heaven-born spirit is fled;
Her wish is accomplish'd at last,
And now she's entomb'd with the dead.
The months of affliction are o'er,
The days and the nights of distress;
We see her in anguish no more—
She's gain'd her happy release.

2 No sickness, or sorrow, or pain,
Shall ever disquiet her now;
For death to her spirit was gain,
Since Christ was her life when below.
Her soul has now taken its flight
To mansions of glory above,
To mingle with angels of light,
And dwell in the kingdom of love.

3 The victory now is obtain'd
She's gone her dear Saviour to see;
Her wishes she fully has gain'd—
She's now where she longed to be.
Then let us forbear to complain,
That she has now gone from our sight;
We soon shall behold her again,
With new and redoubled delight.

*HYMN 571. C. M.   Newton.
Mear. Barby.
1 IN vain my fancy strives to paint
The moment after death;
The glories that surround a saint,
When yielding up his breath.

2 One gentle sigh his fetters breaks,
We scarce can say, "He's gone!"
Before the willing spirit takes
Its mansions near the throne.

3 Faith strives, but all its efforts fail,
To trace the spirit's flight;
No eye can pierce within the veil
Which hides the world of light.

4 Thus much (and this is all) we know,
Saints are completely blest;
Have done with sin, and care, and wo,
And with their Saviour rest.

5 On harps of gold they praise his name,
His face they always view,
Then let us foll'wers be of them,
That we may praise him too.

*HYMN 572. S. M.   Newton.
St. Thomas. Dover.
Balaam's wish. Numbers xxiii. 10.
1 HOW blest the righteous are,
When they resign their breath!
No wonder Balaam wish'd to share,
In such a happy death.

2 "Oh! let me die," said he,
"The death the righteous do;
When life is ended, let me be
Found with the faithful few."—

3 The force of truth, how great,
When enemies confess!
None but the righteous whom they hate,
A solid hope possess.

4 But Balaam's wish was vain—
His heart was insincere;
He thirsted for unrighteous gain.
And sought a portion here.

5 May we, O Lord most high,
Warning from hence receive;
If like the righteous we would die,
To choose the life they live.

*HYMN 573. C. M.   Steele.
Standish. Funeral Hymn.
Death of a young person.
1 WHEN blooming youth is snatch'd away
By death's resistless hand,
Our hearts the mournful tribute pay,
Which pity must demand.

2 While pity prompts the rising sigh,
Oh, may this truth, impress'd
With awful pow'r—" I too must die"
Sink deep in ev'ry breast.

3 The voice of this alarming scene
May ev'ry heart obey;
Nor be the heav'nly warning vain,
Which calls to watch, and pray.

4 Oh, let us fly, to Jesus fly,
Whose pow'rful arm can save;
Then shall our hopes ascend on high,
And triumph o'er the grave.

HYMN 574. C. M.   Steele.
Martyr's. Buckingham.
On the death of a Child.
1 THE once lov'd form, now cold and dead,
Each mournful thought employs:
And nature weeps her comforts fled,
And wither'd all her joys.

2 But wait the interposing gloom,
And lo! stern winter flies;
And, dress'd in beauty's fairest bloom,
The flow'ry tribes arise.

3 Hope looks beyond the bounds of time,
When what we now deplore,
Shall rise in full, immortal prime,
And bloom to fade no more.

4 Then cease, fond nature, cease thy tears;
Religion points on high;
There everlasting spring appears,
And joys which cannot die.

*HYMN 575. L. M.   Newton.
Putney. Darwent. Surry.
1 OFT as the bell, with solemn toll,
Speaks the departure of a soul,
Let each one ask himself,
"Am I Prepar'd, should I be call'd to die?

2 "Only this frail and fleeting breath
Preserves me from the jaws of death;
Soon as it fails, at once I'm gone,
And plung'd into a world unknown.

3 "Then leaving all I lov'd below,
To God's tribunal I must go;
Must hear the Judge pronounce my fate,
And fix my everlasting state."

4 LORD JESUS! help me now to flee,
And seek my hope alone in thee;
Apply thy blood, thy Spirit give—
Subdue my sins and let me live.

5 Then when the solemn bell I hear,
If sav'd from guilt, I need not fear;
Nor would the thought distressing be,
Perhaps it next may toll for me.

TIME AND ETERNITY.

*HYMN 576. C. M.   Hoskins.
Elgin. Wantage. Martyr's.
I Corinthians vii. 29.
1 THE time is short! the season near,
When death will us remove
To leave our friends, however dear,
And all we fondly love.

2 The time is short! sinners, beware,
Nor trifle time away;
The word of great salvation hear,
While it is call'd today.

3 The time is short! ye rebels, now
To Christ the Lord submit;
To mercy's golden sceptre bow,
And fall at Jesus' feet.

4 The time is short! ye saints rejoice—
The Lord will quickly come;
Soon shall you hear the Bridegroom's voice,
To call you to your home.

5 The time is short! it swiftly flies—
The hour is just at hand,
When we shall mount above the skies,
And reach the wish'd for land.

6 The time is short!— the moment near,
When we shall dwell above;
And be for ever happy there,
With Jesus, whom we love.

*HYMN 577. C. M.   Logan.
Elgin. Standish. Aldridge.
Psalm xc. 5, 9.

1 THE mighty flood, that rolls along
In torrents to the main,
The waters lost can ne'er recall,
From that abyss again.

2 The days, the years, the ages dark,
Descending down to night,
Can never, never be redeem'd,
Back to the gates of light.

3 Where are our Fathers?—Whither gone
The mighty men of old!
The patriarchs, prophets, princes, kings,
In sacred books enroll'd?—

4 Gone to the resting place of man,
His long, his silent home;
Where ages past have gone before,
Where future ages come!

HYMN 578. 8s.
Lambeth. Uxbridge.
Job xvi. 22; xvii. 1, 11.

1 I WAIT a few sorrowful years,
And then I no longer shall mourn,
But flee from the valley of tears,
A way I shall never return;
My days are all vanish'd away,
Broke off the designs of my heart,
No longer on earth I delay,
Or linger as loath to depart.

2 My days are extinguish'd and gone—
My time as a shadow is fled,
And gladly I lay myself down
To rest with the peaceable dead:
The dead ever-living attend,
Whose dust is all safe in the tomb,
And many a glorified friend
Is ready to welcome me home.

*HYMN 579. L. M.
Surry. Norfolk.
Eternity
1 ETERNITY is just at hand
And shall I waste my ebbing sand;
And careless view departing day,
And throw my inch of time away?

2 But an eternity there is
Of endless wo, or endless bliss;
And swift as time fulfils its round,
We to eternity are bound.

3 What countless millions of mankind
Have left this fleeting world behind!
They're gone! but where? Ah, pause and see,
Gone to a long eternity.

4 Sinner! canst thou for ever dwell
In all the fiery deeps of hell;
And is death nothing, then to thee;
Death, and a dread eternity?

HYMN 580. C. P. M.   C. Wesley.
Penitent. Pilgrim. Woods.
1 LO! on a narrow neck of land,
'Twixt two unbounded seas I stand,
Yet how insensible!
A point of time—a moment's space—
Removes me to yon heav'nly place,
Or—shuts me up in hell!

2 O God, my inmost soul convert,
And deeply on my thoughtless heart,
Eternal things impress
Give me to feel their solemn weight,
And save me, ere it be too late—
Wake me to righteousness.

3 Before me place, in bright array,
The pomp of that tremendous day,
When thou with clouds shalt come,
To judge the nations at thy bar,
And tell me, Lord, shall I be there,
To meet a joyful doom?

4 Be this my one great business here,
With holy trembling, holy fear,
To make my calling sure!
Thine utmost counsel to fulfil,
And suffer all thy righteous will,
And to the end endure!

RESURRECTION.

HYMN 581.　C. M.
Florence. Steffani's. Clifford.
1 THE winter past, reviving flowers
Anew shall paint the plain;
The woods shall hear the voice of Spring,
And flourish green again.

2 Shall man depart this earthly scene,
Ah! never to return!—
No second Spring of life revive
The ashes of the urn!—

3 'Shall life revisit dying worms,
And spread the insect's wing?
And oh—shall man awake no more,
The Saviour's name to sing?

4 'Cease—all ye vain desponding fears;
When Christ from darkness sprang,
Death, the last foe, was captive led,
And heav'n with praises rang.

5 'The trump shall sound;—the gates of death
Shall make his children way;
From the cold tomb the slumb'rers spring,
And shine in endless day.'

HYMN 582.　C. M.　H. K. White.
Chapel. Aldridge. Wantage.
1 THRO' sorrow's night and danger's path,
Amid the deep'ning gloom,
We, soldiers of an injur'd King,
Are marching to the tomb.

2 There, when the turmoil is no more,
And all our pow'rs decay,
Our cold remains, in solitude,
Shall sleep the years away.

3 Our labors done, securely laid
In this our last retreat,
Unheeded, o'er our silent dust,
The storms of life shall beat.

4 These ashes poor, this little dust,
Our Father's care shall keep,
Till the last angel rise, and break
The long and dreary sleep.

5 Then love's soft dew o'er ev'ry eye
Shall shed its mildest rays,
And the long silent dust shall burst
With shouts of endless praise.

HYMN 583. L. M.
China. Luther's Hymn.
1 THE saints, who now in Jesus sleep,
His own almighty pow'r shall keep,
Till dawns the bright illustrious day.
When death itself shall die away.

2 How loud shall our glad voices sing,
When Christ his risen saints shall bring
From beds of dust, and sleeping clay,
To realms of everlasting day!

3 When Jesus we in glory meet,
Our utmost joys shall be complete;
When landed on that heav'nly shore,
Death and the curse shall be no more.

HYMN 584. L. M.
Babylon. Carthage.
1 OUR life how short! a groan, a sigh;
We live—and then begin to die:
But Oh! how great a mercy this,
That death's a portal into bliss!

2 My soul! death swallows up thy fears,
My grave-clothes wipe away all tears;
Why should we fear this parting pain,
Who die, that we may live again?

3 Oh! how the resurrection light
Will clarify believer's sight;
How joyful will the saints arise,
And rub the dust from off their eyes!

4 My soul, my body I will trust,
With him who numbers every dust;
My Saviour faithfully will keep
His own—their death is but a sleep.

DAY OF JUDGMENT.

HYMN 585. C. M.   Addison.
Martyr's. Windsor. Colchester.
1 WHEN rising from the bed of death,
O'erwhelm'd with guilt and fear,
I see my Maker face to face—
Oh, how shall I appear!

2 If yet, while pardon may be found,
And mercy may be sought,
My heart with inward horror shrinks,
And trembles at the thought:

3 When thou, O Lord! shalt stand disclos'd
In Majesty severe,
And sit in judgment on my soul,
Oh, how shall I appear!

4 Prepare me, Lord, to meet that day,
Ere yet it be too late,
When I shall view these solemn scenes,
And feel their awful weight.

*HYMN 586. C. M.   Watts.
Elgin. Windsor.
Everlasting absence of God intolerable.
1 THAT awful day will surely come,
Th' appointed hour makes haste—

When I must stand before my Judge,
And pass the solemn test.

2 Thou lovely Chief of all my joys,
Thou Sov'reign of my heart,
How could I bear to hear thy voice
Pronounce the sound, *Depart!*

3 The thunder of that dismal word
Would so torment my ear,
'Twould tear my soul asunder, Lord,
With most tormenting fear.

4 What—to be banish'd from my life,
And yet forbid to die!
To linger in eternal pain,
Yet death for ever fly!

5 Oh, wretched state of deep despair
To see my God remove—
And fix my doleful station where
I must not taste his love!

6 Oh, tell me that my worthless name
Is graven on thy hands;
Show me some promise in thy book,
Where my salvation stands.

HYMN 587. 8, 7, 4.
Littleton. Jordan.
Luke xiii. 28.
1 SEE th' Eternal Judge descending—
View him seated on his throne!
Now, poor sinner, now lamenting,
Stand and hear thy awful doom
Trumpets call thee!
Stand and hear thy awful doom.

2 Hear the cries he now is venting,
Fill'd with dread of fiercer pain;
While in anguish thus lamenting,
That he ne'er was born again,
Greatly mourning,
That he ne'er was born again;

3 "Yonder sits my slighted Saviour,
With the marks of dying love;
Oh, that I had sought his favor,
When I felt his spirit move—
Golden moments,
When I felt his Spirit move."

4 Now, despisers, look and wonder!
Hope and sinners here must part,
Louder than a peal of thunder,
Hear the dreadful sound, "Depart!"
Lost for ever,
Hear the dreadful sound, "Depart!"

*HYMN 588. 8, 7.
Northampton Chapel. Tabernacle.
1 SINNERS, take the friendly warning—
Soon that awful day shall break,
And the trumpet with its dawning,
All the slumb'ring millions wake.

2 See assembled ev'ry nation!—
Lofty cities, temples, tow'rs,
Wrapp'd in dreadful conflagration,
Earth and sea the flame devours.

3 Ye, who to the world dissemble,
While you practise deeds of night,
Sinners, now behold and tremble;
All your crimes are brought to light.

4 Lost in ease, or carnal pleasure,
Sporting on the burning brink;
Now, you say, you have no leisure,
You can find no time to think.

5 Ye—who now, conviction stifling,
Waste your time—the loss deplore;
Hear the angel—cease your trifling—
"Time," he cries, "shall be no more."

6 Pause, and hear the voice of reason—
Catch the moments as they fly—
You who lose the present season,—
You must all find time to die.

*HYMN 589. L. M.   Needham.
Surry. Warwick.
The books opened. Revelation xx. 12.
1 ME THINKS the last great day is come;
Me thinks I hear the trumpet sound,
That shakes the earth, rends ev'ry tomb,
And wakes the pris'ners under ground.

2 The mighty deep gives up her trust,
Aw'd by the judge's high command;
Both small and great now quit their dust,
And round the dread tribunal stand.

3 Behold the awful books display'd,
Big with th' important fates of men;
Each deed and word now public made,
As wrote by heav'n's unerring pen.

4 To ev'ry soul, the books assign
The joyous or the dread reward;
Sinners in vain lament and pine—
No plea the Judge will here regard.

5 Lord, when these awful leaves unfold,
May life's fair book my soul approve!
There may I read my name enroll'd,
And triumph in redeeming love!

DEATH AND HEAVEN.

*HYMN 590. C. M.   Collyer.
Elgin. Windsor. Standish.
1 Samuel xv. 32.
1 WHEN, bending o'er the brink of life,
My trembling soul shall stand,
Waiting to pass death's awful flood,
Great God, at thy command!

2 When weeping friends surround my bed,
And close my sightless eyes;
When shatter'd by the weight of years
This broken body lies:

3 When ev'ry long lov'd scene of life
Stands ready to depart;
When the last sigh that shakes the frame
Shall rend this bursting heart:

4 O, thou great source of joy supreme,
Whose arm alone can save,
Dispel the darkness that surrounds
The entrance to the grave!

5 Lay thy supporting gentle hand
Beneath my sinking head;
And, with a ray of love divine,
Illume my dying bed!

6 Leaning on thy dear faithful breast,
May I resign my breath!
And, in thy fond embraces, lose
"The bitterness of death!"

HYMN 591. C. M. Hart.
Bishopsgate. Chapel. Standish.
Preparation for death. Matthew xxiv. 44.
1 VAIN man, thy fond pursuits forbear;
Repent!—thy end is nigh!
Death, at the farthest, can't be far—
Oh, think before thou die!

2 Reflect—thou hast a soul to save:
Thy sins—how high they mount!
What are thy hopes beyond the grave?
How stands that dread account?

3 Death enters—and there's no defence—
His time, there's none can tell;
He'll in a moment call thee hence,
To heaven—or to hell!

4 Thy flesh, perhaps thy chiefest care,
Shall crawling worms consume:
But, ah! destruction stops not there—
Sin kills beyond the tomb.

5 To-day, the gospel calls; to-day,
Sinners, it speaks to you:

Let ev'ry one forsake his way
And mercy will ensue.

*HYMN 592 L. M. Montgomery
Surry. Darwent. Putney.
The Living Know Ecclesiastes ix. 5.
1 WHERE are the dead?—In heav'n or hell
Their disembodied spirits dwell;
Their perish'd forms in bonds of clay,
Reserv'd until the judgment day.

2 Who are the dead?—The sons of time
In ev'ry age, and state, and clime;
Renoun'd, dishonor'd, or forgot,
The place that knew them, knows them not.

3 Where are the living?—On the ground
Where pray'r is heard and mercy found;
Where in the compass of a span,
The mortal makes th' immortal man.

4 Who are the living?—They whose breath
Draws ev'ry moment nigh to death;
Of endless bliss or wo the heirs:
Oh, what an awful lot is theirs.

5 Then, timely warn'd, let us begin
To follow Christ and flee from sin;
Daily grow up in him our head,
Lord of the living and the dead.

HYMN 593. S. M. Montgomery.
Shirland. Berkley.
1 OH, where shall rest be found,
Rest for the weary soul!
'Twere vain the ocean's depths to sound,
Or pierce to either pole.

2 The world can never give
The bliss for which we sigh;
'Tis not the whole of life to live,
Nor all of death to die.

3 Beyond this vale of tears
There is a life above,

Unmeasur'd by the flight of years
And all that life is love.

4 There is a death whose pang
Outlasts the fleeting breath:
Oh! what eternal horrors hang
Around the second death.

5 Lord, God of truth and grace!
Teach us that death to shun:—
Lest we be driven from thy face,
And evermore undone.

6 Here would we end our quest—
Alone are found in thee
The life of perfect love—the rest
Of immortality.

HYMN 594. C. M.   Steele.
Springfield. Rochester. Bray.
Victory over death. I Corinthians xv. 57.
1 DEAR Saviour, thy victorious love
Can all my fears control;
Can bid the pangs of guilt remove,
And cheer the trembling soul.

2 Victorious love! thy wondrous pow'r
From sin and death can raise;
Can gild the dark, departing hour.
And tune its groans to praise.

3 Then shall the joyful spirit soar
To life beyond the sky,
Where gloomy death can frown no more,
And guilt and terror die.

4 No more, O pale Destroyer, boast
Thy universal sway;
To heav'n-born souls thy sting is lost—
Thy night, the gate of day.

HYMN 595. C. M.
Springfield. Keene.
Celestial prospects.
1 SWEET glories rush upon my sight,
And charm my wond'ring eyes;
The regions of immortal light,
The beauties of the skies!

2 All hail! ye fair celestial shores,
Ye lands of endless day;
Swift on my view your prospect pours,
And drives my griefs away.

3 There's a delightful clearness now—
My clouds of doubt are gone;
Fled is my former darkness too—
My fears are all withdrawn.

4 Short is the passage—short the space
Between my home and me;
There! there behold the radiant place
How near the mansions be!

5 Immortal wonders! boundless things,
In those dear worlds appear!
Prepare me, Lord, to stretch my wings,
And in those glories share.

*HYMN 596. C. M.   Watts
Colchester. Springfield.
The everlasting song.
1 EARTH has engross'd my love too long.
'Tis time I lift mine eyes
Upward, dear Father, to thy throne,
And to my native skies.

2 There the blest man, my Saviour, sits:
The God! how bright he shines!
And scatters infinite delights
On all the happy minds.

3 Seraphs, with elevated strains,
Circle the throne around;
And move and charm the starry plains
With an immortal sound.

4 Jesus, the Lord, their harps employs:—
Jesus, my love, they sing!
Jesus, the life of all our joys,
Sounds sweet from ev'ry string.

5 Now let me mount and join their song,
And be an angel too;
My heart, my hand, my ear, my tongue,
Here's joyful work for you.

6 I would begin the music here,
And so my soul should rise;
Oh, for some heav'nly notes to bear
My passions to the skies.

HYMN 597.   8s.   Collyer.
Lambeth. Uxbridge.
The last conflict.
1 I SOON shall accomplish my race,
And soar to the temple on high;
Dear Jesus, beholding thy face,
I cheerfully yield me to die.
Farewell, my distress and my wo—
The storms of existence are o'er;
Though fiercely the tempest may blow,
Its fury appals me no more.

2 More quickly and shorter I breathe—
The dew is o'erspreading my cheek—
I feel the approaches of death,
My heartstrings beginning to break;
A struggle or two and 'tis done—
From earth and its anguish I fly;
The palm of the conqueror won,
I live by submitting to die.

HYMN 598.   8, 7.   C. Wesley.
Sicilian. Northampton Chapel.
The departing saint.
1 HAPPY soul, thy days are ended.
All thy mourning days below:
Go, by angel-guards attended,
To the sight of Jesus, go!

2 Waiting to receive thy spirit,
Lo! the Saviour stands above,
Shows the glory of his merit,
Reaches out the crown of love.

3 Struggle through thy latest passion
To thy dear Redeemer's breast,
To his uttermost salvation,
To his everlasting rest.

4 For the joy he sets before thee,
Bear a momentary pain;
Die, to live the life of glory—
Suffer, with thy Lord to reign.

HYMN 599. 8s. M. De Fleury.
Uxbridge. Dismission.
Panting for Heaven.
1 YE angels, who stand round the throne,
And view my Immanuel's face,
In rapturous songs make him known;
Tune, tune your soft harps to his praise
He form'd you the spirits you are,
So happy, so noble, so good;
When others sunk down in despair,
Confirm'd by his power, ye stood.

2 Ye saints, who stand nearer than they,
And cast your bright crowns at his feet,
His grace and his glory display,
And all his rich mercy repeat:
He snatch'd you from hell and the grave—
He ransom'd from death and despair:
For you he was mighty to save,
Almighty to bring you safe there.

3 Oh, when will the period appear,
When I shall unite in your song?
I'm weary of lingering here,
And I to your Saviour belong!
I'm fetter'd and chain'd up in clay;
I struggle and pant to be free;
I long to be soaring away,
My God and my Saviour to see!

4 I want to put on my attire,
Wash'd white in the Blood of the Lamb,
I want to be one of your choir,
And tune my sweet harp to his name;
I want—Oh, I want to be there,
Where sorrow and sin bid adieu—
Your joy and your friendship to share—
To wonder, and worship with you!

HYMN 600. 7s.
Hotham. Pastoral-Duet.
Heaven. John xiv. 2.
1 HIGH in yonder realms of light,
Dwell the raptur'd saints above,
Far beyond our feeble sight,
Happy in Immanuel's love!
Pilgrims in this vale of tears,
Once they knew, like us below,
Gloomy doubts, distressing fears,
Tort'ring pain and heavy wo.

2 Oft the big, unbidden tear,
Stealing down the furrow'd cheek,
Told, in eloquence sincere,
Tales of wo they could not speak.
But, these days of weeping o'er,
Past this scene of toil and pain,
They shall feel distress no more,
Never—never weep again!

3 'Mid the chorus of the skies,
'Mid th' angelic lyres above,
Hark—their songs melodious rise,
Songs of praise to Jesus' love!
Happy Spirits! ye are fled,
Where no grief can entrance find,
Lull'd to rest the aching head,
Sooth'd the anguish of the mind!

4 All is tranquil and serene,
Calm and undisturb'd repose—
There no cloud can intervene—
There no angry tempest blows:

Ev'ry tear is wip'd away,
Sighs no more shall heave the breast;
Night is lost in endless day—
Sorrow—in eternal rest!

DOXOLOGIES.

L. M.
TO God the Father, God the Son,
And God the Spirit, Three in One,
Be honor, praise, and glory giv'n,
By all on earth, and all in heav'n.

C. M.
LET God the Father, and the Son,
And Spirit be ador'd,
Where there are works to make him known,
Or saints to love the Lord.

S. M.
YE angels, round the throne,
And saints that dwell below,
Worship the Father, praise the Son
And bless the Spirit too.

H. M.
TO God the Father's throne
Perpetual honors raise,
Glory to God the Son;
To God the Spirit praise
With all our powers,
Eternal King,
Thy name we sing,
While faith adores.

7s.
SING we to our God above,
Praise eternal as his love:
Praise him, all ye heavenly hosts,
Father, Son, and Holy Ghost.

8, 7.
MAY the grace of Christ our Saviour,
And the Father's boundless love,
With the Holy Spirit's favor,
Rest upon us from above!
Thus may we abide in union
With each other and the Lord;
And possess in sweet communion,
Joys which earth cannot afford.

Village Hymns for Social Worship

The Hymns Set to the Music Recommended by Asahel Nettleton

William C. Nichols
General Editor

Scott A. Sterner
Musical Arrangements

Dave Belford
Musical Editing

Copyright © 1997 by International Outreach, Inc.

The musical arrangements in this section of the book are copyrighted by International Outreach, Inc. Reproduction of these pages photographically, mechanically, or by any other means is prohibited by the copyright laws of the United States of America and your own integrity.

International Outreach, Inc
P. O. Box 1286, Ames, Iowa 50014
515-233-2932

GOD

Solemn Thoughts of God and Death 1

Luther's Hymn   *Scripture*   Martin Luther

There is a God, who reigns a-bove, Lord of the
There is a law which he has writ, To teach us
There is a gos-pel rich in grace, Whence sin-ners
There is an hour when I must die, Nor do I

heav'n, and earth and seas; I fear his wrath, I
all, what we must do; My soul, to his com-
all their com-forts draw; Lord, I re-pent and
know how soon 'twill come; How man-y, young-er

ask his love, And with my lips I sing his praise.
mands sub-mit, For they are ho-ly, just, and true.
seek thy face, For I have of-ten broke thy law.
much than I, Have pass'd by death to hear their doom.

5. Let me improve the hours I have,
Before the day of grace is fled;
There's no repentance in the grave,
Nor pardon offer'd to the dead.

6. Just as a tree cut down that fell
To north or southward, there it lies;
So man departs to heav'n or hell,
Fixed in the state wherein he dies.

Text: Isaac Watts

GOD

The Eye of God 4

Walsall C. M.   *Proverbs xv. 3; Hebrews iv. 13.*   Anchors' Collection

1. The eye of God is ev-'ry where To watch the sinner's ways; He sees who join in humble prayer, And who in solemn praise.

2. One glance of thine, e-ter-nal Lord, Can pierce and search us thro'; Nor heav'n, nor earth, nor hell afford A shelter from thy view!

3. The un-i-verse, in ev-'ry part, At once before thee lies; And ev-'ry thought of ev-'ry heart Is open to thine eyes.

4. Pre-pare us, Lord, to pray and praise With fervent, holy love; And fit us by thy word of grace To worship thee above.

Text: Steele

5. Angels and men the news proclaim,
Through earth and heaven above.
The joyful and transporting news,
That God, the Lord, is love.

Text: Anonymous

GOD

Trinity

11

Braintree C. M.   *Ephesians ii. 18.*

1. Fa-ther of glo-ry, to thy name Im-mor-tal praise we give, Who dost an act of grace pro-claim, And bid us re-bels live.

2. Im-mor-tal hon-or to the Son, Who makes thine an-ger cease; Our lives he ran-som'd with his own, And died to make our peace.

3. To thine Al-might-y Spir-it be Im-mor-tal glor-y giv'n, Whose in-flu'nce brings us near to thee, And trains us up for heav'n.

4. Let men, with their u-nit-ed voice, A-dore th'e-ter-nal God, And spread his hon-ors and their joys, Thro' na-tions far a-broad.

5. Let faith, and love, and duty join,
One general song to raise:
Let saints in earth and heaven combine,
In harmony and praise.

Text: Isaac Watts

GOD

The Mysteries of Providence   12

St. Anne's C. M.   William Croft

God moves in a mys-te-r'ous way, His wonders to perform; He plants his footsteps in the sea, And rides upon the storm.

Deep in un-fath-om-a-ble mines Of never-failing skill, He treasures up his bright designs, And works his sov-'reign will.

Ye fear-ful saints, fresh cour-age take, The clouds ye so much dread, Are big with mer-cy, and shall break In bless-ings on your head.

Judge not the Lord by fee-ble sense, But trust him for his grace; Be-hind a frown-ing pro-vi-dence He hides a smil-ing face.

5. His purposes will ripen fast,
Unfolding every hour;
The bud may have a bitter taste,
But sweet will be the flower.

6. Blind unbelief is sure to err,
And scan his work in vain;
God is his own interpreter,
And he will make it plain.

Text: William Cowper

Servants of God Always Safe   13

5. In midst of dangers, fears, and deaths,
Thy goodness we'll adore;
We'll praise thee for thy mercies past;
And humbly hope for more.

Text: Addison

UNIVERSAL PRAISE

God Exalted Above All Praise   15

Wells L. M.   Israel Holdroyd

Text: Isaac Watts

Universal Praise

17

Northhampton Chapel 8, 7. Aaron Williams

Saints, with pi - ous zeal at - tend - ing, Now a grate - ful tri - bute raise; Sol - emn songs to heav'n as - cend - ing, Join the un - i - ver - sal
Round Je - ho - vah's foot - stool kneel - ing, Low - ly bend with con - trite souls; Here his mild - er grace re - veal - ing, Here his wrath no thun - der
Ev - 'ry se - cret fault con - fess - ing, Deed un - right - eous, thought of sin, Seize, O seize the prof - fer'd bless - ing, Grace from God and peace with -
Heart and voice with rap - ture swell - ing, Still the song of glor - y raise; On the theme im - mor - tal dwell - ing, Join the un - i - ver - sal

Text: Taylor

UNIVERSAL PRAISE

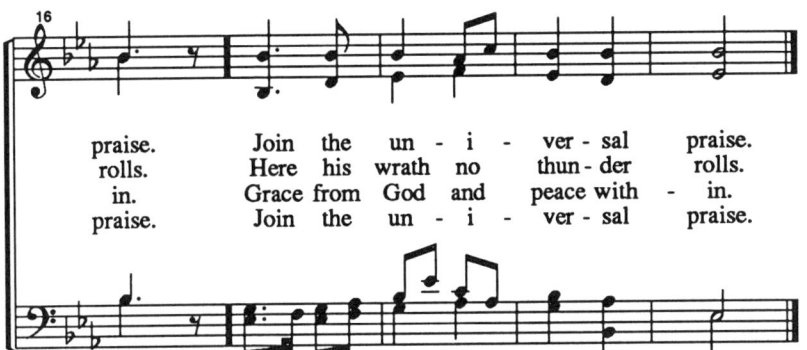

SCRIPTURES

The Book Divine

19

Barby C.M. — William Tansur

How pre-cious is the book di-vine, By in-spi-ra-tion giv'n! Bright as a lamp its doc-trines shine To guide our souls to heav'n.
It sweet-ly cheers our droop-ing hearts, In this dark vale of tears; Life, light, and joy, it still im-parts, And quells our ris-ing fears.
This lamp, thro' all the ted-ious night Of life, shall guide our way, Till we be-hold the clear-er light Of an e-ter-nal day.

Text: Rippon

SCRIPTURES

Heavenly Pages

20

Canterbury C. M.
E. Blancks

Father of mercies, in thy word, What endless glory shines! For ever be thy name ador'd For these celestial lines.
Here, the Redeemer's welcome voice, Spreads heav'nly peace around, And life, and ever-lasting joys Attend the blissful sound.
Oh, may these heav'nly pages be My ever dear delight; And still new beauties may I see, And still increasing light!
Divine instructer, gracious Lord, Be thou for ever near, Teach me to love thy sacred word, And view my Saviour there.

Text: Steele

SCRIPTURES

The Guide to Life 21

Abridge C. M. I. Smith

1. Laden with guilt and full of fears, I fly to thee, my Lord, And not a glimpse of hope appears, But in thy written word.
2. The volume of my Father's grace Does all my grief assuage; Here I behold my Saviour's face Almost in ev'ry page.
3. This is the field where hidden lies The pearl of price unknown; That merchant is divinely wise, Who makes the pearl his own.
4. This is the Judge that ends the strife Where wit and reason fail; My guide to everlasting life, Thro' all this gloomy vale.

Text: Isaac Watts

ALARMING

Few Saved

25

Orange S.M.   *Luke xiii. 23.*   Stone

De - struction's dan - g'rous road What mul - ti -
Be - liev - ers find the way Thro' Christ the
If self must be de - nied, And sin no
En - com-pass'd by a throng, On num - bers
But hear the Sav - iour's word, "Strive for the

tudes pur - sue! While that which leads the soul to
liv - ing gate; But those who hate this ho - ly
more ca - ress'd, They ra - ther choose the way that's
they de - pend; They say, so ma - ny can't be
hea - v'nly gate, Ma - ny will call up - on the

God, Is known or sought by few.
way Com - plain it is too strait.
wide, And strive to think it best.
wrong, And miss a hap - py end.
Lord, And find their cries too late."

6. Obey the gospel call,
And enter while you may;
The flock of Christ is always small,
And none are safe but they.

7. Lord, open sinners' eyes,
Their awful state to see;
And make them, ere the storm arise,
To thee for safety flee.

Text: John Newton

ALARMING

The Sinner Weighed & Found Wanting

Luther's Hymn L. M.   *Daniel v. 27.*   Martin Luther

Raise, thought-less sin-ner, raise thine eye— Be-hold God's bal-ance lift-ed high! There shall his jus-tice be dis-play'd, And there thy hope and life be weigh'd.

See in one scale his per-fect law; Mark with what force its pre-cepts draw: Wouldst thou the aw-ful test sus-tain? Thy works how light! thy thou'ts how vain!

Be-hold, the hand of God ap-pears To trace in dread-ful char-ac-ters; "Sin-ner— thy soul is want-ing found, And wrath shall smite thee to the ground."

Let sud-den fear thy nerves un-brace; Let hor-ror change thy guilt-y face; Through all thy thou'ts let an-guish roll, Till deep re-pen-tance melt thy soul.

5. One only hope may yet prevail;—
Christ hath a weight to turn the scale;
Still doth the gospel publish peace,
And show a Saviour's righteousness.

6. Great God, exert thy power to save;
Deep on the heart these truths engrave;
The pond'rous load of guilt remove,
That trembling lips may sing thy love.

Text: Phillip Doddridge

ALARMING

The Fig Tree

31

Wells L. M.   *Mark xi. 20.*   Israel Holdroyd

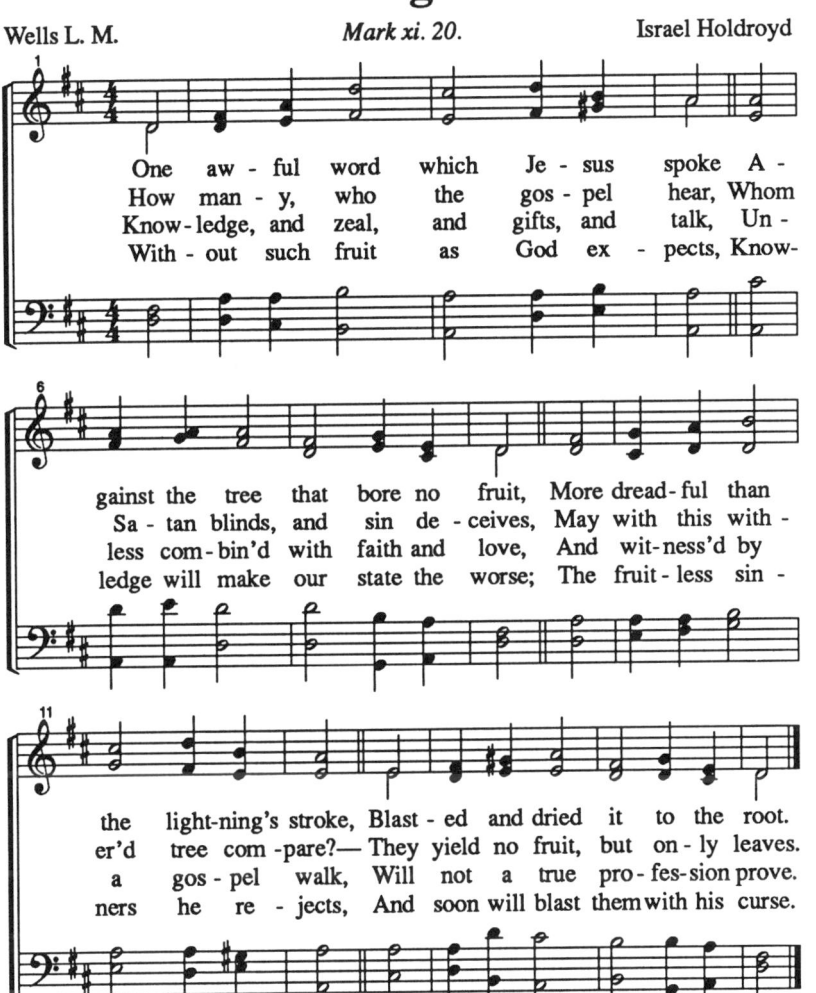

1. One awful word which Jesus spoke Against the tree that bore no fruit, More dreadful than the lightning's stroke, Blasted and dried it to the root.
2. How many, who the gospel hear, Whom Satan blinds, and sin deceives, May with this withered tree compare?— They yield no fruit, but only leaves.
3. Knowledge, and zeal, and gifts, and talk, Unless combin'd with faith and love, And witness'd by a gospel walk, Will not a true profession prove.
4. Without such fruit as God expects, Knowledge will make our state the worse; The fruitless sinners he rejects, And soon will blast them with his curse.

Text: John Newton

ALARMING

The Harvest is Past 33

Wirksworth S. M.   *Jeremiah viii. 20.*   Harmonia Sacra

1. I saw, beyond the tomb, The aw-ful Judge ap-pear, Pre-par'd to scan with strict ac-count, My bless-ings wast-ed here.
2. His wrath like flam-ing fire, Burn'd to the low-est hell— And in that hope-less world of wo, He bade my spir-it dwell.
3. Ye sin-ners, fear the Lord, While yet 'tis call'd to-day; Soon will the aw-ful voice of death Com-mand your souls a-way.
4. Soon will the har-vest close— The sum-mer soon be o'er— And soon, your in-jur'd, an-gry God Will hear your prayers no more.

Text: Timothy Dwight

ALARMING

The Rich Worldling 34

Barby C.M. *Luke xii. 16-21.* William Tansur

"My barns are full, my stores in - crease; And now for man - y years, Soul, eat and drink, and take thine ease, se - cure from wants and fears."
Thus, while a world-ling boast - ed once, As man - y now pre - sume, He heard the Lord him - self pro - nounce His sud - den, aw - ful doom:
"This night, vain fool, thy soul must pass, In - to a world un - known; And who shall then the stores pos - sess, Which thou hast call'd thine own?"
Thus blind - ed mor - tals fond - ly scheme For hap - pi - ness be - low; Till death de - stroys the pleas - ing dream, And they a - wake to wo.

Text: John Newton

ALARMING

Delay No Longer

38

St. Martin's C. M.   *Acts xvii. 30.*   William Tansur

Re - pent, the voice ce - les - tial cries, Nor long - er dare de - lay: The wretch that scorns the man - date dies, And meets a fier - y day.
No more the sov - 'reign eye of God O'er - looks the crimes of men; His her - alds are des - patch'd a - broad To warn the world of sin.
To - geth - er in his pre - sence bow, And all your guilt con - fess; Ac - cept the of - fer'd Sav - iour now, Nor tri - fle with his grace.
Bow, ere the aw - ful trum - pet sound, And call you to his bar: For mer - cy knows th'ap - point - ed bound, And turns to venge - ance there.

5. Amazing love, that yet will call,
And yet prolong our days!
Our hearts, subdu'd by goodness, fall,
And weep, and love, and praise.

Text: Phillip Doddridge

ALARMING

The Wreck of Nature 39

Old Hundred L. M. *Isaiah xxiv. 18-20.* Martin Luther

How great, how ter - ri - ble that God, Who shakes cre - a - tion with his nod! He frowns: earth, sea, all na - ture's frame
Where now, oh, where shall sin - ners seek For shel - ter in the gen - 'ral wreck! Shall fall - ing rocks be o'er them thrown?
In vain for mer - cy now they cry; In lakes of li - quid fire they lie; There on the flam - ing bil - lows toss'd,
But saints, un - daunt - ed and se - rene, With calm - ness view the dread - ful scene; Their Sav - iour lives, the worlds ex - pire;
Je - sus, the hope - less crea - ture's friend, To thee my all I dare com - mend; Thou canst pre - serve my fee - ble soul,

Text: Samuel Davies

ALARMING

Sink　　in　　one　　un - i - ver - sal　　flame.
See　rocks,　like　snow　dis - solv - ing　down.
For　　ev - er—　　oh,　for　　ev - er　　lost!
And　earth　and　skies　dis - solve　in　fire.
When　light-nings　blaze　from　pole　to　pole.

5. Lord, prepare us by thy grace!
Soon we must resign our breath,
And our souls be call'd to pass
Through the iron gate of death.

6. Let us now our day improve,
Listen to the gospel voice;
Seek the things that are above;
Scorn the world's pretended joys.

Text: John Newton

ALARMING

Apostasy

42

Wirksworth S. M. *2 Peter ii. 22.* Harmonia Sacra

Ye, who in form - er days,	Were found at	Zi - on's gate;	Who seem'd to walk in	wis-dom's ways,	And told your hap - py state;
But now to sin draw back,	And love a -	gain to stray,	The nar - row path of	life for - sake,	And choose the beat - en way;
Think not your names a - bove	Are writ - ten	with the saints	The pro - mise of un - chang-ing	love	Is his who nev - er faints.
Your tran - sient joy and peace	Your deep - er	doom have seal'd,	Un - less you wake to	right-eous - ness,	Ere judg - ment is re - veal'd.

Text: Hyde

INVITING

The Saviour's Invitation 44

Clifford C. M. *John vii. 37.*

The Sav-iour calls— let ev - 'ry ear At - tend the heav'n-ly sound; Ye doubt-ing souls, dis - miss your fear, Hope smiles re - viv - ing round.
For ev - 'ry thirst - y, long - ing heart, Here streams of boun - ty flow, And life, and health, and bliss im - part To ban - ish mor - tal wo.
Ye sin - ners, come, 'tis mer - cy's voice; The gra - cious call o - bey; Mer - cy in - vites to heav'n-ly joys— And can you yet de - lay?
Dear Sav-iour, draw re - luc - tant hearts To thee let sin - ners fly, And take the bliss thy love im - parts And drink, and nev - er die.

Text: Steele

INVITING

5. Ye dang'rous inmates, hence depart;
Dear Saviour, enter in,
And guard the passage to my heart,
And keep out every sin.

INVITING

Now is the Time

51

Tunbridge C. M.

1. Now is the time, th'accepted hour, O sinners, come away
The Saviour's knocking at your door, Arise without delay.

2. Oh! don't refuse to give him room, Lest mercy should withdraw
He'll then in robes of vengeance come To execute his law.

3. Then where, poor mortals, will you be, If destitute of grace,
When you your injur'd Judge shall see, And stand before his face.

4. Oh! could you shun that dreadful sight, How would you wish to fly
To the dark shades of endless night, From that all-searching eye?

5. The dead awak'd must all appear,
And you among them stand,
Before the great impartial bar,
Arraign'd at Christ's left hand.

6. Let not these warnings be in vain,
But lend a list'ning ear
Lest you should meet them all again,
When wrapp'd in keen despair.

Text: William Cowper

INVITING

The Contrite Heart

60

Blendon L. M.   *Luke xv. 20-24.*   Giardini

Lo! what a rapt'rous joy possess'd The tender parent's throbbing breast, To see his spendthrift son return, And all his former follies mourn!

So Jesus never will despise The contrite heart for sacrifice; The deep-fetch'd sigh, the secret groan Will rise accepted to the throne.

He meets, with tokens of his grace, The trembling lip, the blushing face; His bowels yearn when sinners pray, And mercy bears their sins away.

Text: Anonymous

INVITING

The Gospel Trumpet 63

Rochester C. M.   *Isaiah lv. 1, 2.*   A. Williams

1. Let ev-'ry mor-tal ear at-tend, And ev-'ry heart re-joice! The trum-pet of the gos-pel sounds, With an in-vit-ing voice.
2. Ho! all ye hun-gry, star-ving souls, Who feed up-on the wind,— And vain-ly strive, with earth-ly toys, To fill an emp-ty mind:—
3. E-ter-nal wis-dom has pre-par'd A soul-re-viv-ing feast; And bids your long-ing ap-pe-tites The rich pro-vi-sion taste.
4. Ho! ye who pant for liv-ing streams, And pine a-way and die; Here, you may quench your rag-ing thirst, With springs that nev-er dry.

5. The happy gates of gospel grace
Stand open all the day;
Lord, we are come to seek supplies,
And drive our wants away.

Text: Isaac Watts

INVITING

Let the Wicked Forsake Their Way 69

Plymouth C. M.   *Isaiah 55:7*   W. Tunsar

Sin - ners, the voice of God re - gard; His mer - cy speaks to - day; He calls you by his sov - 'reign word, From sin's de - struc - tive way.

Like the rough sea that can - not rest, You live de - void of peace: A thou - sand stings with - in your breast, De - prive your souls of ease.

Your way is dark, and leads to hell; Why will you per - se - vere? Can you in end - less tor - ments dwell, Shut up in black des - pair?

Why will you in the crook - ed ways Of sin and fol - ly go? In pain you trav - el all your days, To reap im - mor - tal wo!

Text: Fawcett

INVITING

Healing Virtue in Christ 73

Shoel L. M.   *Luke vi. 19.*   Shoel

Ye mourn-ing sin-ners, here dis-close Your deep com-plaints, your var-ious woes; Approach— 'tis Je-sus, he can heal The pain which mourn-ing sin-ners feel.
Dear Lord, ex-tend thy heal-ing hand; Dis-eas-es fly at thy com-mand; O, let thy sov'-reign touch im-part Life, strength, and health to ev-'ry heart.
Then shall the sick, the blind, the lame, A-dore their great Phy-si-cian's name; Then dy-ing souls shall bless their God, And spread his won-drous praise a-broad.

Text: Steele

INVITING

Gold for Dross?

76

Colchester C. M.
Henry Purcell

Lord, shall we part with gold for dross, With solid good for show! Outlive our bliss, and mourn our loss In everlasting wo!
Let us not lose the living God, For one short dream of joy: With fond embrace cling to a clod, And fling all heav'n away.
Vain world, thy weak attempts forbear, We all thy charms defy; And rate our precious souls too dear For all thy wealth to buy.

Text: Rippon

INVITING

Resolve

77

Windsor C. M.   *Esther iv. 16.*   G. Kirby

5. "I can but perish if I go;
"I am resolv'd to try
"For if I stay away,
"I know I must for ever die."

Text: E. Jones

INVITING

One Thing Demands Our Care 84

Little Marlboro' S. M.   *James iv. 13, 14.*   Williams

To-mor - row, Lord, is thine, Lodg'd in thy
The pre - sent mo - ment flies, And bears our
Since on this wing - ed hour E - ter - ni -
One thing de - mands our care; Oh, be it

sov - 'reign hand; And, if its sun a - rise and
life a - way; Oh, make thy ser - vants tru - ly
ty is hung, Wak - en by thy al - might - y
still pur - su'd— Lest, slight - ed once, the sea - son

shine, It shines by thy com - mand.
wise, That they may live to - day.
pow'r The a - ged and the young.
fair Should nev - er be re - new'd.

5. To Jesus may we fly,
Swift as the morning light,
Lest life's young golden beam should die
In sudden, endless night.

Text: Philip Doddridge

PENITENTIAL

Lord, Help Me to Repent 96

Orange S.M. — Stone

1. Lord, help me to re-pent— With sin for ev-er part; And to thy gra-cious eye pre-sent An hum-ble, con-trite heart.
2. A heart with grief op-press'd, For hav-ing griev'd thy love; A trou-bled heart that can-not rest, Till cleansed from a-bove.
3. Je-sus, on me be-stow The pen-i-tent de-sire; With true sin-cer-i-ty of wo, My ach-ing breast in-spire;
4. With soft-'ning pi-ty look, And melt my hard-ness down; Strike, with thy love's re-sist-less stroke, And break this heart of stone.

Text: Anonymous

PENITENTIAL

Jesus, Full of Truth and Grace   100

Truro L. M. *Hosea xiv. 1, 2.* George F. Handel

O Jesus, full of truth and grace, More full of grace than I of sin; I now would flee to thine embrace; O-pen thine arms and take me in.
The stone to flesh do thou convert; And all my guilt and sin remove; Sprinkle thy blood upon my heart, And melt it by thy dying love.
Give to mine eyes refreshing tears, And kindle my relentings now; Fill all my soul with filial fears: To thy sweet yoke my spirit bow.
O, give me, Lord, the tender heart, That trembles at th' approach of sin; A godly fear of sin impart; Implant and root it deep within!

Text: Anonymous

CHRIST

Transfiguration

108

Malmsbury L. M. *Luke ix. 28-31.*

On Ta-bor's top the Sav-iour stands, His al-ter'd face re-splen-dent shines; And, while he el-e-vates his hands, Lo,

Two heav'n-ly forms de-scend to wait Up-on their suff-'ring Prince be-low; But while they wor-ship at his feet, They

A-mid the lus-tre of the scene, To Cal-va-ry he turns his eyes; And, with sub-mis-sion, all se-rene, He

Then let us climb the mount of prayer, Where all his beam-ing glor-ies shine; And, gaz-ing on his bright-ness there, Our

Text: Collyer

CHRIST

5. Oh, that on yonder heavenly hills,
Where now the risen Saviour stands,
And peace, like softest dew, distils--
I too may elevate my hands.

6. Burning with holy zeal, they spread,
Through distant lands, his word;
And we, like them, with faith and joy
Expect our risen Lord.

Text: Colliver

CHRIST

The Saviour God **121**

Eagle Street H. M.   *Scripture*   I. Smith

1. Come, ev-'ry pious heart That loves the Saviour's name, Your noblest pow'r exert To celebrate his fame: Tell...
2. He left his starry crown, And laid his robes aside; On wings of love came down, And wept, and bled, and died: What...
3. From the dark grave he rose, The mansion of the dead; And thence his mighty foes In glorious triumph led: Up...
4. Jesus, we ne'er can pay The debt we owe thy love; Yet tell us how we may Our gratitude approve: Our...

Text: Stennett

CHRIST

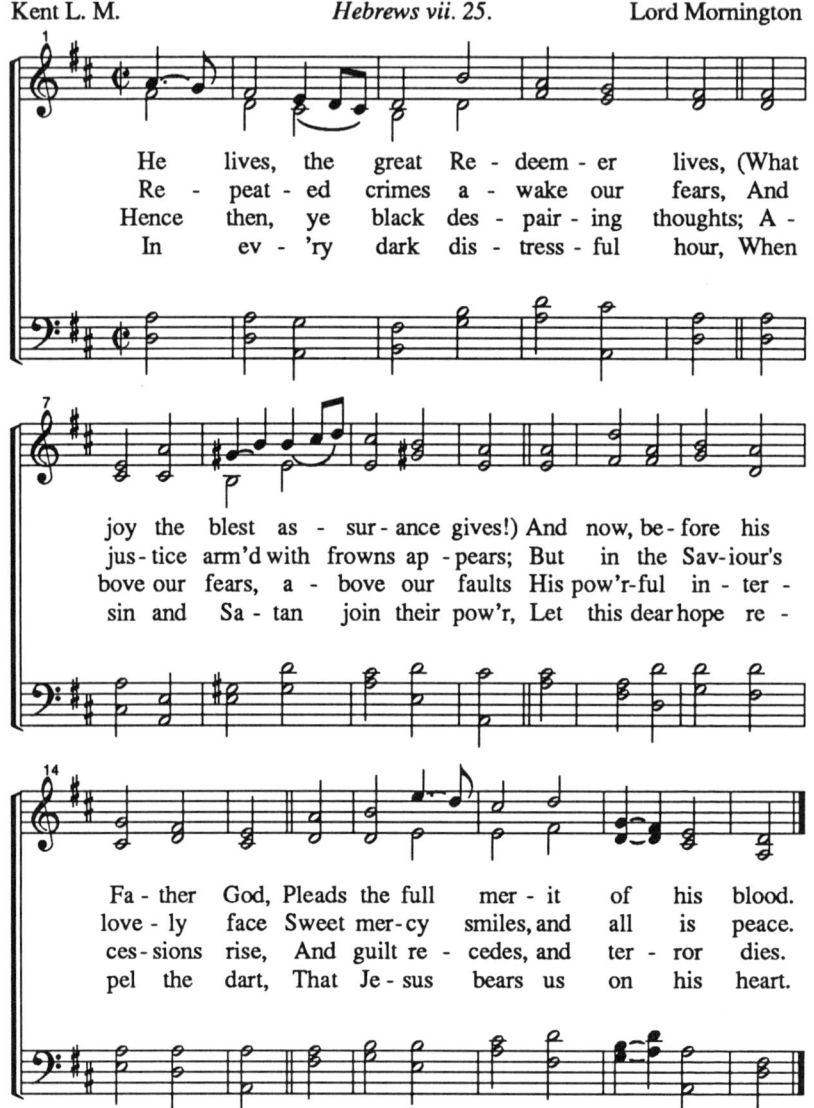

5. Great Advocate, Almighty Friend—
On him our humble hopes depend:
Our cause can never, never fail,
For Jesus pleads and must prevail.

Text: Steele

CHARACTERS OF CHRIST

The Hiding Place

130

Wareham C. M.   Arnold

1. He who on earth as man was known, And bore our sins and pains, Now seated on th' eternal throne— The God of glory reigns!
2. His righteousness to faith reveal'd, Wrought out for guilty worms, Affords a hiding place, and shield, From enemies and storms.
3. When troubles, like a burning sun, Beat heavy on their head, To this high rock his people run, And find a pleasing shade.
4. How glorious He!— how happy they! In such a glorious Friend! Whose love secures them all the way, And crowns them at the end.

Text: John Newton

CHARACTERS OF CHRIST

Friend

Proverbs xviii. 24.

Northhampton Chapel 8, 7. Aaron Williams

One there is, a-bove all oth-ers, Well de-serves the name of Friend, His is love, be-yond a broth-er's, Cost-ly, free, and knows no

Which of all our friends to save us, Could or would have shed his blood? But this Sav-iour died to have us Re-con-cil'd in him to

When he liv-ed on earth a-based, Friend of sin-ners was his name; Now, a-bove all glor-y rais-ed, He re-joic-es in the

Oh, for grace our hearts to sof-ten! Teach us, Lord, at length to love; We, a-las! for-get too of-ten, What a Friend we have a-

Text: John Newton

CHARACTERS OF CHRIST

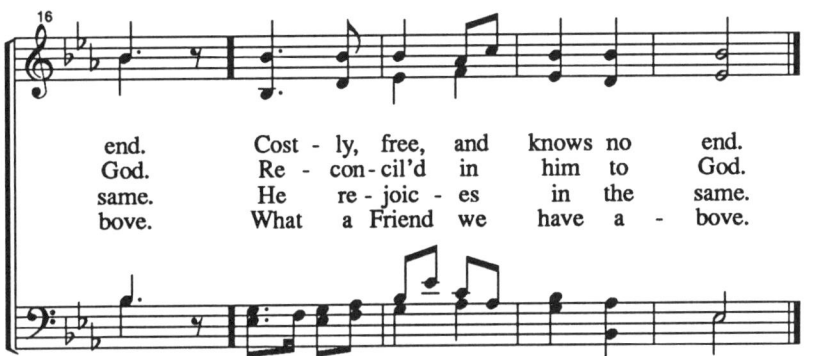

CHARACTERS OF CHRIST

Lamb of God

131

St. Thomas S. M.　　　　　　　　　　　　　　　　　　　　　A. Williams

1. Not all the blood of beasts, On Jewish altars slain, Could give the guilty conscience peace, Or wash away the stain.
2. But Christ, the heav'nly Lamb, Takes all our sins away; A sacrifice of nobler name, And richer blood than they.
3. My faith would lay her hand On that dear head of thine— While like a penitent I stand, And there confess my sin.
4. My soul looks back to see The burdens thou didst bear, When hanging on the cursed tree, And hopes her guilt was there.

5. Believing, we rejoice
To see the curse remove;
We bless the Lamb with cheerful voice,
And sing his bleeding love.

Text: Isaac Watts

CHARACTERS OF CHRIST

Pearl of Great Price

133

Rochester C. M.   *Matthew xii. 46.*   A. Williams

1. Ye glittering toys of earth, adieu; A nobler choice be mine; A real prize attracts my view, A treasure all divine.
2. Begone, unworthy of my cares, Ye specious baits of sense; Inestimable worth appears, The pearl of price immense!
3. Jesus, to multitudes unknown, O name divinely sweet! Jesus, in thee, in thee alone, Wealth, honor, pleasure meet.
4. Should both the Indies at my call, Their boasted stores resign; With joy I would renounce them all, For leave to call thee mine.

5. Should earth's vain treasures all depart, Of this dear gift possess'd, I'd clasp it to my joyful heart, And think myself most bless'd.

6. Dear sov'reign of my soul's desires, Thy love is bliss divine; Accept the wish that love inspires, And bid me call thee mine.

Text: Isaac Watts

CHARACTERS OF CHRIST

Saviour 137

St. Anne's C. M.   *John iv. 42.*   William Croft

1. The Saviour! Oh, what endless charms Dwell in the blissful sound! Its influence ev'ry fear disarms, And spreads sweet peace around.
2. Here pardon, life, and joys divine, In rich effusion flow, For guilty rebels lost in sin, And doom'd to endless wo.
3. Oh, the rich depths of love divine, Of bliss, a boundless store! Dear Saviour, let me call thee mine; I cannot wish for more.
4. On thee alone my hope relies, Beneath thy cross I fall; My Lord, my life, my sacrifice, My Saviour, and my all.

Text: Steele

DOCTRINES

Adoption

141

Shoel L. M.   *John i. 12. I John iii. 1.*   Shoel

Not all the no-bles of the earth, Who boast the hon-ors of their birth, Such re-al dig-ni-ty can claim, As those who bear the Chris-tian name.

To them the priv-i-lege is giv'n To be the sons and heirs of heav'n; All heirs of joys be-yond the sky.

His will he makes them ear-ly know, And teach-es their young feet to go; Whis-pers in-struc-tion to their minds, And on their hearts his pre-cepts binds.

When, thro' temp-ta-tion, they re-bel, His chas-t'ning rod he makes them feel; Then, with a Fa-ther's ten-der heart, He sooths the pain, and heals the smart.

Text:

DOCTRINES

Nearness to God   145

Walsall C. M.
Anchors' Collection

Oh, could I find from day to day, A nearness to my God: Then should my hours glide sweet a-way, And lean up-on his word.

Lord, I de-sire with thee to live A-new from day to day In joys the world can nev-er give, Nor ev-er take a-way.

O Je-sus, come and rule my heart, And make me whol-ly thine, That I may nev-er more de-part, Nor grieve thy love di-vine.

Thus till my last ex-pir-ing breath, Thy good-ness I'll a-dore; And when my flesh dis-solves in death, My soul shall love thee more.

Text: Anonymous

DOCTRINES

Decrees of God

146

St. Anne's C. M.

William Croft

Keep silence, all created things, And wait your Maker's nod: My soul stands trembling, while she sings The honors of her God.

Life, death, and hell, and worlds unknown Hang on his firm decree; He sits on no precarious throne, Nor borrows leave— to be.

Chain'd to his throne, a volume lies, With all the fates of men: With ev'ry angel's form and size, Drawn by th'e-ter-nal pen.

His providence unfolds the book, And makes his counsels shine; Each op'ning leaf, and ev'ry stroke, Fulfils some deep design.

Here, he exalts neglected worms To sceptres and a crown; And there, the foll'wing page he turns, And treads the monarch down.

6. Not Gabriel asks the reason why,
Nor God the reason gives;
Nor dares the fav'rite angel pry
Between the folded leaves.

7. In thy fair book of life and grace,
Oh, may I find my name,
Recorded in some humble place,
Beneath my Lord— the Lamb.

Text: Isaac Watts

DOCTRINES

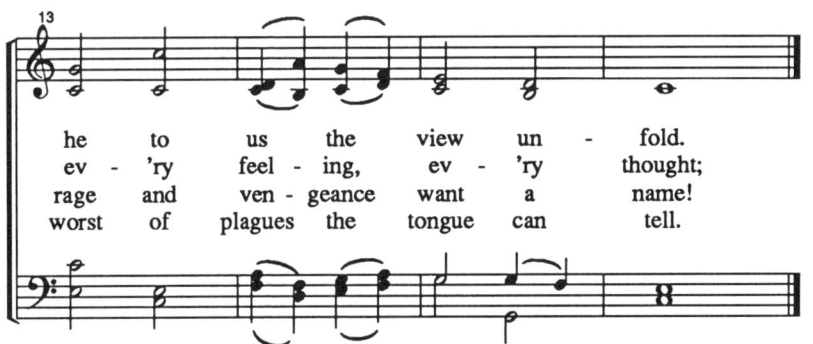

he to us the view un - fold.
ev - 'ry feel - ing, ev - 'ry thought;
rage and ven - geance want a name!
worst of plagues the tongue can tell.

5. Unveil'd and naked ev'ry heart
Before the judgment seat must stand,
Sin act no more a double part,
But meet a death from its own hand.

6. The fiery lake will hotter grow
From the fierce clash of sinful souls;
Each bosom like a furnace glow,
Nor God the rage, or fire control.

DOCTRINES

Sin and Misery Connected 149

Sheerness L. M.   T. Clark

Ah, wretch-ed souls are they, who hear With scorn, the sound of gos-pel grace; For sor-row walks a-long with sin, Al-and peace, Nor

How blind-ly sin-ners grasp their chains, And yet of free-dom vain-ly boast; They look for hap-pi-ness

Ap-proach-ing vice is deck'd in charms, And smiles with pro-mis-es of gain; No soon-er past— Its joys are fled, And

Sin-ners may for a time re-joice— Till storms of threat-en'd wrath a-rise— Till jus-tice grasp th'a veng-ing sword; And

Text: J. Steward

DOCTRINES

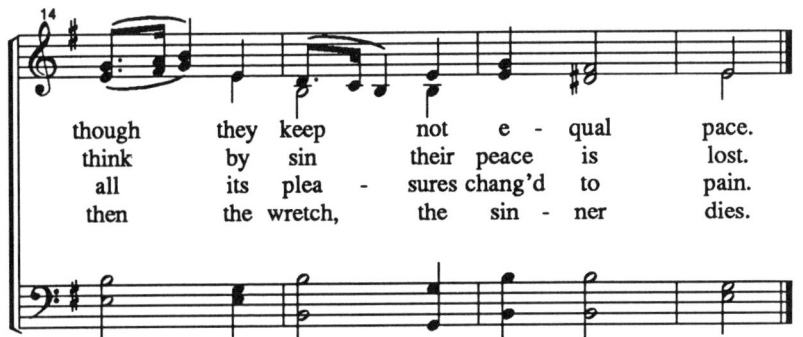

DOCTRINES

Christ, the Believer's Ark 162

Blendon L. M.　　　　　*1 Peter iii. 20.*　　　　　Giardini

The de-luge, at th'Al-might-y's call, In what im-
How dire the wreck! how loud the roar! How shrill the
Yet No-ah, hum-ble, hap-py saint, Sur-round-ed
So may I sing, in Je-sus safe, While storms of

pe-tuous streams it fell! Swal-low'd the moun-
un-i-ver-sal cry— Of mil-lions in
with the cho-sen few, Sat in his ark,
venge-ance round me fall; Con-scious how high

tains in its rage, And swept a guilt-y world to hell.
the last de-spair— Re-ech-o'd from the low'r-ing sky!—
se-cure from fear, And sang the grace that steer'd him thro'.
my hopes are fix'd, Be-yond what shakes this earth-ly ball.

5. Enter thine ark, while patience waits,
Nor ever quit that sure retreat;
Then the wide flood, that buries earth,
Shall waft thee to a fairer seat.

Text: Doddridge

DOCTRINES

Redeemer

164

Stade C. M. — Burney

Plung'd in a gulf of dark des - pair, We
With pi-ty-ing eyes the prince of grace Be-
Down from the shin - ing seats a - bove, With
He spoil'd the pow'rs of dark - ness thus, And

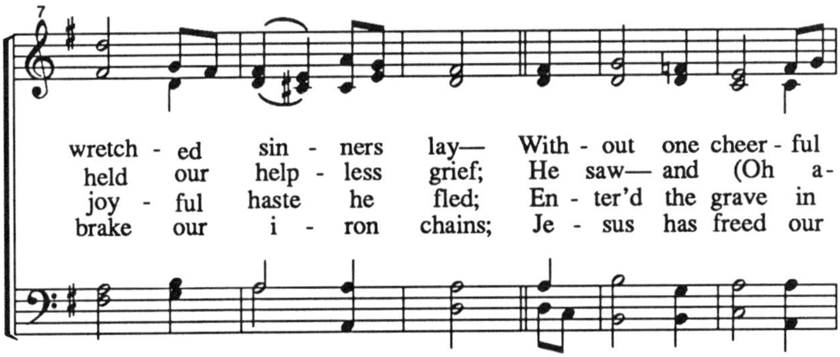

wretch - ed sin - ners lay— With - out one cheer - ful
held our help - less grief; He saw— and (Oh a-
joy - ful haste he fled; En - ter'd the grave in
brake our i - ron chains; Je - sus has freed our

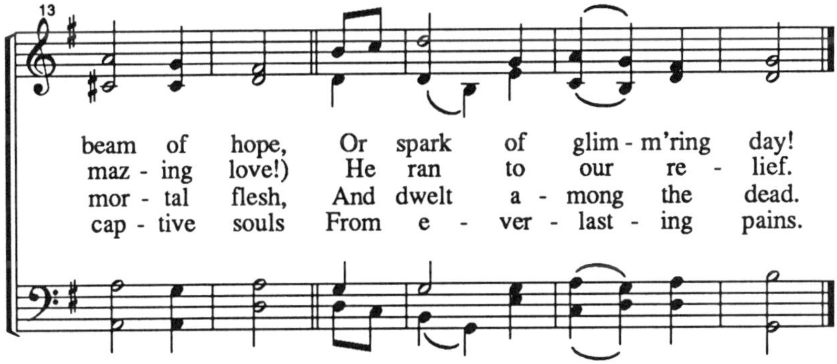

beam of hope, Or spark of glim - m'ring day!
maz - ing love!) He ran to our re - lief.
mor - tal flesh, And dwelt a - mong the dead.
cap - tive souls From e - ver - last - ing pains.

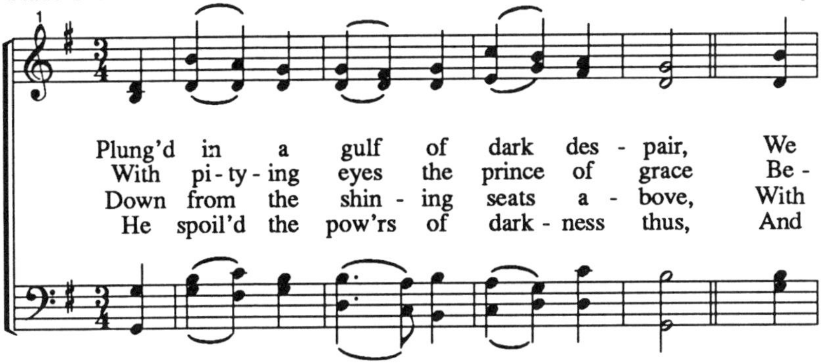

5. Oh, for this love, let rocks and hills
   Their lasting silence break;
   And all harmonious, human tongues
   The Saviour's praises speak.

Text: Isaac Watts

DOCTRINES

Praise to the Redeemer

165

St. Thomas S. M.   A. Williams

1. Pre-pare a thank-ful song To the Redeemer's name; Let his high praise em-ploy our tongue, And ev-'ry heart in-flame.

2. He laid his glor-y by, And bit-ter pains en-dur'd; That reb-els such as you and I, From wrath might be se-cur'd.

3. The Hol-y Ghost he sends, Our stub-born souls to move: To make his en-e-mies his friends, And con-quer them by love.

4. As-sur'd that Christ our King, Will put our foes to flight; We on the field of bat-tle sing, And tri-umph while we fight.

Text: John Newton

DOCTRINES

Regeneration the Work of God 168

Windsor C. M. G. Kirby

Can aught be-neath a pow'r di-vine The stub-born will sub-due? 'Tis thine, e-ter-nal Spir-it, thine To form the heart a-new.

'Tis thine the pas-sions to re-call, And up-ward bid them rise; And make the scales of er-ror fall From rea-son's dark-en'd eyes.

To chase the shades of death a-way, And bid the sin-ner live, A beam of heav'n, a vi-tal ray— 'Tis thine a-lone to give.

Oh, change these wretch-ed hearts of ours And give them life di-vine; Then shall our pas-sions and our pow'rs, Al-might-y Lord, be thine.

Text: Anonymous

DOCTRINES

Efficacious Grace

169

Mear C. M.   *Psalm xiv. 3, 5.*   Aaron Williams

5. Oh, may my humble soul be found
Among that favor'd band!
And I, with them, thy praise will sound
As round the throne we stand.

Text: Wallin

HOLY SPIRIT

Sanctification and Pardon 170

Windsor C. M. G. Kirby

Where shall we sin-ners hide our heads! Can
Is there no shel-ter from the eye Of
Those guard-ian drops our souls se-cure, And
We bless that wond-'rous pur-ple stream, That

rocks or moun-tains save? Or shall we wrap us
an a-veng-ing God? Je-sus, to thy dear
wash a-way our sins: E-ter-nal jus-tice
cleans-es ev-'ry stain: Our souls are yet but

in the shades Of mid-night and the grave?
wounds we fly, Be-dew us with thy blood.
frowns no more, And con-science smiles with-in.
half re-deem'd, If sin, the ty-rant, reign.

5. Lord, blast his empire with thy breath,
That cursed throne must fall;
Ye flatt'ring plagues, that work our death,
Fly, for we hate you all.

Text: Isaac Watts

HOLY SPIRIT

Come, Holy Spirit, Come 179

Watchman S. M.   *John xiv. 26.*   Leach

1. Come, Holy Spirit, come, Let thy bright beams arise; Dispel the sorrow from our minds, The darkness from our eyes.
2. Convince us of our sin; Then lead to Jesus' blood; And to our wond'ring view reveal The secret love of God.
3. 'Tis thine to cleanse the heart— To sanctify the soul— To pour fresh life in ev'ry part, And new create the whole.
4. Revive our drooping faith; Our doubts and fears remove; And kindle in our breasts the flame Of never-dying love.

Text: Hart

GRACES OF THE SPIRIT

Bearing the Cross   183

Bray C. M. *Mark vii. 38.* N. Herman

Didst thou, dear Je - sus, suf - fer shame, And bear the cross for me? And shall I fear to own thy name, Or thy dis - ci - ple be?
For - bid it, Lord, that I should dread To suf - fer shame or loss; Oh, let me in thy foot - steps tread, And glor - y in thy cross.
In - spire my soul with life di - vine, And ho - ly cour - age bold; Let know-ledge, faith, and meek - ness shine, Nor love, nor zeal grow cold.
Say to my soul, "Why dost thou fear The face of fee - ble clay? Be - hold thy Sav - iour ev - er near, Will guard thee in the way.

Text: Kirkham

GRACES OF THE SPIRIT

5. Oh, how my soul would rise aud run,
At this reviving word:
Nor any painful suff'rings shun,
To follow thee, my Lord.

6. Let sinful men reproach, defame,
And call thee what they will,
If I may glorify thy name,
And be thy servant still.

GRACES OF THE SPIRIT

Comforts—True and False 185

Canterbury C. M.   E. Blancks

1. O God, whose fa-vor-a-ble eye The sin-sick soul re-vives; Ho-ly and heav'n-ly is the joy, Thy shin-ing pre-sence gives.
2. This hy-po-crites have ne'er be-liev'd, They judge with grace-less hearts; Swell'd with their pride, they are de-ceiv'd By Sa-tan's wi-ly arts.
3. Un-ho-ly, self-ish joys are theirs; And while they boast their light, And seem to soar a-bove the stars, They're plung-ing in-to night.
4. Lull'd in a soft and for-mal sleep, They sin, and yet re-joice; Were they in-deed the Sav-iour's sheep, They sure would hear his voice.

5. Be mine the comforts that reclaim
The soul from Satan's pow'r;
That make me blush for what I am,
And hate my sin the more.

6. 'Tis joy enough, my All in All,
At thy dear feet to lie
Thou wilt not let me lower fall,
And none can higher fly.

Text: William Cowper

GRACES OF THE SPIRIT

Contrite Heart

188

Plymouth C. M. *Isaiah lvii. 15.* W. Tunsar

1. The Lord will happiness divine On contrite hearts bestow; Then tell me, gracious God, is mine A contrite heart or no?
2. I hear, but seem to hear in vain, Insensible as steel; If aught is felt, 'tis only pain, To find I cannot feel.
3. I sometimes think myself inclin'd To love thee, if I could; But often feel another mind, Averse to all that's good.
4. My best desires are faint and few, I fain would strive for more; But, when I cry, "My strength renew," Seem weaker than before.

5. Thy saints are comforted, I know,
And love thy house of pray'r;
I therefore go where others go,
But find no comfort there.

6. Oh, make this heart rejoice or ache—
Decide this doubt for me;
And if it be not broken, break,
And heal it, if it be.

Text: William Cowper

GRACES OF THE SPIRIT

A Living and a Dead Faith

191

Bath L. M.

James Lyon

The Lord re-ceives his high-est praise, From hum-ble minds and hearts sin-cere While all the loud pro-fes-sor says, Of-fends the right-eous Judge's ear.

To walk as chil-dren of the day, To mark his pre-cepts' ho-ly light, To wage the war-fare, watch and pray, Show who are pleas-ing in his sight.

Not words a-lone it cost the Lord, To pur-chase par-don for his own; Nor will a soul by grace re-stor'd, Rest in mere forms and words a-lone.

Ea-sy in-deed it were to reach A man-sion in the courts a-bove, If wa-t'ry floods and flu-ent speech Might serve in-stead of faith and love.

But none shall gain that bliss-ful place, Or God's un-cloud-ed glor-y see; Who talk of rich and sov-'reign grace; Un-less from sin they are made free.

Text: William Cowper

GRACES OF THE SPIRIT

Holy Fortitude

193

Braintree C. M.

Am I a sol-dier of the cross; A fol-l'wer of the Lamb; And shall I fear to own his cause, Or blush to speak his name?

Shall I be car-ry'd to the skies, On flow-'ry beds of ease, While oth-ers fought to win the prize, And sail'd thro' blood-y seas?

Are there no foes for me to face, Must I not stem the flood Is this vain world a friend to grace, To help me on to God?

Sure I must fight, if I would reign In-crease my cour-age, Lord, To bear the cross, en-dure the shame, Sup-port-ed by thy word.

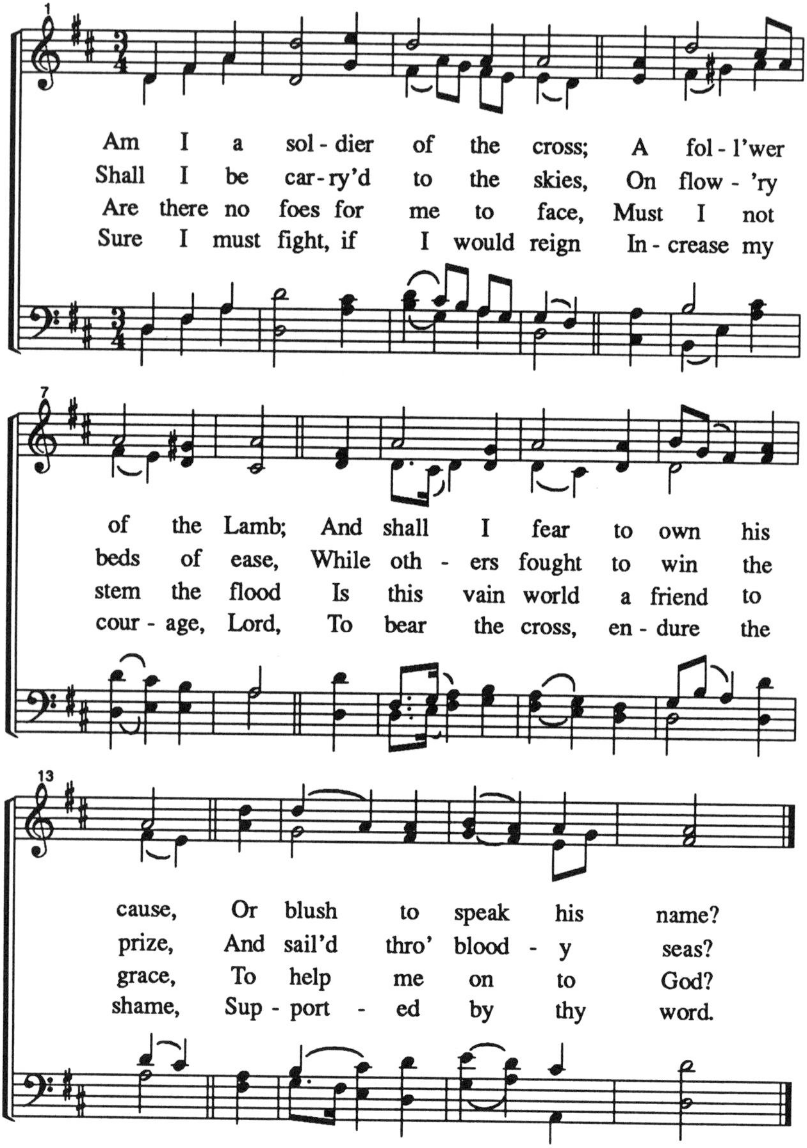

5. The saints, in all this glorious war,
Shall conquer, though they die;
They see the triumph from afar,
With faith's discerning eye.

Text: Isaac Watts

GRACES OF THE SPIRIT

Happy Poverty

196

Blendon L. M.   *Matthew v. 3.*   Giardini

1. Ye hum-ble souls, com-plain no more; Let faith sur-vey your fu-ture store; How hap-py, how di-vine-ly blest, The sa-cred words of truth at-test.
2. When con-scious grief la-ments sin-cere, And pours the pen-i-ten-tial tear: Hope points to your de-ject-ed eyes, The bright re-ver-sion in the skies.
3. In vain the sons of wealth and pride De-spise your lot, your hopes de-ride In vain they boast their lit-tle stores; Tri-fles are theirs, a king-dom yours:
4. A king-dom of im-mense de-light, Where health and peace and joy u-nite; Where un-de-clin-ing plea-sures rise, And ev-'ry want hath full sup-plies.

Text: Steele

GRACES OF THE SPIRIT

Longing for Freedom from Sin

198

Surry L. M.
Costellow

Text: Harrison

GRACES OF THE SPIRIT

The Christian's Hope

199

Truro L. M.   George F. Handel

Text: Isaac Watts

5. Come then, O blessed Jesus, come,
To me thy Spirit give;
Shine through a dark, benighted soul,
And bid a sinner live.

Text: J. Steward

5. That stream doth water paradise;
It makes the angels sing;
One cordial drop revives my heart;
Hence all my joys do spring.

Text: Anonymous

GRACES OF THE SPIRIT

Heavenly Joy on Earth

205

St. Thomas S. M.　　　　　　　　　　　　　　　　　　　A. Williams

1. Come, we who love the Lord, And let our joys be known; Join in a song with sweet ac-cord, And thus sur-round the throne.
2. Let those re-fuse to sing, Who nev-er knew our God; But fav-'rites of the heav'n-ly King Should speak their joys a-broad.
3. The men of grace have found Glory be-gun be-low: Ce-les-tial fruits on earth-ly ground, From faith and hope may grow.
4. The hill of Zi-on yields A thou-sand sa-cred sweets, Be-fore we reach the heav'n-ly fields, Or walk the gold-en streets.

5. Then let our songs abound,
And every tear be dry;
We're marching thro' Immanuel's ground
To fairer worlds on high.

Text: Isaac Watts

GRACES OF THE SPIRIT

Love to God

207

York C. M.   *I Corinthians xiii. 8; Psalm cxxxvii. 5,6.*   John Milton

Hap-py the heart where grac-es reign, Where love in-spires the breast; Love is the bright-est of the train, And streng-thens all the rest.
This is the grace that lives and sings, When faith and hope shall cease; 'Tis this shall strike our joy-ful strings In the sweet realms of bliss.
Be-fore we quite for-sake our clay, Or leave this dark a-bode, The wings of love bear us a-way To see our smil-ing God.

Text: Isaac Watts

GRACES OF THE SPIRIT

Lovest Thou Me?

212

Pleyel's Hymn. 7.   Ignace Pleyel

'Tis a point I long to know, Oft it causes anxious thought Do I love the Lord, or no? Am I his, or am I not?
If I love, why am I thus? Why this dull, this lifeless frame? Hardly, sure, can they be worse, Who have never heard his name.
Could my heart so hard remain, Pray'r a task and burden prove— Ev'ry trifle give me pain— If I knew a Saviour's love?
When I turn mine eyes within, All is dark, and vain, and wild; Fill'd with unbelief and sin— Can I deem myself a child?

Text: John Newton

GRACES OF THE SPIRIT

5. If I pray, or hear, or read,
Sin is mix'd with all I do;
You who love the Lord indeed,
Tell me—is it thus with you?

6. Yet I mourn my stubborn will,
Find my sin a grief and thrall;
Should I grieve for what I feel,
If I did not love at all!

7. Lord decide the doubtful case!
Thou who art thy people's Sun:
Shine upon thy work of grace,
If it be indeed begun.

8. Let me love thee more and more,
If I love at all, I pray;
If I have not lov'd before,
Help me to begin to-day.

GRACES OF THE SPIRIT

Rejoicing

218

Dover S. M.   *Psalm cxxxviii. 5.*   Aaron Williams

1. Now let our voi-ces join To form a sa-cred song; Ye pil-grims, in Je-ho-vah's ways, With mu-sic pass a-long.
2. How straight the path ap-pears How o-pen and how fair! No lurk-ing gins t'en-trap our feet, No fierce de-stroy-er there.
3. But flow'rs of pa-ra-dise In rich pro-fu-sion spring; The Sun of glor-y gilds the path, And dear com-pan-ions sing.
4. All hon-or to his name, Who marks the shin-ing way,— To him who leads the wan-d'rers on To realms of end-less day.

Text: Philip Doddridge

GRACES OF THE SPIRIT

Effectual Means

220

Walsall C. M.   Anchors' Collection

1. Our hearts are fas-ten'd to this world By strong and num-'rous ties, And ev-'ry sor-row breaks a string, And urg-es us to rise.
2. When heav'n would kind-ly set us free, And earth's en-chant-ment end, It takes the most ef-fec-tual means, And robs us of a friend.
3. Re-sign— and all the load of life That mo-ment you re-move Its heav-y tax, ten thou-sand cares De-volve on ONE a-bove.

Text: Young

GRACES OF THE SPIRIT

Self-Denial

221

Bray C. M. *Mark viii. 34.* N. Herman

And must I part with all I have, My dear-est Lord, for thee? It is but right, since thou hast done Much more than this for me. Much
Yes, let it go— one look from thee Will more than make a-mends, For all the loss-es I sus-tain Of cred-it, rich-es, friends. Of
Ten thou-sand worlds, ten thou-sand lives, How worth-less they ap-pear, Com-par'd with thee, su-preme-ly good, Di-vine-ly bright and fair! Di-
Sav-iour of souls, could I from thee A sin-gle smile ob-tain, Tho' des-ti-tute of all things else, I'd glor-y in my gain. I'd

Text: Rippon

GRACES OF THE SPIRIT

more than this for me.
cred - it, rich - es, friends.
vine - ly bright and fair!
glor - y in my gain.

5. Ye dang'rous inmates, hence depart;
Dear Saviour, enter in,
And guard the passage to my heart,
And keep out every sin.

THE SPIRIT

Submission

223

St. Anne's C. M.
William Croft

1. O Lord, my best desires fulfil, And help me to resign to thy will, And make thy pleasure mine.
2. Why should I shrink at thy command, Whose love forbids my fears? Or tremble at the gracious hand That wipes away my tears?
3. No— let me rather freely yield What most I prize to thee; Who never has a good withheld, Or wilt withhold from me.
4. Thy favor, all my journey thro' Thou art engag'd to grant; What else I want, or think I do, 'Tis better still to want.

5. Wisdom and mercy guide my way,
Shall I resist them both?
A poor, blind creature of a day,
And crush'd before the moth!

6. But ah! my inward spirit cries,
Still bind me to thy sway;
Else the next cloud that veils my skies,
Will drive these thoughts away.

Text: William Cowper

GRACES OF THE SPIRIT

God Ruleth All Things Well

227

St. Thomas S. M.   A. Williams

Text: Anonymous

GRACES OF THE SPIRIT

Zeal—True and False

230

Mear C. M.
Aaron Williams

1. Zeal is that pure and heav'n-ly flame, The fire of love sup-plies; While that which of-ten bears the name, Is self in a dis-guise.
2. True zeal is mer-ci-ful and mild, Can pit-y and for-bear; The false is head-strong, fierce and wild, And breathes re-venge and war.
3. While zeal for truth the Chris-tian warms, He knows the worth of peace; But self con-tends for names and forms, Its par-ty to in-crease.
4. Zeal has at-tain'd its high-est aim, Its end is sat-is-fy'd, If sin-ners love the Sav-iour's name, Nor seeks it aught be-side.

5. But self, however well employ'd,
Has its own ends in view;
And says, as boasting Jehu cry'd,
"Come, see what I can do."

5. But self, however well employ'd,
Has its own ends in view;
And says, as boasting Jehu cry'd,
"Come, see what I can do."

Text: John Newton

CHRISTIAN

Indwelling Sin Lamented 234

Plymouth C. M.   W. Tunsar

1. With tears of anguish I lament, Here at thy feet, my God, My passion, pride, and discontent, And vile ingratitude.
2. Sure there was ne'er a heart so base, So false as mine has been; So faithless to its promises, So prone to ev'ry sin.
3. How long, dear Saviour, shall I feel These struggles in my breast? When wilt thou bow my stubborn will, And give my conscience rest?
4. Break, sov'reign grace, O break the charm, And set the captive free: Reveal, Almighty God, thine arm, And haste to rescue me.

Text: Stennent

CHRISTIAN

The Penitent Cleansed

235

Putney L.M.   I. Smith

Lord, I'm defil'd in ev-ery part,
Barren my life, and cold my heart,
Yet some-times thro' thy sov'-reign grace,
I catch a glimpse at Jesus' face.

This gives my drow-sy heart a spring,
I fain would rise, and fain would sing;
But soon a cloud rolls in be-tween,
All black with some in-dwell-ing sin.

My notes then fal-ter on my tongue,
The foul con-ta-gion spoils my song;
But Thou, who dost the world con-trol,
Speak but the word—I shall be whole.

Text: Anonymous

CHRISTIAN

Self-Examination

236

Colchester C. M.   *2 Corinthians xiii. 5.*   Henry Purcell

'Tis first of all thy-self to know, To feel the plague of sin, Expos'd to ever-lasting wo, And nothing good within;

To know thy wretched sinful state, Averse to all that's good; To feel thy guilt exceeding great, Thy heart oppos'd to God:

To know thy law-condemned case, And own thy sentence just; Thy heart subdu'd by sov'reign grace, And humbled in the dust;

To know the pangs of pious grief, For sins against the Lord; To know that nought can give relief, But trusting in his word;

To know that thou art born of God, Thy num'rous sins forgiv'n, Thy soul redeem'd by Jesus' blood, And thou an heir of heav'n.

Text: Anonymous

CHRISTIAN

O That I Were as in Months Past 243

Canterbury C. M.   E. Blancks

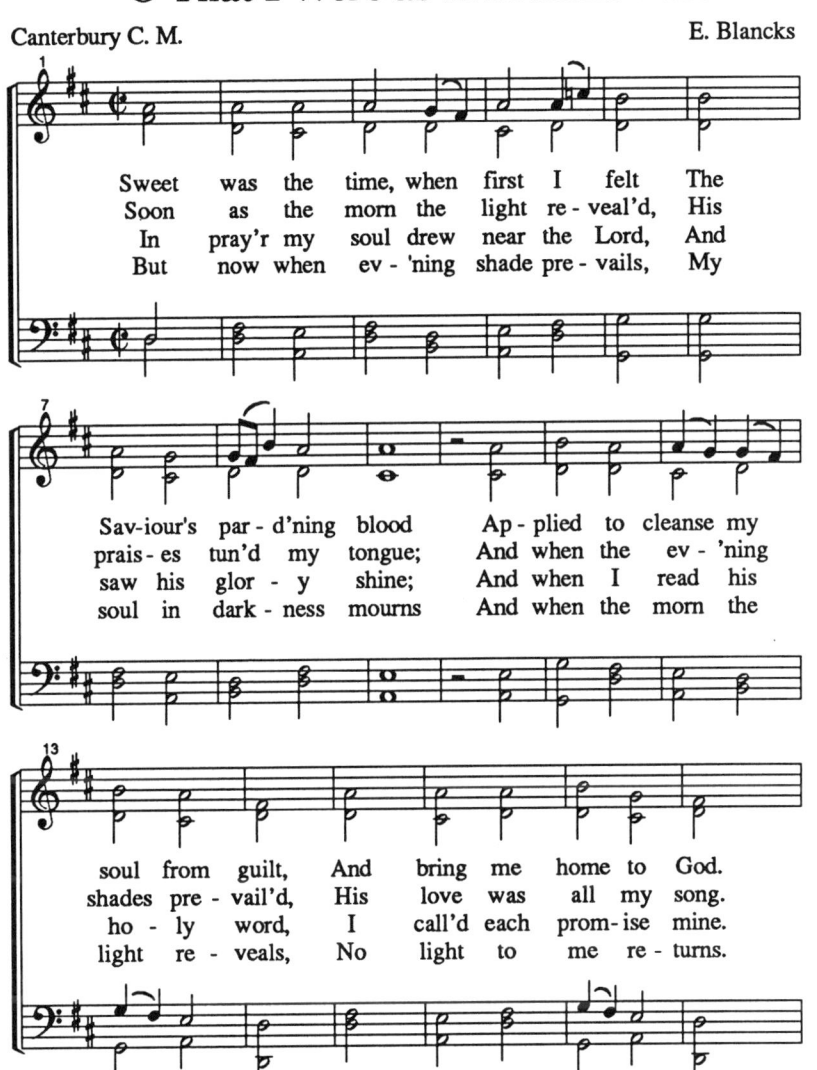

5. My pray'rs are now an empty noise,
For Jesus hides his face
I read— the promise meets my eyes,
But will not reach my case.

6. Rise, Lord, now help me to prevail,
And make my soul thy care;
I know thy mercy cannot fail—
Let me that mercy share.

Text: John Newton

CHRISTIAN

Prayer Answered By Crosses 244

Luton L. M.　　　　　　　　　　　　　　　　　　　　　　　　　　G. Burder

I ask'd the Lord, that I might grow
In faith, and love, and ev-'ry grace;
Might more of his sal-va-tion know,

'Twas he who taught me thus to pray,
And he, I trust, has an-swer'd pray'r;
But it has been in such a way,

I hop'd that in some fav-or'd hour,
At once he'd an-swer my re-quest;
And by his love's re-strain-ing pow'r,

In-stead of this, he made me feel
The hid-den e-vils of my heart,
And let the an-gry pow'rs of hell

Text: John Newton

CHRISTIAN

And seek more earn - est - ly his face.
As al - most drove me to des - pair.
Sub - due my sins, and give me rest.
As - sault my soul in ev - 'ry part.

5. Yea more, with his own hand he seem'd
Intent to aggravate my wo;
Cross'd all the fair designs I schem'd,
Blasted my hopes, and laid me low.

6. "Lord, why is this," I trembling cried,
"Wilt thou pursue thy worm to death?"
"'Tis in this way," the Lord replied,
"I answer pray'r for grace and faith:

7. "These inward trials I employ,
From self, and pride, to set thee free;
And break thy schemes of earthly joy,
That thou may'st seek thy all in me."

The Vanity of the World

250

Wareham C. M.

Arnold

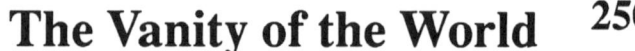

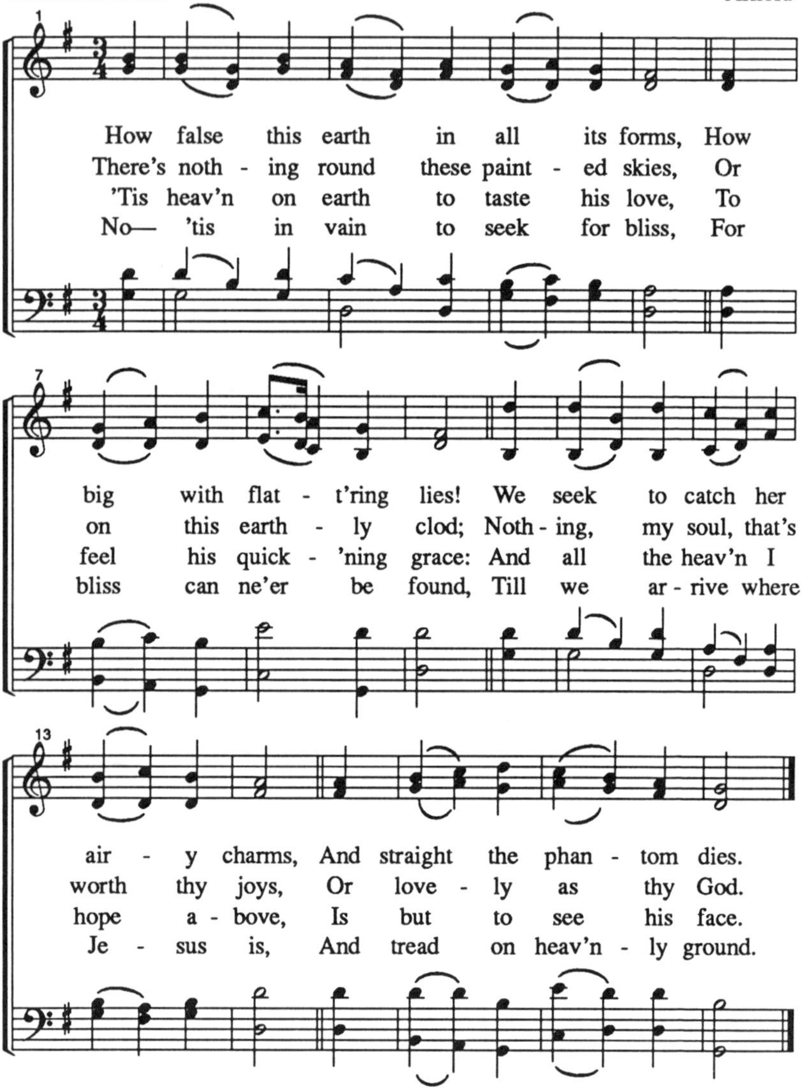

Text: Isaac Watts

CHRISTIAN

"Who Will Show Us Any Good?" 252

Braintree C. M.   *Psalm iv. 6.*

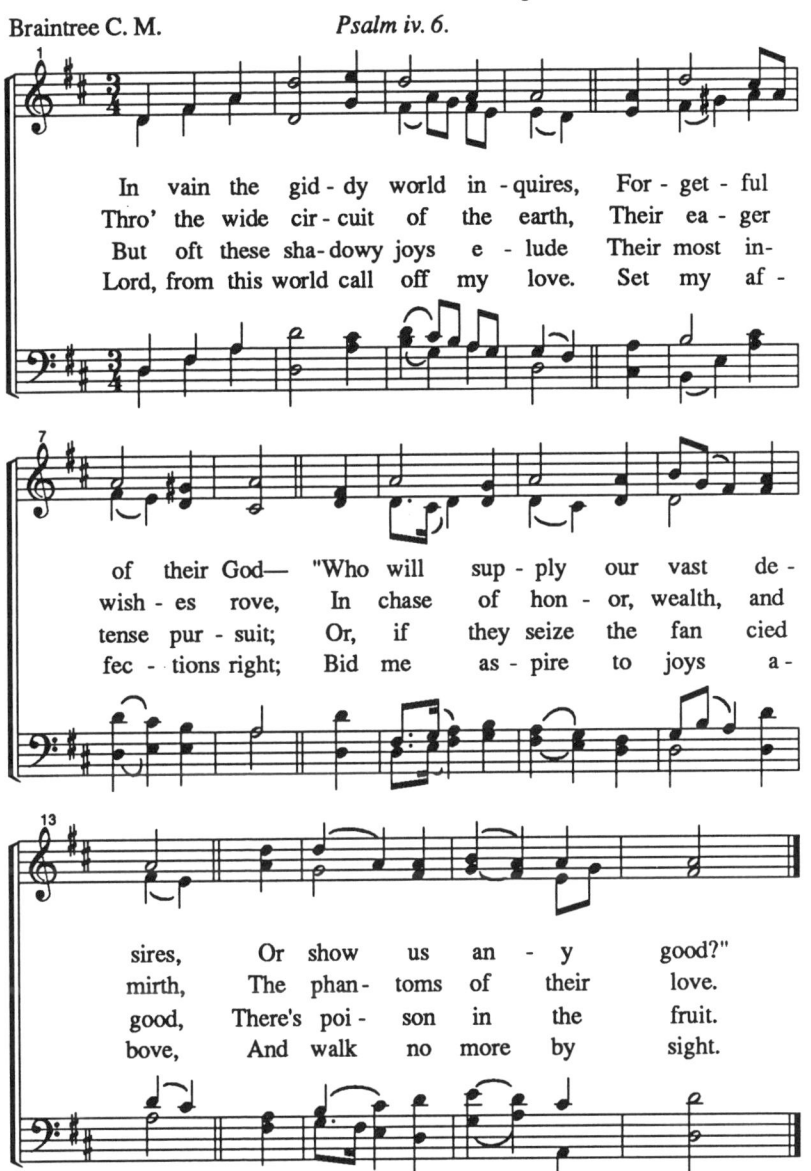

In vain the gid-dy world in-quires, For-get-ful of their God— "Who will sup-ply our vast de-sires, Or show us an-y good?"

Thro' the wide cir-cuit of the earth, Their ea-ger wish-es rove, In chase of hon-or, wealth, and mirth, The phan-toms of their love.

But oft these sha-dowy joys e-lude Their most in-tense pur-suit; Or, if they seize the fan-cied good, There's poi-son in the fruit.

Lord, from this world call off my love. Set my af-fec-tions right; Bid me as-pire to joys a-bove, And walk no more by sight.

Text: Samuel Stennett

CHRISTIAN

Parting with Carnal Joys 253

Evening Hymn L. M.   Thomas Talis

1. I send the joys of earth away; A-way, ye tempters of the mind, False as the smooth deceitful sea, Empty as the whistling wind.
2. Your streams were floating me along, Down to the gulf of black despair; And whilst I listen'd to your song, Your streams had e'en convey'd me there.
3. Lord, I adore thy matchless grace, That warn'd me of that dark abyss; That drew me from those treach'rous seas, And bade me seek superior bliss.
4. Now to the shining realms above, I stretch my hands, and glance my eyes; Oh, for the pinions of a dove, To bear me to the upper skies.

Text: Isaac Watts

CHRISTIAN

Christ Precious

264

Rochester C. M. *I Peter ii. 7.* A. Williams

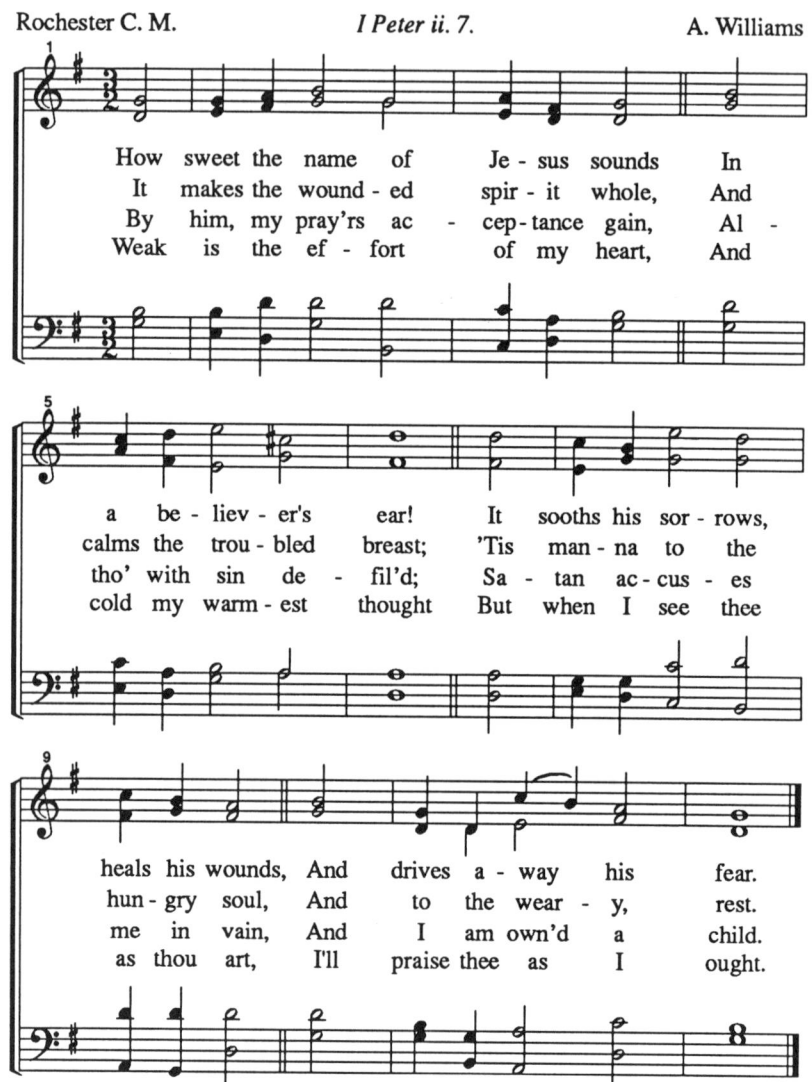

How sweet the name of Jesus sounds In a believer's ear! It sooths his sorrows, heals his wounds, And drives away his fear.

It makes the wounded spirit whole, And calms the troubled breast; 'Tis manna to the hungry soul, And to the weary, rest.

By him, my pray'rs acceptance gain, Although with sin defil'd; Satan accuses me in vain, And I am own'd a child.

Weak is the effort of my heart, And cold my warmest thought But when I see thee as thou art, I'll praise thee as I ought.

5. Till then, I would thy love proclaim,
With ev'ry fleeting breath;
And may the music of thy name
Refresh my soul in death.

Text: John Newton

5. Oh! weak to know a Saviour's pow'r,
To feel a father's care:
A moment's toil, a passing show'r,
Is all the grief ye share.

Text: Logan

CHRISTIAN

The Lord of Light Unveiled 268

Abridge C. M.   I. Smith

The Lord of light, though veil'd a-while He hides his noon tide ray, Shall soon in love l'er beauty smile To gild the closing day:
And, bursting thro' the dusky shroud That dar'd his pow'r invest, Ride thron'd in light o'er ev'ry cloud, Triumphant to his rest:
And there, beneath his beam renew'd, That glorious vale shall shine, So long by trembling hope pursu'd, And now for ever thine.
Then, Christian, dry the falling tear; The faithless doubt remove; Redeem'd at last from guilt and fear, Oh! wake thy heart to love.

Text: Anonymous

5. He wants no pomp nor royal throne,
To raise his figure here,
Content and pleas'd to live alone,
Till Christ his life appear.

Text: Isaac Watts

CHRISTIAN

The Fear of God

275

Clifford C. M.   *Proverbs xxiii. 17.*

Thrice hap-py souls, who, born of heav'n, While yet they so-journ here, Hum-bly be-gin their days with God, And spend them in his fear.

So may our eyes with ho-ly zeal Pre-vent the dawn-ing day; And turn the sa-cred pag-es o'er, And praise thy name and pray.

Midst hour-ly cares may love pre-sent Its in-cense to thy throne; And, while the world our hands em-ploys, Our hearts be thine a-lone.

At night we lean our wear-y heads On thy pa-ter-nal breast; And, safe-ly fold-ed in thine arms, Re-sign our pow'rs to rest.

5. In solid, pure delights, like these,
Let all my days be past;
Nor shall I then impatient wish,
Nor shall I fear the last.

Text: Doddridge

CHRISTIAN

Rising to God

278

Shoel L. M.   *John i. 12. 1 John iii. 1.*   Shoel

Now let our souls, on wings sub-lime, Rise from the
Born by a new ce-les-tial birth, Why should we
Shall aught be-guile us on the road, When we are
Wel-come, sweet hour of full dis-charge, That sets our

van-i-ties of time Draw back the part-ing
grov-el here on earth? Why grasp at tran-si-
walk-ing back to God? For, strang-ers, in-to
long-ing souls at large; Un-binds our chains, breaks

veil, and see The glor-ies of e-ter-ni-ty.
tor-y toys, So near to heav'n's e-ter-nal joys?
life we come, And dy-ing is but go-ing home.
up our cell, And gives us with our God to dwell.

5. To dwell with God, to feel his love.
Is the full heav'n enjoy'd above;
And the sweet expectation now
Is the young dawn of heav'n below.

Text: Gibbons

WORSHIP

Evening Twilight

285

Plymouth C. M.
W. Tunsar

1. I love to steal a-while a-way From ev-'ry cum-b'ring care, And spend the hours of set-ting day, In hum-ble, grate-ful prayer.
2. I love in sol-i-tude to shed The pen-i-ten-tial tear, And all His prom-is-es to plead, Where none but God can hear.
3. I love to think on mer-cies past, And fu-ture good im-plore, And all my care and sor-rows cast On him whom I a-dore.
4. I love by faith to take a view Of bright-er scenes in heav'n; The pro-spect doth my strength re-new While here by tem-pests driv'n.

5. Thus, when life's toilsome day is o'er,
May its departing ray
Be calm as this impressive hour,
And lead to endless day.

Text: B

Social Prayer

286

Bath L. M.

James Lyon

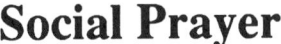

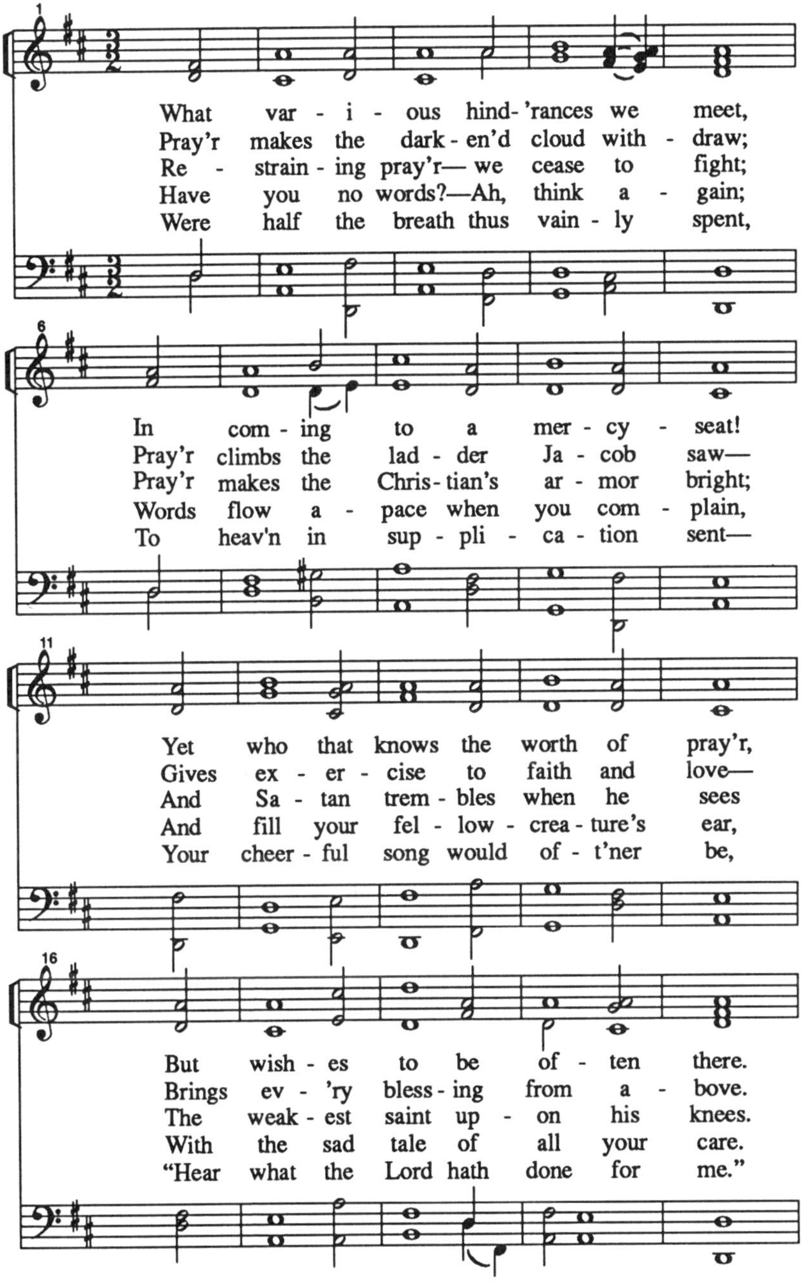

Text: William Cowper

WORSHIP

Pray Without Ceasing 289

Blendon L. M.   *I Thessalonians v. 17.*   Giardini

Pray'r was ap - point - ed to con - vey The
If pain af - flict, or wrongs op - press— If
'Tis pray'r sup - ports the soul that's weak; Tho'

bless - ings God de - signs to give; Long as they live
cares dis - tract or fears dis - may— If guilt de - ject—
tho't be bro - ken - lan - guage lame; Pray, if thou canst,

should Christians pray, For on - ly while they pray they live.
if sin dis - tress, The re - me - dy's be - fore thee—pray.
or canst not speak, But pray with faith in Je - sus' name.

Text: Hart

WORSHIP

The Formalist

291

Little Marlboro' S. M. Job xxvii. 8. Williams

Re - li - gion's form is vain, While we de -
Now he may cre - dit gain, And in his
Then, O what dread sur - prise, What hor - ror
Lord, search and know my heart, And make my

ny its pow'r! What will the hy - po - crite ob -
af - flu'nce roll; But all his pro - fit will be
and dis - may, When death shall o - pen wide his
soul sin - cere; And bid hy - po - cri - sy de -

tain, In death's tre - men - dous hour?
pain, When God shall take his soul.
eyes, And tear his mask a - way!
part, And keep my con - science clear.

Text: Hoskins

WORSHIP

Declension Lamented

298

Northhampton Chapel 8, 7. Aaron Williams

Once, O Lord, thy gar-den flour-ish'd, Ev-'ry part look'd gay and green; Then thy word our spir-its nour-ish'd, Hap-py sea-sons we have greatly nour-ish'd,
But a drought has since suc-ceed-ed, And a sad de-cline we see; Lord, thy help is great-ly need-ed, Help can on-ly come from
Some, in whom we once de-light-ed, We shall meet no more be-low; Some, a-las! we fear are blight-ed, Scarce a sin-gle leaf they
Dear-est Sav-iour, has-ten hith-er, Thou canst make them bloom a-gain.; Oh, per-mit them not to with-er, Let not all our hopes be

Text: John Newton

WORSHIP

Sovereign Grace

WORSHIP
300
Colchester C. M.
Henry Purcell

1. How few the word of God regard,
Or seek their Maker's face!
In vain the gospel is proclaim'd,
If not enforc'd by grace.

2. Almighty God, exert thy pow'r,
And melt the stony breast;
Then shall thy justice be ador'd,
Thy mercy stand confess'd.

3. The scorner then shall mourn in dust,
And put his sins away;
No more resist his Maker's hands,
But lift his own to pray.

Text: Anonymous

WORSHIP

Wheat and Tares

304

Armley L. M.　　　　*Matthew xiii. 37-42.*　　　　Harmonia Sacra

1. Tho' in the earthly church below, The wheat and tares together grow; Jesus ere long will weed the crop, And pluck the tares in anger up.
2. Will it relieve their horrors there, To recollect their stations here? How much they heard how much they knew, How long among the wheat they grew!
3. Oh! this will aggravate their case! They perish under means of grace; To them the word of life and faith Became an instrument of death.
4. We seem alike when thus we meet, Strangers might think we all were wheat; But to the Lord's all-searching eyes, Each heart appears without disguise.

5. The tares are spar'd for various ends, Some for the sake of praying friends; Others, the Lord against their will, Employs his counsel to fulfil.

6. But though they grow so tall and strong, His plan will not require them long; In harvest when he saves his own, The tares shall into hell be thrown.

Text: John Newton

WORSHIP

For Christian Conference 315

St. Anne's C. M.   William Croft

1. O Lord, our languid souls inspire, For here we trust thou art; Send down a coal of heav'nly fire, To warm each waiting heart.
2. Show us some tokens of thy love, Our fainting hope to raise; And pour thy blessing from above, That we may render praise.
3. Within these walls let holy praise, And love and concord dwell: Here give the troubled conscience ease, The wounded spirit heal.
4. The feeling heart, the melting eye, The humble mind bestow; And shine upon us from on high, To make our graces grow.

5. May we in faith receive thy word,
In faith present our pray'rs;
And in the presence of our Lord,
Unbosom all our cares.

6. And may the gospel's joyful sound,
Enforc'd by mighty grace,
Awaken sinners all around
To come and fill the place.

Text: John Newton

THE SINNER AWAKENED

The Awakened Sinner 332

Armley L. M.   Harmonia Sacra

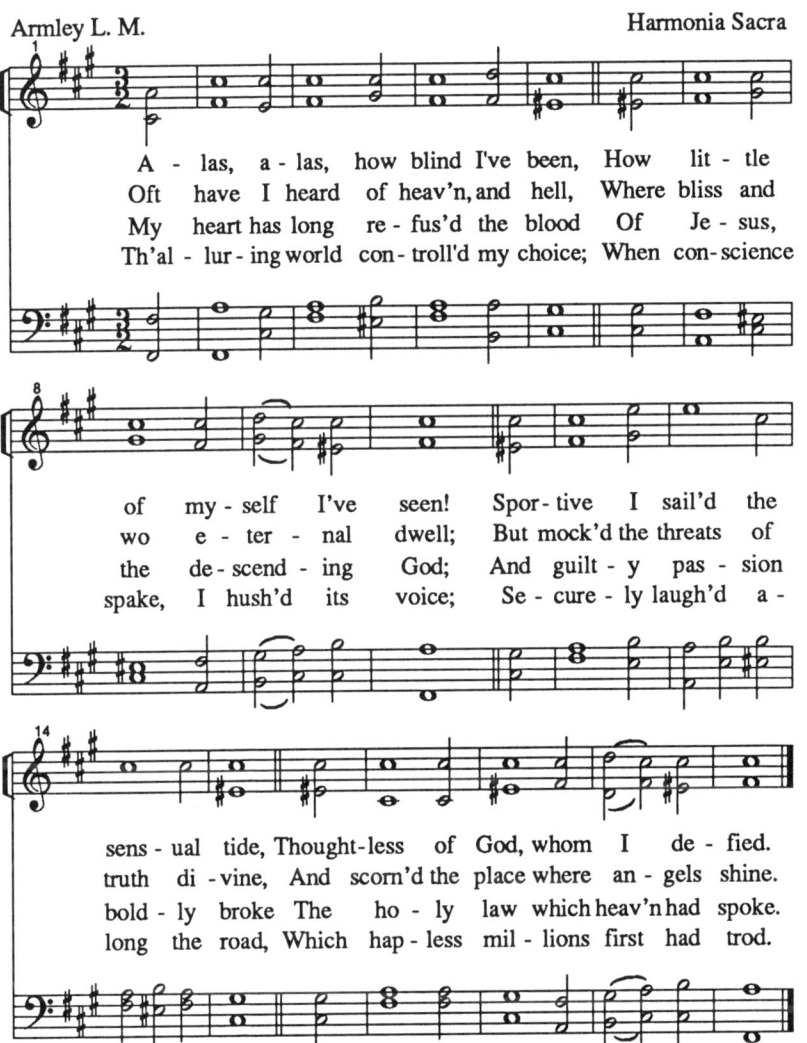

A - las, a - las, how blind I've been, How lit - tle of my - self I've seen! Spor - tive I sail'd the sens - ual tide, Thought-less of God, whom I de - fied.

Oft have I heard of heav'n, and hell, Where bliss and wo e - ter - nal dwell; But mock'd the threats of truth di - vine, And scorn'd the place where an - gels shine.

My heart has long re - fus'd the blood Of Je - sus, the de - scend - ing God; And guilt - y pas - sion bold - ly broke The ho - ly law which heav'n had spoke.

Th'al - lur - ing world con - troll'd my choice; When con - science spake, I hush'd its voice; Se - cure - ly laugh'd a - long the road, Which hap - less mil - lions first had trod.

      5. But now, th'Almighty God comes near
      And fills my soul with awful fear—
      Perhaps I sink to endless pain,
      Nor hear the voice of joy again.

Text: Strong

THE SINNER AWAKENED

My Spirit Shall Not Always Strive 333

Blendon L. M.   *Genesis vi. 3.*   Giardini

1. Say, sinner, hath a voice within,
Oft whisper'd to thy secret soul,
Urg'd thee to leave the ways of sin,
And leave thy heart to God's control?

2. Hath something met thee in the path
Of worldliness and vanity,
And pointed to the coming wrath,
And warn'd thee from that wrath to flee?

3. Sinner, it was a heav'nly voice,
It was the Spirit's gracious call,
It bade thee make the better choice,
And haste to seek in Christ thine all.

4. Spurn not the call to life and light;
Regard in time the warning kind;
That call thou may'st not always slight,
And yet the gate of mercy find.

5. God's Spirit will not always strive
With harden'd, self-destroying man;
Ye, who persist his love to grieve,
May never hear his voice again.

6. Sinner—perhaps this very day,
Thy last accepted time may be;
Oh, should'st thou grieve him now away,
Then hope may never beam on thee.

Text: Hyde

THE SINNER AWAKENED

The Sinner's Complaint 341

Standish C. M. John Tufts

5. Then conscience thunders, Sinai flames
  I try again to rise;
  The trial fails, and conscience blames
  My pray'rs, my tears, my cries.

6. 'Tis thus perplex'd, forlorn, and lost,
  I spend my weary days;
  No Jesus comes, my hopes are cross'd,
  While other's sing, and praise.

Text: Strong

THE SINNER AWAKENED

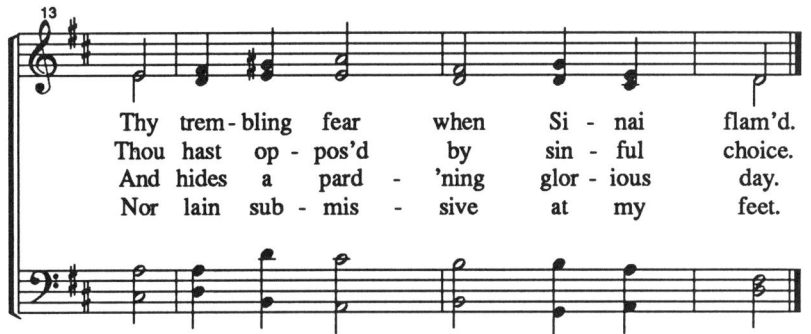

Thy trem-bling fear when Si - nai flam'd.
Thou hast op - pos'd by sin - ful choice.
And hides a pard - 'ning glor - ious day.
Nor lain sub - mis - sive at my feet.

5. Should thy proud will at length submit,
With holy sorrow deeply smit,
Thy voice would be the first to say,
I'm glorious in this long delay.

6. Stay, sinner, cease my grace to chide,
Nor think thy moan such sin can hide,
Delay no more, repent and live,
Or meet the death my wrath must give.

THE SINNER AWAKENED

Who Can Tell? 343

Eagle Street H. M.   *Jonah iii. 9*   I. Smith

Text: Anonymous

THE SINNER AWAKENED

CONVICTION

Under Conviction

344

Wirksworth S. M.　　　　　　　　　　　　　　　　　　Harmonia Sacra

My form-er hopes are fled, My ter-ror now be-gins; I feel, a-las! that I am dead In tres-pass-es and sins.

Ah, whi-ther shall I fly? I hear the thun-der roar The law pro-claims de-struc-tion nigh, And venge-ance at the door.

When I re-view my ways, I dread im-pend-ing doom; But sure, a friend-ly whis-per says, "Flee from the wrath to come."

I see, or think I see, A glimm'ring from a-far A beam of day that shines for me, To save me from des-pair.

5. Forerunner of the sun,
It marks the pilgrim's way;
I'll gaze upon it while I run,
And watch the rising day.

Text: Cowper

CONVICTION

The Heart

345

St. Thomas S. M. *Jeremiah xvii. 9; Matthew xv. 19.* A. Williams

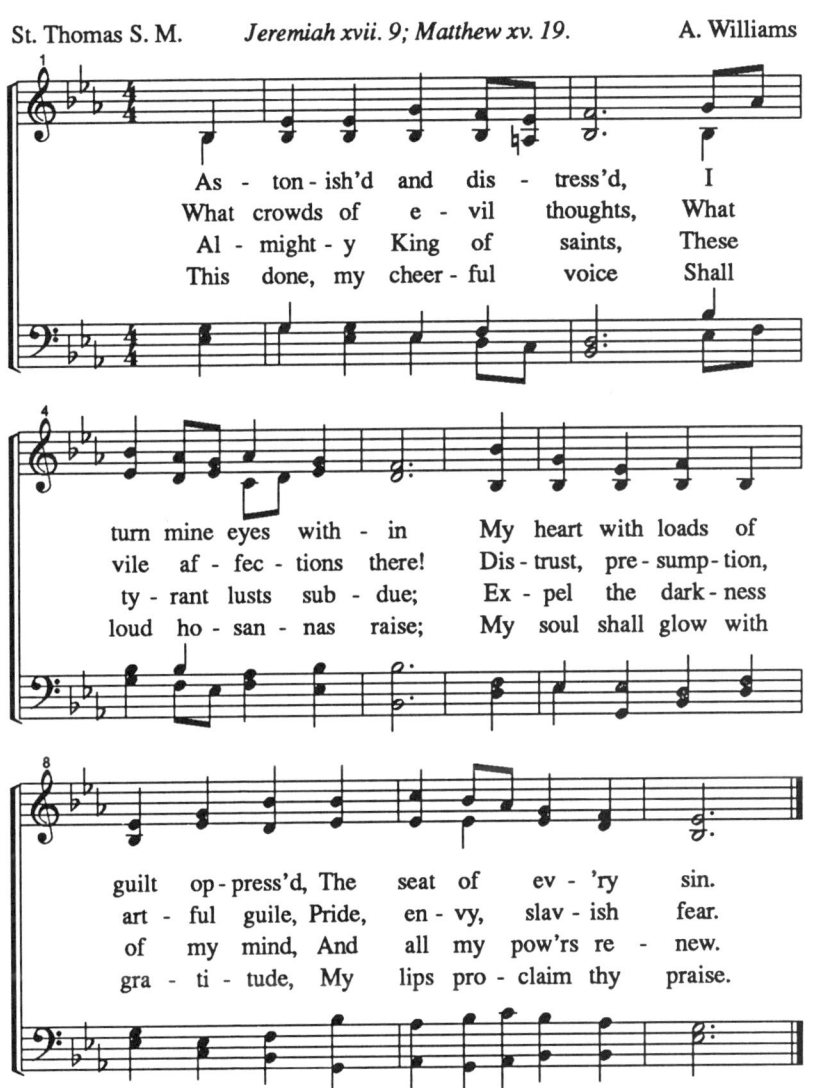

Text: Augustus Toplady

CONVICTION

The Weight of Sin 347

Little Marlboro' S.M.   Williams

1. O Lord, how vile am I, Unholy and unclean! How can I dare to venture nigh With such a load of sin!
2. Is this polluted heart A dwelling fit for thee? Swarming, alas! in ev'ry part, What evils do I see!
3. If I attempt to pray, And raise my soul on high, My thoughts are hurried fast away, For sin is ever nigh.
4. If in thy word I look, Such darkness fills my mind, I only read a sealed book, But no relief can find.

5. Thy gospel oft I hear,
But hear it still in vain:
Without desire, or love, or fear,
Harden'd I still remain.

6. And must I then indeed
Sink in despair and die?
Fain would I hope that thou didst bleed
For such a wretch as I.

Text: John Newton

CONVICTION

God Our Hiding Place

349

St. Anne's C. M.
William Croft

5. "Haste, sinner! haste," the Saviour cried,
"Behold my wounded form!
The cleft of my deep-pierced side
Shall hide thee from the storm."

Text: Haweis

CONVICTION

A Sinner Submitting to God 357

Surry L. M.   Costello w

Wea - ry of strug-gling with my pain, Hope-less to
From my own works at last I cease, God that cre-
Lord, I de-spair my-self to heal; I see my
'Tis thine a heart of flesh to give, Thy gifts I

burst this sin - ful chain, At length I give the
ates must seal my peace; Fruit - less my toil, and
sin but do not feel; Nor shall I till thy
on - ly can re - ceive; Here then to thee I

con - test o'er, And seek to free my-self no more.
vain my care, Un - less thy sov-'reign grace I share.
Spir - it blow, And bid th'o - be - dient wa - ters flow;
all re - sign, To draw, re - deem, and seal is thine.

Text: Anonymous

Conviction and Conversion 361

Luther's Hymn L. M. *Psalm cvii. 17-20.* Martin Luther

The sin-ner's flat-t'ring dreams are fled, De-struc-tion hov-ers o'er his head; And con-science throws her darts a-round, And poi-son ran-kles in each wound.

De-spair and death his heart as-sail, And all his hopes of com-fort fail; Till, deep-ly hum-bled in the dust, He owns his pun-ish-ment is just.

Then Pen-i-tence be-side him stands, With brow se-vere, but heal-ing hands; The wounds she probes, the balm ap-plies, To heav'n di-rects the mourn-er's sighs.

To heav'n his stream-ing eyes he rears, And Mer-cy's ra-diant form ap-pears; She whis-pers peace and hope with-in, His sor-rows cease, his joys be-gin.

Text: Phillip Doddridge

CONVICTION AND CONVERSION

Heart Taken

363

Barby C.M.   *Luke xi. 21, 22.*   William Tansur

1. The castle of the human heart,
Strong in its native sin,
Is guarded well in ev'ry part,
By him who dwells within.

2. For Satan there in arms resides,
And calls the place his own;
With care against assaults provides,
And rules as on a throne.

3. But Jesus, stronger far than he,
In his appointed hour,
Appears to set his people free
From the usurper's pow'r.

4. "This heart I bought with blood," he cries,
"And now it shall be mine;"
His voice the strong man arm'd dismays;
He knows he must resign.

5. In spite of unbelief and pride,
And self and Satan's art,
The gates of brass fly open wide,
And Jesus wins the heart.

Text: John Newton

CONVICTION AND CONVERSION

The Mercy of God in Salvation   364

Dover S. M. Aaron Williams

1. Beneath the poi-s'nous dart Of Satan's rage I fell— How narrowly my feet escap'd The snares of death and hell!
2. Darkness, and shame, and grief Oppress'd my gloomy mind; I look'd around me for relief, But no relief could find.
3. At length, to God I cried; He heard my plaintive sigh; He heard, and instantly he sent Salvation from on high.
4. Oh, may I ne'er forget The mercy of my God! Nor ever want a tongue to spread His loudest praise abroad.

Text: Anonymous

CONVICTION AND CONVERSION

The Prodigal

368

Colchester C. M.   *Luke xv. 11-24.*   Henry Purcell

Thankless— the Prodigal receives
The bounty of his Sire,
Rejoicing only in the hope

And far from home, in climes of vice,
He joins the heedless throng;
Begins in pleasure to rejoice,

But lo, the famine coming on,
Now dies the song profane;—
The youth beholds his substance gone,

The terrors of the world to come
Have struck his pleasures dead—
And far from God— and far from home,

Text: Anonymous

CONVICTION AND CONVERSION

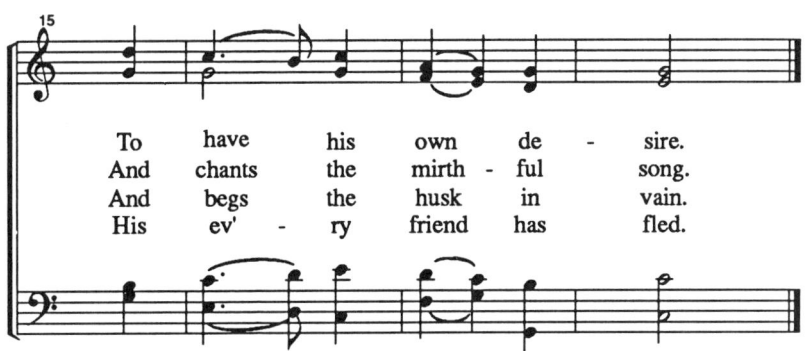

To have his own de - sire.
And chants the mirth - ful song.
And begs the husk in vain.
His ev' - ry friend has fled.

5. The Prodigal, with streaming eyes,
From folly just awake,
Reviews his wand'rings with surprise;
His heart begins to break.

6. I starve, he cries, nor can I bear
The famine in this land;
While servants of my Father share
The bounty of his hand.

7. With deep repentance I'll return
And seek my Father's face;
Unworthy to be call'd a son,
I'll ask a servant's place.

8. Far off He saw him slowly move,
In pensive silence mourn;
The Father ran with arms of love
To welcome his return.

9. Through all the courts the tidings flew,
And spread the joy around;
The angels tune their harps anew;
The Prodigal is found!

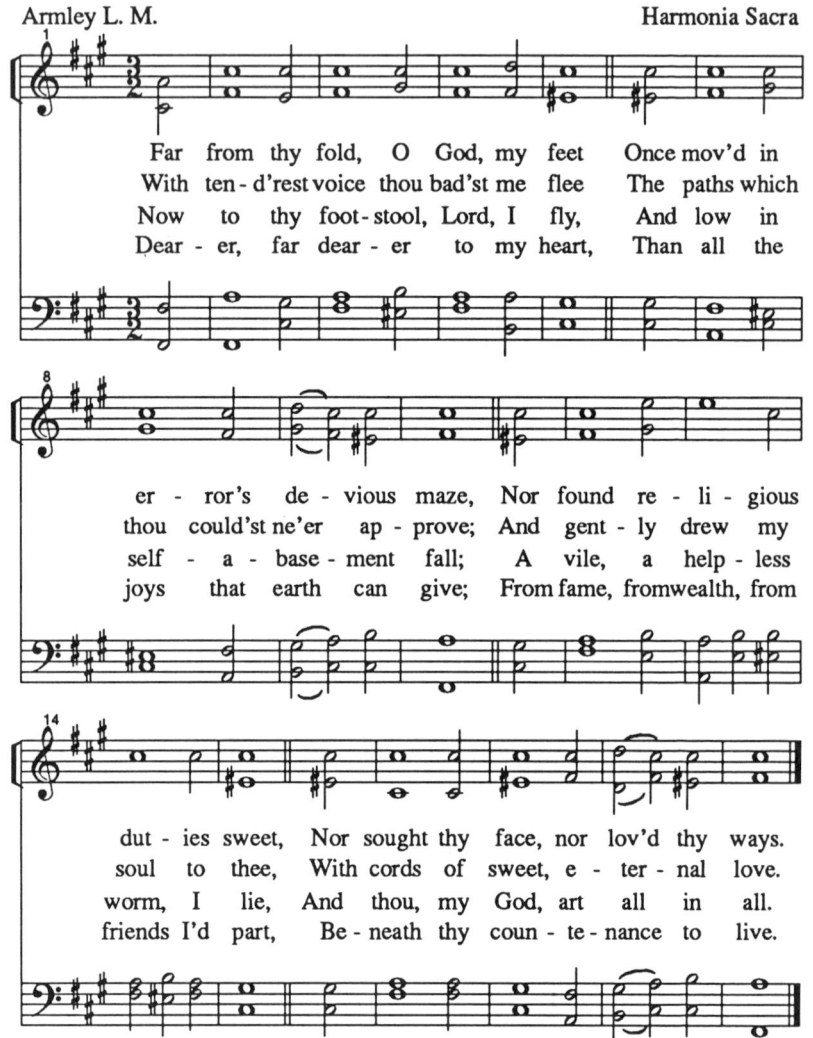

5. And when, in smiling friendship dress'd
Death bids me quit this mortal frame,
Gently reclin'd on Jesus' breast,
My latest breath shall bless his name.

6. Then my unfetter'd soul shall rise,
And soar above yon starry spheres,
Join the full chorus of the skies,
And sing thy praise thro' endless years.

Text: Tatlock

THE CONVERT

And   heard   what   ma - ny   said.
Had   nei - ther   joys   nor   song.
And   thought   that   all   was   right.
Be - fore   they   found   the   way.

5. Ah! then I thought my hopes were vain,
For I had liv'd at ease;
I wish'd for all my fears again,
To make me more like these.

6. I had my wish, the Lord disclos'd
The evils of my heart;
And left my naked soul expos'd
To Satan's fiery dart.

7. Alas! I cried in deep despair,
Borne down with fearful pain!
How can I these fierce terrors bear,
And who will now sustain?

8. Again my Saviour brought me aid,
And when he set me free,
"Trust simply on my word," he said,
"And leave the rest to me."

THE CONVERT

Spiritual Warfare Discovered 393

Shoel L. M.   Shoel

Like Is-rael, safe up-on the shore, Who thought the
But soon, with sick-'ning heart, sur-vey The per-ils
The morn-ing sun that shone so bright Is shroud-ed
But Je-sus calls them to the field: "Come, gird on

con-flict all was o'er, Young con-verts view the
of the de-sert way; The pow'r of sin re-
in the gloom of night; Hope-less the vic-tor's
har-ness, sword and shield; Stand fast in faith, fight

fright-ful train Of all their foes for e-ver slain.
vives a-gain, And all their hopes seem false and vain.
crown to win, They yield ere they the fight be-gin.
for your King, My grace shall strength and vic-t'ry bring."

5. Their daily wants his hands supply,
Their steps he guards with watchful eye,
Leads them from earth to heav'n above,
And crowns them with eternal love.

Text: Samuel Stennett

THE CONVERT

Nature Subdued

395

Luther's Hymn L. M.

Martin Luther

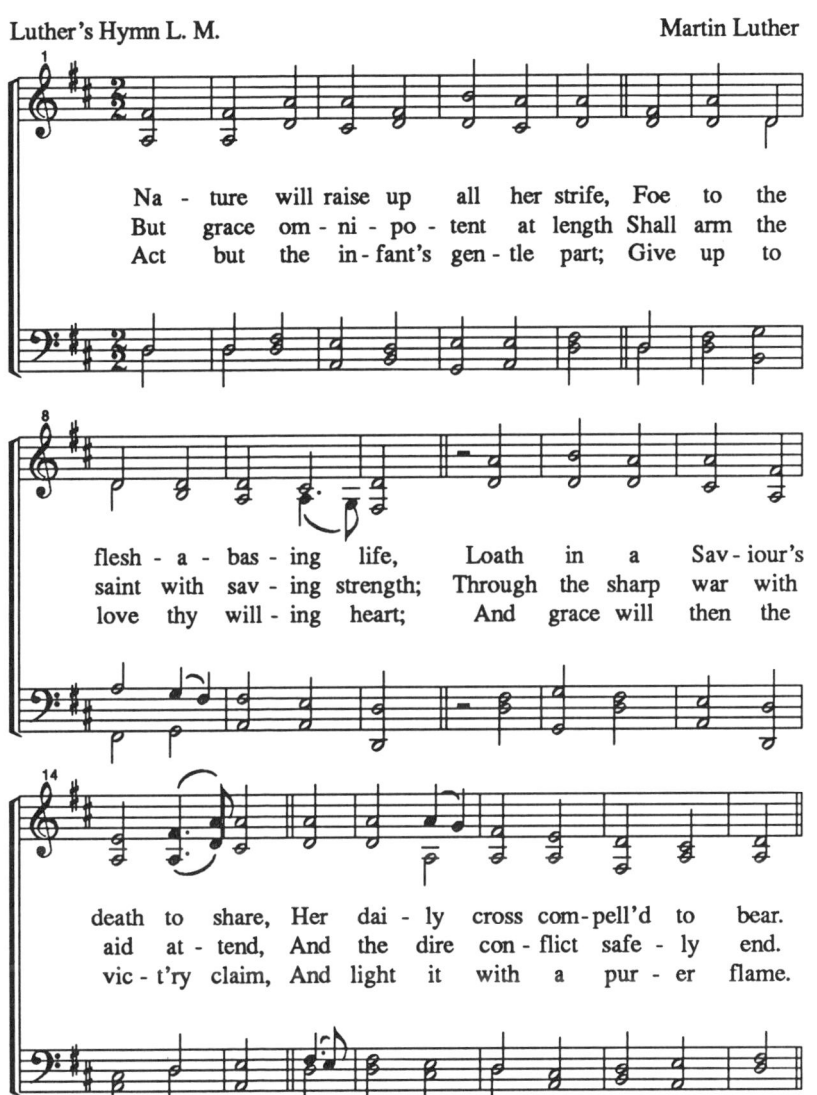

Na - ture will raise up all her strife, Foe to the flesh-a-bas-ing life, Loath in a Sav-iour's death to share, Her dai - ly cross com-pell'd to bear.
But grace om - ni - po - tent at length Shall arm the saint with sav - ing strength; Through the sharp war with aid at - tend, And the dire con - flict safe - ly end.
Act but the in - fant's gen - tle part; Give up to love thy will - ing heart; And grace will then the vic - t'ry claim, And light it with a pur - er flame.

Text: Martin Luther

THE CONVERT

The Boist'rous Seas Stilled 403

Abridge C. M. I. Smith

Our lit-tle bark on boist-'rous seas, By cru-el temp-est toss'd, With-out one cheer-ful beam of hope, Ex-pect-ing to be lost;

We to the Lord, in hum-ble prayer, Breath'd out our sad dis-tress; Tho' fee-ble, yet with con-trite hearts, We begg'd re-turn of peace.

The storm-y winds did cease to blow, The waves no more did roll; And soon a-gain a pla-cid sea Spoke com-fort to each soul.

Oh! may our grate-ful, trem-bling hearts Sweet hal-le-lu-jahs sing, To him who hath our lives pre-serv'd, Our Sav-iour, and our King.

5. Let us proclaim to all the world,
   With heart and voice, again,
   And tell the wonders he hath done
   For us, the sons of men.

Text: Martin Madan

THE CONVERT

Beware of Self-Confidence 409

Orange S.M.   Stone

1. Beware of Peter's word, Nor confidently say, "I never will deny the Lord," But "grant I never may."
2. Man's wisdom is to seek His strength in God alone; And e'en an angel would be weak, Who trusted in his own.
3. Retreat beneath his wings, And in his grace confide; This more exalts the King of kings Than all your works beside.
4. In Jesus is our store; Grace issues from his throne Whoever says, "I want no more," Confesses he has none.

Text: William Cowper

THE CONVERT

We've No Abiding City Here   422

Bath L. M.   *Hebrews xiii. 14.*   James Lyon

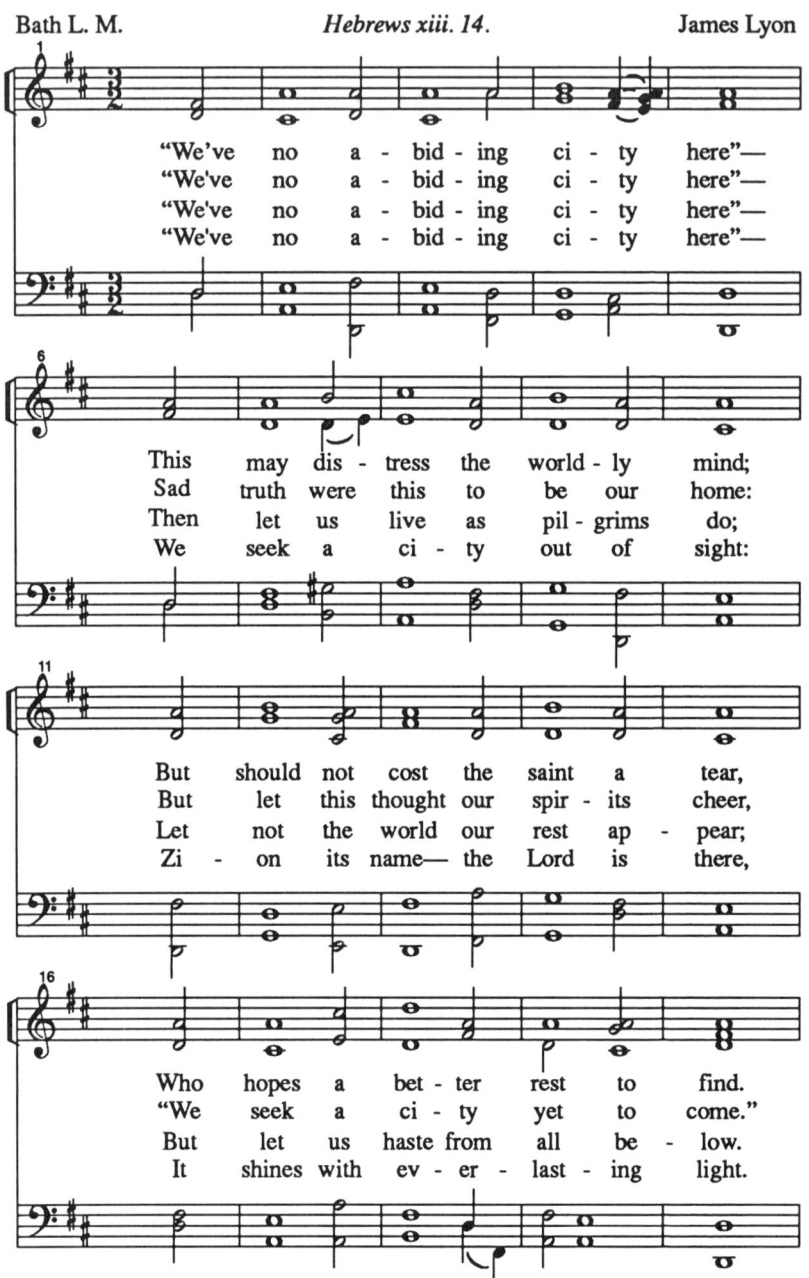

"We've no a-bid-ing ci-ty here"—
"We've no a-bid-ing ci-ty here"—
"We've no a-bid-ing ci-ty here"—
"We've no a-bid-ing ci-ty here"—

This may dis-tress the world-ly mind;
Sad truth were this to be our home:
Then let us live as pil-grims do;
We seek a ci-ty out of sight:

But should not cost the saint a tear,
But let this thought our spir-its cheer,
Let not the world our rest ap-pear;
Zi-on its name— the Lord is there,

Who hopes a bet-ter rest to find.
"We seek a ci-ty yet to come."
But let us haste from all be-low.
It shines with ev-er-last-ing light.

Text: Kelly

THE CONVERT
Headed for Immanuel's Ground 423
Rochester C. M.   A. Williams

1. Our country is Immanuel's ground, We seek that promis'd soil: The songs of Zion cheer our hearts, While strangers here we toil.
2. Oft do our eyes with joy o'er-flow, And oft are bath'd in tears; Yet nought but heav'n our hopes can raise, And nought but sin our fears.
3. Our pow'rs are oft dissolv'd away, In ecstasies of love; And while our bodies wander here, Our souls are fix'd above.
4. We purge our mortal dross away, Refining as we run; But while we die to earth and sense, Our heav'n is here begun.

Text: Barbauld

REJOICING IN A REVIVAL

Sinai and Calvary

435

St. Martin's C. M.
William Tansur

Hark! how from Sinai's mount proceed: The trumpet's awful blast; While yet the heart with anguish bleeds, And sinks in wo at last.

Behold the sinner's fearless soul, Which love could ne'er arrest, With trembling hears the thunder roll, And death approaching fast.

But lo!— what sounds of heav'nly peace, Amid the storm I hear; When howling winds a moment cease, And love succeeds to fear!

Now, on the hill of Calvary, Where Jesus once was slain, Sweet peace, and love, and sympathy, There all unbroken reign.

5. Whene'er the tempest's vengeful voice,
And guilt my soul appal,
I then in Jesus will rejoice,
And mercy's gentle call.

6. And when by care and we oppress'd,
Or storms of sorrow fall,
I'll flee to him and find a rest—
Enjoy in him my all.

Text: Anonymous

REJOICING IN A REVIVAL

Lift Up Your Eyes

442

Luther's Hymn L. M.   *John iv. 35.*   Martin Luther

Lift up your eyes, ye sons of light, Behold the fields already white! The glorious harvest now is come; See ransom'd sinners flocking home.
Mov'd by the Spirit's softest wind, Their hearts are all as one inclin'd; Their former sins and follies mourn; They bow, and to their God return.
Improve the harvest fleeing fast, Ere yet the shining season's past, When all the work of life shall end, The last— the long dark night descend.

Text: Anonymous

MONTHLY CONCERT

Sound Thro' All the Earth 472

Old Hundred L. M. Martin Luther

O Thou, who from thy glor-'ous throne,
Hast sent thy ser-vants to pro-claim
Sal-va-tion to a world un-done,
And sound thro' all the earth thy name;

Suc-ceed their ef-forts who in-vite
The wan-d'ring, wretch-ed out-casts home;
And let thy sov-'reign Spir-it's might
Com-pel the hea-then world to come.

From Af-ric's burn-ing, a-rid sand,
And A-sia's mild, re-splen-dent sky;
Let con-verts, from the hea-then lands,
As doves un-to their win-dows fly.

With Eu-rope may they join to bless
The Sav-iour's name, his praise pro-long;
And Is-lands of the South-ern seas
Join with A-mer-i-ca the song.

Text: Anonymous

MONTHLY CONCERT

Call the Nations

476

Luton L. M.
G. Burder

Look down, O God, with pi-tying eye, And view the de-so-la-tions round; See what wide realms in dark-ness lie, And hurl their i-dols to the ground.

Lord, let the gos-pel-trum-pet blow, And call the na-tions from a-far; Let all the isles their Sav-iour know, And earth's re-mot-est ends draw near.

Let Sa-tan's cru-el king-dom shake,— The realms of dark-ness, and of sin; Mes-si-ah now his em-pire take— In ev-'ry soul his reign be-gin.

Text: Anonymous

MONTHLY CONCERT

Zion's Hill

481

Braintree C. M.   *Micah iv. 1-5.*

Be-hold! the moun-tain of the Lord, In lat-ter days, shall rise A-bove the moun-tains and the hills, And draw the wond'ring eyes.
To this the joy-ful na-tions round, All tribes and tongues, shall flow; "Up to the hill of God," they say, "And to his courts we'll go."
The beams that shine on Zi-on's hill Shall light-en ev'-ry land; The King who reigns in Zi-on's tow'rs, Shall all the world com-mand.
No long-er hosts en-coun-t'ring hosts, Their mil-lions slain de-plore; They hang the trum-pet in the hall, And stud-y war no more.

5. Come then, Oh, come from ev'ry land,
To worship at his shrine:
And walking in the light of God,
With holy beauties shine.

Text: Logan

MONTHLY CONCERT

Thy Kingdom Come 484

Malmsbury L. M.

Bright as the sun's meridian blaze, Vast as the blessings he conveys, Wide as his reign from pole to pole, And permanent as his control:

So, Jesus, let thy kingdom come—Then sin and hell's terrific gloom Shall, at his brightness, flee away, The dawn of an eternal day.

Text: Anonymous

MISSSIONARY MEETINGS

Go, Proclaim

494

Malmsbury L. M.

1. Go, much lov'd brethren, haste and rear
The gospel standard, void of fear:
Go, seek with joy your des-tin'd shore,

2. Yes— Christian Heroes! go, proclaim Salvation through Immanuel's name;
To barren climes the tidings bear, And

3. He'll shield you with a wall of fire, With flaming zeal your breasts inspire,
Bid raging winds their fury cease, And

4. And when our labors all are o'er, Then we shall meet to part no more;
Meet with the blood-bought throng to fall And

Text: Anonymous

MISSSIONARY MEETINGS

view your na - tive land no more.
plant the Rose of Shar - on there.
hush the tem - pests in - to peace.
crown our Je - sus Lord of all!

Go, Ye Messenger

York C. M.

John Milton

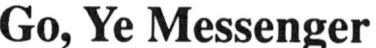

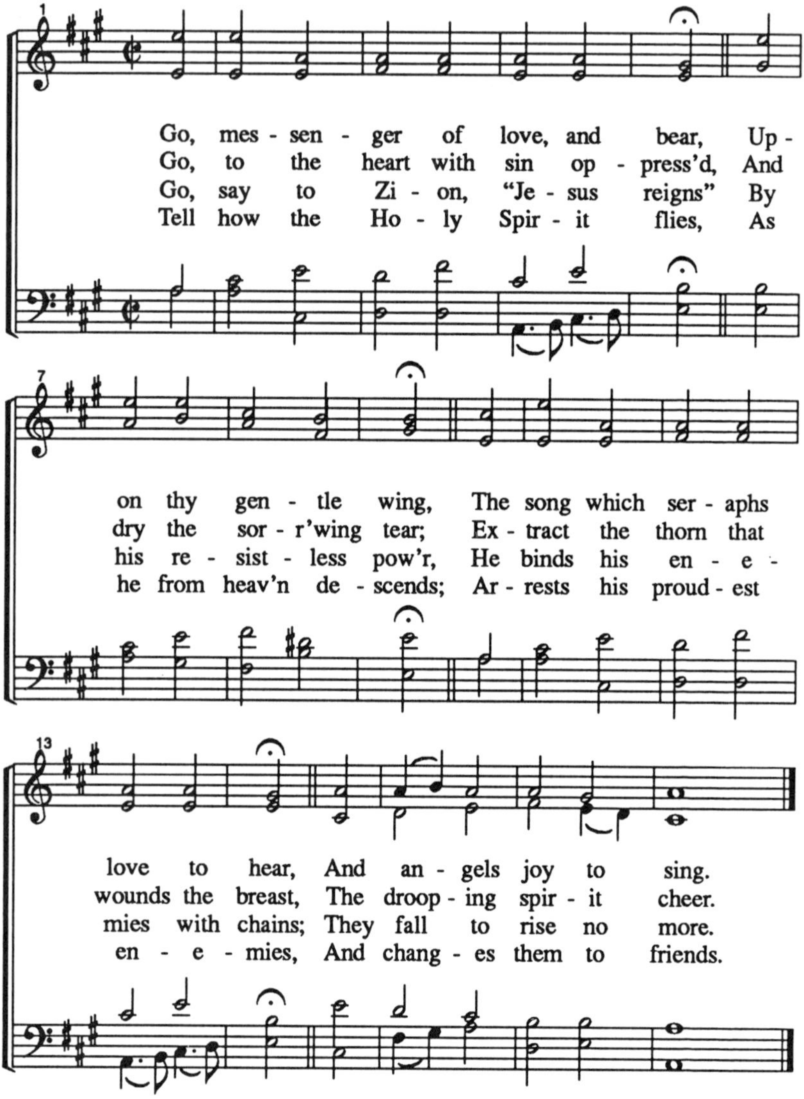

Text: B

TIMES AND SEASONS

Morning

505

Wareham C. M.　　　　　　　　　　　　　　　　　　　　　　　Arnold

When we, with wel - come slum - ber press - ed
Had clos'd our wear - y eyes, A pow'r un - seen
se - cur'd our rest, And made us joy - ful morn - ing light, In death's tre - men - dous gloom.

Num - bers this night have doubt - less met Their
long e - ter - nal doom; And lost the joys of

But life to us its light pro - longs,— Let
warm - est thanks a - rise; Great God, ac - cept our
morn - ing songs, Our will - ing sac - ri - fice.

Text: Anonymous

TIMES AND SEASONS

Before the Throne

511

Mear C. M.

Aaron Williams

O Lord, an-oth-er day is flown, And we, a lone-ly band Are met once more be-fore thy throne, To bless thy fos-t'ring hand.
And wilt thou bend a list-'ning ear To prais-es low as ours? Thou wilt! for thou dost love to hear The song which meek-ness pours.
And, Je-sus, thou thy smiles wilt deign, As we be-fore thee pray; For thou didst bless the in-fant train, And we are less than they.
Oh, let thy grace per-form its part, And let con-ten-tion cease; And shed a-broad in ev-'ry heart Thine ev-er-last-ing peace.

Text: H. K. White

TIMES AND SEASONS

Reflecting on Death   512

Wirksworth S. M.   Harmonia Sacra

1. The day is past and gone, The ev-'ning shades ap-pear; Oh, may I ev-er keep in mind, The night of death draws near.
2. I lay my gar-ments by, Up-on my bed to rest; So death will soon re-move me hence, And leave my soul un-dress'd.
3. Lord, keep me safe this night, Se-cure from all my fears; May an-gels guard me while I sleep, Till morn-ing light ap-pears.
4. And when I ear-ly rise, To view th'un-wear-ied sun, May I set out to win the prize, And af-ter glor-y run:

5. That when my days are past,
And I from time remove,
Lord, I may in thy bosom rest,
The bosom of thy love.

Text: Anonymous

TIMES AND SEASONS

This Day of Heavenly Joy

517

Clifford C. M.

When, on the third au-spi-cious day, While yet the blush-ing dawn Shed forth its ear-liest smil-ing ray To gild the ris-ing morn;

The "ho-ly wom-en" sought the place Where their be-lov'd was laid, And shin-ing an-gels preach'd the grace That rais'd him from the dead;

They hast-ed from the hal-low'd ground, Where his dear flesh had lain, To tell his mourn-ing friends a-round, That Je-sus lives a-gain.

This day, as days of old-er time, Is one of heav'n-ly joy; Good tid-ings reach to ev-'ry clime, And ev-'ry tongue em-ploy.

Text: Anonymous

TIMES AND SEASONS

Evening of the Lord's Day 518

Mear C. M.   Aaron Williams

1. Fre-quent the day of God re-turns To shed its quick-'ning beams; And yet how slow de-vo-tion burns; How lan-guid are its flames!
2. Ac-cept our faint at-tempts to love— Our frail-ties, Lord, for-give; We would be like thy saints a-bove, And praise thee while we live.
3. In-crease, O Lord, our faith and hope, And fit us to a-scend, Where the as-sem-bly ne'er breaks up, The Sab-bath ne'er shall end;
4. Where we shall breathe in heav'n-ly air, With heav'n-ly lus-tre shine; Be-fore the throne of God ap-pear, And feast on love di-vine.

Text: Brown

TIMES AND SEASONS

Spring, or Return of Joy   521

York C. M.
John Milton

At length the wish'd for spring has come; How al-ter'd is the scene! The trees and shrubs are dress'd in bloom, The earth ar-ray'd in green.

I see my Sav-iour from on high, Break thro' the clouds and shine; No crea-ture now more bless'd than I, No song more loud than mine.

Thy word does all my hopes re-vive; It ov-er-comes my foes; It makes my lan-guid grac-es thrive, And blos-som like the rose.

Dear Lord, a mon-u-ment I stand, Of what thy grace can do; Up-hold me by thy gra-cious hand, Each chang-ing sea-son through.

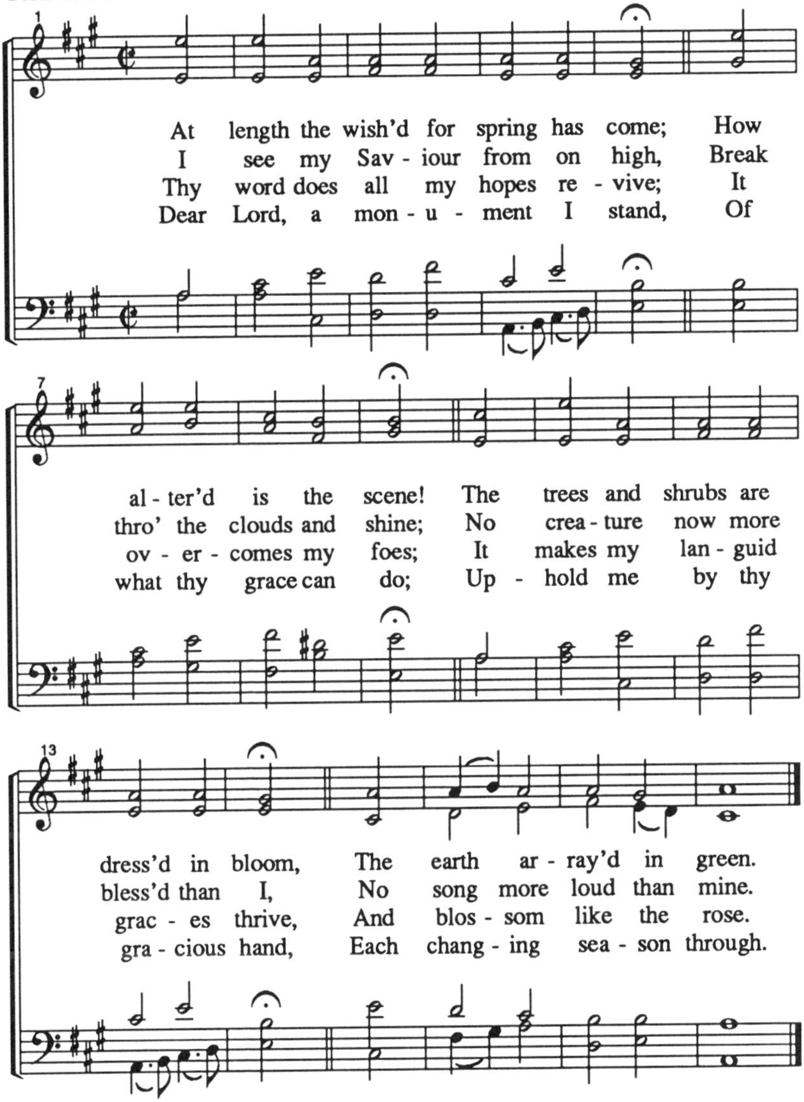

Text: John Newton

TIMES AND SEASONS

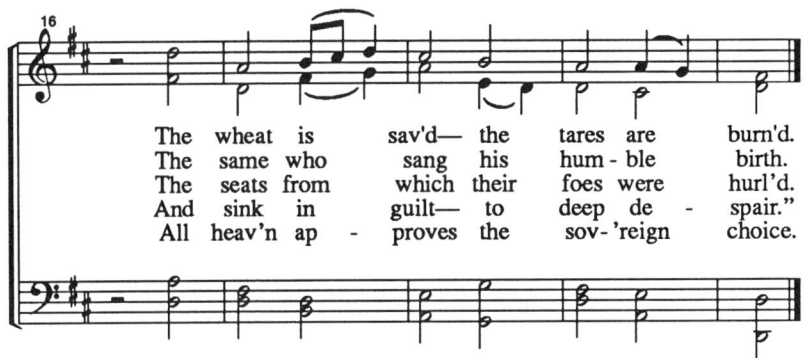

TIMES AND SEASONS

Prepare to Meet Thy God 525

Walsall C. M. Anchors' Collection

Come, Lord, and bless the ris-ing race! Make this a hap-py hour, Ac-cord-ing to thy rich-est grace, And thine al-might-y pow'r.
Dear youth, we know your sin-ful state: May God your hearts re-new! We would a-while our-selves for-get, To pour our pray'r for you.
We see, tho' you per-ceive it not, Th'ap-proach-ing aw-ful doom! Oh, trem-ble at the sol-emn thought, And flee the wrath to come!
Dear Sav-iour, let this new born year Spread an a-larm a-broad; And cry in ev-'ry care-less ear, "Pre-pare to meet thy God!"

Text: William Cowper

TIMES AND SEASONS

The Chief Concern

542

Barby C.M. — William Tansur

Re - li - gion is the chief con - cern Of mor - tals here be - low; May I its great im - por - tance learn, Its sov' - reign vir - tue know!
More need - ful this, than glit - t'ring wealth, Or aught the world be - stows; Nor re - pu - ta - tion, food, or health, Can give us such re - pose.
Re - li - gion should our thoughts en - gage, A - midst our youth - ful bloom; Twill fit us for de - clin - ing age, And for the aw - ful tomb.
O may my heart by grace re - new'd, Be my Re - deem - er's throne; And be my stub - born will sub - du'd, His gov - ern - ment to own.

5. Let deep repentance, faith, and love,
Be join'd with godly fear;
And all my conversation prove
My heart to be sincere.

Text: Isaac Watts

TIMES AND SEASONS

Vanity of the World

545

Armley L. M.   Harmonia Sacra

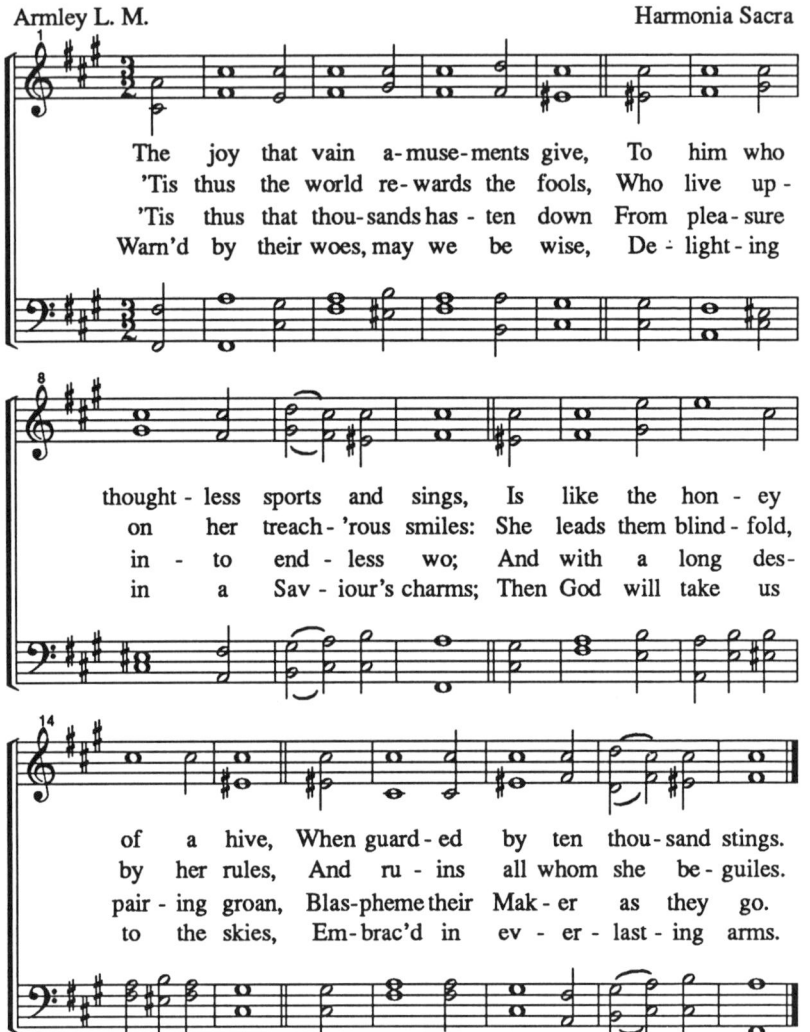

1. The joy that vain amusements give, To him who thoughtless sports and sings, Is like the honey of a hive, When guarded by ten thousand stings.
2. 'Tis thus the world rewards the fools, Who live upon her treach'rous smiles: She leads them blindfold, by her rules, And ruins all whom she beguiles.
3. 'Tis thus that thousands hasten down From pleasure into endless wo; And with a long despairing groan, Blaspheme their Maker as they go.
4. Warn'd by their woes, may we be wise, Delighting in a Saviour's charms; Then God will take us to the skies, Embrac'd in everlasting arms.

Text: William Cowper

TIMES AND SEASONS

The Saviour's Voice   547

Clifford C. M.   *Proverbs viii. 19.*

Ye hearts, with youth-ful vig-or warm, In smil-ing
He, Lord of all the worlds on high, Stoops to con-
"The soul that longs to see my face, Is sure my
What ob-ject, Lord, my soul should move, If once com-

crowds draw near, And turn from ev-'ry mor-tal
verse with you; And lays his ra-diant glor-ies
love to gain; And those that ear-ly seek my
par'd with thee? What beau-ty should com-mand my

charm, A Sav-iour's voice to hear.
by, Your friend-ship to pur-sue.
grace, Shall nev-er seek in vain."
love, Like what in Christ I see?

5. Away, ye false, delusive toys,
Vain tempters of the mind!
'Tis here I fix my lasting choice,
And here true bliss I find.

Text: Doddridge

HOLY SPIRIT

Prayer of a Youth

548

Watchman S. M.   *Psalm cxix. 9.*   Leach

With humble heart and tongue, My God, to
thee I pray; Oh, make me learn while
I am young, How I may cleanse my way.

Make an unguarded youth The object
of thy care; Help me to choose the
way of truth, And fly from ev'ry snare.

My heart, to folly prone, Renew'd by
pow'r divine; Unite it to thyself alone, And make me wholly thine.

Oh, let thy word of grace My warmest
thoughts employ; Be this, through all my
foll'wing days, My treasure and my joy.

5. To what thy laws impart,
Be my whole soul inclin'd;
Oh, let them dwell within my heart,
And sanctify my mind.

6. May thy young servant learn,
By these to cleanse his way;
And may I here the path discern
That leads to endless day.

Text: Fawcett

TIMES AND SEASONS

Public Fast

551

Walsall C. M.   *Joel i. 14.*   Anchors' Collection

1. See, gracious Lord, before thy throne, Thy mourning people bend! 'Tis on thy sov-'reign grace alone, Our humble hopes depend.

2. Tremendous judgments, from thy hand, Thy dreadful pow'rs display; Yet mercy spares this guilty land, And still we live to pray.

3. How chang'd, alas! are truths divine, For error, guilt, and shame! What impious numbers, bold in sin, Disgrace the Christian name.

4. O turn us, turn us, mighty Lord, By thy resistless grace Then shall our hearts obey thy word, And humbly seek thy face.

5. Then, should insulting foes invade,
We shall not sink in fear;
Secure of never failing aid,
When God, our God, is near.

Text: Steele

TIMES AND SEASONS

Perfect Bliss on Earth?   554

Standish C. M.
John Tufts

1. Why should the Christian waste in sighs
The breath that God hath giv'n;
Whom ev-'ry pass-ing hour that flies
Bears on-ward fast to heav'n?

2. Why should we wish for per-fect bliss,
In this dark world for-lorn;
Or seek, a-midst a wil-der-ness,
A rose with-out a thorn?

3. Our Fa-ther God! be ours the grief,
Which to thy sons be-longs;
And let us share in their re-lief,
Their ev-er-last-ing songs.

Text: Anonymous

TIMES AND SEASONS

Joy in Sorrow

557

Standish C. M.
John Tufts

And let this fee - ble bod - y fail, And let it faint or die; My soul shall quit the mourn - ful vale, And soar to worlds on high;

Shall join the dis - em - bod - y'd saints, And find its long sought rest, (The on - ly rest for which it pants,) On the Re - deem - er's breast.

In hope of that im - mor - tal crown, I now the cross sus - tain; And glad - ly wan - der up and down, And smile at toil and pain.

I trav - el my ap - point - ed years, Till my De - liv - 'rer come, And wipe a - way his ser - vant's tears, And take his ex - ile home.

Text: Anonymous

TIMES AND SEASONS

Sick-Bed Reflections 563

Orange S.M. Stone

Just o'er the grave I hung— No par-don met my eyes, As bless-ings nev-er greet the slain, And hope shall nev-er rise.
Sweet mer-cy to my soul Re-veal'd no charm-ing ray; Be-fore me rose a long-dark night, With no suc-ceed-ing day.
Then— Oh, how vain ap-pear'd The joys be-neath the sky! Like vi-sions past, like flow'rs that blow When win-t'ry storms are nigh.
How mourn'd my sink-ing soul The Sab-bath's hours di-vine, The day of grace, that pre-cious day, Con-sum'd in sense and sin.

5. The work—the mighty work
Of life, so long delay'd—
Repentance yet to be begun
Upon a dying bed.

Text: Timothy Dwight

FUNERAL

The New Inhabitant of Bliss 566

Armley L. M.   *Ecclesiastes vii. 7.*   Harmonia Sacra

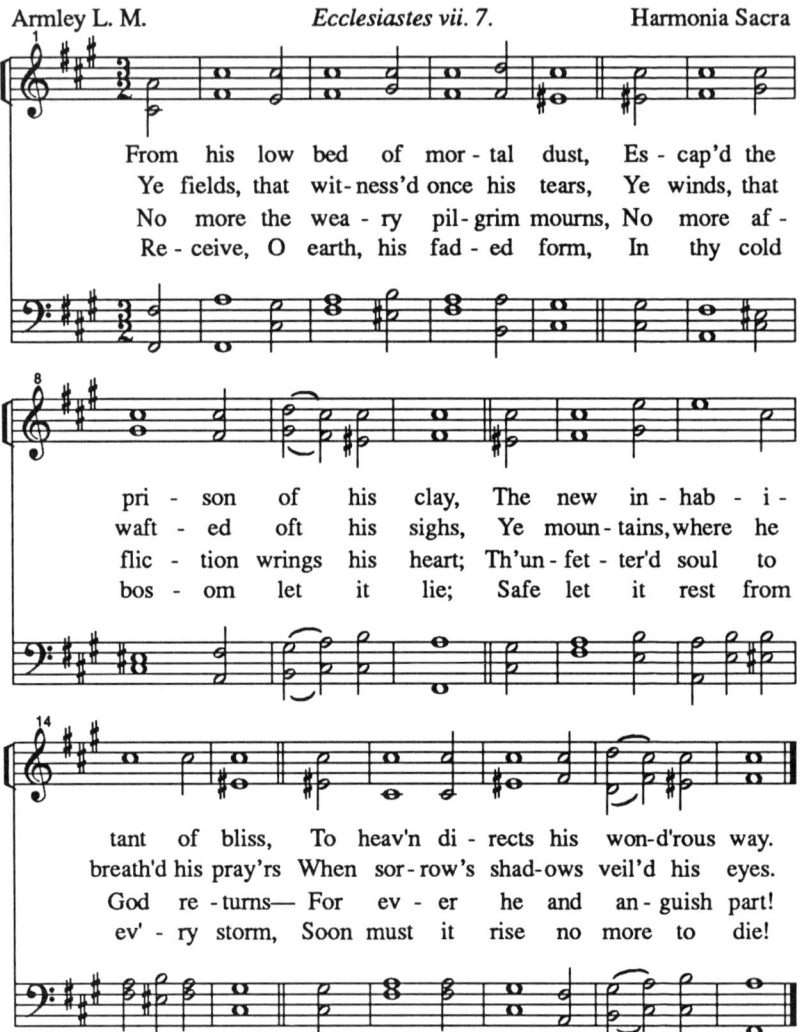

From his low bed of mor-tal dust, Es-cap'd the pri-son of his clay, The new in-hab-i-tant of bliss, To heav'n di-rects his won-d'rous way.
Ye fields, that wit-ness'd once his tears, Ye winds, that waft-ed oft his sighs, Ye moun-tains, where he breath'd his pray'rs When sor-row's shad-ows veil'd his eyes.
No more the wea-ry pil-grim mourns, No more af-flic-tion wrings his heart; Th'un-fet-ter'd soul to God re-turns— For ev-er he and an-guish part!
Re-ceive, O earth, his fad-ed form, In thy cold bos-om let it lie; Safe let it rest from ev'-ry storm, Soon must it rise no more to die!

Text: Collyer

FUNERAL

The Moment After Death 571

Mear C. M.
Aaron Williams

In vain my fan-cy strives to paint The mo-ment af-ter death; The glor-ies that sur-round a saint, When yield-ing up his breath.

One gen-tle sigh his fet-ters breaks, We scarce can say, "He's gone!" Be-fore the will-ing spir-it takes Its man-sions near the throne.

Faith strives, but all its ef-forts fail, To trace the spir-it's flight; No eye can pierce with-in the veil Which hides the world of light.

Thus much (and this is all) we know, Saints are com-plete-ly blest; Have done with sin, and care, and wo, And with their Sav-iour rest.

5. In midst of dangers, fears, and deaths,
Thy goodness we'll adore;
We'll praise thee for thy mercies past;
And humbly hope for more.

Text: John Newton

FUNERAL

Balaam's Wish   572

Dover S. M.   *Numbers xxiii. 10.*   Aaron Williams

How blest the right-eous are, When they re-sign their breath! No won-der Ba-laam wish'd to share, In such a hap-py death.

"Oh! let me die," said he, "The death the right-eous do; When life is end-ed, let me be Found with the faith-ful few."—

The force of truth, how great, When en-e-mies con-fess! None but the right-eous, whom they hate, A sol-id hope pos-sess.

But Ba-laam's wish was vain— His heart was in-sin-cere; He thirst-ed for un-right-eous gain. And sought a por-tion here.

5. May we, O Lord most high,
Warning from hence receive;
If like the righteous we would die,
To choose the life they live.

Text: John Newton

FUNERAL

The Death of a Young Person 573

Funeral Hymn. C. M. — Miller

1. When bloom-ing youth is snatch'd a - way By death's re - sist - less hand, Our hearts the mourn - ful tri - bute pay, Which pi - ty must de - mand.
2. While pi - ty prompts the ris - ing sigh, Oh, may this truth, im - press'd With aw - ful pow'r, "I too must die" Sink deep in ev' - ry breast.
3. The voice of this a - larm - ing scene May ev' - ry heart o - bey; Nor be the heav'n - ly warn - ing vain, Which calls to watch, and pray.
4. Oh, let us fly, to Je - sus fly, Whose pow'r - ful arm can save; Then shall our hopes as - cend on high and tri - umph o'vr the grave.

Text: Steele

FUNERAL

Am I Prepared?

575

Putney L.M.
I. Smith

Oft as the bell, with sol-emn toll,
Speaks the de-par-ture of a soul,
Let each one ask him-self, "Am I

"On-ly this frail and fleet-ing breath
Pre-serves me from the jaws of death;
Soon as it fails, at once I'm gone,

"Then leav-ing all I lov'd be-low,
To God's tri-bu-nal I must go;
Must hear the Judge pro-nounce my fate,

Lord Je-sus! help me now to flee,
And seek my hope a-lone in thee;
Ap-ply thy blood, thy Spir-it give -

Text: John Newton

FUNERAL

Pre - par'd, should I be call'd to die?
And plung'd in - to a world un - known.
And fix my ev - er - last - ing state."
Sub - due my sins and let me live.

5. Then when the solemn bell I hear,
If sav'd from guilt, I need not fear;
Nor would the thought distressing be,
Perhaps it next may toll for me.

TIME AND ETERNITY

The Mighty Flood 577

Standish C. M.   *Psalm xc. 5, 9.*   John Tufts

1. The might-y flood, that rolls a-long In tor-rents to the main, The wa-ters lost can ne'er re-call, From that a-byss a-gain.
2. The days, the years, the a-ges dark, De-scend-ing down to night, Can nev-er, nev-er be re-deem'd, Back to the gates of light.
3. Where are our Fa-thers?— Whi-ther gone The might-y men of old! The pa-tr'archs, pro-phets, prin-ces, kings, In sa-cred books en-roll'd?—
4. Gone to the rest-ing place of man, His long, his si-lent home; Where a-ges past have gone be-fore, Where fu-ture a-ges come!

Text: Logan

DAY OF JUDGMENT

Everlasting Absence of God Intolerable

Elgin C. M.   Scottish Folk Tune

5. Oh, wretched state of deep despair
To see my God remove—
And fix my doleful station where
I must not taste his love!

6. Oh, tell me that my worthless name
Is graven on thy hands;
Show me some promise in thy book,
Where my salvation stands.

Text: Isaac Watts

DAY OF JUDGMENT

Judgment Day

588

Northhampton Chapel 8, 7. Aaron Williams

Sin - ners, take the friend - ly warn - ing Soon that aw - ful day shall break, And the trum - pet with its dawn - ing, All the slum - b'ring mil - lions
See as - sem - bled ev - 'ry na - tion! Loft - y ci - ties, tem - ples, tow'rs, Wrapp'd in dread - ful con - fla - gra - tion, Earth and sea the flame de -
Ye, who to the world dis - sem - ble, While you prac - tise deeds of night, Sin - ners, now be - hold and trem - ble; All your crimes are brought to
Lost in ease, or car - nal plea - sure, Sport - ing on the burn - ing brink; Now, you say, you have no lei - sure, You can find no time to

Text: Anonymous

DAY OF JUDGMENT

5. Ye—who now, conviction stifling,
Waste your time-the loss deplore;
Hear the angel—cease your trifling—
"Time," he cries, "shall be no more.

6. Pause, and hear the voice of reason—
Catch the moments as they fly—
You who lose the present season,—
You must all find time to die.

DEACH AND HEAVEN

The Books Opened

589

Surry L. M.   *Revelation xx. 12.*   Costellow

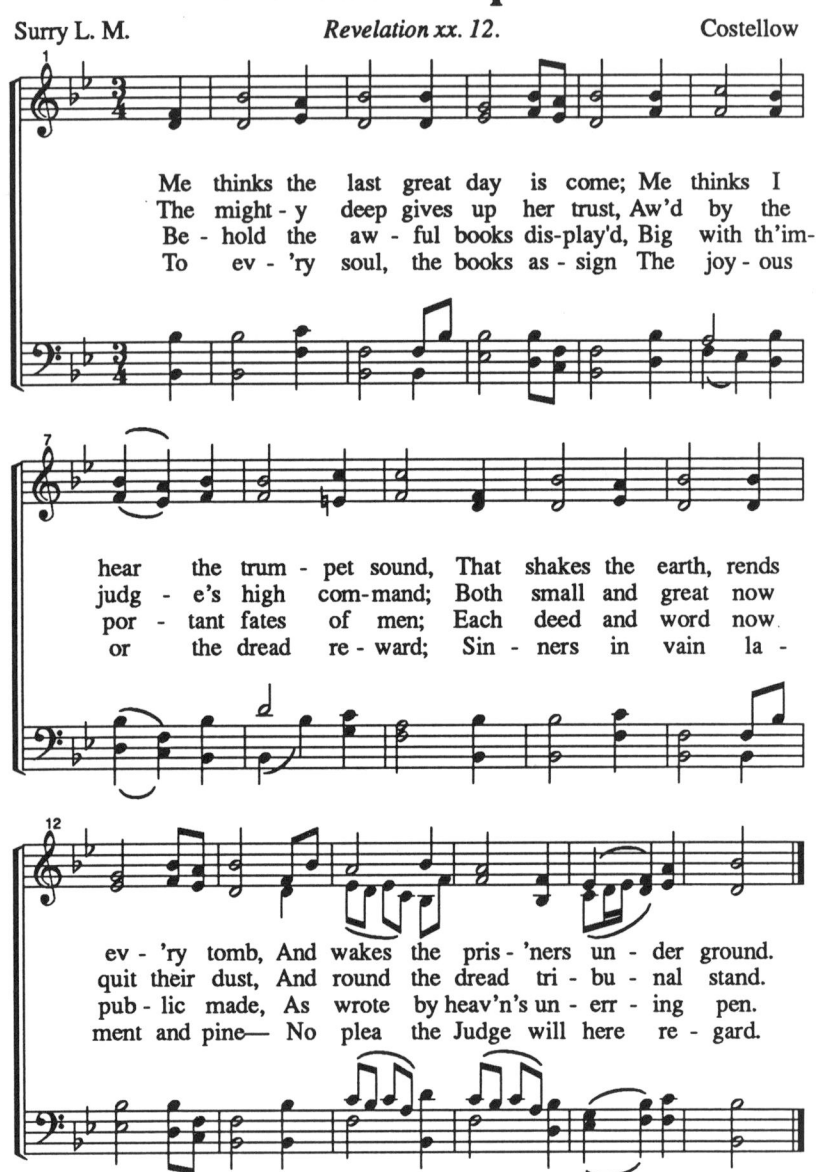

5. Lord, when these awful leaves unfold, May life's fair book my soul approve!
There may I read my name enroll'd, And triumph in redeeming love!

Text: Needham

DEATH AND HEAVEN

Security in Death

590

Standish C. M.

John Tufts

When, bend-ing o'er the brink of life, My
When weep-ing friends sur-round my bed, And
When ev-'ry long lov'd scene of life Stands
O, thou great source of joy su-preme, Whose

tremb-ling soul shall stand, Wait-ing to pass death's
close my sight-less eyes; When shat-ter'd by the
read-y to de-part; When the last sigh that
arm a-lone can save, Dis-pel the dark-ness

aw-ful flood, Great God, at thy com-mand!
weight of years This bro-ken bod-y lies:
shakes the frame Shall rend this burst-ing heart:
that sur-rounds The en-trance to the grave!

Text: Collyer

DEATH AND HEAVEN

The Living Know They Will Die

592

Putney L.M.   *Ecclesiastes ix. 5.*   I. Smith

Where are the dead?— In heav'n or hell
Who are the dead?— The sons of time
Where are the living?— On the ground
Who are the living?— They whose breath

Their dis - em - bod - ied spir - its dwell;
In e - v'ry age, and state, and clime;
Where pray'r is heard and mer - cy found;
Draws e - v'ry mo - ment nigh to death;

Their per - ish'd forms in bonds of clay,
Re - noun'd, dis - hon - or'd, or for - got,
Where in the com - pass of a span,
Of end - less bliss or wo the heirs:

Text: Montgomery

DEATH AND HEAVEN

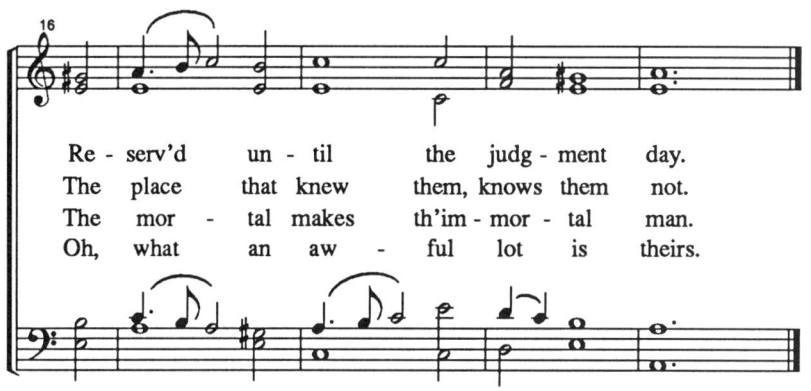

Re - serv'd un - til the judg - ment day.
The place that knew them, knows them not.
The mor - tal makes th'im - mor - tal man.
Oh, what an aw - ful lot is theirs.

5. Then, timely warn'd, let us begin
To follow Christ and flee from sin;
Daily grow up in him our head,
Lord of the living and the dead.

DEATH AND HEAVEN

The Everlasting Song

596

Colchester C. M. Henry Purcell

5. Now let me mount and join their song,
And be an angel too;
My heart, my hand, my ear, my tongue,
Here's joyful work for you.

6. I would begin the music here,
And so my soul should rise;
Oh, for some heav'nly notes to bear
My passions to the skies.

Text: Isaac Watts

THE ARRANGEMENT.

Hymn.	
GOD; - - - from	1 to 13
Universal Praise,	14-18
Scriptures,	19-24
Alarming,	25-43
Inviting,	44-85
Penitential,	86-101
Christ,	102-124
His Birth,	102-104
Life and Ministry,	105-109
Sufferings and death,	110-116
Resurrection,	117
Ascension,	118-121
Intercession,	122
Dominion,	123-124
Characters of Christ,	
in alphabetical order,	125-140
Doctrines of the Gospel,	
in alphabetical order,	141-170
Law and Gospel,	171-173
Holy Spirit,	
His Influences,	174-182
Graces of;	
in alphabetical order,	183-230
The Christian,	231-278
Worship,	279-331
Private,	279-285
Social,	286-291
Ministers,	292-296
The Church,	297-364
Prayer for a Revival,	305-314
Conference Meetings,	315-325
Dismission,	326-331
The sinner awakened,	332-343
Conviction,	344-360
Conversion,	361-371
The Convert,	372-423
Rejoicing in a Revival,	424-445
Baptism,	446-450
Monthly Concert,	451-487
Missionary Meetings,	488-501
Collections,	502-504
Times and Seasons,	505-564
Morning and Evening,	505-515
Sabbath,	516-519
Seasons of the year,	520-523
New Year,	524-527
Marriage,	528-530
Meeting & parting of Friends,	531-537
Youth,	538-548
Middle Age,	549
Old Age,	550
Fast,	551
Affliction,	552-564
Funeral Hymns,	565-575
Time and Eternity,	576-580
Resurrection,	581-584
Day of Judgment,	585-589
Death and Heaven,	590-600

A TABLE OF FIRST LINES.

Ah, what can I, a sinner, do,	337
Ah, who can speak the vast dismay,	35
Ah, why this disconsolate frame,	401
Ah, wretched souls are they who here,	149
Alas, alas, how blind I've been,	332
Alas, and did my Saviour bleed,	86
Alas, what hourly dangers rise,	260
Almighty God of truth and love,	94
All glory to God in the sky,	314
All hail the power of Jesus' name,	123
All ye who laugh and sport with death,	29
Amazing grace! how sweet the sound,	155
Amazing sight! the Saviour stands,	49
Am I a soldier of the cross,	193
An angry God, a Judge severe,	41
And canst thou, sinner, slight,	335
And does the Spirit kindly move,	334
And have I measur'd half my days,	549
And is the gospel peace and love,	106
And let this feeble body fail,	557
And must I part with all I have,	221
And what am I? my soul, awake,	237
And will the Lord thus condescend,	50
And will th' offended God again,	256
Angels! roll the rock away,	117
Another six days' work is done,	516
Anxious, I strove to find the way,	390
A present God is all our strength,	174
Arise, great God, and let thy grace,	467
Arm of the Lord, awake, awake,	477
Ascend thy throne, Almighty King,	483
As in soft silence vernal showers,	307
As once the Saviour took his seat,	90
As on the cross the Saviour hung,	158
Assembled at thy great command,	488
As the serpent, rais'd by Moses,	47
Astonish'd and distress'd,	345
As when the weary traveller gains,	269
At Jacob's well a stranger sought,	80
At length, the wish'd for spring has come,	521
Attend, while God's exalted Son,	167
Attend, ye children of our God,	450
Awake, and sing the song,	375

Awake, awake my sluggish soul,	85	Come, weary souls, with sins distress'd,	58
Awak'd by Sinai's awful sound,	367	Come, we who love the Lord,	205
Awake, my soul, lift up thine eyes,	232	Come, ye, that know and fear the Lord,	7
Awake, my soul, to joyful lays,	9	Come, ye weary, heavy laden,	57
Awake, ye saints, and raise your eyes,	527	Come, ye weary sinners, come,	350
		Convinced of sin, men now begin,	427
BEHOLD a stranger at the door,	48		
Behold high in the midst of heaven,	466	DEAD be my heart to all below,	251
Behold the expected time draw near,	489	Dear Jesus, let thy pitying eye,	246
Behold the genial showers descend,	310	Dear refuge of my weary soul,	254
Behold the glorious dawning bright,	482	Dear Saviour, if these Lambs should	303
Behold the mountain of the Lord,	481	Dear Saviour, thy victorious love,	594
Behold the sons, the heirs of God,	195	Deep are the wounds which sin has	134
Behold the tears that Mary shed,	348	Descend, holy Spirit, the Dove,	180
Begone my worldly cares away,	515	Destruction's dangerous road,	25
Begone unbelief,	228	Did Christ o'er sinners weep?	248
Beneath the poisonous dart,	364	Did I possess the gift of tongues,	213
Beside the gospel pool,	371	Didst thou, dear Jesus, suffer shame	183
Beware of Peter's word,	409	Disconsolate tenant of clay,	559
Blessed Redeemer! how divine,	206	Dismiss us with thy blessing, Lord,	327
Blest be the dear uniting love,	536		
Blest be the tie that binds,	533	EARTH has engross'd my love too	596
Blest Comforter divine,	176	Encompass'd with clouds of	241
Blest is the man whose softening heart,	184	Eternal God, almighty cause,	452
Blest Lord, behold the guilty scorn,	313	Eternal God, enthron'd on high,	550
Blest Saviour, by thy powerful word,	247	Eternal power, whose high abode,	15
Blow ye the trumpet, blow,	432	Eternal Spirit, source of light,	181
Break thro' the clouds, dear Lord, and	552	Eternal Sun of Righteousness,	330
Brethren, belov'd for Jesus' sake,	531	Eternity is just at hand,	579
Bright as the sun's meridian blaze,	484	Eye hath not seen, nor ear hath heard,	208
By whom shall Jacob now arise?	302	Exert thy power, thy rights maintain,	459
CAN aught beneath a power divine,	168	FAITH adds new charms to earthly	192
Children of the heavenly King,	378	Farewell, and what if next we	501
Children of God, who trav'ling slow,	267	Farewell, dear friends, a short farewell,	537
Come, all ye souls by sin oppress'd,	65	Far from afflictions, toil and care,	565
Come, christian brethren, ere we part,	535	Far from my thoughts, vain world	322
Come, every pious heart,	121	Far from the world, O Lord, I flee,	282
Come, gracious Spirit, heavenly dove,	316	Far from the utmost verge of day,	28
Come, heavenly peace of mind,	217	Far from thy fold, O God, my feet,	372
Come, Holy Ghost, my soul inspire,	284	Father, divine, thy piercing eye,	279
Come, Holy Spirit, come,	179	Father, how wide thy glory shines,	5
Come, Holy Spirit, heavenly dove,	177	Father of all, thy care we bless,	290
Come, humble sinner, in whose breast,	77	Father of faithful Abram, hear,	469
Come, let me love, or is my mind,	67	Father of glory, to thy name,	11
Come, let us anew,	526	Father of mercies, God of love,	101
Come, let us now forget our mirth,	538	Father of mercies, in thy word,	20
Come, Lord, and bless the rising race,	525	Father of mercies, send thy grace,	503
Come, Lord, and warm each languid	319	Father, whate'er of earthly bliss,	283
Come, my soul, thy suit prepare,	351	Forgiveness, 'tis a joyful sound,	159
Come, sacred Spirit, from above,	306	Fountain of light, whose copious stream,	271
Come, sinners, attend,	59	Frequent the day of God returns,	518
Come, thou Almighty King,	14	Friend of the friendless, and the faint,	98
Come, thou Fount of every blessing,	439	From Greenland's icy mountains,	492

From his low bed of mortal dust,	566
GAY is thy morning, flattering hope,	539
Gird on, great God, thy sword,	312
Give to the winds thy fears,	227
Glorious things of thee are spoken,	462
Glory to God on high,	331
Go, and the Saviour's grace proclaim,	495
God from his throne with piercing eye,	148
God, in the gospel of his Son,	23
God moves in a mysterious way,	12
God of my life, through all its days,	18
Go, messenger of love, and hear,	496
Go, much lov'd brethren, haste and rear,	494
Go, ye heralds of salvation,	499
Go, ye messengers of God,	498
Grace, 'tis a charming sound,	154
Grant, Lord, I may delight in thee,	187
Great God, preserved by thine arm,	506
Great God, the nations of the earth,	456
Great God, to thee I make,	343
Great God, we to thy honor raise,	325
Great High Priest, we view thee	136
Great Saviour, let thy power divine,	474
Guide me, O thou great Jehovah,	276
HAD I a throne above the rest,	197
Hail, mighty Jesus! how divine,	169
Hail, my ever blessed Jesus,	380
Hail, sov'reign love that first began,	129
Hail, the day that saw him rise,	118
Hail to the Lord's anointed,	445
Happy soul, thy days are ended,	598
Happy the heart where graces reign,	207
Happy the hours, the golden days,	242
Happy the man who finds the grace,	229
Happy the saints, whose lot is cast,	324
Hark, a cry among the nations,	486
Hark, from yon wilds is heard the strain,	441
Hark, hark, the notes of joy,	444
Hark, how from Sinai's mount proceeds,	435
Hark, the glad sound the Saviour comes,	105
Hark, the herald angels sing,	104
Hark, 'tis the prophet of the skies,	480
Hark, the song of Jubilee,	487
Hark, the voice of love and mercy,	113
Hasten; O sinner, to be wise,	30
Heal us, Immanuel, here we stand,	353
Hearts of stone, relent, relent,	150
He dies, the Friend of sinners dies,	115
He lives, the great Redeemer lives,	122
He who on earth as man was known,	130
High in yonder realms of light,	600
Ho! every one that thirsts, draw nigh,	64

Holy be this, as was the place,	320
Holy Ghost, dispel our sadness,	178
How are thy servants blest, O Lord,	13
How blest is our brother bereft	569
How blest the righteous are,	572
How blest the sacred tie that binds	420
How false this earth in all its forms,	250
How far, alas, in sinful ways,	245
How few the word of God regard,	300
How firm a foundation, ye saints of the	161
How great, how terrible that God,	39
How happy are they,	385
How long beneath the law I lay,	172
How lost was my condition,	135
How much the drooping hearts revive,	426
How oft, alas, this wretched heart,	157
How precious is the book divine,	19
How shall I my Saviour set forth,	66
How shall the sons of men appear,	142
How sweet, how heavenly is the sight,	215
How sweet the name of Jesus sounds,	264
How tedious and tasteless the hours,	239
How will my heart endure,	32
I ASK'D the Lord that I might grow,	244
If God had bid his thunders roll,	405
I hear a voice that comes from far,	381
I leave the world with willing feet,	388
I love thy kingdom, Lord,	297
I love to steal awhile away,	285
Indulgent Father, by whose care,	510
Indulgent Father, how divine,	6
Indulgent God of love and power,	490
Indulgent God, to thee we pray,	471
Infinite excellence is thine,	460
Inquire, ye pilgrims, for the way,	421
In sin by blinded passions led,	366
In songs of sublime adoration	151
Inspirer and hearer of prayer,	514
In thy great name, O Lord, we come,	323
In vain my fancy strives to paint,	571
In vain the giddy world inquires,	252
I own my guilt, my sins confess,	358
I saw, beyond the tomb,	83
I send the joys of earth away,	253
I soon shall accomplish my race,	597
It is the voice of love divine,	119
I wait a few sorrowful years,	578
JESUS, and shall it ever be,	410
Jesus, at thy command,	400
Jesus, dear name, how sweet the sound	72
Jesus, full of all compassion,	855
Jesus, great healer of mankind,	560

Jesus, lover of my soul,	255	My barns are full, my stores increase,	34
Jesus, my all, to heaven is gone,	139	My conscious guilt is now so great,	336
Jesus, my King, proclaims the war,	231	My dear Redeemer, and my Lord,	107
Jesus once left his throne on high,	224	My former hopes are fled,	344
Jesus, our best beloved friend,	413	My gracious Redeemer I love;	210
Jesus, Redeemer of mankind,	53	My lovely Jesus while on earth,	508
Jesus, thy blessings are not few,	55	My son, know thou the Lord,	540
Jesus, thy witness speaks within,	22	My soul, be on thy guard,	259
Jesus, who knows full well,	287	My soul doth magnify the Lord,	204
Just o'er the grave I hung,	563	My soul, thy hasty censure spare,	370
		My soul, with humble fervor, raise,	379
KEEP silence all created things,	146	My soul would fain indulge a hope,	202
Kindred and friends and native	500	My times of sorrow and of joy,	219
LADEN with guilt, and full of fears,	21	NATURE will raise up all her strife,	395
Let carnal minds the world pursue,	373	No more I ask or hope to find,	374
Let every mortal ear attend,	63	Not all the blood of beasts,	131
Let party names, no more;	214	Not all the nobles of the earth,	141
Let saints on earth their anthems raise,	485	Not the best deeds that we have done,	190
Let those who bear the Christian name,	222	Now begin the heavenly theme,	163
Let thy returning Spirit, Lord,	398	Now, gracious Lord, thine arm reveal,	524
Let us adore the grace that seeks,	152	Now, he who turns to God, shall live,	70
Let Zion's watchmen all awake,	292	Now is the accepted time,	81
Lift up your eyes, ye sons of light.	442	Now is the time, the accepted hour,	51
Light of those whose dreary dwelling,	132	Now let a true ambition rise,	541
Like her, who in Samaria's bound,	79	Now let our souls on wings sublime,	278
Like Israel, safe upon the shore,	393	Now let our voices join,	218
Long have I walk'd this dreary road,	341	Now may the Lord reveal his face,	153
Long unafflicted, undismay'd,	553	Now the shades of night are gone,	509
Look down, O God, with pitying eye,	476	Now we hail the happy dawning	428
Look down, O Lord, with pitying eye,	309		
Lo! on a narrow neck of land,	580	OBEDIENT to our Zion's King,	446
Lord, at thy feet, we sinners lie,	354	Of all the joys we mortals know,	211
Lord, dismiss us, with thy blessing,	326	Oft as the bell with solemn toll,	57
Lord, help me to repent,	96	O God of sovereign grace,	45
Lord, I am thine, entirely thine,	412	O God, whose favorable eye,	185
Lord, I'm defil'd in every part,	235	Oh, for a glance of heavenly day,	339
Lord, in the temples of thy grace,	318	Oh, for a thousand tongues to sing,	376
Lord, shall we part with gold for dross,	76	O happy soul, that lives on high,	273
Lord, thou with an unerring beam,	3	Oh, could I find from day to day,	145
Lord, when together here we meet,	532	Oh, could I find some peaceful bower,	198
Lost in a labyrinth of sin,	301	Oh, could our thoughts and wishes fly,	258
Love divine, all love excelling,	438	Oh, for a closer walk with God,	143
Lo! what a rapturous joy possess'd,	60	Oh, how divine, how sweet the joy,	425
		Oh, that I knew the secret place,	144
MAJESTIC sweetness sits enthron'd,	127	Oh, that my load of sin were gone,	346
May I resolve with all my heart,	414	Oh, that the Lord would hear my cry,	92
Men of God, go take your stations,	294	Oh, the sharp pangs of smarting pain,	88
Mercy, O thou Son of David,	365	Oh, turn, great Ruler of the skies,	93
Messiah, at thy glad approach,	440	Oh, what amazing words of grace,	45
Methinks the last great day is come,	589	Oh, when shall Afric's sable sons,	457
Millions there are on heathen ground,	475	Oh, where shall rest be found,	593
Mortals, awake, with angels join,	102	O Jesus, full of truth and grace,	100
Mountains of Israel, rear on high,	461	O Lord, another day is flown,	511

O Lord, how vile am I,	347
O Lord, my best desires fulfil,	223
O Lord, our languid souls inspire,	315
O Love divine, what hast thou done,	111
O my soul, what means this sadness,	200
Once I thought my mountain strong,	238
Once more before we part,	329
Once, O Lord, thy garden flourish'd,	298
Once, on the raging seas I rode,	138
One awful word which Jesus spoke,	31
One there is above all others,	126
On Tabor's top the Saviour stands,	108
On the mountain's top appearing,	434
O Sun of righteousness arise,	311
O Sun of righteousness divine,	299
O thou before whose gracious throne,	295
O thou from whom all goodness flows,	562
O thou great Monarch, in thy might,	453
O thou to whose all-searching sight,	257
O thou who dry'st the mourner's tear,	561
O thou who from thy glorious throne,	472
O thou whose tender mercy hears,	87
Our country is Immanuel's ground,	423
Our hearts are fastened to this world,	220
Our life, how short! a groan, a sigh,	584
Our little bark, on boisterous seas,	403
Our souls, by love together knit,	419
O'er the gloomy hills of darkness,	458
O Zion, tune thy voice,	431
PEOPLE of the living God,	415
Pilgrim, burden'd with thy sin,	270
Plung'd in a gulf of dark despair,	164
Poor sinners, little do they think,	340
Praise to the Lord on high,	293
Prayer is the soul's sincere desire,	288
Prayer was appointed to convey,	289
Prepare a thankful song,	165
Prostrate, dear Jesus, at thy feet,	91
RAISE, thoughtless sinner, raise	27
Rejoice, for Christ, the Saviour	430
Rejoice in God, the word commands,	391
Rejoice, the Lord is King,	124
Rejoicing now in glorious hope,	384
Religion is the chief concern,	542
Religion's form is vain,	291
Repent, the voice celestial cries,	38
Return, my roving heart, return,	280
Return, O wanderer, return,	68
Rise, my soul, and stretch thy wings,	277
SAINTS, with pious zeal attending,	17
Saviour, visit thy plantation,	305
Saviour, we wait the day,	261
Saw ye not the cloud arise,	436
Say, sinner, hath a voice within,	333
See from Zion's sacred mountain,	443
See, gracious Lord, before thy throne,	551
See, how rude winter's icy hand,	520
See, how the worthless bramble stands,	36
See human nature sunk in shame,	308
See Israel's gentle Shepherd stand,	448
See th' Eternal Judge descending,	587
Shall I, to gain the world's applause,	411
Shepherd of Israel thou didst lead,	468
Shepherds, rejoice, lift up your eyes,	103
Shepherd, who leadest with tender care,	449
Should God forbid the Sun to rise,	507
Since Jesus freely did appear,	528
Since we and all our treasures too,	194
Sing, how eternal love,	10
Sing, ye redeemed of the Lord,	377
Sinner, art thou still secure,	40
Sinner, behold I've heard thy groan,	342
Sinners, approach your dying Lord,	62
Sinners, behold that downward road,	26
Sinners, obey the gospel word,	61
Sinners, take the friendly warning,	588
Sinners, the voice of God regard,	69
Sinners, this solemn truth regard,	166
Sinners, will you scorn the message,	71
Smote by the law, I'm justly slain,	359
Soft be the gently breathing notes,	386
Sometimes a light surprises,	272
Sound, sound the truth abroad,	497
Sovereign grace hath power alone,	156
Sovereign of worlds above,	454
Sovereign of worlds, display thy power,	473
Sovereign Ruler, Lord of all,	95
Stay, thou insulted Spirit, stay,	182
Stop, poor sinners, stop and think,	43
Stretch'd on the cross, the Saviour dies,	110
Sure the blest Comforter is nigh,	175
Surrounded by a frightful gloom,	383
Sweet glories rush upon my sight,	595
Sweet peace of conscience, heavenly	216
Sweet the moments, rich in blessing,	265
Sweet was the time when first I felt,	243
TEACH us, O Lord, the great concern,	78
Thankless, the prodigal receives,	368
That awful day will surely come,	586
That mighty angel to whose hand,	465
The billows swell, the winds are high,	558
The castle of the human heart,	363
The christian voyager strikes the rock,	399
The day is drawing nigh,	437

The day is past and gone,	512	'Tis finish'd, the conflict is past,	570
The day, the gospel day draws near	418	'Tis first of all thyself to know,	236
The deluge at th' Almighty's call,	162	'Tis hard from those we love, to go,	564
The eye of God is every where,	4	'Tis midnight—and on Olive's brow,	109
The flow'ry spring, at God's command,	523	'Tis ours to sojourn in a waste,	321
The giddy world, with flattering tongue,	387	'Tis past—the dreadful stormy night,	402
The God of my salvation lives,	226	To-day, if ye will hear his voice,	83
The God who once to Israel spoke,	543	To God I cried when troubles rose,	160
The grave is now a favor'd spot,	567	To-morrow, Lord, is thine,	84
The happy in Jesus may sleep,	397	To the cross where Jesus dies,	116
The joy that vain amusements give,	545	To whom, my Saviour, shall I go,	408
The Lord of life, the Saviour dies,	89	Trembling before thine awful throne,	97
The Lord of light, tho' veil'd awhile,	268		
The Lord on mortal worms looks down,	491	UNHAPPY city, hadst thou known,	52
The Lord receives his highest praise,	191	United prayers ascend to thee,	447
The Lord will happiness divine,	188	Unveil thy bosom, faithful tomb,	568
The Lord will not forget the grace,	470		
The mighty flood that rolls along,	577	VAIN man, thy fond pursuits forbear,	591
The mighty frame of glorious grace,	120		
The moment a sinner believes,	189	WAIT, O my soul, thy Maker's will,	147
The new-born child of gospel grace,	389	Weary of struggling with my pain,	357
The night shall hear me raise my song,	513	"We've no abiding city here,"	422
The once-lov'd form now cold and dead,	574	Welcome, welcome, dear Redeemer,	360
The prodigal, with streaming eyes,	369	Welcome, ye hopeful heirs of heaven,	417
The ransom'd spirit to her home,	209	Were once our vain desires subdued,	555
There is a fountain fill'd with blood,	128	We wander in a thorny maze,	546
There is a God who reigns above,	1	What is the thing of greatest price,	75
There is a voice of sovereign grace,	46	What jarring natures dwell within,	233
The saints who now in Jesus sleep,	583	What must I do? the Jailor cries	362
The Saviour calls, let every ear,	44	What shall the dying sinner do,	173
The Saviour, Oh, what endless charms,	137	What sinners value I resign,	199
The sinner's flattering dreams are fled,	361	What think ye of Christ? is the test,	140
The sovereign Father, good and kind,	396	What, tho' the arm of conquering death,	296
The Spirit breathes upon the word,	24	What various hind'rances we meet,	286
The summer harvest spreads the field,	522	When any turn from Zion's way,	406
The time is short, the season near,	576	When bending o'er the brink of life,	590
The trump of Israel's Jubilee,	463	When blooming youth is snatch'd away,	573
The voice that bids us all repent,	338	When frowning death appears,	37
The winter past, reviving flowers,	581	When gathering clouds around I view,	186
Thine earthly Sabbaths, Lord, we love,	519	When I can read my title clear,	274
This God is the God we adore,	328	When I survey the wondrous cross,	262
Tho' in the earthly church below,	304	When I the blest Redeemer see,	263
Tho' now the nations sit beneath,	464	When Jesus bade me leave the world,	416
Thou great Physician of the soul,	352	When Jesus dwelt in mortal clay,	502
Thou only Sovereign of my heart,	407	When languor and disease invade,	556
Thrice happy souls, who born of heaven,	275	When low'ring clouds deform the sky,	349
Thro' all the changing scenes of life,	225	When on the third auspicious day,	517
Thro' Christ when we together came	534	When night descends in sable guise,	394
Thro' sorrow's night and danger's path,	582	When renovating grace begins,	392
Thro' this wide wilderness I roam,	266	When rising from the bed of death,	585
Thy people, Lord, who trust thy word,	451	When the Eternal bows the skies,	2
Thy presence, gracious God, afford,	317	When the poor leper's case I read,	74
'Tis a point I long to know,	212	When we with welcome slumber,	505
'Tis finish'd, so the Saviour cried,	114	When will the happy trump proclaim,	479

When with my mind devoutly press'd,	404
Where are the dead? in heaven or hell,	592
Wherefore should man, frail child of	203
Where is my God? does he retire,	125
Where is now our boasted Saviour,	240
Where shall we sinners hide our heads?	170
While I to grief my soul gave way,	424
While life prolongs its precious light,	82
While Sinai roars, and round the earth,	171
While the heralds of salvation,	504
Whilst thee I seek, protecting Power,	281
Who but thou, Almighty Spirit,	478
Why should the christian waste in sighs,	554
Why sinks my weak desponding mind,	201
With cheerful voices rise and sing,	530
With conscious guilt and bleeding heart,	99
With grateful hearts and tuneful lays,	529
With humble heart and tongue,	548
With kind compassion hear my cry,	356
With reverend awe, tremendous Lord,	433
With tears of anguish, I lament,	234
World, adieu, thou real cheat,	249
YE angels, who stand round the	599
Ye dying sons of men,	56
Ye glittering toys of earth, adieu,	133
Ye hearts, with youthful vigor warm,	547
Ye humble souls, complain no more,	196
Ye lovely bands of blooming youth,	544
Ye messengers of Christ,	493
Ye mourning sinners, here disclose,	73
Ye saints, assist me in my song,	382
Ye servants of God,	16
Ye sons of men, with joy record,	8
Yes, we trust the day is breaking,	429
Ye, who in former days,	42
Ye wretched, hungry, starving poor,	54
Yonder, amazing sight! I see,	112
ZEAL is that pure and heavenly flame,	230

A TABLE

Book	Ch.	ver.	Hymn #
Genesis.			
	5.	24.	143.
	6.	3.	333.
			334.
	18.	19.	290.
	24.	56.	416.
	28.	17.	320.
Numbers.			
	6.	25, 26.	330.
	13.		384.
	23.	10.	572.
Deuteronomy.			
	8.	2.	266.
	33.	27.	254, 255.
Joshua.			
	24.	15.	414.
Judges.			
	16.	20.	174.
Ruth.			
	1.	16-19.	415.
1 Samuel.			
	1.	12.	439.
	15.	32.	590.
	30.	6.	201.
1 Kings.			
	18.	44.	436.
1 Chronicles.			
	28.	9.	540.
Nehemiah.			
	5.	19.	562.
Esther.			
	4.	16.	77.
Job.			
	3.	17.	567.
	14.	2.	539.
	16.	22.	578.
	17.	1-11.	578.
	23.	3.	144.
	27.	8.	291.
	29.	2.	243.
Psalms.			
	4.	6.	252.
	6.	92.	
	7.	11.	41.
	13.		398.
	32.	7.	349.
	34.		225.
	36.	9.	271.
			272.
	37.	4.	187.
	42.	5.	200.
	43.	5.	392.

45.	3-5.	169.		-	7.	69.
		312.		55.	7.	70.
48.	14.	276.		-	10-11.	310.
51.	9-13.	93.		-	12-13.	440.
-	11.	182.		57.	15.	188.
65.	11.	523.		58.	1.	294.
85.	6.	305.		60.	1.	431.
87.	3.	462.				480.
90.	59.	577.		-	2.	464.
103.	14.	379.		-	8.	437.
104.	34.	556.		63.	7.	9.
107.	17-20.	361.		66.	2.	2.
-	30.	399.	Jeremiah.			
		400.		3.	22.	157.
-	31.	8.		8.	20.	33.
112.	4.	561.		-	22.	134.
119.	9.	548.				135.
-	67.	553.		17.	5, 6.	36.
-	158.	308.		-	9.	345.
133.	1.	215		23.	29.	433.
137.	5-6.	297.		31.	3.	151.
138.	5.	218.		-	6.	463.
139.	3.			-	18-20.	68.
Proverbs.			Ezekiel.			
3.	13.	229.		36.	8.	461.
4.	7.	78.		-	37.	306.
8.	17.	547.		37.	3.	309.
15.	3.	4.	Daniel.			
18.	24.	126.		5.	5, 6.	340.
23.	17.	275.		-	27.	27.
Ecclesiastes.			Hosea.			
9.	5.	592.		14.	1, 2.	100.
12.	7.	566.		-	4.	157.
Canticles.			Joel.			
3.	11.	123.		1.	14.	551.
5.	10.	127	Amos.			
Isaiah.				7.	2.	302.
2.	2.	486.	Jonah.			
9.	2.	132.		3.	9.	343.
12.	2.	228.	Micah.			
24.	18-20.	39.		4.	15.	481.
36	1-2.	418.	Habakkuk.			
30.	33.	28.		2.	17, 18.	226.
32.	2.	129.				272.
		130.	Haggai.			
33.	20-21.	462.		2.	7.	460.
35.	10.	377.	Zechariah.			
		378.		12.	10.	86, 88.
44.	23.	5.		13.	1.	128.
51.	9.	477.				443.
52.	7.	434.	Malachi.			
-	10.	429.		3.	16.	491.
53.	1.	300.				
55.	1-2	63, 64.				

Matthew.			
	2.	1, 2.	138.
	5.	3.	196.
	6.	6.	279.
			280.
	-	10.	483.
		33.	484.
			541.
	7.	12.	206.
	-	13, 14.	26.
	8.	2, 3.	74.
	-	24.	399.
	11.	28.	350.
			351.
	-	28, 30.	57, 58, 59.
	13.	39.	522.
	-	37-42.	304.
	-	46.	133.
	15.	19.	45.
	22.	42.	140.
	24.	44.	591.
	26.	41.	259, 260.
	26.	41.	261.
	28.	18.	474.
Mark.			
	1.	35.	508.
	8.	34.	221.
	-	36.	75, 76.
	-	38.	183.
			410, 411.
	9.	43, 44.	28.
	10.	14.	448.
			449.
	-	48.	355.
			356.
			365, 475.
	11.	20.	31.
	16.	15.	498.
Luke.			
	1.	46.	204.
	-	78.	482.
	2.		814.	103.
				104.
	6.	19.	73.
	7.	36-50.	90.
	-	37-50.	348.
	-	47.	159.
	9.	28-31.	108.
	10.	30-37.	503.
	11.	21-22.	363.
	12.	16-21.	34.
	13.	23.	25.
	-	28.	587.
	14.	17.	61.
		22.	54, 55, 56.
		23.	65.
	15.	10.	425.
	-	11-24.	368.
			369.
			370.
	-	20-24.	60.
	18.	1-7.	287.
	19.	41.	248.
	-	42.	52,53.
			156.
	23.	39-43.	158.
	4.	50, 51.	119.
John.			
	1.	12.	141.
	-	29.	131.
	-	39.	72.
	3. 5-7.	166.	
			168.
	-	14.	47.
		4.	79, 80.
	4.	35.	442.
	-	42.	137.
	-	46-49.	560.
	5.	2-9.	371.
	6.	67-69.	406.
			407.
			408.
	7.	37.	44, 45, 46.
	9.	4.	85.
			549.
	14.	2.	600.
	-	6.	139.
			142.
	-	16, 17.	175.
	-	26.	179.
			180.
	19.	30.	113.
			114.
	20.	28.	140.
	21.	15.	212.
Acts.			
	8.	8.	426.
	9.	11.	288.
	10.	38.	502.
	16.	30, 31.	362.
	17.	30.	38.
	24.	16.	216.
Romans.			
	1.	16.	173.
		17.	189.
	3.	16.	37.
	5.	21.	153.
	7.	9.	359.

	8.	14.	316.	James.		
	10.	1.	467, 468.		4.	13, 14.	84.
			469.	1 Peter.		
	13.	11.			2.	7.	264.
1 Corinthians.					3.	20.	162.
	2.	9.	208.		5.	8.	394.
	4.	7.	151.	2 Peter.		
	6.	19.	256.		1.	4.	161.
	7.	29.	576.		2.	22.	42.
	13.	1-3.	213.	1 John.		
	-	8.	207.		2.	1.	125.
	15.	57.	594.		3.	1.	141.
2 Corinthians.					4.	8.	7.
	2.	15, 16.	293.		-	10.	382.
	4.	6.	392.	Revelation.		
	-	18.	258.		3.	20.	48, 49.
	5.	17.	373.				50, 51.
			374.		14.	2, 3.	487.
			404.		-	6.	465.
	6.	2.	81, 82, 83.				466.
	-	17, 18.	152.		15.	3.	375.
	13.	5.	286.		20.	11.	32.
			237.		-	12.	589.
Galatians.					21.	4.	559.
	3.	28.	214.		22.	17.	45
			215.				
	6.	14.	262.				
Ephesians.							
	2.	5.	154.				
			155.				
	-	18.	11.				
	4.	30.	335.				
	6.	13-17.	231.				
Philippians.							
	1.	6.	160.				
	2.	8, 9.	120.				
	4.	4.	124.				
	-	8.	222.				
Colossians.							
	2.	2.	419.				
		15.	120.				
	3.	1.	450.				
1 Thessalonians.							
	5.	17.	289.				
Hebrews.							
	4.	7.	30.				
	-	9.	519.				
	-	13.	4.				
	-	15.	186.				
	7.	25.	122.				
	12.	5-11.	552.				
	-	22-24.	267, 268.				
	13.	14.	422.				
	-	17.	292.				

INDEX OF SUBJECTS.

A.
Absence from God, 407, 408.
Accepted time. 51, 81-85.
Adieu, vain world. 249, 252.
Adoption, 141.
Advocate. Christ our, 122, 125.
Afflictions needful, 552-555.
   resignation to, 219, 220, 223.
   support under, 556, 559 561.
   sweetened, 556.
Age, middle. 549.
   old, 550.
Africa, prayer for, 457.
Alarm, the, 43.
Alarming, 25-43, 585-589.
All things ready, 61.
Alms, 502-554, 184.
Angel flying, 465, 466.
Angels ready, 61.
Ark for believers, 162.
Ascension of Christ, 118-121.
Ashamed, not, 183, 410, 411.
Atonement, 142, 262-265, 110, 116, 131.
Attributes of God 3, 4.
Awakened sinner, 332-343.

B.
Backsliding, danger of, 409.
   and returning, 245-248.
   prayer against, 406-409.
Balaam's wish, 572.
Baptism, 446-450.
   adult, 446, 450.
   household 447, 448.
   infant, 448, 449.
Bartimeus, 365.
Bethlehem, Star of, 135.
Bramble, 36.
Brazen Serpent, 47.
Broad and narrow way, 25, 26.
Brotherly love, 214, 215, 419.

C.
Call, the Lord's, 152.
Calvary, 111-114.
   voice from, 381.
   and Sinai, 435.
Canaan, way to, 139.
Carnal joys, 253, 573.
Characters of Christ, 12-140.
Charity, 184.
Children, baptized, 448, 449.
   of the church, prayer for, 303.
   death of 574.

Christ, 102-140.
   advocate, 125.
   ark for believers, 162.
   ascension of, 118-121.
   ashamed, of not, 410, 411.
   characters of, 125-140.
   coronation of, 123.
   crucified, 110-112.
   death and resurrection of, 110-116.
   desire of all nations, 460.
   example, 106, 107.
   excellencies of, 66.
   finishing his work, 113, 114.
   fountain 128, 443.
   friend, 126, 127.
   in Gethsemane, 109.
   hiding-place, 129, 130, 349.
   intercession of, 122.
   inviting sinners, 44-46.
   kingdom of, 124, 314, 483, 484.
   knocking at the door, 48-51.
   lamb of God, 131.
   light, 132.
   love to, 210-212.
   message of, 105.
   my Lord and my God, 140.
   nativity of, 102.
   pearl of great price, 183.
   physician 73, 74, 134, 135, 371.
   precious, 264.
   priest, 136.
   prince of peace, 485.
   redeemer, 164, 165, 167.
   reigning, 115, 444, 445, 486, 487.
   refuge, 254, 255.
   resurrection of, 117.
   Saviour, 137.
   Star of Bethlehem, 135.
   submission to, 224.
   sufferings of, 110-116.
   transfiguration of, 108.
   trust in, 225.
   way to Canaan, 139.
   weeping, 52, 53, 248.
Christian, backsliding and returning, 245-247.
   bidding adieu to the vain world, 249, 252, 273, 274.
   in darkness, 283, 240.
   encouraged, 201.
   enjoying light, 271-273.
   examination, 212, 236, 237.
   his faith fainting, 241.
   fearing God, 275.
   forsaken, yet hoping, 242.

hope of, 199.
inviting sinners 54, 56-59.
has joys unseen, 258.
journeying to heaven, 423.
mariner, 400.
mourning, 234, 235.
parting with carnal joys, 250.
pilgrim, 266, 270.
rejoicing in a revival, 424-445.
rising to God, 278.
singing, 277.
sitting at Jesus' feet, 265.
supported by hope, 274.
trembling, 202.
watching and praying, 259, 261.
Christian love, 214, 215, 419, 420, 531, 537.
friends welcomed, 531.
—parting, 532-537.
Church, love to, 297.
prayer for 483, 484, 314 302.
glory of, 479-482, 486, 487.
wheat and tares in, 304.
meetings, 303, 205, 307.
City of God, 462.
of refuge, 418.
no abiding, 422.
wept over, 52.
Collections, 502-504, 184, 489-492.
Come and see, 72.
Comfort of forgiveness, 159, 97, 379.
from hope of heaven, 274.
true and false, 184.
Communion with God, 143, 145.
with saints, 419, 420, 214, 215.
Company, evil, 287.
Concert, monthly, 451-487.
Conference, 315-324.
Confession, 86-101.
Confidence in Christ, 186.
Conscience, peace of, 216, 273, 131, 217.
tender, 94.
Contrite heart, 96, 188.
Contributions, 502-504, 184.
Conversion, 361-371.
effected by divine power, 366.
gives joy to saints, 425, 426.
necessity of, 367.
Convert, 372-423.
in darkness, 391-397.
humbled, 389, 390.
true, 404, 405.
Conviction, 344-361.
and conversion, 361-371.
Coronation of Christ, 123.

Cross of Christ, 110-116.
our glory, 181.
crucifixion to the world by it, 262, 263.
D.
Danger, of delay, 33, 51.
of death, 85.
of hell, 28, 29.
Darkness, Christian in, 238-240.
new convert in, 391-397.
light in, 561.
Day of Judgment, 585-589.
of glory to the church, 479.
Death, approaching, 85.
of a child, 574.
of Christ, 110-115.
of a brother, 569.
of men, 565-575.
preparation for, 591.
of a minister, 296, 565, 566.
of a saint, 571, 572.
of the sinner, 37.
of a sister, 570.
of a person, 573.
Death and Heaven, 590, 600.
Declension lamented, 298-392.
Decrees of God, 146, 147.
Dedication, self, 412, 413.
Delay, 33, 51, 333-336.
Deliverance from evil companions, 387, 388.
Satan, 363.
sin, 364.
temptation, 388.
Depravity, 148-150, 308, 309, 345.
Desert, wandering in, 394.
Destruction, escaping from, 26.
multitudes in the way of, 25.
Devotion, secret, 279, 280.
Dismission, 326, 331.
Doctrines, 141-170.
Door, 48-51.
Dress, 195, 203.
E.
Efficacious grace, 169.
Eternity, 579, 589.
Evening, 510-514.
and morning, 6.
Saturday, 515.
Sabbath, 518.
Examination, self, 212, 236, 227.
Example of Christ, 106, 107.
F.
Faith, connected with salvation, 190.
conquering, 189.
fainting, 241.

living and dead, 191.
Faith, power of, 192.
  in suffering, 308.
Fall of man, 308, 309.
Family worship, 290.
Fathers, where, 577.
Fear of God, 275.
Feast of the gospel, 54.
  invitation to, 63.
Fellowship with christians, 214, 215, 419, 420, 531-537.
Few saved, 25, 26.
Fields white for harvest, 442.
Fig-tree, 31.
Finished, 113, 114.
Flood, 162.
Forgiveness of sin, 389.
  joy of, 97, 379, 159.
Forms without love, 291, 213.
Fortitude, holy 193.
Fountain, 79, 80, 204.
  opened in Zion, 443.
Frailty of life, 577, 539, 584.
Friend, Christ our, 126, 127, 48.
Friends welcome, 531.
  parted with, 532-537.
Funeral, 82, 84, 85, 565-575.
  of ministers, 565, 296, 566.
  of a saint, 566, 571.
  of a child, 574.
  of a youth, 573.

G.
Garden of Gethsemane, 109, 136.
Gideon, 389.
GOD, 1-13.
  angry with the wicked, 41.
  communion with, 143-145, 187.
  condescension of, 2.
  decrees of, 146, 147.
  dedication to, 412-414.
  delight in, 187.
  eternal and exalted, 15.
  fear of, 275.
  fountain of light, 271, 272.
  glorified in redemption, 5-6.
  goodness and mercy of, 8.
  love to, 207-209, 225.
  love and mercy of, 10.
  is love, 7, 8.
  loving-kindness of, 9.
  omniscience and omnipresence, 3, 4.
  people of, 415.
  pilgrim's guide, 276.
  praised, 16-18.
  providence, mysteries of, 12.
  rising to, 278.
  servants of, always safe, 13.
  temple of, our bodies, 256.
  trust in, 226-228.
Gospel, doctrines of, 141, 170.
  excellence of, 21.
  and law, 171-13.
  free offer of, 64.
  power of, 22, 173.
  pool, 371.
  prayer for spread of, 451-459, 464, 471-477.
  suited to our wants, 45, 55.
Grace, efficacious, 169.
  and nature, conflict of, 395.
  miracle of, 380.
  necessity of, 300.
  prayer for, 257.
  reigning, 153.
  salvation by, 154-156.
  sovereign, 156.
Graces of the Spirit, 183-230.
Gratitude, humble, 194.
Grave, the, 567, 568.
Gravity and decency, 195,

H.
Happiness in God only, 273.
Happy change, 366.
  poverty, 196.
Hardness of heart, 338, 339.
Harvest, fields white for, 442.
  past, 33.
  the great, 522.
Hatred of sin, 197, 198.
Heart contrite, 188.
  given to God, 373.
  hard, 338, 339.
  sinful, 345.
  taken, 363.
Heaven, hope of, 274.
  panting for, 599.
  prospect of, 384, 595.
  song of, 596.
Heavenly joy on earth, 205.
Hell, 28, 29.
Hiding-place, 129, 130, 319.
Hinder me not, 416.
Holy Spirit, breathing after, 177.
  graces of, 183.
  influences of, 175, 306, 307, 309, 310.
  insensibly withdrawn, 174.
  invocation to, 176.
  joy in, 204.
  prayer to, 178-182, 316.

prayer for, 478.
Hope, christian, 199.
  encouraged, 200, 201.
  a support, 274.
  trembling, 202.
Humility, 203.
Hypocrite, 291, 185.
I.
Indwelling sin lamented, 234, 235.
Intercession of Christ, 122.
Inviting, 44-85.
Invitations of Christ to sinners, 44-51, 57, 64.
Invocation of the Holy Spirit, 176-182.
Israel, prayer for, 467-469.
  restoration of 461, 463, 470.
J.
Jacob, by whom arise, 302.
Jailor, 362.
Jerusalem, wept over, 52.
Jesus, (see Christ).
Jews, (see Israel).
Joy in sorrow, 557.
Judgment day, 32, 39, 40, 522, 585-589.
Justice and equity, 206.
K.
Kingdom of Christ, 124.
  love to, 297.
  prayed for, 314, 483, 484.
  triumphant, 479-482, 486, 487.
Knocking at the door, 48-51.
Knowledge vain without love, 213.
L.
Lamb of God, 131.
Law and Gospel, 171-173, 435.
Leper healed, 74.
Life, the accepted time, 82.
Light, Christ the, 132.
  in darkness, 561.
Living and dead faith, 191.
Lord's Supper, 417, (see sacramental).
Love to God, 207-209, 225.
  to the Church, 297.
  to Christ, 210-212.
  nothing without, 213.
  to Christians, 214, 215, 419, 420.
  redeeming, 382.
  divine 111, 438.
Loving-kindness, 9.
M.
Mariner, 13, 138, 399, 403.
Marriage, 528-530, 420, 316.
Mary, 90.
  weeping, 348.
Mercies remembered, 439.

Mercy of God, 10, 354-356.
  message of, 71.
Messiah, his reign, 440, 441.
Midnight, 109.
Millennium, 479-487.
Ministers, watchmen, 202.
  loss of, 296.
  a sweet savor, 293.
  sick, prayer for, 295.
  rejoicing, 426.
  their work, 204.
  funeral of, 565, 296.
Misery and sin, 148-150.
Missionary meetings, 488-501, 294.
  collections, 502, 504.
Missionaries, ordination of, 493-498.
  departure of, 493-498.
  farewell of, 500, 501.
  farewell to, 490.
Monthly concert, 451-487.
Morning, 505-509, 275.
  and evening, 6, 275.
Multitude in the road to destruction, 25, 26.
N.
Narrow way, 26.
Nature and grace, 395, 396.
New birth, 73.
  necessity of, 367.
  convert humbled, 389, 390.
New-Year, 524-526.
  close of, 527.
Night, coming, 85.
  Saturday, 515.
Nightingale, 282.
Noah, 162.
O.
Ordination of ministers, 292-294, 431.
  of missionaries, 493-498.
P.
Pardon, 137, 379, 380, 111.
  for the greatest sins, 159.
  and sanctification, 170.
Peace of conscience, 216, 217.
Penitential, 86-101.
Penitent, the, 90, 91.
  prayer of, 92-101.
Pearl of great price, 133.
Perseverance, 160-162.
Physician, Christ the, 73, 74.
  of souls, 134, 135, 371.
Pilgrim, 266-270, 276.
  rejoicing on his way, 218, 377, 379.
  asking the way to Zion, 421.
  his guide, 276.

seeking a city, 422, 423.
his song, 277.
Pleasures unseen, 258.
Pool, the gospel, 371.
Poor, the friends of, 184.
Poverty, happy, 196.
Praise, universal, 14-18.
to God, 17-18.
to the Trinity, 14.
to the Redeemer, 385.
for redemption, 382, 383.
Prayer for Africa, 457.
answered, 364, 365.
prayer answered by crosses, 244.
for Christ's presence, 315, 318, 319.
for children, 303.
exhortation to, 108, 286-289.
for the kingdom of Christ, 314, 451-459, 464-477.
to be kept from backsliding, 406-409.
for the Spirit, 478.
to the Spirit, 176-182, 316.
for deliverance from sin, 94.
of a parent, 560.
for peace of mind, 217.
to be remembered, 562.
for a revival, 305-312.
for opposers of revivals, 313.
for repentance, 96.
for mercy, 354-356, 365.
for the spread of the gospel 451-459, 464, 471-477.
for spiritual healing, 352, 353.
for sinners, 300.
for the Jews, 467-469.
and watchfulness, 259-261, 270.
Pride, folly of, 203.
Priest, Christ our, 136.
Prince of Peace, 485.
Prodigal, 368, 370.
returning, 369, 60.
Profession, false, 31.
Promises, precious, 461.
Prospect of heaven, 384.
Providence, 12.
R.
Redeeming love, 382, 163.
Redemption by Christ, 163-165.
exhibits the glories of God, 5.
Redeemer, his message, 105.
Reflections, sick-bed, 563, 564.
Refuge, 254, 255.
city of, 418.
Regeneration, 166-168.

Rejoicing, 218, 377, 378.
in a revival, 424-445.
Religion, 78, 542.
a revival of, 424-445.
prayed for 305-314.
triumph of, 441.
vain without love, 213.
its support, 274.
Repentance, 38, 86-95.
Resignation, 219, 220, 223.
Resolution noblest, 414.
Resolve, 77.
Resurrection, 581-584.
of Christ, 117, 120, 121.
Returning sinner, 372.
backslider, 245, 246.
to Zion, 377.
Revival of religion, 424-445.
prayed for, 305-314.
beginning, 427-432, 436, 437.
enjoyed, 424-445.
Riches, their vanity, 36.
danger of, 34-36.
Rich sinner dying, 34, 35.
Rising to God, 278.
S.
Sabbath, 516, 517.
the eternal, 519.
Sabbath evening, 518.
Sacramental, 412, 413, 417, 419, 420, 89, 109-116.
Sacrifices, 131, 89, 112.
Saint, (see Christian and Convert).
Saints and sinners in the wreck of nature, 39.
Sailors, 13, 138, 399-403.
Salvation, by grace, 154-156.
connected with faith, 190.
Sanctification and pardon, 170.
Samaria, woman of, 79, 80.
Satan subdued, 363.
Saturday Night, 515.
Saviour, (see Christ).
Scoffer addressed, 29, 398.
Scriptures, 19-24.
excellence of, 21, 20.
a lamp, 19.
glory of, 24.
attended with the Spirit, 22.
reveal Christ, 23.
Seasons, 523.
Secret devotion, 279-285.
Self-denial, 221.
Self examination, 212, 236, 237, 202.
Servants of God always safe, 13.

should praise him, 16.
Serpent raised by Moses, 47.
Shame, 183, 410, 411, 562.
Sick-bed reflections, 563, 564.
Sincerity and truth, 222.
Sinai, 171, 583, 7.
   and Calvary, 435.
Sin bewailed, 351.
Sin and misery, 148-150.
   effects of it, 352, 308, 309.
   forgiven, 97, 379.
Sin, hatred of it, 198, 197.
   indwelling, 234, 235.
Sinner addressed, 26-30, 38, 40, 43, 56-62.
   awakened, 332-343.
   burdened, 346, 350.
   complaint of, 341.
   confessing his sin, 50.
   convicted, 344-348.
   condemned, 41.
   cured, 371.
   in danger by delay, 51.
   expostulation with, 71.
Sinner, forgiven, 379, 380.
   friend of, 126, 127.
   God's answer to, 342.
   hiding place for, 349.
   invited by Christ, 48-52, 44.
   invited to Christ, 45-74.
   invited by Christians, 54, 56-59.
   in the hour of death, 33, 37.
   in the judgment, 39, 51.
   looking back, 42.
   lamenting, 332, 334, 336, 337.
   the hardness of his heart, 339, 345, 347.
   mourning, invited, 73.
   must be born again, 367.
   prayer of a penitent, 92-95, 350-356.
   prepare to meet God, 40.
   prayer to Christ for, 53.
   repenting, 86-91.
   resolving to go to Christ, 77.
   returning, 72.
   requested to stop, 43.
   slain and reviving, 359.
   submitting to God, 357, 358.
   trembling, 340, 343, 344.
   sitting at Jesus' feet, 265.
Song, the pilgrim's, 277.
   of Moses and the Lamb, 375.
Sorrow, joy in, 557.
Soul, its worth, 75, 76.
Spirit, Holy, his influences, 306, 307, 309, 310.
Spring, 521.

Star of Bethlehem, 138.
Storm at Sea, 13.
   hushed, 402.
   refuge from, 254, 255, 349.
Submission, 223, 219, 220.
   to Christ, 224.
Sufferings and death of Christ, 110-116.
   faith in, 398.
Summer, 522.
Surrender, the, 360.
T.
Temptations, 388.
   billows of, 558.
Tender conscience, 93, 94.
Thanksgiving, 439, 523, 379, 6, 8, 18, 194, 375, 376, 158.
Thief, 128, 156, 158.
Thunder, 349, 433, 171.
Time and eternity, 476-480.
Times and Seasons, 505-564.
Today, 80, 81, 83-85.
   the accepted time, 81, 83-85.
Tomorrow, 84.
Transfiguration, 108.
Traveller, 13, 267, 268, 275, 277.
Trinity, 11, 14.
Trust in Christ, 223.
Trust in God, 225-227.
Truth and sincerity, 222.
Twilight, 285.
U.
Unbelief, 228.
Universal praise, 14-18,
Unseen pleasures, 258.
V.
Vanity of the world, 545.
Vision of dry bones, 309.
W.
Water of life, 79, 80.
Wanderer, 546.
   invited to return, 68.
   restored, 439.
Warfare, the Christian, 231-233, 395, 396.
Watch and pray, 258-261.
   and knock, 270.
Watching for souls, 292.
Wicked, God angry with, 41.
   way of, 69.
Wheat and tares, 304.
Winter, 520.
Wisdom, true, 229
Who can tell, 343.
Woman of Samaria, 79, 80.
Word of God, its efficacy, 443.

World, crucified to, 262, 263.
    end of, 39.
    not our home, 422, 423.
    vanity of, 545.
Worldling, 34-36.
Worship, 279-331.
    private, 279-285.
    family, 290.
    social, 286-289.
    public, 317-331.
    place of, 325, 318-321.
    beginning of, 317, 320, 323.
    preparation for, 322.
    delightful, 322, 324.
    formality in, 291.
    dismission of, 326-329, 71, 587, 588.
Wrath, coming, 41.
Wreck of nature, 29.
Y.
Year, New, 524-526.
    seasons of, 523, 520-522, 527.
Youth, 538-548.
    prayer for, 303.
    prayer of, 548.
    invitation to, 83.
    death of, 573.
Z.
Zeal, true and false, 230.
Zion, gate of, knocking at, 270.
    returning to, 377.
    asking the way to, 421.
    restored, 434.
    fountain in, 443.
    prospects of, 479.
    thing spoken of, 462.
    arise and shine, 480.

A TABLE OF TUNES.

LONG METRES.

Sharp Key.

All Saints
Angel's Hymn
Antigua
Bath
Bedford
Bicester
Blendon
Brentford
Castle Street
Chatham
China
Cumberland
Dresden
Evening Hymn
Gloucester
Green's 100th
Halifax
Haverhill
Hinton
Islington
Italy
Kent
Leeds
Leyden
Loving kindness
Luther's Hymn
Luton
Lutzen
Malmsbury
Moreton
Morning Hymn
Nantwich
New Hundredth
Old Hundred
Philadelphia
Pleyel's
Portugal
Quercy
Quito
Richmond
Rothwell
Shoel
Sicilian
Sterling
St. Catharine's
St. Peter's
Spring
Tallis' E. H.
Truro
Vanhall's H.
Wells
Winchester

Flat Key.

Antworth
Armley
Babylon
Brookfield
Darwent
Geneva
German
Kingsbridge
Limehouse
Limerick

Munich
Norfolk
Putney
Sheerness
Surry
Virginia
Warwick
Washington

COMMON METRES.
Sharp Key.

Abingdon
Abridge
Arlington
Arundel
Barby
Bedford
Bradford
Braintree
Bray
Brighton
Canterbury
Carthage
Christmas
Clarendon
Clifford
Colchester
Dundee
Exeter
Florence
Harborough
Herman
Hymn 2d.
Invitation
Irish
Keene
Mear
Missionary
Newark
New Cambridge
Newmark
Newton
Parma
Plymouth
Rochester
Swanwick
St. Ann's
St. Asaph's
St. Martin's
Springfield
Stade
Steffani's
Tempest

Wareham
Washington
York
Zion

Flat Key.

Bangor
Buckingham
Cambridge
Chapel
Dorset
Elgin
Funeral Hymn
Fiducia
Lebanon
Martyr's
Mitcham
Reading
St. Mary's
Standish
Tunbridge
Walsal
Wantage
Windsor

SHORT METRES.
Sharp Key.

Colchester
Dover
Durham
Eastburn
Froome
Lisbon
Lowel
Northampton
Peckham
Pelham
St. Thomas
Shirland
Sicily
Silver Street
Watchman

Flat Key.

Aylesbury
Bridgeport
Bingham
Dunbar
Guilford
Little Marlboro'
Maryland

St. Bridges			Drummond		Love Divine
Wirksworth			Eastarbook		Northampton Chap.
Yarmouth			Gethsemane		Sicilian Hymn
			Good Shepherd		Tabernacle
Hallelujah Metres.			Hampshire		
Allerton		Bethesda			
Eagle Street		Jubilee	7, 6		
Portsmouth		Providence			
Psalm 148th		Triumph	Amsterdam		Hymn 5th
Troy		Watchman	Brighthelmstone		Kingswood
Weymouth		Whitechurch	Entreaty		Lancaster
			Fairlax		Margate
Sevens.			Newton		Romain
Alcester		Alsen	8, 7, 4.		
Anna's Lute		Bath Abbey			
Condolence		Cookham	Calvary		Kershaw
Easter Hymn		Epiphany	Dismission		Littleton
Fairfax		Falmouth	Farnsworth		Tamworth
Hampton		Hotham	Helmsley		Wilna
Magdalen		Middleton	Jordan		
Pastoral Duet		Pilgrim's Hymn			
Pleyel's		Redeeming Love	5, 6.		
Somerset		Sovereign Grace			
Trevecca			Chestnut		Locke
			Devonshire		New Castle
6 Line 7s.			Harwich		Sussex
			Walsal		
Bloxham		Finedon			
Montpelier		Mount Calvary	11.		
Turin			Hinton		St. Dennis
			Idumea		Walsal
Eights.					
			6, 4.		
Bethany	Franklin	Consolation			
Lambeth	Mitcham	New Jerusalem	Bermondsey		St. Clemens
Uxbridge	Dismission		Bridgeton		Trinity
L. P. M.			5, 6, 9.		
Carolans	Eaton	St. Helen's	Feversham		Salem
Clapton	Exeter	Sheffield			
Claybury	Quincy	Harlington	5, 6, 11.		
Cumberland					
			Amesbury		New Year
C. P. M.					
Abby	Chapel	Ganges	11, 8.		
Aithlone	Chilton	Kew			
Penitent	St. John's		Solicitude		Zion's Pilgrim
Pilgrim	Willowby				
8, 7.					
Carlisle		Ingatestone			

Asahel Nettleton:
Sermons From the Second Great Awakening

Over 50 Sermons of Reverend Asahel Nettleton, many never before published. Christian History magazine estimates that over 30,000 people were genuinely led to Christ through Nettleton's ministry during the Second Great Awakening. This book includes most of Nettleton's sermons which have survived. Almost all are evangelistic sermons. Subjects include Death, the Final Judgment, Regeneration, Repentance, the Rich Man and Lazarus, the Unclean Spirit, Hypocrisy in Religion, Mortification of Sin, The Perseverance of the Saints, etc. 500 pages.

True Religion Delineated
by Joseph Bellamy

A classic work on the nature of true religion as distinguished from all counterfeits. One of the best works on the depravity of the heart of man and the religion of self ever written. Bellamy was a student of Jonathan Edwards and active in the Great Awakening. The Preface to this work was written by Jonathan Edwards who states, "They, therefore, who bring any addition of light to this great subject—the nature of true religion, and its distinction from all counterfeits—should be accepted as doing the greatest possible service to the church of God." 384 pages.

The Soul's Preparation for Christ
by Thomas Hooker

Must the heart be broken for sin before it is prepared for the entrance of Jesus Christ? Does God use means to convict the sinner of his sins and break his heart for them? In this classic work, which went through seven printings in the first eleven years after its release in 1632, Thomas Hooker details the process by which God breaks the heart of a sinner preparatory to His giving of life to him. The doctrines set forth in this book should clearly show us how modern evangelism has grievously erred in its slight view of conviction of sin. 204 pages.

International Outreach, Inc.
P. O. Box 1286, Ames, Iowa 50014 USA
(515/233-2932)
http://home.navisoft.com/outreach/NarrowWay.html